Questions & Answers
Family Law

Carolina Academic Press
Questions & Answers Series

Questions & Answers
Family Law

THIRD EDITION

Multiple-Choice and Short-Answer
Questions and Answers

Mark Strasser
TRUSTEES PROFESSOR OF LAW
CAPITAL UNIVERSITY LAW SCHOOL

CAROLINA ACADEMIC PRESS
Durham, North Carolina

ISBN 978-1-5310-0948-9
eISBN 978-1-5310-0949-6
LCCN 2018950234

Carolina Academic Press, LLC
700 Kent Street
Durham, North Carolina 27701
Telephone (919) 489-7486
Fax (919) 493-5668
www.cap-press.com

Printed in the United States of America

To my family
George, Emma, and Nathan

Contents

Preface

Traditionally, family law is a matter of state rather than federal concern, so it is of course true that family law is not uniform across the states. Nonetheless, many matters are treated similarly whether because of federal constitutional law, statutory law, or uniform laws, or because states have learned from each other, or simply because of shared experiences in handling the kinds of issues that arise in families. The law represented here does not focus on that of a particular jurisdiction but instead represents the laws that might be found in a variety of states.

This volume has two kinds of questions — short answer and multiple choice. As a general matter, they will involve fact scenarios from invented jurisdictions, an approach that highlights: (1) the similarities and differences among the states, and (2) the importance of considering the background law of the jurisdiction in which the events occur. Because choosing the appropriate forum can itself be a very important issue, some of the questions focus on jurisdictional rather than substantive law.

This volume covers a variety of areas covered in family law courses. As a general matter, federal and state statutes and case law are used as supporting authority in the answers. The aims of the volume are twofold: (1) to improve test-taking skills, and (2) to help students understand and apply the substantive law by highlighting some of the obvious and less obvious points that may be important when resolving some of the kinds of difficulties that might arise in family law.

Mark Strasser
Capital University Law School
mstrasser@law.capital.edu
Columbus, Ohio
May 2018

About the Author

Mark Strasser has a B.A. from Harvard College, an M.A. and Ph.D. from the University of Chicago, and a J.D. from Stanford Law School. He is the Trustees Professor of Law at Capital University Law School in Columbus, Ohio, where he teaches courses in Family Law and Constitutional Law. He has published extensively in Constitutional Law and Family Law broadly construed.

Questions

Minor Marriages

1.   Ann Adamson, age 17, lives with her boyfriend, Bryan Boyton, age 19, in an apartment. Brian attends Old York State University. In the state of Old York, the age of consent is 18 and minor marriages are voidable. One day, Ann and Brian go to a Justice of the Peace, lie about Ann's age, and marry. They have a little celebration but tell no one about their marriage. They continue to live together. A year and a half later, Brian tells his parents that he and Ann were married by a Justice of the Peace. The Boytons are furious and immediately consult their attorney about whether they can have the marriage annulled. What should their attorney tell them?

   (A)   Because Old York treats minor marriages as voidable, the Boytons can have the marriage annulled by a court.

   (B)   Because Bryan and Ann lied about her age, the marriage will be treated as void, so there is no need for the Boytons to have the marriage annulled.

   (C)   While the Boytons will not be able to have the marriage annulled, Ann's parents can have the marriage annulled because Ann was a minor at the time of the marriage.

   (D)   Because Ann and Bryan continued to live together after Ann had attained majority, the marriage was ratified and it is no longer subject to annulment.

2.   Carrie Collingwood, age 18, and Daniel Davidson, age 17, are domiciled in the state of Massecticut, where the age of consent is 18 and minor marriages are voidable. While Carrie and Daniel are on their week-long senior class trip, they impetuously decide to marry. They easily fool the Justice of the Peace, because they both appear to be in their early twenties. They marry and spend the night together. Regrettably, by the end of the trip, they are not speaking to each other. They go back to their respective homes and do not mention the marriage to their parents. Three years later, Carrie inherits a substantial amount from her grandmother. Unfortunately, she dies in a tragic car accident the following year. She never made a will. Daniel consults an attorney to see whether he should be awarded part of Carrie's estate. What should the attorney tell Daniel?

   (A)   Because Daniel and Carrie never ratified their marriage after they both had attained majority, their marriage was never valid and thus he has no claim to any part of the estate.

   (B)   Because Daniel and Carrie had both reached age 18 before she died, the validity of their marriage cannot be contested, which means that the marriage is valid and Daniel must receive his intestate share.

(C) Because Daniel and Carrie married without Daniel's parents' consent, the marriage was void and Daniel will not be entitled to inherit.

(D) Because a voidable minor marriage is valid until annulled by a court and because the marriage ends upon the death of one of the parties to the marriage and is no longer subject to challenge, Daniel is likely eligible to receive a share of the estate.

3.   John, age 17, and David, age 17, live in Marryvania where the age of consent is 18 and where minor marriages without parental consent are void rather than voidable. John and David decide that they will marry when they go on a skiing vacation. During that vacation, they go to a Justice of the Peace. David has a false ID listing his age as 19 and John has forged his father's signature on a statement of consent. The Justice of the Peace marries them. Regrettably, the marriage falls apart before the vacation is over. John and David go their separate ways. Two years later, John wishes to marry someone else and he consults an attorney to find out whether he must divorce David. What should the attorney say?

(A) While it might be safer to have a court declare the marriage between John and David null and void, the marriage never existed in the eyes of the law so it is not necessary to have a court annul the marriage.

(B) The marriage is null and void. However, if John and David had lived together after attaining majority, the marriage would thereby have been ratified and would be valid.

(C) Because John forged his father's signature to fool the Justice of the Peace, he cannot now benefit by avoiding the time and expense of having the marriage annulled or dissolved. Unless he gets a court declaration establishing the nonexistence of the first marriage, he cannot marry anyone else.

(D) As a general matter, as long as both parties agree that the marriage was a mistake, there is no need to have a court declare the marriage's invalidity.

4.   Zeke, age 18, marries Yolanda, age 12, with the permission of Yolanda's parents. The marriage comes to the attention of the local prosecutor, who decides to charge Zeke with engaging in unlawful relations with a minor. Is Zeke likely to be convicted?

(A) No. Zeke cannot be convicted of having consensual relations with his wife.

(B) No. While Zeke would have been subject to prosecution had he married Yolanda without her parents' consent, he cannot be prosecuted after having secured her parents' consent.

(C) Yes. Had Yolanda been older, the marriage might have immunized his having consensual relations with her but his having sexual relations with a 12-year-old is subject to prosecution, marriage notwithstanding.

(D) Yes. No one who marries a minor can claim the marriage as a defense to a prosecution because minors are incapable of legally consenting to sexual relations.

5.   David, age 19, and Zena, age 17, have been dating for a few years. Zena is pregnant and David and Zena would like to marry before the birth of their child. But Zena has a friend her age, Wanda, who has been told that she cannot marry until she reaches her eighteenth birthday. Zena consults an attorney to find out what her options are. What should the attorney tell her?

ANSWER:

Bigamous Marriages

6.   Jordan's spouse, Riley, is on Safetyair Flight 1607 from London after having delivered a paper at an international conference. The plane disappears without a trace. All are presumed dead.

Seven years later, Jordan starts dating and eventually marries Dakota. All is going well until Riley appears three years later. Apparently, several on the flight had survived the crash but had been stranded on an island for years. Jordan consults an attorney to find out which marriage is valid and whether a bigamy charge might be forthcoming. What should the attorney say?

(A) Because Riley, Jordan's spouse, is still alive, Jordan never ended the first marriage through divorce or dissolution, and Jordan nonetheless intentionally married Dakota, Jordan's second marriage is void and Jordan is subject to a charge of bigamy.

(B) Because Jordan's second marriage was contracted when Jorden did not know that Riley was still alive, the second marriage will be treated as void but Jordan is not at risk for being charged with bigamy.

(C) Because Jordan did not attempt to remarry until seven years had passed after Riley's having disappeared, Jordan is not subject to a bigamy charge and the second marriage will likely be treated as valid.

(D) Because Jordan reasonably believed that Riley was dead, no one would entertain a bigamy prosecution and the first marriage will be treated as if it had ended when Riley allegedly died.

7.   Addison and Bailey are married. One day, Bailey empties the joint bank account and disappears without offering anyone any explanation. Three years later, Addison meets Casey. A relationship develops. Because Addison has heard nothing from or about Bailey for more than three years, Addison assumes that Bailey has died and feels free to develop a relationship with Casey. Soon, Casey proposes to Addison and Addison accepts. One month after the wedding, Addison wins $10 million in the state lottery. Suddenly, Bailey appears, claiming an interest in the lottery winnings. Addison consults an attorney to find out whether Bailey's claim has any merit. What should the attorney say?

(A) By virtue of emptying the bank account and disappearing without a trace, Bailey abandoned the marriage and thus has no claim to the lottery proceeds.

(B) Assuming that the lottery winnings are viewed as marital property and a search of the relevant records reveals that neither Addison nor Bailey ever ended their marriage, Bailey may well be entitled to a share of the lottery winnings.

7

(C) Because Addison sincerely believed that Bailey was no longer alive, the second marriage will be treated as valid and Bailey will have no claim to any property accrued after Bailey's disappearance.

(D) Because Addison entered into a marriage with Casey, the second marriage will be irrebuttably presumed to be valid, which means that the initial marriage will not be recognized and Bailey's claim will be viewed as without merit.

8.   Emerson and Jamie married 15 years ago, although their marriage has been rather rocky for at least two years now. After one very serious and acrimonious argument, Emerson says, "I can't stand this. I want a divorce." Jamie laughs. "No need to get a divorce because we never had a valid marriage." Jamie explains that he had never divorced Kendall (who is still alive), so that his marriage to Emerson is null and void. The next day, Emerson consults an attorney to find out the implications of Jamie's revelation. What should the attorney say?

(A) Because Emerson and Jamie's marriage was celebrated when one of the parties still had a living spouse, the marriage is null and void and there will be no marital property to distribute or possible spousal support to order.

(B) Because Emerson had married Jamie in good faith and had no idea that Jamie had never divorced his first spouse, Emerson's marriage is valid and Emerson will be able to seek a division of marital property and, possibly, spousal support.

(C) Assuming that Jamie and Kendall never divorced, Jamie's marriage to Emerson is void. However, Emerson may still be able to seek a division of property and possible support depending upon local law. Further, Jamie may be estopped from denying the validity of the second marriage.

(D) Because Emerson and Jamie's marriage was celebrated more than seven years ago, the validity of that marriage can no longer be challenged.

9.   Madison and Paris celebrated their marriage 10 years ago and have lived together ever since, treating each other as spouses and holding themselves out to the community as spouses. Madison is thankful that this marriage is working out so well after that disaster of a first marriage with Harlow. If Harlow had not filed for divorce, Madison certainly would have.

Paris dies in an auto accident. To Madison's surprise, Paris's brother, Francis, claims to be Paris's sole surviving relative. After having performed a search of the relevant records, Francis can establish that Harlow was never granted a divorce from Madison and that Madison never sought or received a divorce from Harlow. Harlow had been Madison's lawfully wedded spouse until Harlow's death five years after Madison and Paris had celebrated their marriage, which made Paris's marriage to Madison void *ab initio*. After recovering from the shock of losing Paris and from the revelation that Harlow had never followed through on getting the divorce, Madison consults an attorney to find out whether Francis is indeed Paris's sole remaining relative. What should the attorney say?

(A) Madison will be viewed as Paris's former spouse because Francis cannot attack the validity of that marriage now that Paris has died.

(B) Madison will be viewed as Paris's former spouse because Francis was not a party to the marriage and thus cannot challenge its validity.

(C) Madison will be viewed as a legal stranger to Paris because bigamous marriages are void *ab initio*.

(D) Madison may be considered Paris's legal spouse notwithstanding that their ceremonial marriage was void if the state in which Madison and Paris were living recognizes common law marriage.

10. William and Miranda were married in the backyard of their home in front of all their friends and family and were devoted to each other ever since. Miranda died while working for her employer and William sought workers' compensation benefits. Those benefits were denied because it had been proven that Miranda's marriage to her first husband, Zeno, had never formally ended and Zeno had not died until five years after Miranda had married William. William consults an attorney to explore his options. What should the attorney say?

ANSWER:

Incestuous Marriages

11. Alexander, age 25, and Cassandra, age 25, are first cousins. They are in love and seek to marry, but their state, Nomarritania, prohibits first cousins from marrying each other. Undaunted, Alexander and Cassandra go to the neighboring state of Tennicticut, where such marriages are permitted, and marry. They then come back to Nomarritania and consult an attorney to find out whether Nomarritania will recognize their marriage. What should the attorney say?

   (A) Because the marriage was valid in Tennicticut where it was celebrated, it will be recognized in Nomarritania.

   (B) Because the marriage was prohibited in Nomarritania where Alexander and Cassandra were domiciled at the time of the marriage and where they continue to be domiciled, the marriage will not be recognized in Nomarritania.

   (C) Because Alexander and Cassandra married in Tennicticut in accord with local law, the marriage will be valid as long as Tennicticut did not preclude individuals from marrying there when the marriage could not be celebrated in the couple's domicile.

   (D) Because they were domiciled in Nomarritania at the time of the marriage and continue to be domiciled there, the validity of the marriage will be determined in light of Nomarritania's laws regarding marriages prohibited locally but validly celebrated elsewhere.

12. Julian, age 45, has a half-brother, Kevin, who is age 25. Kevin is in love with Julian's adopted daughter, Loren, age 25. Kevin has asked Loren to marry him. Loren would like to marry Kevin but wants to make sure that the marriage will be recognized. They consult an attorney. What should the attorney say?

   (A) Because the state treats uncle-niece marriages as void and of no legal effect, this marriage will be invalid.

   (B) Because the state law prohibiting uncle-niece marriages does not in addition specify that marriages between a half-uncle and a half-niece are prohibited, the state must recognize the marriage.

   (C) If there is a statute or case law specifying that individuals related by half-blood will be treated in the same way as individuals related by whole blood, then this marriage will only be recognized if the state permits uncle-niece marriages.

(D) While this is a matter of state law and so of course must be researched, the marriage may be recognized even if the state precludes uncle-niece marriages and even if the state does not distinguish between half- and whole-blood.

13.   Tracy, age 25, marries Sasha, age 45, who has a child, Ryan, age 15, from a previous marriage. Five years later, Sasha dies in a car accident. Tracy and Ryan are devastated. A few years later, Tracy and Ryan marry. Tracy dies in a helicopter crash and Tracy's brother, Payton, claims that Tracy and Ryan's marriage is void because parents (including stepparents) cannot marry their children. Will Tracy and Ryan's marriage be held void just as it would have been had Ryan been Tracy's biological child?

(A) No. Because stepparents are not biologically related to the children they are helping to raise, no state precludes a stepparent from marrying his/her stepchild. The validity of Tracy and Ryan's marriage will be upheld.

(B) Yes. Because no state permits a parent to marry his/her child, the marriage between Tracy and Ryan will be held void.

(C) Yes. Assuming that the statute banning incestuous marriages between parents and children includes stepparents, the marriage will be held null and void.

(D) Maybe. Even if stepparents are included within the statutory prohibition, the marriage may nonetheless be held valid if Tracy is no longer viewed as Ryan's stepparent once the marriage between Tracy and Sasha has ended.

14.   Harper and Indigo live together without benefit of marriage, along with Indigo's child, Jesse, age 23. Jesse starts a new job and moves out to live with roommates in an apartment. Several months later, Harper and Jesse go out to dinner while Indigo is at a conference. Sparks fly. Not long after that, Harper moves out of the apartment shared with Indigo. Eventually, Harper and Jesse marry. Local law prohibits stepparents from marrying their children. Is Harper and Jesse's marriage void? Why or why not?

ANSWER:

Marriage and Sexual Relations

15. Shawn, who is incapable of having sexual relations due a terrible accident, marries Robin. A few months later, Shawn cashes his paycheck and uses some of those funds to buy some lottery tickets. Shawn wins $4 million in the lottery. A year later, Robin files for divorce, claiming irreconcilable differences and contending that the lottery winnings are marital property subject to distribution. Shawn admits that the lottery winnings would be subject to distribution were the marriage valid, but contends that the marriage should be annulled due to lack of consummation and thus that the lottery tickets are not marital property. What result?

   (A) While nonconsummation can be a ground for annulment as a general matter, it would be unlikely to be such a ground in this case where both parties knew prior to the marriage that certain kinds of sexual relations would be impossible.

   (B) Because Shawn and Robin never consummated the marriage, it will be annulled.

   (C) While nonconsummation would be a ground for annulling the marriage, annulments are disfavored when the marriage can be ended on a no-fault basis like irreconcilable differences.

   (D) While Shawn could not be granted the annulment based on nonconsummation, Robin would have been accorded the annulment on that basis.

16. Nico and Parker Regan have been trying to conceive for years. Their inability to have children has adversely affected their relationship. Eventually, they consult a fertility doctor to figure out whether anything can be done to increase their chances of having a child together. They learn that Nico is sterile. Nico suggests that they can still adopt children but Parker is inalterably opposed to adopting a child. Their arguments about whether or how they might have children only lead to further anger and alienation. Several months after their last visit to the fertility specialist, Parker seeks to annul the marriage, citing the statutory ground of impotency. Nico seeks a divorce based on irreconcilable differences. What is the likely result?

   (A) Parker will win because but for Nico's sterility they would have had a child.

   (B) Assuming that the marriage cannot be salvaged, Nico will win, because impotence as a ground for annulment was not intended to capture this kind of case.

   (C) Parker will win if but only if she can provide good reasons justifying her opposition to adoption.

   (D) Nico will win but only if he was in no way responsible for his own sterility.

17.   Jungmin is an international student at the college Dominique attends. Jungmin is attractive and somewhat conservative, and Dominique and Jungmin begin to spend a lot of time together. They are married by a Justice of the Peace, although Jungmin says that they cannot have sexual relations until Jungmin's parents formally welcome them into the family. Dominique repeatedly suggests that they have been waiting long enough to consummate their marriage, although Jungmin replies that patience is required. Eventually, Dominique grows tired of waiting when no date has been set for the formal welcoming and seeks an annulment. What result?

(A)   The annulment will likely not be granted because Jungmin did not refuse to consummate the marriage in the future but is merely waiting for the proper time.

(B)   The annulment will likely not be granted unless Jungmin can be shown to be impotent.

(C)   The annulment will likely be granted because the marriage was never consummated despite Dominique's repeated requests and because there seems to be no attempt to bring about the formal welcoming that has been set as a condition for engaging in sexual relations.

(D)   The annulment will likely be granted only if there is an additional reason that the marriage should not be recognized.

18.   Cameron and Dallas have been married for a year and have not yet consummated the marriage. On their wedding night, Dallas was too drunk to engage in sexual relations and they never tried again. While Dallas claims to be interested in having sexual relations, no time has been the right time, although the reasons for refraining have varied from fatigue to being too stressed from work to feeling poorly. Cameron consults an attorney to find out whether the marriage can be annulled. What should the attorney say?

ANSWER:

Marriage and Competency

19.   Zena and Yuri live together in Strictland, which does not recognize common law marriages. They have decided to marry. Zena is quite aware that Yuri is not competent when he is off his medication, so she made him promise to take his medication every morning. Regrettably, because there is so much to do the last few days before the wedding, Yuri forgets to take his medication a few days in a row. By the time that the ceremony is to take place, Yuri is not competent. However, rather than call off the wedding, Zena decides to go through with it. Yuri acts rather strangely but they finally make it through the event.

A week later, after Yuri has been back on his medication for several days, Zena explains what has happened. Yuri is very happy that he and Zena are now married, although he is disappointed that he remembers nothing of what happened on his wedding day.

Years later, Yuri dies intestate. Tatum, Yuri's sole surviving family member by blood, has heard many times about Yuri's rather unusual wedding. Tatum claims that the wedding never took place because Yuri was unable to give consent and thus Tatum is entitled to Yuri's estate. What result?

   (A)   Tatum is entitled to everything. Because Yuri had been unable to give consent, the marriage was never celebrated and Zena is a legal stranger to Yuri.

   (B)   Zena is entitled to the widow's share because her decision to go through with the wedding was reasonable in light of the wedding expenses that had already been incurred and because Yuri rather than Zena was responsible for his not being competent at the time of the wedding.

   (C)   Tatum cannot now challenge the wedding because he had been on notice for years that Yuri had not been competent to consent and Tatum had said nothing during all of those years.

   (D)   Assuming that Strictland treats marriages involving an incompetent as voidable rather than void, the marriage between Yuri and Zena will be treated as valid because ratified after the wedding and Tatum may well be precluded from challenging the validity of the marriage after Yuri's death.

20.   Bacchus and Modesta are finally celebrating their marriage. Bacchus, who is a little nervous and has not eaten all day, has a drink to steady his nerves. He sees his future father-in-law, who has never been particularly friendly, and has another drink. Fearing that the guests will be able to tell that he has had a drink, he has another to bolster his courage. By the time that

he is asked to make his marital vows, he cannot stand by himself and is slurring his words, although his "I do" is discernible. Thankfully, the ceremony is soon over. Six months later, Bacchus seeks to have the marriage annulled, claiming that he had not been competent during the ceremony. Modesta seeks a divorce based on irreconcilable differences. What result?

(A) Modesta will likely be able to establish irreconcilable differences, given that both parties seek to end the marriage. However, Bacchus will likely not be granted an annulment, because he understood what he was doing during the ceremony, even if he slurred his words and was unable to stand by himself.

(B) Bacchus will likely be granted the annulment. He was obviously drunk and so could not be thought competent to consent.

(C) Bacchus will likely be granted the annulment. His having had nothing to eat that day adds credibility to the claim that he was drunk and not competent to consent.

(D) Bacchus will likely not be granted the annulment because, although inebriated, he seemed to understand what he was doing. Modesta will likely not be granted the divorce, because they have not lived apart for a sufficiently long period.

21. Hayden, 75, has married Jamie, 40, much to the consternation of Hayden's family. Hayden is rather wealthy, but was not competent at the time of the wedding and never became competent after the wedding. Hayden's family members themselves disagree about whether Jamie understands that Hayden has never been competent during their relationship. Before family members can agree about what to do, Hayden dies of a heart attack. Greer, Hayden's son, challenges the validity of the marriage. What result?

(A) Because Hayden was never competent and thus could never ratify the marriage, the state may well treat the marriage as void and subject to challenge and annulment even after Hayden's death.

(B) Hayden's marriage can only be successfully challenged after Hayden's death if Jamie can be shown to have known that Hayden was not competent at the time of the wedding.

(C) Whether or not Jamie knew of Hayden's incompetence, no state would permit the marriage to be challenged now that one of the parties is no longer living.

(D) The marriage can be challenged because Jamie is so much younger than Hayden (which suggests fraud). Had they been closer in age, the challenge would have been barred after Hayden's death.

22. Casey and Drew have been living together and have finally decided to tie the knot. Casey is so nervous that he has several shots of whiskey for breakfast and continues drinking throughout the day. When standing (with help) before the clergyperson officiating, Casey is so drunk that he does not seem to understand where he is or what he is doing. The sounds that he makes before, during, and after the clergyperson speaks are unintelligible. Nonetheless, the clergyperson pronounces Casey and Drew married.

Drew is utterly mortified and swears not only to divorce Casey but to punish him any way that she can. Casey and Drew are never again in the same room after the wedding unless accompanied by their respective attorneys. Anticipating that Drew will seek a divorce based on their living separate and apart, Casey seeks to have the marriage annulled. What result?

(A) Because Casey and Drew had long wanted to marry and had planned the wedding, Casey cannot now claim not to have wanted to marry Drew, so Casey cannot now have the marriage annulled.

(B) Because Casey and Drew lived together before the marriage, Casey cannot claim lack of consortium and he will be unable to have the marriage annulled.

(C) Because Casey was so drunk that he could not stand without help, he was obviously incompetent and the annulment will be granted.

(D) Because Casey was so drunk that he did not understand what he was doing, he will likely be granted the annulment, especially because there was never any ratification after the wedding.

23. Lynn and Finley have been dating for months. Some of their friends are marrying, which has sometimes led them to discuss marriage. Neither seems to support marriage as an institution and neither considers the other marriage material. Nonetheless, after attending a wedding reception in Las Vegas where they have plenty to drink and after continuing the celebration with friends post-reception, Lynn and Finley overcome their reservations about marriage, go to an all-night wedding chapel, and make their vows. The next morning, they are both shocked by what they have done, but decide that they will try to make their marriage successful. Six months later, Lynn and Finley are both convinced that their marriage cannot be saved. Lynn consults an attorney to see whether the marriage can be annulled. What should the attorney say?

ANSWER:

Cohabitation and Prenuptial and Postnuptial Agreements

24. Bobby and Chris have been living together for two years. Bobby, who has repeatedly promised that they will marry one day, has not yet consulted an attorney about divorcing his current spouse. Chris no longer believes that Bobby will ever get a divorce and decides to deliver an ultimatum. Unless Bobby promises to support Chris in the style to which he has grown accustomed, Chris will end the relationship immediately. To Chris's surprise, Bobby agrees readily.

    Another three years go by and Bobby's ardor has cooled. Bobby no longer promises an imminent divorce, and Bobby and Chris no longer go out or entertain as they once did. Bobby has been staying at the office in the evening a little too frequently. Finally, Bobby announces that their relationship is over and tells Chris to move out by the end of the week. Chris consults an attorney to find out whether the oral agreement for support is enforceable. What should the attorney say?

    (A) Because the agreement was made under duress—Chris threatened to end the relationship if Bobby refused—the agreement is unenforceable. But for Chris's threatening Bobby, the agreement would likely have been enforceable.

    (B) Chris will likely be successful as long as the agreement is not viewed as solely based on meretricious concerns.

    (C) Chris will likely not be successful because states as a general matter refuse to enforce agreements between non-marital cohabitants.

    (D) While this is a matter of state law, there are many aspects of the case that make the agreement less likely to be enforceable, including the fact that Bobby is still married to someone else and enforcement might compromise the spouse's rights, the agreement was oral rather than written, and in some states cohabitation agreements are not enforceable as a general matter.

25. Erin and Greer have each married and divorced before. They also each believe that their prior failure to specify with particularity the expectations, rights, and responsibilities of the parties to the relationship led to the breakdown of their respective relationships and to an unfair distribution of the marital assets. While Erin and Greer have sworn off marriage, they are each willing to give a serious relationship another try. Before moving in together, they specify how property acquired during the relationship will be divided in the event of a break-up

and the conditions under which partner support should be paid. They also specify the respective duties of the parties, including the minimum number of times per month sexual relations will take place. Ten years later when the relationship founders, Greer seeks to enforce the agreement. What result?

(A) Because both of the parties were sophisticated and knew what they wanted, the agreement will be enforceable in all of the states.

(B) Because the agreement was too specific by including, for example, who would take out the trash, none of it is enforceable.

(C) Because the provisions regarding support too closely emulate the approach that might have been taken had the couple married, no state would permit that provision to be enforced.

(D) Even if the state enforces cohabitation agreements as a general matter, an additional obstacle to enforcement in this case involved the specification involving the frequency of sexual relations, which might make the agreement wholly unenforceable because it would be treated as based on meretricious considerations.

26. Leslie and Morgan treat each other as if they are spouses and hold themselves out to the community as having a marriage-like relationship, but recognize that they are not married because their state does not permit common law marriages to be contracted. Whenever either is asked to describe their relationship, the response is always "meretricious." After 10 years together, Leslie announces that it is time to divide up the property acquired during the relationship and start new lives. Morgan, who is surprised and hurt by Leslie's rejection, is unwilling to split any property held in her own name. Morgan correctly notes that there was never any express agreement to divide up the property upon a breakup of the relationship and she is unwilling to make such an agreement now. How should this dispute be resolved?

(A) Because Leslie and Morgan have always admitted that their relationship is meretricious, no state will require Morgan to give any of the property in her name to Leslie.

(B) Because there is no express agreement to divide up the property, no state will require Morgan to give any of the property in her name to Leslie.

(C) Because as a matter of fairness Leslie must be given some of the property acquired during the relationship, states as a general matter will require Morgan to give some of the property in her name to Leslie to achieve an equitable result.

(D) Depending upon local law, the property acquired during the relationship might be distributed either because of an implied agreement to do so or because in some states when relationships qualifying as meretricious end, the property acquired during the relationship may be subject to distribution.

27. Dallas and Emerson are thinking about marrying. However, they are of different faiths and Dallas will only marry if any children of the marriage are raised in her faith. Emerson does

not particularly care about religious issues and very much wants to marry Dallas. Dallas and Emerson sign a prenuptial agreement specifying that in the event of divorce whoever has custody of the children will raise them in Dallas's faith. When Dallas and Emerson divorce, Emerson is awarded custody of the children and does not want to raise them in Dallas's faith. Dallas seeks to enforce the prenuptial agreement. What result?

(A) Dallas will likely be unsuccessful because enforcement of prenuptial agreements as a general matter is contrary to good public policy.

(B) Because Emerson does not care about religion one way or the other and because Dallas would never have agreed to marry in the first place if there had been any question about the religious teaching of the children, the prenuptial agreement will be enforced.

(C) Dallas will likely be unsuccessful because a prenuptial provision requiring that children be raised in a certain faith is unenforceable, even though other provisions, for example, about the division of property, might well be enforceable.

(D) The prenuptial agreement will likely be enforceable unless Emerson has undergone a religious awakening and Emerson's current religious beliefs are incompatible with Dallas's.

28. Parker and Quinn are considering marrying. But Parker is watching her sister's wrenching divorce in which there is a bitter custody dispute. Because Parker simply cannot imagine having minor children living in the world but not having them live with her, she makes clear that she will not consider marrying unless Quinn signs a prenuptial agreement specifying that in the event of divorce Parker will have custody of any children born of the marriage. Quinn signs the agreement. Parker and Quinn marry and have three children. Regrettably, the marriage breaks down. When Quinn broaches the question of who should have custody, Parker responds that the issue has already been resolved in the prenuptial agreement. Parker consults an attorney to find out if the prenuptial agreement is enforceable. What should the attorney say?

(A) Yes, the agreement is enforceable unless Parker can be shown to be an unfit parent.

(B) No, the agreement is not enforceable because custody should be determined in light of what would best promote the children's interests rather than in light of a provision in an agreement made prior to the children's birth.

(C) Yes, the agreement is enforceable because Parker's having insisted on the provision is a great way to show that she cares about the children and Quinn's having been willing to sign such an agreement establishes that Quinn does not care very much about the children.

(D) No, the agreement is not enforceable because there was no consideration.

29. Storm has mentioned several times that he wants Tate to sign a prenuptial agreement. Two weeks before the wedding, Storm shows the agreement to Tate. But Tate has filled up the last two weeks with social engagements and last-minute preparations for the wedding and so does

not have time to consult an attorney. Tate explains the problem to Storm, but Storm insists and Tate signs the agreement.

Years later, when Storm and Tate divorce, Tate seeks to have the prenuptial agreement set aside because Tate did not have time before the wedding to show it to an attorney. What result?

(A) Absent fraud, unconscionability, or lack of full disclosure, this agreement is not likely to be set aside merely because Tate claims that it was signed under duress.

(B) Because it was too late to cancel the wedding without incurring significant financial penalties, the prenuptial agreement will likely be held unenforceable because signed under duress.

(C) Because Storm had mentioned several times that a prenuptial agreement would be presented prior to the wedding, Tate was on notice that there would be one and so cannot claim duress. However, had Storm not given those warnings, the agreement would likely have been held unenforceable because signed under duress.

(D) Because Storm and Tate are competent adults who signed an agreement, that agreement cannot now be held unenforceable years after it was signed.

30. Brett and Blair are both very successful attorneys. Before they marry, they sign a prenuptial agreement specifying that neither will be required to pay spousal support in the event of divorce. They stay together for several years. When they divorce, Brett challenges the nonsupport provision of the prenuptial agreement. Brett, who is undergoing extensive chemotherapy, claims that it would be unconscionable to enforce the nonsupport provision because he can no longer work and medical costs have depleted all of his assets. What result?

(A) Brett is unlikely to be successful because this eventuality was foreseeable at the time the agreement was signed.

(B) Brett is likely to be successful because there had been no cancer diagnosis at the time the agreement was signed.

(C) Brett is unlikely to be successful because an individual provision of an agreement cannot be held unenforceable — either the entire agreement is enforceable or none of it is.

(D) While the unconscionability standard is very difficult to meet, Brett may well be successful either because local law prohibits provisions waiving support or because unconscionability is to be determined at the time of enforcement and this agreement would be unconscionable to enforce because Brett would then be eligible for public support.

31. Darby and Eden are getting ready to marry each other. Each has children from a previous marriage. Each had a bitter divorce and each wants to avoid some of the difficulties incurred earlier. To that end, each waives spousal and child support, perhaps because neither intends to have any more children. Nonetheless, when they are ready to divorce 10 years later, two children have been born into the marriage. Darby and Eden have agreed that Eden will have custody of the two children. Eden seeks child support from Darby, prenuptial provision to the contrary notwithstanding. What result?

(A) Unless there is some other basis upon which to invalidate the prenuptial agreement, the agreement will be enforced—avoidance of litigation was one of the primary reasons that the agreement was signed in the first place.

(B) The agreement is unenforceable because Darby and Eden did not know at the time that they signed it that they would have any children of the marriage.

(C) The agreement is enforceable. If it were held unenforceable, then Darby might not have been willing to agree to Eden's having custody, and bitter custody disputes are bad for everyone.

(D) The child support provision is unenforceable because it is against public policy.

32. Jordan and Kelly are living together. They have a very comfortable relationship, although neither wants to marry the other. But Jordan is fired one day and will lose health insurance unless something is done quickly. Jordan and Kelly agree that they will go to a Justice of the Peace and marry so that Jordan can be on Kelly's insurance. However, they also agree that this purported marriage is not a real marriage and sign a writing to that effect.

Jordan eventually gets another job and is able to pay Kelly back for all of the costs incurred by having Jordan on her insurance. All goes well until Jordan buys a winning lottery ticket and Kelly seeks her share of the winnings. Jordan files to have the marriage declared null and void so that he does not have to share his lottery winnings. What result?

(A) The marriage will be declared null and of no legal effect. Jordan and Kelly knew all along that the marriage was only for show and Kelly cannot now claim that the marriage is valid.

(B) The marriage will be declared a nullity because Jordan and Kelly in effect contracted with each other to pretend to be married.

(C) Jordan will be unsuccessful in his attempt to have the marriage declared invalid and he will likely have to share his lottery winnings because he used proceeds from a paycheck to buy the winning ticket.

(D) Jordan will be unsuccessful in his attempt to have the marriage declared invalid because he did not seek to annul it once he no longer needed the insurance benefits.

33. Alex and Cassidy have been having marital difficulties. Alex has indicated that she wants a divorce but Cassidy believes that the marriage can be salvaged. Alex agrees to try in good faith to save the marriage, but only if Cassidy is willing to gift some of Cassidy's separate property to Alex. Cassidy agrees and Alex tries in good faith to save the marriage. One year later, Alex files for divorce and claims that the gifted property is her separate property. What result?

(A) The agreement to gift the contested property is likely to be treated as unenforceable for lack of consideration.

(B) The agreement to gift the contested property is likely to be treated as unenforceable because made under duress.

(C) The agreement to gift the contested property is likely to be treated as enforceable because the parties understood what they were doing.

(D) The agreement to gift the contested property is likely to be treated as enforceable because the agreement was knowing and voluntary, and there was consideration in that Alex refrained from filing for divorce earlier and instead tried in good faith to save the marriage.

34. Mickey and Montana Monaldo have been married for several years. Mickey has decided to end the marriage, but would like to secure the most advantageous distribution of property possible. He tells Montana that he plans on filing for divorce, although he hints that he might be induced to change his mind. Montana offers to convey to him Montana's separate property if Mickey will give the marriage a chance. He agrees. Two days after they sign the postnuptial agreement he files for divorce. Montana argues that the postnuptial agreement is unenforceable. What result?

(A) Montana knew that the marriage might not survive, so the knowing and voluntary transfer of property will be upheld.

(B) Because Mickey did not act in good faith and did not even try to save the marriage, the postnuptial agreement may well be held unenforceable.

(C) The postnuptial agreement will be enforceable, assuming that Mickey did not acquire so much of Montana's separate property as to make enforcement of the agreement unconscionable.

(D) The agreement will be held unenforceable because the property transferred was Montana's separate property. If the property had been jointly held by both of them, however, then the agreement would have been enforceable.

35. Luella and Phil have been married for years. Once again, Phil is utterly contrite for having strayed during a business trip. Luella says that she will give him one more chance. However, she wants him to sign a postnuptial agreement specifying that if he commits adultery any time after the agreement is signed, she will have their vacation cabin as her separate property. Luella knows that Phil loves that cabin and believes that he will not dare have another affair if he knows that the cabin is at risk. Luella and Phil sign and date the postnuptial agreement. Regrettably, within a year, Phil is discovered in flagrante delicto with his secretary when firemen break down a hotel room door in response to a call about a fire. When Luella and Phil divorce, he claims that the postnuptial agreement is unenforceable on equal protection grounds among others. What result?

(A) The agreement is unenforceable. Because the agreement specifies what will happen if he breaks his marriage vows but says nothing about what will happen if she breaks hers, the agreement is unfair and unenforceable.

(B) The agreement is unenforceable because it lacks consideration.

(C) The agreement is enforceable only if it can be shown that at the time it was made Phil had no intention of staying true to his marriage vows.

(D) The agreement is enforceable assuming that there are no other grounds upon which it might not be enforced, e.g., fraud or unconscionability.

36. Vick and Whitney are considering marriage. However, many of their friends have divorced and Vick and Whitney understand that they too might ultimately divorce. Their ideas about childrearing coincide—they believe that children should be raised by their mother and that children should receive extensive religious training. Because Vick and Whitney both believe in the importance of independence and hard work, they completely reject the idea behind spousal support. Their prenuptial agreement reflects these shared beliefs. Vick and Whitney marry and have two children. Regrettably, their life plans do not proceed as hoped. Although they were making roughly the same salary when they wed, when they are divorcing 10 years later Whitney's salary has increased by tens of thousands of dollars while Vick's has essentially stagnated. Vick seeks custody, at least in part, because he gets much more satisfaction out of parenting than he does out of his job. Vick remains quite religiously observant, while Whitney's religious views have changed. Vick argues that the only enforceable provision of the prenuptial agreement involves the children's religious education, while Whitney argues that the only provision that is *not* enforceable involves the children's religious education. What result?

(A) Because the prenuptial agreement was informed and voluntary and because its enforcement at the time of divorce would not be unconscionable, all provisions are enforceable.

(B) Because one cannot tell prior to the children's birth which parent's having custody would best promote the children's interests, that provision is unenforceable but the others will likely be enforced.

(C) Because the state cannot force a custodial parent to give his or her children extensive religious training, that provision is unenforceable, although the others can be enforced.

(D) The only provision that might be enforceable is the provision regarding spousal support, although even that provision is unenforceable in some states.

37. Alice and Bevan sign a premarital agreement specifying that Alice will have custody of any children born of the marriage, that the children will receive extensive religious training, and that neither will be required to pay spousal support. Alice and Bevan live happily and are fortunate to have three children. Tragically, one of the children dies in an auto accident. Alice becomes despondent and eventually loses her faith. When Alice and Bevan divorce, Alice seeks to enforce the provision involving her having custody and Bevan seeks to enforce the provision involving religious training. Which of the premarital agreement provisions, if any, will be enforced?

ANSWER:

Marriage and Fraud

38.   John and Karen met through an Internet dating service. John has made clear that he could never have a serious relationship with anyone who was not wealthy. Karen makes clear that she is an only grandchild and that her terminally ill grandfather is extremely wealthy. Two months after John and Karen marry, Karen's grandfather dies, leaving all of his money to a foundation devoted to animal welfare. When John asks Karen whether she is surprised by her grandfather's not having left her anything in his will, she replies that she knew all along that he was devoted to animals and that she never expected him to leave her anything. John seeks to annul the marriage, claiming that he was fraudulently induced to marry Karen. What result?

    (A)   The annulment will likely not be granted on the basis of fraud because Karen never stated that she would inherit anything and hence did not defraud John.

    (B)   The annulment will be granted because Karen knew that it was very important to John that he marry someone who was wealthy and that she was not and was unlikely to become wealthy.

    (C)   The annulment will likely not be granted because in most, if not all, states, even express misrepresentations of one's wealth will not provide a basis for annulment.

    (D)   The annulment will likely be granted because an implied misrepresentation about something one knows to be important to one's (future) marital partner might forever undermine trust, an essential element of a successful marriage.

39.   Adrian and Bevan had dated for several months, with each claiming to want very much to have children. After they marry, Adrian refuses to have sexual relations without using contraception because he admits to never having wanted to have children. Bevan seeks an annulment. What result?

    (A)   The annulment will likely be granted because attitudes toward having children go to the essentials of marriage.

    (B)   The annulment will likely not be granted because there are many matters that individuals might misrepresent, and granting an annulment in this case would open up the floodgates to individuals seeking annulments based on any of a number of claimed misrepresentations.

    (C)   The annulment will likely be granted because Bevan had made clear to Adrian the importance to her of having children.

(D) The annulment will likely not be granted because it is not clear that Adrian and Bevan would have been able to have children even if they had tried.

40.   While Cassidy and Dana are dating, Cassidy makes clear that she believes that having a healthy sexual relationship is an important part of a marriage. Dana agrees. After their marriage, Cassidy and Dana have sexual relations a few times, but after that Dana is never in the mood. Eventually, Dana admits that he simply is no longer interested in having sexual relations. Cassidy files for an annulment. What result?

(A) The annulment will likely be granted. Dana knew beforehand that one of the conditions of marrying was having a healthy sexual relationship and that condition simply is not being met.

(B) The annulment will likely not be granted. Once they had sexual relations once, this ground was no longer available.

(C) The annulment will likely be granted because decisions about sexual relations are included within those going to the essentials of marriage and thus can be the basis of an annulment.

(D) The annulment will likely not be granted in this case. While decisions about whether to have sexual relations go to the essentials of marriage, there is no evidence that Dana defrauded Cassidy by misrepresenting his views prior to the marriage. If his views changed after the marriage, there was no fraudulent inducement to marry.

41.   Phoenix never tells Quinn that he married previously, although Quinn has said on numerous occasions that she believes that marriage is for life and that she would never marry anyone who has been married before. After they married, Quinn seeks an annulment upon learning that Phoenix married previously. What result?

ANSWER:

Common Law Marriage

42. Addison and Bobby live in a state that recognizes common law marriages. Addison and Bobby view each other as spouses and are treated by all who know them as spouses. Indeed, all of their friends and family believe that Addison and Bobby were married by a Justice of the Peace. While Addison and Bobby had not in fact participated in a marriage ceremony because the Justice of the Peace had suddenly gotten sick just before their ceremony was to begin, Addison and Bobby were sufficiently confident in their feelings for each other that such a technicality did not bother them.

     One day, Addison came home from work to discover that Bobby and all of Bobby's belongings had vanished. There was no note and none of Addison and Bobby's friends had any idea about where Bobby had gone. Now, Addison feels some comfort in knowing that they had never celebrated a marriage.

     A few years later, Addison meets Cameron. Their relationship becomes quite serious. This time, Addison actually goes through a ceremony. Addison and Cameron live together quite happily for a year until Addison has a heart attack and dies. Suddenly, out of nowhere, Bobby shows up claiming to be entitled to the surviving spouse's share of Addison's estate. What result?

     (A) Cameron will be treated as Addison's former spouse. Bobby, who abandoned the marriage, cannot now claim to have been Addison's spouse after that abandonment.

     (B) Cameron will be treated as Addison's former spouse. Bobby and Addison informally contracted a marriage by living together and holding themselves out as married, and informally ended that marriage by no longer living together and no longer holding themselves out as married.

     (C) Bobby will be treated as Addison's former spouse, assuming that a record search indicates that the marriage was never formally ended.

     (D) Bobby will be treated as Addison's former spouse unless Bobby had had a settled and firm intention never to return to the marriage.

43. Sloan and Tate live in Wedyvania, which recognizes common law marriages. They participate in a marriage ceremony in front of all of their friends and family. Three years later, Sloan dies intestate. To Tate's chagrin, Sloan's long-lost brother, Morgan, announces that he can prove that Sloan had been married to Reese until Reese's death, which had not taken place until one year after Sloan and Tate had celebrated their marriage. Morgan claims to be Sloan's

sole remaining relative and thus to be entitled to Sloan's estate. Tate consults an attorney. What should the attorney say?

(A) Because Sloan and Tate contracted a marriage while Sloan had a living spouse, Sloan and Tate's marriage is void and Sloan and Tate are legal strangers.

(B) Because Sloan and Tate treated each other as spouses, were viewed by the community as married, and could legally marry once Reese died, Sloan and Tate may well have contracted a common law marriage.

(C) Because Tate married Sloan in good faith, the marriage they celebrated must be recognized as valid now that Reese has died.

(D) Whether or not Sloan and Tate's marriage is valid, Morgan does not have standing to challenge the marriage now that Sloan has died.

44.   Piper and Quinn live in Kanana, which recognizes common law marriage. They treat each other as spouses and are viewed by the community as spouses. However, they cannot celebrate a marriage because Piper still has a living spouse, Montana. Montana dies. Piper, who learns of Montana's death, says to Quinn that they now really are married, giving Quinn a ring to represent that their relationship is now on a different footing. Two years later, Piper is in a car accident where the other driver plows into Piper's car while Piper is stopped at a red light. Quinn sues the other driver, Motorona, for loss of consortium. Motorona argues that Piper and Quinn did not establish a common law marriage because when they began living together and holding themselves out as married, Piper still had a living spouse. Will Quinn be successful in suing Motorona for loss of consortium?

(A) No, because at the time Piper and Quinn allegedly contracted their common law marriage, Piper had a living spouse, Montana, which means that their common law marriage was null and void.

(B) Yes, all states recognizing common law marriage would recognize the union between Piper and Quinn because (1) they treated each other as spouses, (2) they held themselves out as married, and (3) there is no current bar to their marrying.

(C) No, because when Piper and Quinn started living together their relationship was adulterous and allowing such a relationship to ripen into a valid marriage would be contrary to good public policy.

(D) Yes, because they not only treated each other as spouses and held themselves out to the community as married, but they recognized and signified that their relationship was on a different footing once the impediment to their marriage no longer existed.

45.   Aubrey and Bailey are married by Dana in what turned out to be an off-script, very unusual ceremony. All attendees were quite surprised and believed that this was one of the most memorable ceremonies they had ever witnessed.

A year after the ceremony, Aubrey read in the local newspaper that Dana is a fraud who is not authorized by the state to perform weddings. The article noted that this fraud could have significant consequences and that those who were married by Dana should have another ceremony.

Aubrey and Bailey are pleased to reaffirm their vows. But Bailey suddenly becomes very sick and is rushed to the emergency room. Fortunately, Bailey makes a full recovery after a stay in the hospital. However, because Bailey is insured by virtue of being Aubrey's lawful spouse and because Bailey's marriage to Aubrey is allegedly not recognized by the state, the insurance company refuses to pay Bailey's medical bills. Aubrey and Bailey consult an attorney. What should the attorney say?

ANSWER:

46.   Scout and Taylor live together in Marryvania where they have always lived. Marryvania does not permit common law marriage to be celebrated within the state but will recognize such a marriage if validly celebrated elsewhere. Scout and Taylor treat each other as spouses, are thought by all who know them to be spouses, and are legally permitted to marry. However, they have always resisted going through a formal ceremony and see no reason to do so now. Every year, they spend several weeks vacationing in Texarkana, which does recognize common law marriages.

One day, while crossing a street at the stoplight near their home in Marryvania, Scout is hit by a car that goes through a red light. While Scout will eventually recover, Taylor wishes to sue the negligent driver for loss of consortium. When conferring with an attorney, Taylor is told that there is no cause of action under Marryvania law unless Scout and Taylor are married. What result?

(A) Taylor will not be successful when suing the negligent driver. Scout and Taylor refused to celebrate a ceremonial marriage even when they knew (or should have known) that Marryvania does not permit common law marriages to be contracted within the state. Now, they have an additional reason to wed once Scout recovers.

(B) Taylor is likely to be successful when suing the negligent driver. Although Marryvania does not permit common law marriages to be contracted within the state, other states do, so Marryvania is likely to recognize that Scout and Taylor are married.

(C) Because Taylor and Scout have always been domiciled in Marryvania and because Marryvania does not permit common law marriages to be contracted within the state, Taylor and Scout will not be recognized as spouses. Taylor will be unsuccessful unless Marryvania relaxes the conditions under which individuals can successfully sue for loss of consortium.

(D) Taylor might be successful if (1) Texarkana permits common law marriages to be contracted by non-domiciliaries under certain conditions, (2) Taylor and Scout met those conditions, and (3) Marryvania will recognize common law marriages celebrated elsewhere even when the parties were not domiciled in the state permitting common law marriages to be contracted.

47. Jean and Greer live in a state permitting common law marriages to be contracted. They treat each other as if they were spouses and are known in the community as spouses. But Jean and Greer never formally married and Jean has always thought that there was something lacking because they never went through a ceremonial marriage. At first, Greer promised that they would have a wedding someday. But after a few years, Greer stopped even saying that and Jean gave up hope that they would ever have a real wedding. Eventually, Jean simply left and moved to a different part of the state. About a year after leaving Greer, Jean met Harlow. The relationship got rather serious and Jean and Harlow celebrated a wedding. They lived together for about a decade when Jean suddenly had a heart attack and died intestate. Clark, Jean's brother, claimed that Harlow's marriage to Jean was void and that Clark is Jean's sole remaining relative. Clark can establish that Greer, who was still living when Jean and Harlow celebrated their wedding, never filed for divorce and that Jean never filed for divorce. Clark can also establish that Greer predeceased Jean by a year. Harlow has never heard anything about Greer and consults an attorney. What result?

(A) Harlow is entitled to a share of the estate. In Jean's eyes, Jean and Greer never had a real marriage because they never had a wedding, so Jean had never been married prior to meeting Harlow.

(B) Harlow will not receive any of Jean's estate. Because Jean and Greer contracted a common law marriage and because it can be shown that the marriage was never formally dissolved, Harlow's marriage to Jean was null and void.

(C) Harlow is entitled to a share of the estate. Because there is a presumption that the last-in-time marriage is valid, Harlow will be presumed to be Jean's former spouse and hence Harlow will be entitled to a share of the estate.

(D) Harlow will likely be entitled to a share of the estate if under local law the removal of an impediment validates the marriage.

Civil Unions

48. Rory and Ryan are living together and have entered into a civil union in Vermington. Four years later, Rory announces to all his friends and family that his relationship with Ryan is over. Rory moves out and starts a new life. Eventually, he meets Skylar and they remain in a committed relationship until Rory's death. While Rory did not enter into a civil union with Skylar, Rory did make a will leaving everything to Skylar. After Rory's death, Ryan contests the will, claiming that he is entitled to a share of the estate. What result?

   (A) Because everyone, including Ryan, knew that the relationship between Rory and Ryan had ended, Ryan will not be entitled to any of Rory's estate.

   (B) Because Rory and Ryan never formally ended their civil union, Ryan is entitled to the same rights to which he would have been entitled had Rory and Ryan married and their union had never been formally dissolved. Ryan is entitled to elect against the will.

   (C) Because Ryan never claimed any rights related to the civil union while Rory was alive, Ryan cannot claim them now.

   (D) Ryan will only be entitled to a share of Rory's estate if Vermington law provides for putative spouses.

49. Jean and Jillian enter into a civil union in New Vermshire. While they are reasonably happy there, they both have wonderful job opportunities in the neighboring state of Traditionaland. While they assume that their civil union would travel with them just as would have been true had they married, they consult a Traditionaland attorney just to make sure. What should the attorney say?

ANSWER:

Divorce

50. Alexander and Bethany are married. They get along when Alexander is sober, although Alexander has been violent several times when drunk. He is always very sorry once he becomes sober, promising never to hit her again. This time, Alexander comes home slurring his words and yelling about how everything is Bethany's fault. Before Alexander even gets in the same room with Bethany, she slips out the back door with pre-packed suitcases in hand and goes to her mother, who lives in another state. When Alexander is sober, he calls Bethany, asking her to come back and promising never to drink again. Bethany says that she will never come back. A year later when Bethany still has not come back, Alexander files for divorce, claiming abandonment. In response, Bethany claims that she rather than Alexander has been abandoned. What result?

    (A) Because Bethany has remained out of state for a year after announcing her settled intent not to return, Alexander will be granted the divorce based on abandonment.

    (B) Because Bethany left because she reasonably and genuinely feared for her safety, she, but not he, will likely be granted the divorce based on abandonment.

    (C) Because Bethany remained away even after Alexander promised to remain sober, Alexander will likely be granted the divorce based on abandonment.

    (D) The divorce cannot be granted on this ground to either party because both parties are at fault.

51. James has noticed that Sarah is paying more attention to her appearance and seems happier. He knows that she has been assigned to an important project at work and is spending a lot of time working with Herman, sometimes into the evening. Sarah admits that she and Herman have been going out to dinner when working late and that she finds him amusing. James looks up Herman up on the company website and sees that Herman is attractive. James suspects that Sarah is having an affair. He decides to file for divorce after one particular incident. Sarah and Herman were on a business trip. James called her room late one evening and there was no answer. He tried her cell phone and that call remained unanswered as well. When she returned home, James accused her of having an affair. Sarah denied the allegation, explaining that she had unplugged the hotel phone and muted hers so that she could get a good night's sleep the evening before her important presentation. James does not believe a word of what she has said and files for divorce, claiming adultery. What result?

    (A) Because James merely must show an adulterous inclination and a reasonable opportunity to follow that inclination, he will be able to establish Sarah's adultery. Herman is attractive, Sarah has admitted that she enjoys his company, and she and Herman were away on a business trip.

(B) Because adultery is a serious charge, James will need eyewitness testimony of Sarah's adultery. His claim that she committed adultery will be rejected as unsubstantiated.

(C) Because adultery can be established through circumstantial evidence and because of all of the circumstances, including Sarah and Herman spending many evenings together, their having gone away on a business trip together, Sarah's admission that she enjoys Herman's company, and Sarah's having answered neither her cell phone nor her hotel phone on that one occasion, James's charge of adultery will be sustained.

(D) Because adultery is a serious charge, it is necessary to show an adulterous inclination and that an innocent explanation cannot explain the circumstantial evidence. James's charge of adultery will likely not be sustained, because there is no evidence of adultery or an adulterous inclination beyond James's suspicion.

52. Mary has decided that she is no longer willing to put up with her husband Peter's infidelity. He swore that his infatuation with Katherine was in the past and that he would never see her again. But he has allegedly been staying late at the office and never answers the phone when she calls. She hired a private investigator who followed Peter on several occasions to an apartment complex where Katherine lives. While the investigator could see that the lights were dimmed in Katherine's apartment each time, he could not see into the apartment because the shades were drawn. Peter always stayed a few hours and then came home. A few times, he seemed to be rearranging his clothing as he came out the main entranceway to the apartment building. On the occasions when Mary mentions that she called him at work and he did not answer his phone, he always says that he must have been talking to someone else in a different office. He never admits to being anywhere other than his office on any of those evenings. Mary consults an attorney to see whether she has enough evidence to file for divorce asserting adultery as a ground. What should the attorney say?

(A) Mary does not have enough evidence to establish adultery because the private investigator never saw Peter commit adultery with Katherine.

(B) Mary does not have enough evidence to establish adultery because there is a possible explanation for Peter's behavior—he claimed to be at work because he knew that Mary would be too apt to jump to the wrong conclusion about his innocent visits with his friend, Katherine.

(C) Mary likely has enough for a court to find that Peter has committed adultery.

(D) While Mary had enough to establish his adultery earlier, once she forgave him for straying, she was forever barred from asserting that he committed adultery with Katherine.

53. William and Zelda are often seen in public together in restaurants, shows, and nightclubs. Further, they have been seen on several occasions in a parked car for several minutes at a time, although this was always during daylight hours in a public place. William and Zelda

admit that they are very attracted to each other and have engaged in activities that are sexual in nature, but both deny that they have ever had intercourse. Esmerelda, William's wife, files for divorce, claiming adultery. What result?

(A) Because no one saw William and Zelda engage in intercourse and because there was no evidence that either had gone to the other's home or that they had shared a hotel room, Esmerelda will likely be unable to establish that William committed adultery.

(B) Esmerelda will be successful because it is clear that William and Zelda have lusted in their hearts even if they have not engaged in intercourse.

(C) Esmerelda will likely be unable to establish that William and Zelda committed adultery because these facts do not establish an adulterous inclination, but merely somewhat of an attraction.

(D) Esmerelda may well be successful on these facts because William and Zelda have admitted to their attraction to each other and their having engaged in activities of a sexual nature, and they may well not be believed that they never had intercourse while parked in a car on one of those occasions.

54. David and Ellen are married, although they are at best civil to each other. They would like to divorce, although their domicile requires that they live separate and apart for a year before they can end their marriage. Unfortunately, there is little available housing, and that which is available is very expensive. David and Ellen divide up their apartment, some of which is designated as hers and some of which is designated as his. They have different times for kitchen use and differing refrigerator shelves assigned to each of them. In short, they have very little contact beyond what is absolutely necessary. After living this way for 13 months and after having had no marital relations for at least two years, David files for a divorce. What result?

(A) Because they live in the same apartment, no jurisdiction would permit them to end their marriage based on the ground of living separate and apart.

(B) Because their lives are about as separate and independent as possible, all of the jurisdictions would permit them to divorce so that David and Ellen could get on with their lives.

(C) While jurisdictions differ with respect to the conditions that must be met to establish that a couple has lived separate and apart for the required period, many jurisdictions would permit them to divorce, reasoning that David and Ellen's lives have been sufficiently separate and apart for the requisite period.

(D) Although they might have been granted a divorce on this ground had they lived in different apartments in the same building, their living in the same apartment, coupled with their having some contact with each other, means that their lives are not sufficiently separate to permit them to be divorced on this ground.

55. Harper and Lee are married. While their marital relations with each other continue to be extremely satisfying, Harper and Lee find that they are utterly incompatible in all other respects. They decide to divorce. Harper moves out and lives in a different apartment in the

same building. However, Harper and Lee continue to have sexual relations regularly. After the requisite period for living separate and apart has been met, Harper files for divorce. Will the divorce be granted even if their continuing to have sexual relations regularly comes to light?

(A) Yes, because Harper and Lee have been living in separate residences for the requisite period.

(B) No, because their living separate and apart requires that they live separate lives, a condition that includes their not regularly engaging in sexual relations.

(C) Yes, because even if they are having sexual relations, they live apart and their marriage is irretrievably broken.

(D) No, because their living in the same apartment complex means that they have not made the requisite psychological break to satisfy the separate and apart ground.

56. Rowan and Shannon have been married for several years, although the last few have been rather rocky. They both care deeply for each other, but each believes that the marriage is not salvageable. They have been living apart for a year. Shannon is getting ready to file for divorce based on their living separate and apart for a year. However, just to be sure that divorce is the right choice, Rowan and Shannon have one final date. They have dinner, drinks, and wind up spending the night. The next morning, they are both sure that divorce is the right choice, although Shannon is now worried that their having spent the night together will mean that they will have to live separate and apart for another year before they can divorce on that ground. Shannon consults an attorney. What should the attorney say?

(A) The ground of living separate and apart requires that the members of the couple live separate lives, and a resumption of marital relations means that they are not living separately in the relevant sense. Rowan and Shannon will have to wait another year before filing.

(B) The ground of living separate and apart requires the couple to live separate lives. As long as Rowan and Shannon are living in separate residences and have done so for more than a year, they meet the requirements for obtaining a divorce on this ground.

(C) While state law varies with respect to the requirements for meeting the ground of living separate and apart, several states will not treat one instance of marital relations, especially when seeking to assess whether the marriage is salvageable, as requiring the couple to restart the clock with respect to the requisite period for living separate and apart.

(D) While state law varies with respect to the requirements for meeting the ground of living separate and apart, states as a general matter preclude individuals who are continuing to have marital relations as a general matter from being awarded a divorce on this ground.

57. Shawn and Tate have been married for 20 years. For as long as either can remember, Shawn has complained about Tate's homemaking skills and Tate has complained about Shawn being a poor provider. One day, Tate threatens to file for divorce, stating that he is unwilling to put

up with Shawn's abuse any longer. Tate consults with an attorney to find out whether Shawn's history of complaining suffices to establish the ground of cruel and abusive treatment. What should the attorney say?

(A) Given that Tate has put up with these criticisms for 20 years, it is simply too late in the day to assert this ground now.

(B) Tate has undergone this treatment for a very long time and should be commended for the patience thus far shown. Tate should of course be awarded a divorce on this ground.

(C) Tate is unlikely to be able to get a divorce on this ground, absent some evidence of significant mental or emotional harm that this abuse allegedly caused.

(D) Tate is likely to be granted a divorce on this ground because the marriage is obviously irretrievably broken.

58. Drew and Finley have been married for three years but their marriage has been pretty rocky from the start. Drew sometimes drinks too much and has occasionally gotten violent. After Drew's most recent drinking binge during which there was yet another violent episode, Finley files for divorce, asserting cruel and inhuman treatment. What result?

(A) Finley has already manifested a willingness to put up with Drew's drinking, so it cannot now be asserted as a basis for divorce.

(B) Finley can get a divorce on this ground unless Finley was guilty of provoking Drew.

(C) Finley cannot secure a divorce on this ground because the most recent episode of violence did not differ in kind or degree from those that had already been countenanced.

(D) Finley will likely be awarded a divorce based on cruel and inhuman treatment because physical violence is one of the paradigmatic bases to support securing a divorce on this ground.

59. Alice and Brian Matthews have been married for 10 years. They have gradually gone in different directions and now find themselves in a loveless marriage. Neither has committed a marital fault but they both want to end the marriage. They agree that Alice should have custody of their one child, Carol, while Brian will have liberal visitation. Will they be able to dissolve their marriage?

(A) Yes. However, they should not assume that they will be able to end it immediately merely because they both agree that the marriage is irretrievably broken.

(B) No. While some couples can end their marriages on no-fault grounds, that option is not open to couples who have a child born of the marriage.

(C) Yes. Because they are certain that their marriage is over, they will be able to end it immediately in all of the states.

(D) No. A divorce on this ground would not be available unless both parties were willing to forego spousal support.

60.   Fred has finally decided that he cannot remain married to his wife, Henrietta. They share no interests and have no feelings for each other. When he mentions this to her, he discovers to his surprise that she does not want a divorce and does not even believe that their marriage is troubled. She instead attributes his feelings of emptiness and loneliness to changes in his testosterone levels. She assures him that he will get over his bad feelings soon, and suggests that he talk to his physician about getting a prescription. Fred consults his attorney instead. What should the attorney say about Fred's getting a divorce?

(A)   The attorney should say that if Fred is sure that the marriage is irretrievably broken, then it does not matter that Henrietta disagrees with him. Those states recognizing irretrievable breakdown of the marriage as a ground of divorce do not distinguish between cases in which one of the spouses asserts that the marriage cannot be saved and cases in which both spouses assert that the marriage cannot be saved. In both kinds of cases, one spouse saying that the marriage is over is all that is required.

(B)   The attorney should tell Fred that a divorce cannot be granted on the ground that the marriage is irretrievably broken unless both parties to the marriage agree that the marriage cannot be saved.

(C)   The attorney should explain that states differ about whether it matters that only one of the parties believes that the marriage cannot be saved, so the attorney will have to do some research to determine the implications of Fred and Henrietta disagreeing about whether the marriage is salvageable (unless the attorney already knows how the jurisdiction treats this issue).

(D)   The attorney should explain that, absent Henrietta's agreement about the state of the marriage, Fred will have to use a different ground and live separate and apart from her for the requisite period.

61.   In February, John is very excited about a new job offer in the state of Penntucky that he has received and he cannot wait to tell his wife, Karen, about it. He has been saying for a long time that they should leave the state of Minnegan where they currently live, and this new job pays more, has better benefits, and will be more satisfying. Karen is pleased for him but does not seem anxious to move, at least in part, because she wants their children to finish their next year in their current schools. John does not have the option of deferring the job offer. They take out a mortgage on a house in Penntucky, and he looks forward to having his family join him in 16 months or so. He understands that he will likely not see his family very much during the interim, because of the great distance between the two states, respective job responsibilities, and plans that have already been made for the children during the intervening summer.

Fourteen months later, Karen files for divorce in Penntucky, claiming that the parties have lived separate and apart for the 12 months required under Penntucky law, even though they have not been living separate and apart for the 24 months year required under Minnegan law. John argues that Karen, who is domiciled in Minnegan, cannot file for divorce in

Penntucky and, in any event, has not met her domicile's required period for living separate and apart. What result?

(A) John is correct. Karen cannot file in Penntucky because she is not domiciled there.

(B) While Karen can file for divorce in Penntucky because John is domiciled there, a divorcee can only be granted on the ground of living separate and apart if she meets her domicile's requirement of living apart for 24 months.

(C) Penntucky can grant the divorce and can apply its own law when deciding whether the applicable ground has been established because Penntucky has personal jurisdiction over both parties—John is there and Karen filed there.

(D) Unless a Penntucky statute says otherwise, because one of the parties has met the residency requirement and is domiciled in Penntucky, the divorce can be granted as long as the Penntucky statutory requirement for living separate and apart has been met.

62. Alexander and Zelda have been fighting constantly and each lacks confidence that their marriage will survive. They agree that Alexander should go stay with his brother, Maxwell, to give Alexander and Zelda a break. Alexander stays with his brother for 14 months. Alexander and Zelda talk frequently, although Zelda is equivocal on the phone about whether she thinks the marriage can be saved. Unbeknownst to Alexander, Zelda has already filed for divorce, having provided constructive notice in the local paper. Because the statutorily required period for living separate and apart had already been met, Zelda was granted the divorce. Two months after the decree became final, Zelda was hit by a car and died. Regrettably, Zelda left no will. Yolanda, who was Zelda's last remaining blood relative, claims to be entitled to Zelda's estate. Alexander returns, claiming to be entitled to his share as Zelda's surviving spouse. What result?

(A) Because the divorce was already final by the time Zelda died, Alexander was no longer her husband and can assert no rights with respect to her estate.

(B) Because Zelda knew where Alexander was living, her having published notice in the local paper will not suffice to meet the notice requirement, which can result in the divorce being declared invalid and Alexander being recognized as a surviving spouse.

(C) Because constructive notice of the divorce was given and because the divorce was already final, Alexander was not Zelda's husband at the time of her death and is not entitled to any of the estate.

(D) Because the required period for living separate and apart where Maxwell lived (and where Alexander was staying) was 24 months, the required time apart had not been met and the divorce will be invalidated for failure to establish the asserted ground.

63. Ellis and Drew are married and have a child, Finley. Ellis has been terribly unhappy for years and has long believed that the marriage to Drew is irretrievably broken. Ellis, who has been spending more time with Robin recently, is beginning to have feelings (for Robin) that have

long been dormant. Ellis consults an attorney to find out whether it is necessary to wait until Ellis and Drew have formally separated before seeing if the relationship with Robin has any potential. What should the attorney say?

(A) Because Ellis is terribly unhappy and the marriage to Drew is irretrievably broken, Ellis has nothing to lose by exploring whether a relationship with Robin might become serious.

(B) Once Ellis and Drew have started living separate and apart, there can be no adverse effects of Ellis's starting a serious relationship with Robin.

(C) Once Ellis has explained to Drew that their marriage is over and cannot be saved, then there will be no adverse effects flowing from Ellis's exploring with Robin the possibility of their having a serious relationship.

(D) Some research may be necessary because in some states Ellis's exploring a potential relationship with Robin even after Ellis and Drew separate might adversely affect custody, the distribution of property, or spousal support in the event that Ellis and Drew actually divorce.

64. Jordan and Kennedy have legally separated, and Kennedy is confident that they will never again live together as a married couple. Kennedy meets Lee and they start dating. Jordan files for divorce, claiming adultery. Kennedy consults an attorney to find out whether dating Lee could be the basis of the divorce from Jordan. What should the attorney say?

(A) Some research may be necessary because in some states Lee's having begun a relationship while separated from Jordan could have important consequences. Consummating such a relationship while separated might not only provide the ground for the divorce, but might affect the award of spousal support.

(B) Because Kennedy and Jordan already separated before Kennedy began seeing Lee romantically, Kennedy's relationship with Lee will have no effect on Kennedy's divorce from Jordan.

(C) Lee's relationship with Kennedy will have no effect on the divorce as long as Kennedy and Lee had not even met prior to Kennedy's legal separation from Jordan.

(D) Lee's relationship with Kennedy cannot play a role in the divorce from Jordan as long as the marriage was irretrievably broken before Kennedy began dating Lee.

65. Lynn, who is transgendered, is married to John. Lynn and John agreed that they never wanted to have children but Lynn never divulged to John her transgender status and is now afraid to do so. John finds out anyway and feels angry and hurt. John consults an attorney to find out whether he can have the marriage annulled or, if not, whether a divorce can be secured. What should the attorney say?

(A) The marriage cannot be annulled because both same-sex couples and different-sex couples may marry in all of the states.

(B) The marriage cannot be annulled merely because Lynn's transgender status was very important to John as long as John never mentioned those beliefs and feelings to Lynn.

(C) The marriage may be annulled if Lynn knew that her transgender status was very important to John.

(D) The marriage may be annulled if transgender status goes to one of the essentials of marriage. If it does not, then a divorce or dissolution might be secured based on irreconcilable differences or, perhaps, on living separate and apart for the requisite period.

Divorce Defenses

66. Addison and Ashley Anderson live in Marrylandia. They have always taken separate vacations and have found that their marriage was strengthened by their having some time apart. This time is a little different. Ashley is spending several months in the state of Divorca on a job assignment. Seven weeks after Ashley left, Addison is surprised when he is personally served notice that Ashley is seeking a divorce in Divorca. Addison decides not to contest the divorce in Divorca because he assumes that there has been a mistake and, in any event, he would have to travel 1,000 miles in order to make a personal appearance there. Ashley, who has met the required residency period, is awarded a divorce based on irreconcilable differences.

    When her job assignment is over, Ashley returns to Marrylandia, staying at her sister's house. Addison files suit in Marrylandia, challenging the validity of the divorce granted in Divorca. What result?

    (A) Addison will likely be successful if Marrylandia does not recognize irreconcilable differences as a ground upon which a divorce can be granted.

    (B) Addison will likely be successful if he has evidence that they did not have irreconcilable differences under Divorca law.

    (C) Addison will likely be successful if he can show that he was not guilty of committing any marital faults.

    (D) Addison will likely be successful if he can establish that the Divorca court did not have jurisdiction to grant the divorce because neither he nor Ashley was ever domiciled in Divorca.

67. Cameron and Casey Cunningham have always lived in Texahoma, although they have been living for the year in Divorca where Casey has a job assignment. After six months, Casey files for divorce. At trial, Cameron challenges the court's jurisdiction to grant the divorce because neither Cameron nor Casey is domiciled in Divorca. The court nonetheless grants the divorce.

    Cameron moves back to Texahoma. After the job assignment ends, Casey moves back to Texahoma as well. Cameron challenges the divorce in Texahoma, arguing that because neither Cameron nor Casey was domiciled in Divorca, the Divorca court lacked jurisdiction to grant the divorce. What result?

ANSWER:

68.   Gene and Gillian live in the state of Cementington. While the state does not require one of the parties to commit a marital fault before a divorce will be granted, the state requires couples to live separate and apart for two years before they can be granted a no-fault divorce. Gene and Gillian recognize that their marriage is not salvageable and do not want to wait two years before getting on with their lives. They agree that one of them will appear to commit a marital fault so that they both can be free. Gene hires a private investigator to follow Gillian. The next week, Gillian meets a friend, Harvey, at a cheap motel one day after work. They rent a room. Harvey has agreed to appear shirtless by the window, to close the curtains, and to spend a few hours there watching a movie. They repeat the exercise the following week.

Gene files for divorce, alleging adultery, and seeks an inordinate share of marital property as the wronged spouse. Gillian denies having committed adultery and claims that her actions had simply been designed to appear to have committed adultery so that she and Gene could get out of a loveless marriage. What result?

(A)   If Gillian is believed that she and Gene colluded and that she only appeared to commit adultery, the divorce will likely not be granted because the relevant ground will not have been met.

(B)   If Gillian is believed that she and Gene colluded, then the divorce cannot be granted even if she and Harvey in fact committed adultery.

(C)   If Gillian is not believed that she and Gene colluded, then the divorce must be granted even if Harvey is believed that no adulterous relations took place.

(D)   If Gillian is not believed that she and Gene agreed to stage the alleged adultery, then the divorce must be granted based on her having engaged in recrimination.

69.   Angel and Erin Smith have lived apart for three years now. Each has dated various individuals over the years, although Angel's current relationship is becoming quite serious. Angel files for divorce—Erin and Angel have more than met the state's requirement of living separate and apart for a year. To Angel's surprise, Erin indicates that she will seek a divorce on the ground of adultery, and will seek a greater share of marital assets than she might have gotten based on the couple having lived separate and apart. Angel consults with his attorney to consider the next step. What should the attorney advise?

(A)   Angel should admit the adultery and consider the unequal distribution of marital assets a price of his current relationship.

(B)   Angel should withdraw his divorce petition. It is clear that Erin is not yet ready to take that step and will make it very expensive for Angel to proceed before Erin is ready.

(C)   Angel should plead the defense of recrimination, although that will mean that the divorce cannot be granted.

(D)   Angel should plead the defense of recrimination, which will still allow the divorce to be granted, e.g., on the ground of having lived separate and apart, but which also might prevent Erin from reaping a windfall in the division of marital assets.

70. Brian and Brianna Bellwhether live in Consolatania. Brianna had an affair with a former co-worker, Lothario, that she deeply regrets. She admits to Brian what she has done and promises never to stray again. He forgives her. She meets Lothario to tell him that she will never see him again. He is inconsolable. She tries to comfort him. She feels so sorry for him that she has sexual relations with him this one last time.

    By the time she comes home, she is filled with remorse. Now she is inconsolable. When Brian understands what happened, he tries to comfort her, notwithstanding his own hurt. They have marital relations. The next morning, however, Brian is very angry because he feels that he can never again trust Brianna. He consults an attorney about getting a divorce, fault-based if possible. What should the attorney say?

    (A) Because Brianna committed adultery, Brian can of course get a fault-based divorce.

    (B) Because Brian forgave Brianna that first time after she had sexual relations with Lothario, Brian forever lost the ability to get a divorce from Brianna based on adultery.

    (C) Because Brian had sexual relations with Brianna after her second indiscretion was revealed, he thereby condoned her behavior and cannot now get a divorce.

    (D) Brian may still be able to divorce Brianna on a fault-based ground if his having sexual relations with her is not construed as forgiving her and, in any event, may well be able to divorce her on a no-fault ground even if the marital relations are construed as condonation.

71. Devon and Dallas have been living separate and apart for several years now. They have not communicated with each other in a long time. In fact, Dallas did not even know that Devon had filed for divorce until a friend had mentioned it. Apparently, Devon had published a notice in the local newspaper to give constructive notice, even though he had Dallas's actual address and phone number. He had even remarried and but had not said a word about it.

    Dallas was almost pleased that Devon had remarried. In fact, a short time later, Dallas married Harlow, who regrettably died in a car crash shortly after the marriage.

    Ten years later, Devon won $10 million in the state lottery and Dallas consulted an attorney to find out whether she could claim any of the winnings. What should the attorney say?

    (A) Because Dallas did not receive actual notice of the divorce, the divorce is invalid, Dallas and Devon are still married, and Dallas is entitled to one-half of the lottery winnings.

    (B) Because Dallas has long known of Devon's having divorced her without having done a thing about it and, further, because Dallas acted in a way that assumed the validity of the divorce, Dallas will likely be viewed as having sat on her rights and will likely be barred by laches and estoppel from asserting a claim to the lottery winnings.

    (C) Devon's having married without having first secured a valid divorce from Dallas makes him guilty of recrimination, which will bar him from contesting Dallas's right to some of the lottery winnings.

(D) Dallas's having known of the second marriage without having done anything about it amounts to condonation and she will thus be barred from challenging its validity now.

72. John and Joanna are in a loveless marriage. John would like to divorce Joanna, but does not want her to have the marital property that she would likely be awarded. However, a provision of their prenuptial agreement states that if the couple divorces because of a marital fault, the party at fault will not be awarded any of the marital property to which he/she would otherwise have been entitled. John hires Brennan to seduce Joanna, so that John can divorce her on the fault-based ground of adultery. All goes according to plan. However, shortly before trial, Joanna learns that Brennan had been hired by John to seduce her. What defense of her actions can she offer?

(A) Connivance, because John acted to bring about Joanna's committing adultery.

(B) Recrimination, because John acted wrongly by paying Brennan to seduce her.

(C) Collusion, because John and Brennan colluded to deprive her of the marital property to which she would have been entitled.

(D) Condonation, because John does not object to Joanna's having an affair if he was willing to take an active part in helping to make that happen.

73. Alice and Bernard Cartwright have been estranged for years. They have finally decided to divorce. However, their domicile, Almostforeverland, does not permit couples to divorce based on irreconcilable differences or irretrievable breakdown of the marriage. Instead, they must live separate and apart for two years. Alice and Bernard believe that two years is simply too long to wait, so Alice decides to go to the state of Eezeebreak and establishes residence within a week. She then files for and receives a divorce after having served Bernard with actual notice.

Alice then goes back to Almostforeverland, where she marries her long-time paramour. Not to be outdone, Bernard marries his long-time paramour.

Alice's second marriage is quite successful but Bernard's is not. When his current spouse files for divorce, Bernard responds that the second marriage is void because the first marriage was never validly dissolved. What result?

(A) Because Alice was not domiciled in Eezeebreak, the divorce decree secured there is not entitled to full faith and credit. The divorce will be considered invalid, which means that both Alice's and Bernard's second marriages are void.

(B) The Almostforeverland court must recognize the Eezeebreak divorce out of comity, which means that Bernard's second marriage will be recognized as valid.

(C) The Almostforeverland court must recognize the Eezeebreak divorce as a matter of full faith and credit.

(D) While the Almostforeverland court might estop Bernard from challenging the validity of the first divorce, especially because he implicitly accepted its validity when marrying a second time, the Almostforeverland court might also hold that the first divorce was void.

74. Donald and Evelyn Fredericks have been married for several years. Donald is abusive, which has resulted in Evelyn's having sought comfort and affection elsewhere. Donald is suspicious that Evelyn is having an affair, which makes him all the more abusive. He frequently says that if she tries to divorce him, he will make sure that she gets no property and no support. Evelyn has not worked outside the home in years, and she is not at all confident that anyone would be willing to hire her at this point. Evelyn consults an attorney to explore her options. What should the attorney say?

ANSWER:

Recognition of Foreign Marriages and Divorces

75. Angel, age 22, and Brett, age 21, are in love and wish to marry. However, they are first cousins and their domicile, Limitania, does not permit them to marry, although the adjoining state, Freeland, does permit first cousins to marry. Angel and Brett go to Freeland and marry in accord with local law. They then return to Limitania to live. A few years later, Angel dies intestate. Brett seeks the share due a spouse but Angel's brother, William, argues that the marriage between Angel and Brett is void and of no legal effect. What result?

   (A) The Limitania court cannot recognize the marriage because such marriages are not permitted under local law.

   (B) The Limitania court must recognize the marriage because it is valid under Freeland law.

   (C) The Limitania court will likely not recognize the marriage because it falls within the incest limitations imposed by the state.

   (D) Notwithstanding that this marriage falls within the incest limitation imposed by the state, the marriage may nonetheless be recognized if such marriages are thought not to violate an important public policy of Limitania.

76. When Louisa and Marcel were domiciled in Freeland (which permits common law marriages to be contracted), they treated each other as spouses and held themselves out to the community as married, but never married there. They later moved to Limitania, which does not permit common law marriages to be contracted. Two years later, Louisa was killed in a terrible auto accident, where the other driver was clearly at fault. Marcel sues for wrongful death, claiming to be Louisa's lawful spouse by virtue of their common law marriage established in Freeland. What result?

   (A) The marriage will not be recognized because common law marriages are not permitted in Limitania.

   (B) The marriage will be recognized because Louisa and Marcel treated each other as spouses in a state permitting common law marriages to be contracted.

   (C) The marriage will not be recognized because Louisa and Marcel should have fulfilled the formal requirements for marriage in Limitania if they wished to have the legal benefits of that relationship in that state.

   (D) The common law marriage is likely to be recognized, assuming that Marcel can establish that he and Louisa contracted such a marriage in Freeland while they were domiciled there.

77.   Monty and Madeline Mains have been married for 10 years in Matriland. They are both ready to go their separate ways but the state requires couples to lives separate and apart for a year before they can end their marriages. Monty has no desire to wait so long. While on an extended business trip where he more than meets the residency requirement in Libertania, he gives Madeline actual notice that he intends to file for divorce and then does so. He is granted a divorce and eventually returns to Matriland.

Monty is living in an apartment. After several months, he meets Agatha and begins a serious relationship with her. By this time, Monty and Madeline have lived separate and apart for 14 months. One month later, Madeline files for divorce, asserting adultery as the ground in the hopes that a fault-based divorce would inure to her benefit in the division of marital property or in the award of spousal support. She argues that the Libertania divorce was invalid and not subject to full faith and credit. What result?

ANSWER:

78.   Zenia and Wallace Thomas have a child, Sarah. They later adopt a child, Max, who is Sarah's age. Sarah and Max get along very well but go their separate ways when they reach adulthood. They meet again when each is 30 years old. They begin to spend much time together and eventually decide that they wish to marry. Their state, Tradington, does not permit siblings to marry, so they go to the neighboring state, Newageland, and marry in accord with local law. They then go back to Tradington and consult an attorney to find out whether their marriage will be recognized. What should the attorney say?

ANSWER:

Property

79.   John and Mary are married, although they have wildly different aesthetic tastes. One day, John goes into a local gallery and purchases a painting for $10,000. Mary is livid because they cannot afford such an extravagance and because she hates the painting. John assures her that the painting will greatly increase in value and that one day she will thank him for his having made such a prudent investment.

The next year, when John and Mary are running short of money, Mary goes to an art dealer she knows to inquire about the painting's market value. She is told that while the painter was very popular, he is now considered by the cognoscenti to be second-rate and that the painting is probably only worth $1,000. This is the last straw. Mary consults an attorney about filing for divorce and wants to know in particular whether John's purchase of the painting would be considered dissipation of marital asserts. What should the attorney say?

(A)   Yes, John is guilty of dissipation of marital assets because he has wasted scarce marital funds.

(B)   Yes, John is guilty of dissipation of marital assets by buying the painting that he knew Mary would not like.

(C)   No, he is not guilty of dissipation of marital assets because even experts do not always know which artwork will appreciate in value over time.

(D)   No, he is not guilty of dissipation of marital assets because he did not spend marital assets on himself rather than on the parties to the marriage and because the challenged spending was not at a time when he knew or strongly suspected that the marriage would soon come to an end.

80.   Alex and Beatrice Cunningham have worked hard all of their lives, conscientiously saving for their retirement. Regrettably, Alex makes some very bad investment decisions, seriously depleting their savings. When Alex and Beatrice divorce, Beatrice argues that Alex has dissipated the marital assets and that the resources he wasted should be attributed to him when the marital assets are distributed. What result?

(A)   Because Alex wasted their hard-earned savings leaving Beatrice in the same position that she would have been in had he simply spend those resources on illicit drugs for himself, Alex should have those wasted assets attributed to his share of the marital assets.

(B) Because Alex was at the very least negligent with respect to how he invested their hard-earned monies, he should be held responsible for his poor decision-making and have those funds attributed to his share of the marital assets.

(C) Because Alex was attempting, however inartfully, to increase marital assets, he is unlikely to be found to have dissipated those assets and is unlikely to be forced to bear that burden entirely on his own shoulders.

(D) Because the losses occurred before Beatrice and Alex were actually divorced, they both must bear the burden of that loss equally.

81. Mickey and Nevada have been unhappily married for years and have finally decided to divorce. Mickey decides that this is the perfect opportunity to go on a gambling trip. He empties the joint savings account and goes to a nearby casino where he quickly loses everything. When Mickey and Nevada divorce, Nevada argues that Mickey has dissipated marital assets and all of those losses should be attributed to him when the marital property is divided. Mickey argues that the remaining assets should be divided equally. What result?

(A) Because Mickey and Nevada were still married when the gambling losses accrued, Mickey and Nevada must bear the burden of those losses equally.

(B) Because Mickey knew that the marriage was over and then went on a gambling spree to satisfy his own selfish desires, Mickey will likely be found to have dissipated the marital funds and will have those losses solely attributed to him when the marital assets are distributed.

(C) Because Mickey did not intentionally lose the monies but instead was merely gambling, which might, after all, have resulted in increased wealth, Mickey is unlikely to be found to have dissipated the marital funds.

(D) Because Mickey acted in a way that substantially decreased the marital assets, he is likely to be found to have dissipated marital resources and to be solely responsible for that loss.

82. Piper and Pat have been married for a long time. They have little in the way of marital assets other than a savings account containing $100,000. Pat sees the writing on the wall—the marriage is over. Pat empties the savings account and spends it on a wild weekend. When Piper and Pat divorce, Piper not only wants to receive all of the marital property but also wishes to be awarded some of Pat's separate property. What result?

(A) Wild weekend notwithstanding, marital property is to be divided equitably upon divorce. Whatever marital property remains should be divided evenly between Piper and Pat.

(B) While Pat's separate property is not subject to distribution, Piper can be awarded all of the marital property.

(C) Not only can Piper be awarded all of the marital property but, depending upon the jurisdiction, Pat's separate property can also be distributed to achieve an equitable result.

(D) Piper can only receive a disproportionate share of the marital property if Pat is at fault for the break-up of the marriage.

83. Assume the same facts as in Question 82, although Pat's sole separate property involves ownership of real property in another state. What result?

(A) Because the court cannot transfer title to real estate located in a different state, it can only award Piper a disproportionate share of the marital estate.

(B) The court can order Pat to sell the property and split the proceeds or, in the alternative, can order Pat to transfer title of the property to Piper.

(C) The court can transfer ownership of the property from Pat to Piper.

(D) The court can punish Pat by awarding custody of the children to Piper, even if the children's best interests would be better served were Pat to have custody.

84. Reese and Riley Robinson have been married for several years. During their marriage, Reese inherits a cabin in the woods from Aunt Mathilda. Reese and Riley frequently use the cabin when they go on vacation. When Reese and Riley divorce, Riley argues that because the cabin was inherited during the marriage and because it was used by both Reese and Riley during the marriage, it is marital property and it (or its value) is subject to distribution. Reese argues that the cabin is separate property and not subject to distribution. What result?

(A) Because the property was inherited during the marriage, it is marital property subject to distribution. However, Reese does not have to sell the cabin as long as Riley can receive one half the value of the cabin in some other way.

(B) Because the cabin was inherited during the marriage and used by the couple during the marriage, the cabin is marital property. Unless some other arrangement can be made, Reese may be forced to sell the cabin so that Riley can receive what is owed.

(C) The cabin will be treated as separate property only if Riley's share of the cabin was gifted to Reese.

(D) Because Reese alone inherited the cabin from Aunt Mathilda, it will be treated as separate property and will likely not be subject to distribution.

85. Scout and Tracy are married but have been living separate and apart for several months. On a whim, Scout cashes that week's salary check and buys several lottery tickets among other items. One of the lottery tickets has a $1 million payout. When Scout and Tracy divorce, Tracy claims that the lottery winnings are marital property subject to distribution, while Scout claims that the winnings are separate property and not subject to distribution. What result?

(A) Absent case law or a statute specifying otherwise, the winnings will likely be treated as marital property subject to distribution because Scout and Tracy were still legally married when the winning ticket was purchased.

(B) Because Scout and Tracy were living separate and apart when the lottery ticket was purchased, the earnings are separate property not subject to distribution.

(C) Those winnings distributed before the divorce is final are marital and subject to distribution, whereas those winnings distributed after the divorce is final are separate and not subject to distribution.

(D) If the ticket was purchased when both parties understood that the marriage was over, then the winnings will be treated as separate property; otherwise, it will be treated as marital property.

86. Wyatt and Yvette are married. Wyatt inherits from Uncle Jackson an expensive modernist painting that Yvette hates, which is nonetheless prominently displayed in the house. Yvette buys a Corvette out of monies from her salary, a purchase that is way beyond their means. Wyatt is resentful that Yvette made such an extravagant purchase, and Yvette is resentful that she must see a painting that she hates whenever she walks by the living room. When they divorce, Wyatt and Yvette can agree about everything except how to categorize the painting and the car. The characterizations will affect how other marital assets are distributed. What result?

(A) The Corvette is separate property because it was purchased only using funds from Yvette's salary and because only she drives it. The painting is marital because it was acquired during the marriage and, in addition, is prominently displayed in the marital home.

(B) The Corvette is marital property because it was acquired during the marriage with funds coming from Yvette's salary, notwithstanding that Yvette is the only person who drives it. The painting is separate property because it was inherited solely by Wyatt, notwithstanding that Yvette sees it numerous times a day in their marital home.

(C) The Corvette is separate property because it was purchased only using funds from Yvette's salary and is only driven by Yvette, and the painting is separate property because it was inherited solely by Wyatt.

(D) Both the Corvette and the painting are marital because both were acquired during the marriage.

87. Carmen and Miguel are married. Carmen uses marital funds to buy an expensive painting in commemoration of their anniversary, which she presents to Miguel as a surprise. When they divorce, they cannot agree about the appropriate characterization of the painting. What result?

(A) Because this was a gift to Miguel, it will be treated as separate property not subject to distribution.

(B) Because this was to commemorate their marriage, it cannot be construed as a gift (and Miguel's separate property) when the marriage itself is ending.

(C) Because it was bought with marital funds, it cannot be construed as Miguel's separate property.

(D) Absent a statutory presumption or sufficient evidence of an intent to make the painting Miguel's separate property, the painting will likely be treated as marital property, whose value is subject to distribution.

88. Wesley and Whitney Wellington have a huge wedding in Whitney's house, which she inherited from her grandmother a few years before she met Wesley and which is titled solely in Whitney's name. The house is maintained using funds from Whitney's trust fund, which had been set up years before the marriage. Ten years later, Whitney and Wesley plan to divorce. Wesley claims that the house where he has been living for the past 10 years is a marital asset subject to distribution. What result?

   (A) The house has become a marital asset by virtue of Wesley's having lived there for the past 10 years. One-half of the current market value of the house must be distributed to Wesley.

   (B) The house will likely be treated as Whitney's separate property, assuming that she did not implicitly or explicitly gift any interest in it to Wesley or to the marital estate.

   (C) Because all funds used to maintain a house during a marriage are considered marital regardless of their source, at least some of the house must be considered marital property subject to distribution.

   (D) Because the house was titled solely in Whitney's name, the house is her separate property regardless of whether funds used to maintain or even improve the house were separate or marital.

89. Casey Cassingham and Emerson Emening marry later in life. Before their marriage, each acquired an apartment building. (Neither made an express or implied gift of the apartment building to the marital estate.) During the marriage, Casey has a management team taking care of all aspects of management and maintenance, and the payment of all related expenses, including taxes, fees, etcetera, comes out of rental receipts. Emerson works full time managing and maintaining the building that he owns. When Casey and Emerson divorce, they can agree about everything except how to characterize the apartment buildings for marital versus separate property purposes. What result?

   (A) Because both apartment buildings were acquired prior to the marriage, both are separate property and no apartment-related compensation is owed to either party.

   (B) Both apartment buildings are marital property because both were owned for a substantial period during the marriage.

   (C) While it is not clear how to characterize the buildings, it is clear that they should be characterized in the same way.

   (D) Because Casey did not invest marital time, energy, or money in the apartment building, it remains separate property. However, because Emerson invested marital time and energy in managing and maintaining the building, the marital estate may well be thought to have acquired an interest in the building or Casey may be thought entitled to some compensation for Emerson's having invested marital time and energy managing the building.

90.   Chris and Morgan are married. For a long time, Chris has been interested in attending law school and he has decided that it is finally the time to do so. After some family consultation, Chris and Morgan decide that Chris will attend law school full-time, which means that Morgan will not only be the primary wage-earner, but will also be responsible for almost all of the day-to-day household caretaking duties.

Chris graduates at the top of his class and begins a prestigious clerkship. He falls in love with one of the other clerks and he announces to Morgan that he wants a divorce. When they divorce, Chris and Morgan can agree about everything, except Morgan claims that some kind of compensation is owed for the sacrifices made so that Chris could go to law school, whereas Chris claims that no compensation is owed for the sacrifices made so that he could earn his degree and, further, that there is no marital interest in the law degree. What result?

(A)   Because the degree was earned by Chris alone and because degrees are not transferable, no compensation will be owed to Morgan for the sacrifices made to enable Chris to go to law school. Further, the degree will not be treated as marital property.

(B)   Because Chris likely would have been working had he not gone to law school full-time, Morgan will be credited with one half of what Chris would have earned had he instead been working full-time.

(C)   Because there is no way to accurately assess the value of a law degree, Morgan will not be entitled to any compensation.

(D)   Many jurisdictions would permit Morgan to be compensated in some way, although very few jurisdictions treat a professional degree as property subject to distribution.

91.   John Jones has been working at the Forever Corporation since he was 25 years old. John married Matthew McDirkson when each was 45 years old. John, who retired this year now that he is 65 years old, is divorcing Matthew. They can agree about all property issues except for Matthew's share, if any, of John's pension benefits. To what degree, if any, are the pension benefits subject to distribution?

(A)   Because John alone earned those benefits, they are not subject to distribution.

(B)   Because a substantial portion of the pension benefits were earned during the marriage, they are marital property subject to equitable distribution. Matthew should receive one-half of those benefits.

(C)   Matthew will not receive any pension benefits as long as he was working outside the home and also earned pension benefits.

(D)   The pension benefits earned *during the marriage* are marital property subject to distribution so Matthew will be entitled to roughly one-quarter of the pension benefits.

92. William and Wanda Weatherspoon live in the state of Wordaho. They have been having marital difficulties, at least in part, because William wants to accept a job opportunity in New Arizico more than 1,000 miles away. William accepts the job and moves to New Arizico, confident that Wanda will eventually agree to join him there. William leases an apartment for a year, opens a bank account, gets a new driver's license, and registers to vote. Several months later, Wanda tells him that she has never set foot in New Arizico and never will. Not long after that, William files for divorce, making sure that Wanda is served with actual notice. He has more than met New Arizico's residency requirement. When the divorce is granted, the judge divides some of the marital property located in Wardaho. Wanda does not wish to contest the divorce, but she does want to contest the property division. She consults an attorney to find out what can be done. What should the attorney say?

    (A) In order to challenge the property division, Wanda will also have to challenge the validity of the divorce, e.g., by arguing that William had not established domicile in New Arizico.

    (B) Because the New Arizico court had jurisdiction to grant the divorce, the court also had jurisdiction to divide up the property, so there is no basis for challenging the property division.

    (C) If Wanda had wanted to protect her rights, she could have easily made an appearance at the New Arizico proceeding. By failing to make an appearance, she lost her opportunity to contest the decision later.

    (D) While the New Arizico court likely had jurisdiction to grant the divorce, it likely did not have jurisdiction to divide the property located in Wardaho, so Wanda can challenge the property division even if she has no basis upon which to challenge the divorce.

93. Same question as 92, except this time the only property division by the court involved property located in New Arizico. What result?

    (A) Because the New Arizico court did not have jurisdiction over Wanda, it could neither grant the divorce nor divide marital property.

    (B) The court could grant the divorce because William was a domiciliary of New Arizico who had met the residency requirement and who had given actual notice to Wanda. However, courts are split with respect to whether a court has the power to distribute marital property located in that state under these circumstances.

    (C) If Wanda had wished to contest the divorce or protect her property interests, she should have hired an attorney to represent her interests in New Arizico. She lost her opportunity to contest the decision when she decided not to go to New Arizico.

    (D) While the New Arizico court clearly had jurisdiction to grant the divorce, it did not have jurisdiction over Wanda and thus could not distribute any marital property under these circumstances.

94. Bailey and Blair Billingswood live in New Vermshire, a common law state. Bailey purchases a painting with monies coming from his paycheck. The Billingswoods then move to the state of Orington, a community property state. Ten years later, they divorce. They can agree about the property division with respect to everything except the painting. How should it be characterized?

    (A) It should be characterized as separate property because it was bought with funds solely from Bailey's paycheck.

    (B) It should be characterized as community property because it was bought with funds from Bailey's paycheck earned while he was married to Blair.

    (C) It should be characterized as marital property because it was bought in a common law state with funds from Bailey's paycheck earned while he was married to Blair.

    (D) It should be characterized as quasi-community property because it would have qualified as marital property had they remained in New Vermshire but they are divorcing in Orington, a community property state.

95. Ashton buys a very expensive watch for his spouse, Brett, using monies from a joint checking account, while Brett gives Ashton a car (with a value roughly equal to that of the watch) also purchased from that account. When Ashton and Brett divorce years later, they disagree about how these gifts should be characterized. What are the appropriate characterizations of the watch and the car?

ANSWER:

96. Harlow owns her own home, although she still has to pay off a substantial mortgage. When she marries Scout, they decide to live in Harlow's home. During the marriage, Harlow continues to make the mortgage payments, which come out of her salary. When Harlow and Scout divorce 10 years later, Harlow argues that the house is her separate property and is not subject to distribution. Scout argues that the house is Harlow's separate property but that the marital estate must be reimbursed for all the mortgage payments. How should this be resolved?

ANSWER:

Custody/Visitation

97. John and Joanna Smith are married and raising two of John's children from a previous marriage, Matthew, age 8, and Marilyn, age 6. Regrettably, John and Joanna are divorcing and each seeks custody. Marilyn has not adopted the children and the state in which they all live does not recognize *in loco parentis*, de facto parent, functional parent, or psychological parent status. Nor does it accord stepparents any special rights via statute. John and Joanna are both fit parents. Who is likely to be awarded custody of the children?

    (A) John will likely be awarded custody of the children only if their best interests would be promoted by his having custody.

    (B) Joanna will likely be awarded custody if her having custody would promote the best interests of the children.

    (C) John will likely be awarded custody as long as his having custody would not be detrimental to the children.

    (D) Custody will likely be decided in accord with the stated preferences, if any, of Matthew and Marilyn.

98. Alexander Adamson, age 34, and Alice Adamson, age 28, live in the state of Missabama, with their two children, Bobby, age six, and Beatrice, age five, both of whom would prefer to live with their mother. Missabama recognizes a tender years presumption.

    Alice appeals Alexander's having been awarded custody of their two children in their divorce, claiming that the trial court did not give adequate weight to the tender years presumption, given that both Alexander and Alice are fit parents. Is Alice's challenge likely to be successful?

    (A) Because the presumption suggests that a teenage parent is presumed to be disfavored in a custody dispute if the other parent is older, the presumption is not triggered and the appeal will be dismissed.

    (B) Because the presumption suggests that children who are very young are insufficiently mature to have their preferences given weight, the trial court correctly employed the presumption and the appeal will not be successful.

    (C) Because the state employs a rebuttable presumption that a mother should be awarded custody of young children, the trial court opinion may be reversed and remanded, absent some evidence that the presumption has been rebutted.

(D) Because the presumption is irrebuttable that the mother should be awarded custody of young children, the trial court decision will be reversed and Alice will be awarded custody.

99. Chicago and Nevada are married and have two children, Dakota, age 15, and Phoenix, age 14. Both Dakota and Phoenix have expressed a preference to live with Chicago and the court nonetheless granted custody to Nevada. Chicago appeals, claiming that the trial court did not give adequate weight to the children's express preferences. What result?

(A) Because the express preferences of children at least 14 years of age are dispositive, the trial court grant of custody to Nevada will be reversed.

(B) Because children are minors, their preferences have no legal weight and the appeal will be dismissed.

(C) Custody will be awarded to the parent who would promote the best interests of the child, and a mature child's express preferences will be overridden if there is reason to believe that granting those preferences would not promote the child's best interests. The disposition of this case will depend in part upon why the trial court rejected the children's stated preferences.

(D) Because trial court custody decisions are intensely fact-dependent, the trial court cannot be reversed on this basis.

100. Arthur and Betty Donaldson have been married for 10 years. Each thinks the other a horrible person and an even worse parent. They are divorcing and each seeks custody of their eight-year-old daughter, Carol. Both are fit parents who love Carol. At trial, Arthur's attorney suggests that Arthur should get custody because Arthur would promote Carol's having a good relationship with Betty, while Betty would do her utmost to prevent Arthur from having any relationship with their daughter. To what degree, if any, should such a factor play in the determination of who should have primary custody?

(A) The factor is irrelevant. The dispositive issue is which parent's having custody would best promote the child's interests.

(B) The factor is dispositive because children do best when they have good relationships with both (fit) parents.

(C) The ability to promote the child's having a good relationship with the noncustodial parent is one factor among many to consider when making a custody determination.

(D) The ability to promote the child's having a good relationship with the noncustodial parent is a factor than can only be used as a tiebreaker when the other factors do not favor one parent over the other with respect to who should have custody.

101. Nancy and Oscar Palmer are divorced. Nancy has custody of their child, Robert. Oscar seeks a modification of custody, claiming that his increased salary is a material change in circumstances justifying the modification. The trial court agrees and Nancy appeals. What result?

(A) This is a paradigmatic example of a material change, because Oscar now earns substantially more, which constitutes a significant change in the ability of a parent to provide material support. The appeal will likely be dismissed.

(B) While states generally require a material change in circumstances to modify custody, they do not merely mean an increase in salary. Rather, what must be shown is a significant change that adversely affects the child. An increase in Oscar's salary would not constitute an adverse change, especially because that increase in salary might help Robert even if Nancy retains custody, for example, if Oscar's child support obligation is increased.

(C) A material change in circumstances is any change that either parent believes significant. Oscar obviously believes the change significant, so the trial court modification will likely be upheld if Oscar is better able to provide for Robert's needs and desires.

(D) A material change in circumstances is any change that the child believes is significant. If Robert believes that Oscar's increase in salary is important, then the appeal will likely be dismissed.

102. Adrian are Bevan are divorced, and Bevan has custody of their child, Chris. Adrian seeks to modify custody, accusing Bevan of parental alienation. What effect, if any, might there be on the custodial arrangement if Adrian's allegation is true?

(A) There will likely be no effect on the custodial arrangement. Divorced parents often do not get along and may well be alienated from each other long before the divorce.

(B) There will likely be no effect on the custodial arrangement, absent indications of harm to Chris. It is not uncommon for parents to be temporarily alienated from the children in their care and this is not a matter of concern unless that alienation has a significant and deleterious effect on the child.

(C) This will likely result in a change of custody if Bevan is so alienated from parenting that Bevan cannot perform those tasks that must be performed if Chris is to thrive.

(D) In extreme cases, one parent's alienating the child from the other parent can result in a modification of custody.

103. Charlie and Skyler are married and live in New Caledonia with their two children, Ann and Devon. Charlie and Skyler divorce, with Charlie being awarded custody of the children. Skyler moves to Old Jersey to start a new job, where he meets and marries Casey. Skyler seeks a modification of custody in Old Jersey, claiming that his new job and new spouse constitute a material change in circumstances justifying his having custody. What is the likely result?

(A) Skyler's request is likely to be denied assuming that Charlie has also remarried and advanced professionally.

(B) Skyler's request is likely to be granted if he can show that he is now able to provide a good home for his children.

(C) As to whether Skyler's request will be approved, this will depend upon whether Ann and Devon get along with Casey.

(D) Skyler's request is likely to be dismissed because it should have been filed in New Caledonia under the New Caledonia and Old Jersey versions of the Uniform Child Custody and Jurisdiction Enforcement Act (UCCJEA).

104. Suppose that the facts of Question 103 are modified in the following way: Both Charlie and Skyler remain in New Caledonia, and Skyler files in New Caledonia for a modification of custody in light of his new job and spouse, Casey. What result?

(A) Skyler's request is likely to be denied, assuming that Charlie has also remarried and advanced professionally.

(B) Skyler's request is likely to be granted if he can show that he is now able to provide a good home for his children.

(C) As to whether Skyler's request will be approved, this will depend upon whether Ann and Devon get along with Casey.

(D) As to whether Skyler's request will be granted, this will depend upon whether Skyler can show that there has been a material change in circumstances adversely affecting the children and that his having custody would best promote their interests.

105. Denver and Dakota Donaldson are married and live in the state of West Delolina. They divorce and Denver is awarded primary physical custody of their two children, Zachary and Yolanda. Denver is given permission to move with the children to the neighboring state of Florabama.

On a few different occasions, Denver has heard some disturbing stories from Zachary and Yolanda when they returned from visiting Dakota in West Delolina. Dakota denies that anything untoward has happened. Denver files in a Florabama court to restrict Dakota's visitation rights. What result?

(A) Assuming that these stories do not allege something that would endanger the children, Denver's request will be denied because it is the word of children against the word of an adult.

(B) Even assuming that these stories do not allege something dangerous, Denver's request will likely be granted if the allegations involve something that would be contrary to the children's best interests.

(C) Even assuming that these stories do not allege something dangerous, the Florabama court will have jurisdiction to decide this issue because Florabama is the children's home state, although it is unclear what the court will do.

(D) Assuming that these stories do not justify the Florabama court's having jurisdiction, e.g., because of an emergency exception, Denver will have to seek to modify visitation in West Delolina, where Dakota still lives.

106. Paris and Pat Parkington are divorced and live in Old York. Paris has custody of their two children. Pat sees the children infrequently, often canceling his scheduled time for visitation at the last minute. Paris has received a wonderful job offer in New Calington, which is 3,000 miles away. Pat objects to Paris's taking the children so far away, because it will make visitation with them too difficult. Paris points out that New Calington has much better schools and that Paris's new position would be both better-paying and allow more time with the children. Further, most of the extended family on both sides live in New Calington. Finally, Pat has not been taking advantage of visitation opportunities now, so it could not plausibly be said that the move would undermine Pat's strong relationship with the children. What result?

(A) Paris will not be permitted to move because the children living so far away would impair their relationship with Pat.

(B) Paris will be permitted to move with the children because preventing such a move would abridge her right to travel.

(C) Paris will not be allowed to move because she is obviously moving to advance her career.

(D) Paris is likely to be allowed to move as long as she is able to establish why the move would promote the best interests of the children.

107. Robert and Sarah Tarkington are divorced and live in Delington. Robert has custody of their two children, Wyatt and Yolanda, although Sarah sees the children frequently. While Robert and Sarah both have good relationships with their children, they cannot stand each other. Robert has been offered in excellent job in New Vermshire. He would be making significantly more money and be in a location with a significantly lower cost of living. The schools are better there and they would be moving closer to family. Sarah opposes the relocation, claiming that Robert's primary purpose in moving is to undermine her relationship with the children. What result?

(A) If Robert has a genuine offer with a significantly higher salary in a place with a lower cost of living, the increased income will likely inure to the benefit of the children. The request will likely be granted.

(B) If Sarah is correct that Robert's primary reason for moving is to undermine the children's relationship with her, then the request will likely be denied.

(C) If Robert is accurate when claiming that the schools are better and that the children will be much closer to family, then the move would benefit the children and likely be approved.

(D) The request will likely be rejected, because Sarah would not be able to see the children as frequently if they moved.

108. Ulysses and Ursula Underwood are divorced and live in New Mexizona. Ulysses has custody of their two children, Alice and Beatrice. Ulysses plans to remarry and his betrothed has a wonderful job in East Jersey, which is more than 1,000 miles away. Ulysses seeks permission

to relocate with the children. Ursula opposes the relocation and instead requests a modification of custody. She notes that Ulysses has not been very good at promoting the children's relationship with her and fears that a move so far away would make it even more difficult for her to have a good relationship with the children. She further notes that the children have many cousins in New Mexizona and are flourishing in their current schools. What result?

(A) Relocation is not in and of itself a significant change in circumstances, so Ursula will not be permitted to seek a custody modification.

(B) As long as Ulysses is not seeking to relocate in bad faith, he cannot lose custody of his children merely because he wants to live with his new spouse together with the children.

(C) If the custodial parent is benefited, then the children are benefited too, so a proposed relocation is unlikely to be viewed as sufficiently detrimental to justify a custody modification.

(D) A proposed relocation may well justify a change in custody if the children's moving would undermine their relationship with the noncustodial parent and extended family and would also remove them from an environment in which they were thriving.

109. Reese and Robin Rohrington are going through a divorce after Robin discovered that Reese has had an affair. Both parents have a good relationship with their 10-year-old child, Brian, and both seek primary custody. Robin claims that Reese's having committed adultery demonstrates that Reese should not have custody, whereas Reese claims that Robin is so angry that Robin will be unable to promote a relationship between Reese and Brian and thus should not be awarded custody. What result?

ANSWER:

110. Alfred, age 14, and Beatrice, age 15, live with their mother, Carla, who has recently married their stepfather, David. Regrettably, Alfred and Beatrice have a very strained relationship with David and, in fact, are afraid of him. Alfred and Beatrice's father, Gerry, has also remarried. Alfred and Beatrice get along very well with their stepmother, Henrietta. Alfred and Beatrice have explained to their father that while they do not want to hurt their mother, they would much prefer to live with him. Gerry files for a modification of custody. What result?

ANSWER:

111. Alex and Barbara are divorced and Alex has custody of their son, Ronald. One weekend while visiting with Barbara, Ronald mentions that he is excited because Alex is going to marry Justice, who will be moving into the house. Barbara had no idea that Alex and Justice were going to marry. She disapproves of the relationship and files to modify custody. What result?

ANSWER:

112. Charlie and Murphy are unmarried and living together in the state of Massecticut with Robert, a child born to Murphy through artificial insemination. Charlie adopts Robert, as is permitted under state law. After several years, Charlie and Murphy decide to end their relationship. Each has a good relationship with Robert and each seeks primary physical custody of Robert. How should this be resolved?

ANSWER:

113. Ramsey and Sidney are married and raising Nancy, Sidney's child from a previous marriage, in the state of New Arizico. After several years, Ramsey and Sidney divorce, each seeking primary physical custody of Nancy. Each has a good relationship with Nancy. What result?

ANSWER:

114. Finley and Dominique are married and living in in the state of Idoming. They are both fit parents and have two children, Icarus and Penelope. When they divorce, Finley seeks custody of Icarus whereas Dominique seeks custody of both children. What result?

ANSWER:

115. Leslie and Salem are living together without benefit of marriage and raising Leslie's son, Nathaniel, in Massecticut. While local law permitted Salem to adopt Nathaniel, Salem never did so. Salem and Nathaniel have a good relationship and Nathaniel views Salem as one of his parents. Leslie and Salem are ending their relationship, and each seeks custody of Nathaniel. What result?

ANSWER:

116. Arthur and Alexandra Zanington, who live in Minnegan, have been trying to conceive for a long time. They finally consult a fertility specialist and discover that Alexandra is unable to have children. They contract with a surrogate, who will be artificially inseminated with Arthur's sperm and who will then surrender the child. Sarah Surrogate is artificially inseminated, becomes pregnant, and carries the child to term. After giving birth to Marshall, Sarah is unable to surrender him. Arthur and Alexandra sue to force Sarah to relinquish the child. What result?

ANSWER:

117. Carl and Doris Ellington live in East Monaho and have been trying to have a child without success. They discover that while Doris can produce eggs, she cannot carry a pregnancy to term. They decide to use in vitro fertilization whereby embryos will be created from their genetic material and those embryos will be implanted in a surrogate. They contract with Mary Moore to be their gestational surrogate. When Mary gives birth to twins, she finds that she

is unable to surrender them. Carl and Doris sue to force Mary to surrender the children. What result?

ANSWER:

118. Maxwell and Melinda Mallington live in the state of Pennsyltucky. They are divorcing, and each seeks custody of their child, Norman. Maxwell and Melinda are both fit parents and each would promote a good relationship with the other parent. However, shared parenting is not an option. Melinda is awarded custody.

Alice Attorney, representing Maxwell Mallington, challenges the awarding of custody to Melinda, claiming that custody is disproportionately awarded to mothers rather than fathers. In support of her contention that the custody award must be reversed, Alice notes that the Pennsyltucky Supreme Court has struck down the state's tender years presumption as a violation of the equal protection guarantees of the state constitution. What result?

ANSWER:

Support

119. Norman and Nancy Newington are married and living in Nebransas, which requires couples to live separate and apart for two years before they can before they can end their marriages on a no-fault ground. Norman wants to end his marriage more quickly than that and so goes to the state of Freedamia, which has a one-week residency requirement and has the reputation of being a divorce mill. He establishes residency, gives Nancy actual notice, and secures a divorce.

   Norman goes back to Nebransas, where he meets Paula Pringley, a divorcee who has been receiving spousal support and will continue to receive that support until her death or remarriage. Norman explains that he was married but that he secured a quickie divorce in Freedamia. Paula admires Norman's initiative and marries him, which pleases Peter Pringley, who is now relieved of a support obligation.

   One year after Nancy finds out that Norman has remarried, she challenges the validity of the divorce judgment that Norman secured in Freedamia, claiming that the Freedamia court did not have jurisdiction to grant the divorce. The Nebransas court holds that the divorce is not entitled to full faith and credit, which makes Norman's marriage to Paula invalid because Norman is still married to Nancy. Paula, who now never wants to see Norman again, seeks to have Peter's support payments reinstated because her marriage to Norman was void from the beginning. What result?

   (A) Because Paula's marriage to Norman was void *ab initio*, Peter's support payments may well be reinstated.

   (B) Because Paula was willing to forego those support payments by marrying Norman, no jurisdiction would be willing to reinstate the support payments on these facts.

   (C) Because the harm to Paula should have been foreseen by Nancy when she waited to challenge the validity of Norman's divorce, Nancy will be responsible for making up the payments that Paula lost.

   (D) Because Norman knew that Paula's support payments would end were she to marry him, Norman will now be responsible for making the support payments to Paula.

120. Rhonda Robertson and Seth Seligson have been unhappily married for several years in the state of Old York. Seth discovers that Rhonda has been having an affair and is awarded a divorce and spousal support.

   Seth meets and starts to date Tania Thomas, who has told him that she would love to have a large family. Seth, who has always wanted a large family, eventually proposes and he and Tania marry. To Seth's surprise, Tania now says that she has never wanted children and she will only have sexual relations with Seth if they are using contraception. Seth consults an attorney to find out if he can have the marriage annulled and the support payments reinstated. What should the attorney say?

(A) Because it is unclear whether Seth and Tania would have been able to have children even if they had sexual relations without using contraception, Seth will be unable to secure an annulment and will also be unable to have the support payments reinstated.

(B) Seth is likely to be able to have the marriage annulled. While his ability to have the support payments reinstated is a matter of local law and so will have to be researched, some jurisdictions refuse to reinstate such payments if the second marriage is voidable, even if the payments would have been reinstated had the second marriage been void *ab initio*.

(C) Seth is unlikely to be able to have the marriage annulled unless he explicitly told Tania that he would marry her only if she were willing to have a large family. If he is able to get the marriage annulled, then he of course can have the support payments reinstated.

(D) Assuming that Seth ends his marriage to Tania, his ability to have the support payments reinstated will depend solely upon whether Rhonda has taken on additional financial responsibilities in the interim.

121. Cora and David Ellington have been married for 25 years. Their youngest child, Simone, has just graduated from college and David has announced that he wants a divorce from Cora. Cora had the primary responsibility for taking care of the children and never worked outside of the home. She consults an attorney to find out whether she will be entitled to permanent support. The attorney responds that several factors make it likely that she will be entitled to receive such support. Which of the following would be unlikely to be considered when determining whether permanent support should be ordered?

(A) The significant likelihood that, even with training, Mary would be unable to enter the job market.

(B) The length of the marriage.

(C) The ages of the couple's children.

(D) The standard of living to which the couple has become accustomed.

122. Alex Aronson is going through a divorce and he is seeking permanent rather than rehabilitative support. Which of the following, if true, would provide support for Alex?

(A) Evidence establishing that Alex does not need psychological counseling to help him recover from emotional abuse.

(B) Evidence establishing that Alex does not need physical therapy to help him recover from physical abuse.

(C) Evidence establishing that because Alex had been out of the job market for so long while he was staying home raising the children, he will be unable to reenter the labor market even with training.

(D) Evidence establishing that Alex was an innocent spouse and has no need to be rehabilitated.

123. Bernard and Bernice Benington are going through a divorce. Bernard has threatened to seek custody of their two children unless Bernice agrees to forego both spousal and child support. Both Bernard and Bernice have good jobs, so it is not as if the children will suffer if Bernard does not pay support. Bernice is willing to forego any support from Bernard as long as he will not seek custody. Is the court likely to enforce the agreement that Bernard pay no support assuming that no fraud, coercion, or duress can be established?

(A) The court is likely to enforce the agreement because Bernard is refraining from doing something that he clearly has the right to do, namely, seek custody.

(B) The court is unlikely to approve any agreement with respect to either child or spousal support because all monies coming into the custodial home would benefit the children.

(C) While the court might normally order child support, it will enforce their agreement that no such support be paid in this case because Bernice makes enough for the children to be comfortable.

(D) The court is unlikely to enforce the agreement that Bernard not child pay support, both because such an agreement would not promote the children's interests and because Bernice cannot bargain away child support in exchange for uncontested custody. However, the court might approve Bernice's not receiving spousal support.

124. Emerson and Dakota Samuelson were married and had two children. Emerson and Dakota divorced with Emerson being awarded custody. Regrettably, Emerson and Dakota made no specification at the time of divorce about who, if anyone, would contribute to the costs of the college educations of their children. Now, the children are ready to go to college and Emerson wants Dakota to help bear that financial burden. Dakota has thus far refused and Emerson consults an attorney to find out what the options are. What should the attorney say?

(A) While Emerson and Dakota could have specified in their divorce agreement that each would be responsible to contribute to the children's college educations, it is now too late and Dakota cannot be forced to contribute.

(B) Depending upon local law, Dakota might be responsible for paying some of the college education costs, lack of specification to that effect in the divorce decree notwithstanding.

(C) Because a college education is now viewed as a necessity just as a high school education was viewed generations ago, all states require parents to make reasonable contributions to their children's college education costs.

(D) Assuming that the children are 18 years of age now that they are ready to go to college, Dakota cannot be forced to contribute to their college educations because the children have attained majority.

125. Sidney and Leslie are married and have twins. When Sidney and Leslie divorce, Sidney agrees that he will contribute to reasonable college costs assuming that he has a say in where the children go to school. When the children are college age, they receive acceptances from several schools, including Very Expensive College, Prestigious State University and Very Good State University, the flagship school of the state in which they live. Sidney urges the children to go to Very Good State University, which he asserts is the best value. However, the children want to attend Very Expensive College. Sidney consults his attorney to find out whether he must pay his share of the expenses at Very Expensive College. What should the attorney say?

(A) The attorney should say that Sidney has had his say when suggesting that the flagship state school was the best value and that he will have to pay his share of college costs for whatever school his children ultimately attend.

(B) The attorney should say that the agreement about college expenses is only aspirational, so Sidney will only have to pay whatever he believes is appropriate.

(C) The attorney should explain that his agreement to share college expenses implicitly only requires him to pay state university expenses, so he will be responsible for his share of Prestigious State University costs, even though the flagship university of their state is significantly less expensive than the costs of Prestigious State University.

(D) The attorney should say that Sidney's failure to specify that he would only pay the costs of a state university may obligate him to pay more, although there may well be case law or a statute specifying that he will only be responsible for in-state tuition. His case is especially strong because of the quality of the flagship and because he included the requirement that he have some say in the ultimate decision.

126. John and Melinda Nickerson have been trying to conceive for several years but have been unsuccessful. They both undergo fertility testing and discover that John is sterile. They agree that Melinda should undergo artificial insemination. Melinda becomes pregnant and eventually delivers a child, Oscar.

Five years later, John and Melinda divorce, in large part because John feels no connection to Oscar. John objects to paying child support because he has no emotional or genetic connection to Oscar. Melinda argues that he must pay support because he is Oscar's legal parent. What result?

(A) Because John is neither emotionally nor genetically related to Oscar, he should neither be accorded visitation rights nor support obligations.

(B) Because he agreed to the artificial insemination and because the child was born into the marriage, John is likely to be ordered to pay support.

(C) Because John was married to Melinda at the time of Oscar's conception and birth, John is legally responsible for Oscar and so can be ordered to pay support.

(D) Because John agreed to the artificial insemination so that he could have a child with whom he would bond and because that bonding did not occur notwithstanding John's good faith efforts, John cannot now be forced to pay support for someone whom he views as a complete stranger.

127. Norman and Penelope have been having trouble conceiving. They find out that Norman is sterile and they decide to use artificial insemination. Penelope begins that process and, before too long, discovers that she is pregnant. Penelope gives birth to a little girl, Sarah.

When Norman and Penelope divorce shortly after the birth, Noman argues that he should not have to pay support for Sarah with whom he has never bonded. Norman presents evidence establishing that Sarah is genetically related to Penelope's paramour, Thomas. Penelope argues that genetics is unimportant, because Norman agreed to the artificial insemination. What result?

(A) Because Norman is not genetically related to Sarah, he is not responsible for her support.

(B) Because Norman agreed to the artificial insemination, he is responsible for Sarah's support.

(C) Norman will likely be ordered to pay child support because it would be in Sarah's best interests to receive that support.

(D) Norman would be unlikely to be ordered to pay support if the pregnancy had not resulted from artificial insemination. However, the answer is much less clear if it can be shown that the standard procedures for artificial insemination were followed, e.g., if they had used a doctor as an intermediary, and the sexual relationship between Penelope and Thomas began after the pregnancy had begun.

128. Skyler and Dominique have been married for several years. During that period, two children were born, Abigail and Bertrand, and Skyler had assumed that he was genetically related to each of them. Skyler had very good relationships with both children until discovering that each child was the result of an extramarital affair. Once the children's parentage came to light, Skyler wanted to have nothing to do with Dominique, Abigail, or Bertrand. Will the judgment granting a divorce likely impose a duty of support on Skyler?

(A) Skyler is likely to be ordered to pay child support because Skyler's financial support would promote the children's interests.

(B) Skyler is unlikely to be ordered to pay support for children conceived as a result of extra-marital relations because he cannot be held financially responsible for children fathered by someone else.

(C) Skyler is likely to be ordered to pay support only if he earns more than Dominique does.

(D) Jurisdictions differ about whether a support obligation should be imposed on an individual who had maintained parent-child relationships in the good faith but mistaken belief that he was genetically related to the children.

129. Apollo and Beatrice have been married for several years. Two children were born of the marriage, Cleo and Diane. Apollo has an excellent relationship with the children, which Beatrice always encouraged. However, recently, Apollo and Beatrice have often been fighting and during one heated exchange Beatrice reveals that Apollo is not the father of either child. When they divorce, Apollo seeks custody of the children. Beatrice argues that Apollo should neither have support obligations nor the right to have any contact with the children. What result?

(A) Because Apollo is not genetically related to the children and has not adopted them, he is a legal stranger to them and will be denied both parental rights and parental responsibilities.

(B) Because Beatrice encouraged Apollo to believe that he was the children's father, she will likely be estopped from denying his relationship to them now.

(C) Because on these facts Apollo likely would have been able to seek to avoid paying child support, it is only fair that Beatrice be afforded the opportunity to prevent him from having any parental rights or obligations.

(D) Because Apollo has no genetic connection to the children and thus cannot be required to pay support, he also should not be able to seek visitation or custody privileges.

130. Grant and Hermione have been dating for several months. Hermione would very much like to have a child, although Grant is adamantly against becoming a father. In fact, Grant refuses to have unprotected sexual relations. One day, Hermione announces that she is pregnant and that she wants to carry the child to term. She explains that she has not had sexual relations with anyone other than Grant and that no form of contraception is foolproof. After giving birth to John, Hermione seeks child support from Grant. Grant is willing to pay support until he finds out that Hermione had lied to him about using contraception and that the pregnancy was due to their having had unprotected sexual relations. What result?

(A) While Grant would have been responsible for child support had the pregnancy resulted from contracepted sexual relations, he cannot be required to pay support when he in effect was fraudulently induced to become a father.

(B) Assuming that Grant is the father, he will likely be required to pay child support, misrepresentation about contraception notwithstanding.

(C) Grant will only be required to pay child support if Hermione is unable to provide for John's needs on her own.

(D) Grant will not be required to pay support only if Hermione had actual notice that he refused to have unprotected sexual relations and if she expressly lied about using contraception.

131. John and Karen are unmarried and have been dating for more than a year. Karen became pregnant and she told John that he was the father. When Bobbi was born, John acknowledged paternity and became responsible for child support. When Bobbi was older, John realized that she looked nothing like him. He had a DNA test performed and he has been excluded as Bobbi's possible father. Karen admitted that he was not the father but told him that he would have to continue to pay anyway. He now seeks to disestablish paternity. What result?

    (A) Because John acted in a timely way once he became suspicious that he was not Bobbi's father and because his acknowledgment was based on Karen's misrepresentation that he was Bobbi's father, he may well be permitted to disestablish his paternity.

    (B) Because John voluntarily acknowledged paternity, he cannot now take back that acknowledgment.

    (C) John will be allowed to disestablish paternity only if he can demonstrate that Karen knew all along that he was not Bobbi's father.

    (D) John will be permitted to disestablish paternity only if he can demonstrate who Bobbi's biological father is.

132. Craig and Diane both have well-paying jobs. They are married and have two children, Edward and Fiona. Craig and Diane's marriage has been rather rocky for a long time and they decide to divorce. Diane is awarded primary physical custody of the children and Craig is ordered to pay support. Ever since the divorce, Craig has felt extremely alienated from his family and his job. He quits his job and moves back into his parents' house. He has looked for a job that would be more rewarding but has not yet been successful in finding one. Because he has no income, he files to modify his support payment. He notes that the children's needs are more than met based on Diane's salary alone. What result?

    (A) Because Craig has no income, he cannot be forced to pay child support. His child support obligation will be terminated, although it may be reinstated once he finds work.

    (B) Because Craig has lost his job and has been looking for another job, his support obligation will be suspended until he finds one, at which point his support obligation will be reinstated in light of his new salary.

    (C) Because the children's needs have not changed, Craig's support obligation will not be changed.

    (D) Because Craig voluntarily quit his job without adequate justification knowing that he had child support obligations, the court might well refuse to reduce the amount he must pay in child support.

133. Methuselah was 15 years older than Sarah when they married, and Sarah was already well into her late thirties by the time they made their vows. Two children were born to the marriage. Regrettably, their marriage has come to an end. They agreed that Sarah would have

primary physical custody of the children. Methuselah's support obligation was set in light of his income. A few years later, Methuselah seeks to modify his support obligation because he is already over age 65 and has decided to retire. Sarah argues that support should not be modified because the children's financial needs have not decreased. What result?

(A) Because Methuselah is not retiring early but instead is retiring at an appropriate age, his support obligation will likely be reduced to reflect his lower income.

(B) The determination of whether his support obligation will be modified will depend in part on whether the retirement is voluntary and on whether he is retiring in order to reduce his child support payments.

(C) Because his children's financial needs have not decreased, Methuselah's support obligation is unlikely to be reduced.

(D) Because Sarah knew that Methuselah would be retirement age before any of their children would reach majority, she cannot now contest his seeking to lower his support payments now that he is in fact retiring.

134. Casey and Robin divorce. Casey is awarded primary physical custody of the children, Oscar and Penny, and Robin is required to pay child support. Casey's overtime pay has been cut back significantly, so Casey seeks an increase in support from Robin. In the meantime, Robin has had twins, whom she supports. Robin opposes the support increase because she now has responsibility for two additional children. What result?

(A) Robin's having had twins is irrelevant because she had them knowing that she already had duties of support for Oscar and Penny.

(B) Robin's support obligation must be increased because of the decrease in Casey's annual salary.

(C) Robin's support obligation may well not be increased because she has a legal obligation to support the twins.

(D) Because Casey is not at all responsible for Robin's having had additional children, Casey's family cannot be forced to incur opportunity costs just because Robin decided to take on additional obligations. Robin's support obligation will be increased.

135. Dakota and Phoenix have one child. When they divorce, Dakota is awarded primary physical custody and Phoenix is ordered to pay child support. Phoenix remarries and has a child. Phoenix decides to quit her job to stay home and take care of her newborn. Phoenix seeks to terminate her child support obligation until she no longer needs to stay home with her youngest child. Dakota opposes any change in the support obligation. What result?

ANSWER:

136. Charlie and Skyler are married, live in New Mexizona, and have one child, William. Upon their divorce, Charlie is awarded primary physical custody of William and Skyler is ordered

to pay support. Skyler decides to start a new life in Washifornia, where she has a wonderful job. Regrettably, Skyler is laid off due to a downturn in the economy. Skyler files in Washifornia to have her support obligation reduced, which Charlie opposes. New Mexizona and Washifornia each have versions of the Uniform Interstate Family Support Act, which mirror each other and the Uniform Act. What result?

(A) Skyler is likely to be successful because her being laid off was not her fault.

(B) Skyler is unlikely to be successful because William's needs have not diminished merely because Skyler was laid off.

(C) Because Charlie made a personal appearance to oppose the modification, the Washifornia court is likely to address Skyler's request on the merits in light of Washifornia law.

(D) Skyler is unlikely to be successful on the merits because, under UIFSA, Washifornia does not have subject matter jurisdiction to modify child support.

137. Reese and Riley Robertson are married and living in the state of Monaho. When they divorce, Reese is ordered to pay spousal support to Riley. Reese receives and accepts a wonderful job offer in Old York. Regrettably, the company goes out of business a few years later because one of the officers misappropriated large sums of money. Reese is one of the many innocent people to lose a job as a result of the officer's wrongdoing. Reese, who has been diligently searching for a new job but has been unable to find one, files in Old York to have the spousal support obligation suspended until Reese is employed again. Riley appears and opposes the modification. Monaho and Old York each have versions of the Uniform Family Support Act, which mirror each other and the Uniform Act. What result?

(A) Because Reese was not at all responsible for becoming unemployed, the support obligation will be suspended until Reese is able to find another job.

(B) Because Riley's financial needs have not changed, Reese will simply have to borrow money or sell personal assets to pay the spousal support obligation, which will not be modified.

(C) Because Riley appeared to contest the modification, the Old York court will have to weigh Riley's needs against Reese's ability to pay and decide what would be equitable in light of all of the circumstances.

(D) Reese is unlikely to be successful because, under UIFSA, Monaho rather than Old York has jurisdiction to decide whether the spousal support obligation should be modified.

138. Parker and Phoenix Pellington have lived their entire lives in the state of West Pennio. Both of their families have been there for generations. Parker receives a wonderful job offer in Michisota and Parker and Phoenix decide to move there. Parker is quite happy to be away from West Pennio but Phoenix is homesick and, further, has had some difficulty in finding a job. Phoenix's father is sick and Phoenix decides to go back home to take care of him. Phoenix remains in West Pennio much longer than anticipated and realizes that moving to Michisota was a mistake. In the meantime, Parker has started having an affair. Phoenix and Parker

decide to end their marriage. When Phoenix files for divorce in West Pennio seeking spousal support, Parker argues that West Pennio has jurisdiction to grant the divorce but not to order spousal support because Parker is not domiciled in West Pennio. How will the support issue be resolved?

(A) Because a state does not need have to have personal jurisdiction over both parties to a marriage in order to grant a divorce, the West Pennio court will be able to grant the divorce. However, because the court must have personal jurisdiction over both parties to order spousal support, the court will not have jurisdiction to order that support.

(B) Because Parker is not domiciled in West Pennio, the West Pennio court does not have jurisdiction to grant the divorce, his willingness to permit the court to end the marriage notwithstanding.

(C) If a state has jurisdiction to grant a divorce, it also has jurisdiction to order spousal support. The West Pennio court will likely both grant the divorce and order support.

(D) Assuming that Phoenix is now domiciled in West Pennio and has met the residency requirement, the West Pennio court can grant the divorce because at least one of the parties has met the residency requirement and is domiciled there, and the court can order support because it has jurisdiction over Parker via the state's long-arm statute.

139. Tatum and Scout Riverington have two children, Quentin and Penelope. When Tatum and Scout divorce, Tatum is awarded primary physical custody and Scout is ordered to pay support. After two years have passed, both Scout and Tatum have received substantial raises, although the children's needs have not changed. Tatum seeks an increase in child support, which Scout opposes because the current support order more than covers the children's reasonable needs and wants. What result?

(A) Tatum will be unsuccessful. Because the children's needs have not changed, there is no reason to modify the support obligation.

(B) Because Tatum's salary has also increased, there is no need to modify Scout's support obligation. If Scout's salary had increased while Tatum's had remained constant, then an increase in support would have been ordered.

(C) Because there has been a substantial change in Scout's salary and because a child's station in life should not be tied to the child's station in life at the time of divorce, Scout's support obligation will likely be increased.

(D) Whether Scout's support obligation will increase will depend upon whether Scout's salary increase was greater than Tatum's.

140. John and Jillian Kenworthy had quadruplets, Alex, Brian, Carl, and David. John and Jillian then divorced with Jillian having custody and receiving support. The quadruplets are now 17 years of age and John argues that he should not have to pay any child support because all four of his children are emancipated. Which of the following children is least likely to be found emancipated?

(A)   Alex, who serves full time in the Army.

(B)   Brian, who married his high school sweetheart.

(C)   Carl, who is self-supporting and living in his own apartment.

(D)   David, who has impregnated his girlfriend.

141.   Baylor and Emery, age 16, have loved each other for as long as they can remember. One day, they go to a Justice of the Peace, lie about their age, and marry. When Emery's father, Thomas, hears the news, he is pleased. He immediately files to have his child support obligation ended because of Emery's emancipation through marriage. Emery's mother, Trudy, has the marriage annulled. Emery is living with Trudy, and Trudy seeks to have Thomas's support obligation reinstated. Thomas argues that his support obligation ended when Emery became emancipated. What result?

(A)   Thomas's support obligation ended when Emery married and that obligation cannot now be reinstated merely because the marriage did not work out.

(B)   Because the marriage was annulled, Emery may no longer be viewed as emancipated and the child support obligation may well be reinstated.

(C)   Because Emery and Baylor were minors and because neither Emery's nor Baylor's parents consented to the marriage, there never was a valid marriage and the child support payments should not have been terminated in the first place.

(D)   Emery became emancipated by virtue of marrying. While Trudy is free to allow her emancipated child to live with her just as she would be free to allow her adult child to live with her, Thomas cannot be forced to subsidize Trudy's willingness to have Emery come back.

142.   Campbell and Murphy Wellington are married and living in Georabama. They divorce with Campbell required to pay spousal support until Murphy's death or remarriage. Murphy meets Casey and falls head over heels in love. Murphy and Casey marry. Campbell celebrates because he no longer has to pay spousal support.

Murphy discovers that Casey has no interest in having sexual relations. Murphy has the marriage annulled because of this fraud going to the essentials of marriage, and then seeks to have the spousal support reinstated. What result?

(A)   Because the marriage was declared void by a court, it does not exist in the eyes of the law and the spousal support obligations must be reinstated.

(B)   While this is a matter of state law, the Georabama court might well refuse to reinstate the spousal support because Murphy's marriage to Casey was voidable rather than void and thus existed until declared void by a court.

(C)   Whether the spousal support is reinstated will depend solely upon whether Campbell took on new legal obligations, detrimentally relying on the termination of the spousal support order.

(D) While states differ about whether a support obligation can be reinstated, no state will distinguish based upon whether the second marriage is voidable rather than void, because either way the payor (first) spouse might reasonably have relied on the termination of the support obligation once the second marriage ceremony took place.

143. Baylor and Emery are married in New Coloco. They divorce, with Baylor paying support until Emery's death or remarriage. Emery has started cohabiting with Denver, and Baylor consults an attorney about ending the support obligation, given Emery's marriage-like relationship with Denver. What should the attorney say?

(A) If Baylor had wanted Emery's cohabitation with someone to trigger the termination of spousal support, that should have been included in their separation agreement. Now, all Baylor can do is hope that Baylor and Denver marry.

(B) Because Denver and Emery are in effect married even if they have not had a wedding ceremony, Baylor should file to have spousal support terminated at the earliest opportunity.

(C) Whether spousal support can be terminated will depend solely upon whether New Coloco recognizes common law marriage.

(D) Jurisdictions differ about whether spousal support will end upon cohabitation even where there was no specification to that effect included in the divorce decree, so the attorney will have to do some research to find out what New Coloco does in this situation (assuming that she does not know already).

144. Casey Cassingham is a highly paid attorney who has been paying child support to ex-spouse, Kim, for their child, Andrew. Casey decides that serving the poor would be much more gratifying, and so quits the firm and begins working at Legal Aid at a greatly reduced salary. Casey seeks to have the child support obligation reduced, which Kim opposes. What result?

ANSWER:

145. Frankie and Dakota are divorced with Frankie ordered to pay Dakota $2,000/month until Dakota's death or remarriage. Two years after the divorce, Frankie secures a new job paying twice as much as Frankie had previously earned. Dakota seeks to have the spousal support increased in light of Frankie's new salary. Frankie opposes any increase. What result?

ANSWER:

146. Oakley and Justice are divorced, with Justice having custody of their child, Baylor, and Oakley paying child support. Three years later, Oakley is earning substantially more than during the marriage. Justice seeks an increase in child support, which Oakley opposes. What result?

ANSWER:

147. Alex and Beverly have lived together for 10 years. They have been trying to have a child together but have not been successful. They agree that Beverly should undergo artificial insemination

Beverly undergoes artificial insemination, eventually becomes pregnant, and gives birth to a child, Danielle. By the time that Danielle is born, Beverly and Alex have already broken up. Beverly had been having an affair with Carl and Alex suspects that Carl is Danielle's father. In any event, Alex did not agree that Beverly should undergo artificial insemination just so that she could raise the child with someone else. Alex refuses to pay support or have anything to do with Beverly or Danielle. Beverly seeks to establish Alex's duty of support. What result?

ANSWER:

148. Kai and Kelly are divorced, with Kelly having custody of their child and Kai ordered to pay child support. Three years after their divorce was final, Kelly wins $1 million in the state lottery and Kai seeks a reduction in child support in light of Kelly's increased wealth. Kelly opposes any reduction. What result?

ANSWER:

149. Lee and Robin Nelson are married and live in Pennsyltucky. Lee requires medical treatment, which he approves and receives. But Lee does not have enough money to pay his medical bills and the hospital sues Robin. Robin, who did not personally approve the procedure, denies financial responsibility. What result?

(A) Because Lee rather than Robin approved the procedure, only Lee can be held responsible for the medical bills.

(B) Assuming that Pennsyltucky recognizes the doctrine of necessaries and applies it in a gender-neutral fashion, Robin may well be responsible for Lee's medical bills.

(C) Because the case does not involve food, clothing, or housing, the doctrine of necessaries is not applicable and Robin cannot be forced to pay anything.

(D) If it can be shown that Robin thought a less expensive procedure or practitioner more suitable, then the doctrine of necessaries only requires Robin to pay for the lower costs associated with the preferred procedure/practitioner.

150. Jody and Jesse Johnson were married for several years. When they divorced, Jody was ordered to pay Jesse permanent support. Jody now wishes to retire and needs to find out whether the support obligation can be modified to account for the sharp reduction in income that retirement would cause. What should the attorney say?

ANSWER:

Family Privacy and the Constitution

151. Daniel and Ellen dated for several months. Then, Daniel abruptly stopped taking Ellen's calls or returning her texts. Ellen is pregnant, but she has given up trying to tell Daniel. When she gives birth, she puts the child up for adoption, claiming not to know who the father is. The child is placed. One year after the adoption has been finalized, Daniel discovers that he has fathered a child and consults an attorney to determine whether the adoption can be annulled. What should the attorney say?

    (A) Daniel can have the adoption annulled only if he himself is seeking custody of the child.

    (B) Daniel can have the adoption annulled only if he and Ellen would be raising the child together.

    (C) Because of his fundamental interest in parenting, Daniel can have the adoption annulled as long as he acts in a timely fashion now that he has learned that he is a father.

    (D) Absent statutory or state constitutional guarantees offering additional protections, Daniel will be unlikely to be able to have the adoption annulled.

152. Kevin and Leslie have been living together for a few years. Leslie announces that she is pregnant and their relationship begins to change. They argue frequently and never seem to agree about anything. Leslie gives birth to a daughter, Melissa, and Kevin is listed as the father on the birth certificate. Leslie and Kevin argue even more and Leslie moves out to live with her sister. Kevin and Leslie do not contact each other and Kevin neither sees nor supports Melissa. After a few years, Leslie meets Samuel. After a whirlwind courtship, Leslie and Samuel marry. A year later, Samuel wishes to adopt Melissa. Kevin is notified but he objects to the adoption. What result?

    (A) The adoption will not take place, although Kevin may now have to begin paying child support.

    (B) The adoption will take place because Leslie, the custodial parent, believes that the adoption would be in Melissa's best interest.

    (C) The adoption will not take place unless the state permits the child to have more than two parents.

    (D) The adoption is likely to take place. Because Kevin has neither paid support nor established an emotional relationship with Melissa, he is unlikely to be permitted to block the adoption.

153.   Peter and Roberta are married and living in the state of Famland. During a low point in their relationship, Roberta had a brief affair with Paul, resulting in her becoming pregnant. Peter and Roberta start to see a marriage counselor. By the time that the child, Veronica, is born, Peter and Roberta's relationship has been restored. Paul seeks custody of or visitation with Veronica, which is opposed by Peter and Roberta. Famland law does not provide unwed fathers any protections not provided by the United States Constitution. What result?

ANSWER:

154.   Jesse and Kelsey are married and Kelsey has just discovered that she is pregnant. However, she is not yet ready to have a child and wants to abort. Jesse is quite ready to be a parent and offers to be the primary caretaker if Kelsey will carry the child to term. Kelsey considers the offer but ultimately decides to abort. Seeing no other option, Jesse seeks to enjoin Kelsey from obtaining an abortion. What result?

   (A)   The injunction is likely to be granted. Just as Kelsey could not put a child up for adoption without the consent of the other (fit) parent, the mother cannot abort without the consent of the other parent. When the parents' rights cancel each other out, the child's best interest (here, to be born) will win the day.

   (B)   The court will not issue an injunction. A woman's right to abort is fundamental and cannot be restricted by the state or a spouse.

   (C)   The injunction is likely to be issued. Kelsey has offered no important reasons to justify an abortion, e.g., medical risks involved in continuing the pregnancy, especially given Jesse's announced willingness to take on primary caretaking duties. The state's interest in the life of the child will tip the balance in favor of the injunction.

   (D)   The injunction will likely not be granted. The United States Constitution requires that the pregnant woman be permitted to make the ultimate decision in this kind of case, assuming that the fetus is not yet viable.

155.   Paula, 17 years old, is pregnant. She wishes to obtain an abortion, but her parents are adamantly opposed to abortion and local law requires parental permission before an abortion can be obtained. Paula challenges the law as a violation of her constitutional rights. What result?

   (A)   The parental consent provision will likely be upheld. Just as parental consent may be required before a minor marries, parental consent may be required before a minor obtains an abortion.

   (B)   The law is likely to be struck down because minors have constitutional rights just as adults do.

   (C)   The law is likely to be upheld because parents have a fundamental interest in the care of their children and because parents are presumed to know what is best for their children.

(D) The law is likely to be struck down because it does not include a judicial bypass option whereby a pregnant minor is afforded the opportunity to show that she is sufficiently mature and informed to make her own decision about whether to have an abortion.

156. Carol and Donald Evington have been married for several years and have been unable to conceive. They try IVF (in vitro fertilization). They harvest several eggs from Carol and fertilize them with Donald's sperm. Three embryos are implanted in Carol and the rest are frozen.

Carol becomes pregnant with twins. Only after Carol is pregnant does it become clear that Carol and Donald have very different understandings of parenting and family. They begin to fight a lot and they divorce shortly after the twins are born. Carol and Donald can agree about everything except about what to do with the frozen embryos—Carol wants them destroyed and Donald wants them implanted, possibly in a surrogate. What result?

(A) The court is likely to award roughly half of the remaining frozen embryos to Donald and half to Carol. Neither Carol nor Donald will be permitted to seek support from the other parent for any live births resulting from the use of the frozen embryos.

(B) The court will likely award the embryos to Carol. Just as Carol would have had the final word on whether to abort, she will likely have the final word on whether any of the frozen embryos will be thawed and implanted.

(C) The court is unlikely to award the embryos to Donald, instead either preserving the status quo by keeping them frozen or awarding them to Carol. Because there was no agreement about what to do with the remaining embryos and no apparent reason that Donald would be precluded from creating different embryos, the court is unlikely to force Carol to become a parent of additional children against her will.

(D) The court is likely to award the frozen embryos to Donald because doing so presents the only realistic opportunity for them to be implanted and result in live births.

157. The state of Wishio criminalizes exposure of a third-trimester fetus to certain controlled substances. Alice Anderson uses cocaine during the third semester of her pregnancy and is charged with violating the law. Alice challenges the law as a violation of her privacy rights under the Fourteenth Amendment. What result?

(A) The law will likely be struck down because it implicates privacy interests involving pregnancy and children.

(B) Because the state has a compelling interest in protecting fetal health, the statute will likely be subjected to strict scrutiny and found to pass muster.

(C) The law will likely be struck down because women have a fundamental interest in deciding what they do with their own bodies.

(D) The law will likely be upheld because the right to privacy does not prevent the state from protecting the health of fetuses that have attained viability as long as the state is not thereby endangering the life or health of the pregnant woman.

158. The Texarkana Legislature has criminalized partial birth abortion without including an exception for procedures that would protect the life or health of the pregnant woman. The statute is challenged as a violation of Fourteenth Amendment guarantees. What result?

ANSWER:

159. Jan and Leslie have been having an affair. Jordan, Leslie's spouse, files for a divorce as soon as the affair comes to light. The divorce is granted and Leslie is denied any spousal support because of the affair. Leslie challenges the denial of support, claiming that the right to privacy precludes the imposition of such a penalty. Is the denial of support likely to be found a violation of constitutional guarantees?

(A) Yes, this penalty is likely to be struck down because the federal Constitution requires the state to treat married and unmarried individuals alike.

(B) The challenge is unlikely to be successful because states have plenary power over marriage and divorce.

(C) The penalty is likely to be struck down as a violation of constitutional guarantees because the Constitution protects the right of both a married and an unmarried adult to engage in consensual relations with another adult.

(D) The challenge is unlikely to be successful unless the state constitution provides more robust protection than does the federal Constitution.

160. The town of Famvalington has adopted a zoning ordinance that limits occupancy of dwellings to single families in a certain part of town. Family is defined as:

> One or more persons related by blood, adoption, or marriage, living or cooking together as a single housekeeping unit. A number of persons, not exceeding two, living and cooking together as a housekeeping unit, though not related by blood, adoption, or marriage, shall be deemed to constitute a family.

Arnold Adamson lives with Sandra Smith and her three minor children in a house in the restricted area. Sandra is told that Arnold must move elsewhere because they do not constitute a family for purposes of the ordinance. Arnold and Sandra challenge the constitutionality of the ordinance. What result?

(A) The ordinance is clearly constitutional and in fact the United States Supreme Court has upheld a similar zoning ordinance.

(B) The ordinance is clearly unconstitutional and in fact the United States Supreme Court has struck down a similar ordinance because it too narrowly defined family.

(C) This ordinance will likely be struck down because any ordinance defining family will violate associational rights protected by the First Amendment to the United States Constitution.

(D) It is unclear whether this ordinance will be upheld in light of federal guarantees. While these individuals are not all related by blood, it is nonetheless true that the association of persons at issue here more closely resembles a family than some of the associations of individuals that the United States Supreme Court in the past has suggested may be regulated.

161. Jordan and Mickey are married, although their marriage has been rocky for years. Jordan is living at a friend's house in the state of Marryvania while trying to sort everything out. One morning, Jordan realizes that it is time to start over and consults an attorney about filing for a divorce. However, Marryvania requires married parties to live separate and apart for two years before they can make use of the no-fault ground, as does the state of Foreverland, where Jordan and Mickey had been living. That is simply too long to wait, so Jordan challenges the constitutionality of the waiting period. What result?

(A) The two-year residency requirement is likely to be struck down because the right to marry is fundamental.

(B) The two-year residency requirement is likely to be struck down because imposing such a long waiting time infringes on the right to travel.

(C) The residency requirement is likely to be upheld because states have plenary power over marriage and divorce.

(D) The residency requirement is likely to be upheld because such a waiting period merely delays rather than prevents the divorce and because the state has an important interest in preventing fraud.

162. Zena Youngstone is in her thirty-ninth week of pregnancy. Her doctors have advised her to have a caesarean both for her own health and for the health of the fetus, but she has religious objections to undergoing such a procedure. While no one questions her competency, the hospital nonetheless seeks a court order requiring her to have a caesarean. What result?

(A) The court is unlikely to force Zena to have a caesarean because she is competent and because this is a very invasive procedure.

(B) The court is unlikely to force Zena to have a caesarean because Zena has the right to make whatever reproductive decision she believes best.

(C) The court is likely to force Zena to have a caesarean because such a procedure would promote both her own and the fetus's health.

(D) The court will likely force Zena to have a caesarean because the fetus is viable and Zena's not having the caesarean might adversely affect the fetus's health.

163. Zachariah and Constance Smith are deeply religious. One of their faith's tenets is that medicine is to be avoided and that prayer will cure whatever needs to be cured. The Smiths' daughter, Ruth, is very ill. Normally, someone with Ruth's condition would be administered strong antibiotics. However, no antibiotics are administered and Ruth eventually dies. The

Smiths are charged with manslaughter and they claim that they cannot be prosecuted because the First Amendment immunizes their practice of religion. What result?

(A) The Smiths are protected by the First Amendment and cannot be prosecuted for acting in accord with their sincere religious beliefs.

(B) The Smiths' claim will likely be rejected. While parents are permitted to believe as they wish, the Constitution does not immunize parents who cause their children great harm merely because the parents were acting out of their sincere religious beliefs.

(C) The Smiths cannot be prosecuted as long as Ruth shared her parents' religious beliefs.

(D) While parents are entitled to believe as they wish, the state is always free to second-guess parental decisions because of the state's special interest in children.

164. Alice is a beautiful 18-year-old who has a mental age of three and is very compliant. Alice's parents are fearful that someone will take advantage of her sexually and they have been told by her physicians that it would be devastating for Alice if she were to become pregnant. While Alice's parents are doing everything they can to protect her from sexual assault, they also are seeking court permission to have her sterilized. What is the likely result?

(A) Because the right to procreate is a fundamental interest, a court would be very unlikely to permit Alice to be sterilized.

(B) Because Alice's becoming pregnant would be very difficult for her parents and, in addition, Alice and her child would likely become public charges, Alice's parents will be allowed to have her sterilized.

(C) Because Alice could not give informed consent to the sterilization procedure itself, a court would be very unlikely to permit such a procedure to be performed.

(D) A court would be likely to authorize such a procedure if it can be established that such a procedure would be in Alice's best interests and she, if competent for a few minutes, would choose to have such a procedure performed for herself (her own incompetency notwithstanding).

165. Betty Cunningham, a mature 17-year-old, is living in Massecticut with a terrible disease. With very invasive treatment, her chances of recovery are approximately 20 percent. Without such treatment, her chances of living more than a year are less than one percent. The proposed treatment violates the sincere religious beliefs of Betty and her family. The state seeks to appoint a guardian to consent to treatment. Betty and her family oppose such an appointment. What result?

(A) The guardian is likely to be appointed because Betty has virtually no chance of long-term survival without the relevant treatment.

(B) The guardian is unlikely to be appointed because Betty and her family agree that no such appointment should be made.

(C) The guardian is likely to be appointed because Betty, as a minor, cannot make the relevant decision and because Betty's parents do not have the right to sacrifice their child, sincere religious beliefs notwithstanding.

(D) The guardian is unlikely to be appointed if it can be shown that Betty is sufficiently mature and informed to make that decision for herself and Massecticut recognizes the mature minor doctrine.

166. Thomas and William Jones-Smith hire Daniella Davidson to be their gestational surrogate in the state of Nebradaho. They use donated eggs and William's sperm to create the embryos, which are implanted in Daniella. Daniella becomes pregnant and eventually delivers a little boy, Norman, whom she refuses to relinquish. Thomas and William seeks to establish their parental rights. What result?

(A) Because Daniella would never have become pregnant but for her agreement to surrender Norman, she will be forced to relinquish him.

(B) Because Daniella was a gestational surrogate, she will be forced to surrender Norman. Had she been a traditional surrogate with a genetic connection to the child, she would have been recognized as the child's mother and custody would have been determined in light of the child's best interests.

(C) Because surrogacy contracts are void as a matter of public policy, the court will treat this custody dispute as if it were between members of a non-marital couple.

(D) While jurisdictions vary about whether and which surrogacy agreements are enforceable and so this will be decided in light of Nebradaho law, gestational surrogacy agreements are often found enforceable. However, it is no longer so clear that traditional surrogacy agreements will be found void and unenforceable, so it is not even clear that the contract would have been void and unenforceable had it involved a traditional surrogacy arrangement.

167. Wanda Williams calls the Department of Family Services to report possible abuse of a child, Beatrice Billingsley, who lives next door. Wanda calls three more times on three different occasions. Finally, someone from the Department checks the Billingsley home but is refused admittance. The social worker receives the same treatment on two more occasions. A week after the last attempt, Beatrice is rushed to the hospital, where she dies from a severe beating. Brian Billingsley, Beatrice's father, sues the Department of Family Services, claiming that they were responsible for his daughter being deprived of the liberty guaranteed under the Fourteenth Amendment because they knew (while he did not) that his ex-wife and her paramour were abusing Beatrice. What is the likely result of the suit?

ANSWER:

168. Peter and Ruth have been married for a few years. Peter frequently complains that they have sexual relations too infrequently. On one occasion when he had too much to drink, Peter

forced himself upon his wife. Ruth pressed charges and Peter claimed that the United States Constitution protects marital privacy and thus he was immune from prosecution. What result?

ANSWER:

169. Kevin and his wife, Laura, are divorcing. Laura wishes to submit into evidence some statements that Kevin made to Laura. However, Kevin seeks to invoke marital privilege to prevent Laura from testifying against him. What result?

ANSWER:

170. The United States Supreme Court has held that individuals have a fundamental interest in marriage. What implications does that holding have?

   (A) States cannot restrict who may marry whom without violating constitutional guarantees.

   (B) An individual who contracts a marriage in one state is entitled to have that marriage recognized in all of the states.

   (C) States must permit individuals to end their marriages when they wish to do so because otherwise their right to marry someone else would be infringed.

   (D) While states are permitted to regulate marriage, those regulations must promote sufficiently important interests and must be closely tailored to promote only those interests.

171. Frank and Gertrude Hillshire have one daughter, Monica, who is in need of a bone marrow transplant. Neither Frank nor Gertrude is a suitable match. However, there is some hope that John, Frank's 10-year-old son with his ex-wife, Samantha, might be a match. Samantha, who has custody of John, refuses to have him tested. Frank is confident that the reason Samantha objects to having John tested is that she still harbors resentment because of their less than amicable divorce years ago. Believing that Samantha does not have a good reason to prevent John from helping his half-sister, Frank seeks a court order requiring that John be tested for his suitability as a bone marrow donor for Monica. What result?

ANSWER:

172. Wendy Washington has just given birth to her daughter, Melissa. For some reason, Wendy is unable to breastfeed her daughter and Wendy has sincere religious objections to using animal by-products. Melissa is allergic to soy products and many other milk substitutes. While Wendy does her best to assure that Melissa has enough protein in her diet, Wendy's efforts fall short and, eventually, Child and Family Services removes Melissa from the home. Wendy challenges the action as a denial of her constitutionally protected right to practice her religion and raise her child. What result?

ANSWER:

173. Jesse Johnson and Lee Logan wish to marry in accord with their religious beliefs. Jesse already has a spouse, Kim Kennedy, but their religion permits individuals to have more than one spouse. The state in which they reside, Udaho, does not permit individuals to have more than one spouse at a time, sincere religious beliefs notwithstanding. Jesse, Kim, and Lee all seek a declaratory judgment that the Udaho law violates constitutional guarantees. What result?

(A) The court is likely to hold that the Udaho law abridges the fundamental right to marry and hence is unconstitutional.

(B) The court is likely to hold that the Udaho law violates free exercise guarantees and hence is unconstitutional.

(C) The court is likely to uphold the constitutionality of the law because the United States Constitution nowhere expressly mentions the right to marry.

(D) The court is likely to uphold the law, notwithstanding that states are not permitted to impose certain other restrictions on the right to marry.

174. The South Minnegan State Legislature seeks to reduce expenses after numerous citizen complaints about the high state taxes. After holding hearings to find ways to save money, the Legislature decides to make it more difficult for individuals to marry who are behind on their child support payments and who cannot show that they will be able to meet their support obligations in the future. The Legislature reasons that the number of children needing state support will likely not increase as much if those already behind on support are deterred from marrying and then having even more children in need of support.

Sarah Stone is a noncustodial parent who is behind on support. She wishes to marry Robin Richards but is precluded by the law from doing so. Sarah challenges the law as a violation of federal constitutional guarantees. What result?

ANSWER:

Parenting Relationships

175. Norman Nottingham and Penelope Pringle have lived together for years in Kanaska, which does not recognize de facto, functional, or psychological parent status. They have been trying to have a child but have not been successful. They consult a specialist and discover that Norman is sterile. They agree that Penelope should be artificially inseminated with sperm from an anonymous donor. Eventually, Penelope becomes pregnant and gives birth to a daughter, Rachel. During this period, Norman and Penelope start to grow apart. Shortly before Rachel's second birthday, Penelope and Rachel move into Penelope's sister's house. Penelope refuses to let Norman see Rachel, and Rachel consults an attorney to find out the likelihood of his being awarded custody of or visitation with Rachel. What result?

(A) An unmarried man cannot be recognized as a child's father if his partner was artificially inseminated with another man's sperm.

(B) While this is a matter of state law, Norman may well not succeed. His parental rights would have been more secure had he adopted Rachel or had he married Penelope before Rachel's birth.

(C) As long as Rachel views Norman as her father, Norman must be awarded visitation at the very least.

(D) As long as the court finds that Rachel's best interests would be promoted by continuing to have contract with Norman, Norman will be awarded visitation at the very least.

176. Alex and Betty are married. They have been trying to have a child without success. After testing reveals that Alex has a very low sperm count, they agree that Betty should be artificially inseminated. Betty becomes pregnant and delivers a little boy, Ronald. Regrettably, Alex and Ronald do not bond and Alex and Betty have grown estranged. When they divorce, Alex contests having to pay support for Ronald. What result?

(A) To establish paternity, a man must establish a genetic connection with a child plus a financial or emotional relationship with that child. Because these conditions have not been met, Alex will not be forced to pay child support.

(B) Assuming that Alex's consent to the insemination was in writing, he will likely be forced to pay support.

(C) That Alex and Betty were married at the time of Ronald's birth is enough to justify requiring Alex to pay child support.

(D) Alex will likely not be required to pay support as long as he does not request visitation.

177.   Benita is not in a dating relationship currently, although she has decided that she wishes to have a child. She talks to one of her best friends, Alfred, explaining that she wants him to provide sperm so that she can be artificially inseminated. He agrees and eventually Benita becomes pregnant and delivers a child, Zia.

Alfred wants to be a father to Zia, which Benita opposes. Benita refuses to allow Alfred near Zia, and Alfred consults an attorney to establish visitation, although he does not seek custody. What should the attorney say?

(A)   Because Alfred is not Benita's spouse and because Benita became pregnant through artificial insemination rather than coital relations, Alfred is unlikely to be recognized as having parental rights.

(B)   Assuming that Alfred can establish that he has a genetic connection to Zia, he will likely be recognized as Zia's father.

(C)   Because Benita will have custody of Zia, the degree to which Alfred has any involvement with Zia must be left up to Benita's judgment about what would promote Zia's best interests.

(D)   Whether Alfred is recognized as having any parental rights will likely depend, at least in part, on the explicit or implicit agreement that he and Benita made when he provided the sperm, assuming that the process used by Alfred and Benita did not meet the state law's requirements for Alfred's being considered a sperm donor with no parental rights.

178.   Mary Mooney and Nancy Newington are married and living in New Caledonia. Mary and Nancy orally agree that they want to raise a child and Nancy is artificially inseminated. Nancy gives birth to a child, Thomas. Three years later, Mary and Nancy are divorcing and Nancy wants to preclude Mary from having any contact with Thomas. Mary seeks to vindicate her parental rights in court. What result?

(A)   Mary's parental rights will likely be recognized by virtue of their agreement that Nancy should be artificially inseminated or, perhaps, because of the presumption that a child born during the marriage is a child of the marriage. In the alternative, Nancy might be estopped from denying Mary's parental rights.

(B)   Because Mary is not genetically related to Thomas and because she did not carry him to term, she will not be recognized as one of his parents.

(C)   Mary cannot benefit from the presumption of paternity because that is only for fathers and she will not be protected by the agreement regarding artificial insemination because it was not in writing.

(D)   Mary will be recognized as a parent if and only if Thomas recognizes her as one of his parents.

179.   Jordan and Kelly Monroe have been foster-parenting Thomas, age three, for the past two years. They wish to adopt Thomas, whose mother, Zena, still has parental rights. In one

proceeding, Zena's parental rights are terminated and the Monroes become Thomas's adoptive parents. On appeal, the trial court decision is reversed. Which of the following rationales might plausibly account for the appellate court's decision?

(A) Because Thomas is too young to express a preference, the adoption must be deferred until he can offer an informed and deliberate decision about who his parents should be.

(B) Because Zena opposed the Monroes' adopting Thomas, the adoption had to be vacated.

(C) Because the Monroes had already been foster-parenting Thomas for two years, they had an unfair advantage — Thomas should have been placed with someone else when Zena's parental rights were terminated.

(D) Because Zena's parental rights were terminated in the very proceeding in which the adoption was granted, it might have been too tempting for the court to compare Zena's parenting skills to those of the Monroes when deciding whether her parental rights should be terminated.

180. Leslie and Kim Jordan wish to adopt a child. They are introduced to Beatrice Babcock, who is pregnant and interested in placing her unborn child, Elizabeth, in an adoptive home. Beatrice and the Jordans agree to have an open adoption.

All goes well until a year after the adoption is finalized. Beatrice criticizes the Jordans for some of their parenting choices and the Jordans refuse to permit Beatrice to see Elizabeth. Beatrice seeks to have the open adoption agreement enforced or, in the alternative, the adoption declared void. What result?

(A) Because open adoptions are those that have not yet been finalized, Beatrice will likely be successful in having the adoption set aside.

(B) Because states vary with respect to how and whether open adoptions are enforceable, Beatrice's remedies, if any, will depend upon local law.

(C) Because open adoptions are simply those adoptions where the child's biological family's medical history is made available (with identifying information redacted), Beatrice is unlikely to be afforded any remedy on these facts.

(D) Because open adoptions permit the biological parent to retain parental rights, Beatrice will likely be successful in her attempts either to have some say in how Elizabeth is raised or, perhaps, to have the adoption vacated.

181. Jody Johnson and Kelly Kennedy are married. Each has children from a previous relationship (and both of their ex-spouses have died). Jody and Kelly want to avail themselves of the stepparent exception. What does the stepparent exception allow them to do?

(A) The stepparent exception allows an adult unrelated to children in the home to act as a parent with respect to those children without incurring obligations to support those children should the adults' relationship end.

(B) The stepparent exception establishes that stepparents have no legal obligations with respect to children living in the home.

(C) The stepparent exception allows a parent's spouse to adopt the parent's children without the parent having to have his or her parental rights terminated.

(D) The stepparent exception imposes obligations on the stepparent with respect to the care and support of children living in the home even if the stepparent has no legally recognized relationship with those children.

182. Betty Bunderson has agreed to place her newborn child with the Williams family, who have agreed to pay Betty whatever would be permissible in light of local law (which mirrors the law of most states). How much, if anything, can the Williams family give to Betty?

(A) Nothing, because any money changing hands would be treated as payment for a child and would violate baby-selling laws.

(B) The Williams family can pay whatever the parties think appropriate as long as the adoption itself promotes the best interests of the child.

(C) The Williams family can pay the reasonable expenses associated with the birth as well as reasonable attorney and, perhaps, counseling fees.

(D) While the Williams family cannot pay Betty anything, there are no limitations on how much the attorneys helping to arrange the adoption can be paid.

183. Taylor and Tracy Torrington lived in the state of New Texaho. They had agreed to adopt Owen, who had been living with them and their other children since he was a small child. However, they never got around to formally adopting him. Regrettably, they died intestate. Owen argues that he was equitably adopted and thus is entitled to a share in the estate, although the other Torrington children disagree. What result?

(A) Assuming that New Texaho recognizes equitable adoption, Owen will likely be successful. Because an equitable adoption is simply an adoption that would be fair to recognize and because it would only be fair for a child treated as a member of the family to be recognized as one, Owen will likely be held entitled to the same share of the estate as are each of the other children.

(B) Owen is unlikely to be successful even if New Texaho recognizes equitable adoption. Someone equitably adopted is entitled to the share of an estate to which that person would have been entitled had that person been legally adopted. However, equitable adoptions must be fair to all interested parties and it would hardly be fair to diminish the shares of all of the other children when Owen is not even recognized as a legal child of the Torringtons.

(C) Owen is unlikely to be successful even if equitable adoption is recognized in New Texaho. An equitable adoption permits functional parents to be given a preference when a child is available for adoption so, for example, foster parents would be afforded a preference when attempting to adopt the child whom they are fostering.

(D) Assuming that New Texaho recognizes equitable adoption, Owen is likely to be successful. An equitable adoption involves someone who was not formally adopted, despite an agreement to do so, who nonetheless was treated as if he or she had been formally adopted. Someone equitably adopted can inherit from those who had agreed to adopt him/her.

184. Robin and Parker Nevington have agreed to adopt Monica, who has lived with them since she was a small girl. However, they never formally adopted her. When they died in a car crash, Monica was found to have been equitably adopted and was found to be the Nevingtons' sole relative. Two years later, Monica's biological father, Carl, wins the lottery. He is so excited that he has a heart attack and Monica seeks her share as one of his surviving children. What result?

ANSWER:

185. Shannon and Tory both lost spouses to deadly car accidents and both have sworn never to marry again. They each have children from a previous marriage. They are now living together in New Vermshire and are planning to spend their lives together. They consult an attorney to find out whether each can adopt the other's children even though they themselves will not be married to each other. What should the attorney say?

ANSWER:

186. John and Sarah are married and have lived for years with Sarah's son from a previous marriage, William. William's father died the previous year when William turned 18. John and William would like to formalize their parent-child relationship. John consults an attorney to find out whether he can adopt William, notwithstanding the fact that William is now an adult. What should the attorney say?

ANSWER:

187. Alice Adamson and Bob Berenson had two children together, Carla and David. Alice has custody of the children. Over the years, Bob has paid child support occasionally and has spoken to the children a few times a year. Alice wishes to have Bob's parental rights terminated because of abandonment so that her current spouse, Lee, can adopt the children. Bob denies having abandoned the children and opposes the adoption. What result?

(A) Because Bob never left the children without appropriate supervision, he is unlikely to be found to have abandoned them.

(B) Because the child support has been occasional and the phone contact rare, he may well be found to have abandoned the children and so be precluded from blocking the adoption.

(C) Bob cannot be found to have abandoned his children unless he can be shown to have had a settled intent never to see or support them anymore.

(D) Because Bob has paid some support and maintained some contact, he is unlikely to be found to have abandoned them.

188. Norman and Olga live with Olga's children from a previous marriage, Penny and Quentin. The children see their father, Robert, periodically. One day, Olga is killed in a car accident and both Norman and Robert seek custody of the children. The guardian ad litem suggests that Norman has a better relationship with the children than Robert does, although the children would not be harmed were they to live with Robert. Both Norman and Robert admit that they do not have a good relationship with each other. What result?

(A) As the sole legal parent, Robert must be awarded custody.

(B) Assuming that the guardian ad litem's testimony is accepted as accurate, Norman is likely to be awarded custody because his having custody would better promote the children's interests.

(C) Absent statute or case law to the contrary, Robert is likely to be awarded custody because doing so would not be harmful, although the court still might order that Norman be accorded visitation privileges.

(D) Under these circumstances, the court is likely to order shared custody.

189. Kendall lives in Marryvania with two children, Thomas and Sarah, from a previous marriage. The parental rights of Kendall's ex-spouse have been terminated. Kendall meets and marries Jody. After several years, the marriage falls apart. Marryvania recognizes de facto parentage, and Jody qualifies as a de facto parent. Both Kendall and Jody have good relationships with the children and they both seek custody. What result?

(A) Absent statute to the contrary, custody will be awarded to the parent whose having custody would best promote the interests of the children.

(B) Kendall will most likely be awarded custody and will be permitted to decide whether Jody can have visitation privileges.

(C) Jody will likely be awarded visitation at the very least, although a separate question to be decided in light of Marryvania law will be whether Jody and Kendall will be able to compete on a level playing field for custody.

(D) Assuming that Jody's having custody would best promote the children's interests, Jody will be awarded custody and will be permitted to decide whether Kendall will have visitation privileges.

190. Robin and Lee live together with Robin's children from a previous relationship in the state of New Udaho, which does not recognize de facto, functional, or psychological parent status. They are all together for several years. When Robin and Lee separate, Lee seeks visitation, which Robin opposes. Both Lee and Robin have good parenting skills and good relationships with the children. What result?

(A) Because both are fit parents, Robin is likely to be awarded custody and Lee visitation.

(B) Because both have good parenting skills and good relationships with the children, the court is most likely to impose a shared parenting arrangement.

(C) Absent statute or some showing of exceptional circumstances, Lee may well not even be awarded visitation in this scenario.

(D) Robin is likely to be awarded custody and Lee visitation but only if no other adult, e.g., Robin's former partner, seeks visitation.

191. Jan has two children, Alice and Bernard, from a previous relationship. Jan recently married Kelly, who gets along quite well with Alice and Bernard. Jan, Kelly, Alice, and Bernard all live in the state of Yorkavania, which recognizes psychological parent status.

When Jan and Kelly divorce, Kelly (as a psychological parent) seeks visitation. Jan opposes visitation but also suggests that if Kelly is awarded visitation rights, then Kelly should also be required to pay child support. What result?

(A) If granted visitation, Kelly will also be required to pay child support.

(B) Because Jan, the legal parent, opposes Kelly's being's awarded visitation, Kelly will neither have visitation rights nor duties of support.

(C) Kelly, as a psychological parent, may well be awarded visitation. However, Kelly is unlikely to be required to pay child support unless having done something unusual.

(D) Kelly is unlikely to be awarded visitation over Jan's objections. However, Kelly may well be ordered to pay support because Jan does not oppose that.

192. Casey and Dana are married, although they have different religions. They have two children, Avery and Brett. Unfortunately, Casey and Dana eventually decide to divorce. Casey agrees that if she is awarded custody she will teach them about Dana's religious views.

Casey is awarded custody. However, after the divorce, her religious views evolve, and she now believes that exposing the children to Dana's beliefs would put them in serious spiritual jeopardy. She stops discussing Dana's beliefs. Dana seeks to have their agreement about religious education enforced or, in the alternative, a modification of custody because of a material change in circumstances. What result?

(A) The court is likely to order Casey to abide by the agreement or risk losing custody of the children.

(B) The court is unlikely to order Casey to teach the children Dana's beliefs and, further, will not order a change in custody merely because of her refusal to do so.

(C) The court will not order Casey to teach Dana's beliefs to the children because Casey's religious views have changed since the divorce. However, had there been no change in beliefs, Casey would have been held to her agreement.

(D) Casey's refusal to teach Dana's beliefs constitutes a material change in circumstances justifying a reconsideration of custody.

193. Jody and Harlow, who were raised in different faith traditions, have two children, Vince and Wanda. The children are raised in both traditions. When Jody and Harlow divorce, Jody is awarded custody with Harlow being awarded liberal visitation. Jody becomes concerned after the children report that they learned the past weekend that they would likely burn in everlasting hell. Wanda begins having nightmares where she is trapped in a room that is ablaze. Jody seeks to enjoin Harlow from exposing the children to these unsettling beliefs. What result?

(A) Because the custodial parent determines the children's religious upbringing, Jody is likely to be successful.

(B) Jody is likely to be successful if Harlow is exposing the children to teachings that cause or are likely to cause them significant harm.

(C) Jody is unlikely to be successful because any limitation would undermine Harlow's free speech rights.

(D) Jody is unlikely to be successful because any limitation would implicate Harlow's rights to the free exercise of religion.

194. Mary and Norman have been dating for a few months when Norman receives a text announcing that Mary is pregnant. Norman asks who the father is, although he then texts that he would be willing to contribute to the costs of an abortion. Mary does not respond.

Mary does not communicate with Norman during the entire pregnancy. When she gives birth, she puts the child up for adoption, claiming not to know the identity of the father. Not long after the adoption is finalized, Norman happens to learn from a friend that Mary had given birth and had surrendered the child for adoption. Norman consults an attorney to find out whether he can find out if he is the father and, if so, establish his parental rights. What should the attorney say?

ANSWER:

195. Andrew and Barbara have been dating. Barbara tells Andrew that she is pregnant and Andrew responds that they should start preparing for the baby's arrival. Barbara does not wish to move in with Andrew and Andrew starts giving Barbara financial support. However, Andrew does not have much money so the support that he offers is limited.

Barbara is not in love with Andrew and does not wish to remain with him. She also does not wish to raise a child. Andrew says that he will raise the child. Barbara does not respond.

A few weeks before she is due, Barbara disappears. Andrew asks their mutual friends where she is but no one seems to know and Barbara's family does not seem to know either.

Andrew soon discovers where Barbara is, although she has already given birth and surrendered the child to a would-be adoptive couple. Andrew consults an attorney to find out whether he can block adoption of his child. What should the attorney say?

ANSWER:

Tort Actions

196. Abby and Bertram are married and live in South Carobama, which recognizes actions for criminal conversation. Bertram is having an affair with Charlie, a co-worker who is also married. They often work late into the evening and sometimes have sexual relations in the office when no one else is around. At other times, they rent a hotel room. Eventually, they empty their respective family checking accounts, quit their jobs, and move to another part of the state to begin new lives. Abby consults an attorney to find out whether state law affords her any remedies in addition to a divorce, property division, and possible spousal support. What should the attorney say?

    (A) Abby may well be able to sue for civil damages by establishing that Bertram and Charlie engaged in criminal conversation by having sexual relations while Abby and Bertram were still married.

    (B) Abby may well be able to have Bertram and Charlie prosecuted for criminal conversation, assuming that they spoke to each other about raiding the family checking accounts.

    (C) Abby may well be able to have Bertram and Charlie prosecuted for engaging in criminal conversation if they had sexual relations while Bertram and Abby were still married.

    (D) Abby may well be able to sue for civil damages by establishing that Bertram and Charlie engaged in criminal conversation when discussing their plan to raid the family checking accounts.

197. Carol and Dallas are married and live in Texarkana, which has abolished the tort of criminal conversation but still recognizes alienation of affections. Casey and Dallas's marriage has been rocky for some time now. Eventually, Casey starts a relationship with someone else. Casey and Dallas divorce and Dallas consults an attorney to find out whether to sue for alienation of affections. What should the attorney say?

ANSWER:

198. Skyler, a single parent, is parked at a red light when Negligent Driver slams into the car, causing Skyler serious injuries. Skyler's child, John, sues Negligent Driver for loss of consortium. What result?

    (A) Because loss of consortium as traditionally understood involves the loss of marital relations, this cause of action cannot be brought by a child.

(B) While this is a matter of state law, many states permit a child to bring a loss of consortium claim when deprived of the comfort and counseling of a parent.

(C) Loss of consortium is a cause of action available to anyone who has lost a loved one.

(D) Because loss of consortium as traditionally understood involves the loss of marital relations, this cause of action is available to anyone who can establish that he or she had a committed, sexual relationship with the victim.

199. Casey and Drew have been dating for several months when Casey proposes marriage and Drew accepts. Casey gives Drew a ring. Ever since then, Casey has become more and more certain that the marriage is not a good idea after all. A month before the wedding is to take place, Casey calls everything off and asks Drew for the ring back. Drew refuses. Casey sues for return of the ring. What result?

(A) Drew may well be ordered to return the ring, although some jurisdictions will not require the ring's return if the individual who gave the ring is responsible for the breakdown of the relationship.

(B) Because the ring was given in anticipation of the marriage, it belongs to both. The ring should be sold with the proceeds split between Casey and Drew.

(C) Because Casey is calling off the wedding, Drew should be able to keep the ring.

(D) Because Casey gave the ring to Drew, it should be treated as a gift and remain Drew's regardless of why the wedding is being called off.

200. Mary and Nicholas Oppenheimer each have members of their extended families with a particular dread disease. Mary and Nicholas undergo genetic testing to discover whether any child they conceived would have an increased risk of being afflicted with that disease. They are told that they are not more likely than anyone else to have a child afflicted with that disease.

The Oppenheimers have a child who, regrettably, has the disease. They later discover that those doing the genetic testing had mislabeled the blood samples, which meant that they were wrongly told that they did not have an elevated risk of producing a child with the disease and another couple was wrongly told that there was an elevated risk that any child produced would have the disease. The Oppenheimers sue for damages. What result?

(A) The Oppenheimers will likely be successful as long as they can establish that they would have avoided conceiving a child if they had been apprised of the increased risks and that they have suffered emotional and financial harm as a result of the negligent testing.

(B) The Oppenheimers are unlikely to be successful because having a child cannot constitute a harm.

(C) The Oppenheimers are likely to be successful because they had a child with the dread disease, which is exactly what they were hoping to avoid.

(D) The Oppenheimers are unlikely to be successful because no parents are guaranteed that their child will be perfect.

201. Abby is pregnant. She and her spouse, Blair, are expecting their first child in the state of Pennland. Abby wants to make sure that the fetus is healthy and so has her doctor perform a variety a tests. Abby is relieved when she is told that all is well. When Abby gives birth, she discovers that her child has a terrible congenital condition that should have been detected in the first trimester. Abby and Blair sue for wrongful birth. What result?

(A) Even if Pennland recognizes wrongful birth actions, Abby and Blair are unlikely to be successful because the physician did not cause the child to have the congenital condition.

(B) Because it is better to live than never to have been born at all, Abby and Blair are unlikely to be successful because they are unlikely to be able to establish harm.

(C) Assuming that Pennland recognizes wrongful birth actions, Abby and Blair are likely to be successful as long as they can establish that their physician was negligent when performing the tests during the pregnancy.

(D) Assuming that Pennland recognizes wrongful birth actions, Abby and Blair are likely to be successful if they can establish the physician's negligence, their emotional and financial harm, and that they would have aborted the pregnancy if they had learned of the congenital condition in a timely way.

202. Teresa and William Underwood live in Winnegan with their four children. They are having great difficulty making ends meet. Teresa has a tubal ligation to prevent her becoming pregnant again. However, the tubal ligation is performed improperly and Teresa becomes pregnant again. She gives birth to a healthy baby. She and William sue the physician who negligently performed the tubal ligation. What result?

(A) Because the birth of a healthy baby is a boon rather than a harm, no jurisdiction would permit recovery on these facts.

(B) Because the Underwoods clearly did not want to have another child and because they would not have had another child but for the negligence of the physician, most jurisdictions would permit recovery of child-raising costs on these facts.

(C) Because Teresa could have aborted the pregnancy, she will be found to have failed to mitigate the harm and thus will be precluded from recovery.

(D) While this will be a matter of Winnegan law, those jurisdictions allowing recovery would likely only permit some of the costs associated with the pregnancy rather than the costs of raising a child.

203. Samantha Smith teaches first grade in Illitucky, which recognizes wrongful birth as a cause of action. Samantha has just learned that she is pregnant and she remembers that one of her students had rubella earlier that term. She asks her doctor whether that is a cause for concern

and she is assured her that she has no reason to worry. When Samantha gives birth, she discovers that her child has severe birth defects most likely caused by exposure to German measles during the first trimester of pregnancy. Samantha sues for wrongful birth. What result?

(A) Samantha will likely be successful because she mentioned that one of her students had rubella.

(B) Samantha will likely be successful if she can establish not only that she had mentioned the possible exposure, but also that she would have aborted had she been apprised of the severe risks associated with exposure to rubella.

(C) Samantha will be unlikely to be successful unless she can establish that the exposure to rubella was in her doctor's office.

(D) Samantha will likely be successful only if she can establish that the doctor could have done something during the pregnancy to reduce the risk that her child would be harmed by the exposure to rubella.

204. Emerson is the custodial parent of Sarah, who is an adventurous four-year-old. One day, Emerson is engrossed in a phone conversation and does not notice that Sarah has gone into the backyard near the pool. Sarah falls into the pool. A neighbor rushes over and saves Sarah, but not before Sarah suffers serious injuries. Emerson's ex-spouse, Dana, sues Emerson on behalf of their daughter for negligent supervision. What result?

(A) The suit will be dismissed. Were parents subject to suit for their alleged parenting errors, the courts would be swamped with suits.

(B) The suit will likely be successful. But for Emerson's failure to supervise Sarah properly, Sarah would never have been harmed.

(C) The suit may be successful depending upon whether the jurisdiction has abrogated parent-child immunity for negligence.

(D) Whether or not the jurisdiction has abrogated parent-child immunity, the suit is likely to be dismissed because Sarah assumed the risk by voluntarily going into the pool.

205. Mary lives with her mother, Alice, and stepfather, William. William has been sexually abusing Mary for years. As soon as Mary turns 18 and moves out of the house, she sues William. William argues that he is immune from suit because the jurisdiction recognizes the parental immunity doctrine. What result?

(A) William is immune from suit because of the parental immunity doctrine.

(B) Because William is not Mary's biological or adoptive parent but instead her stepparent, the parental immunity doctrine will not protect him.

(C) William will be liable but only if he is criminally prosecuted and convicted.

(D) William may well be liable because many of the states recognizing parental immunity do not extend that immunity to suits involving intentional torts.

206.   Cameron and Casey are married and live in Tenntucky, a comparative negligence state that has recently abrogated interspousal immunity. As they are discussing what kind of wine to bring to a dinner party, another car driven by Nancy Negligent approaches and runs into them. Cameron might have been able to avoid the accident by turning sharply away a little earlier.

The jury finds Nancy to be 90 percent and Cameron 10 percent responsible for the accident. Casey, who was injured in the accident, is suing Nancy for damages. What effect, if any, will the state abrogation of interspousal immunity have on this case?

(A) By abrogating interspousal immunity, the state abolished the privilege that Casey might otherwise have enjoyed not to testify at the trial.

(B) By abrogating interspousal immunity, the state made it possible for Nancy to sue Cameron for contribution.

(C) The abrogation of interspousal immunity will have no effect on this case — Casey did not want to sue Cameron anyway so the state's policy with respect to interspousal immunity is irrelevant.

(D) Because Cameron is partially responsible for Casey's injuries and because Casey and Cameron are married, the abrogation of interspousal immunity in effect bars Casey from suing Nancy.

207.   Frank is excited. A new family has moved into the neighborhood and their little boy, Robert, is Frank's age. Frank's mother, Gladys, is hopeful that Frank will have a new playmate and best friend.

Regrettably, Frank and Robert's first playdate is their last, as has happened to Frank so many times before. When they were at the local playground a block away, Frank pushed Robert off the slide, resulting in a broken collarbone. Robert's parents are considering whether to sue Gladys and Gladys consults an attorney. What should the attorney say?

(A) Gladys is strictly liable for any injuries Frank causes.

(B) Gladys is liable for any injuries that Frank intentionally or negligently causes.

(C) Gladys may well be liable if she did not adequately supervise Frank and Robert's injuries were reasonably foreseeable.

(D) Gladys cannot be held liable for any injuries caused by Frank as long as she did not encourage him to cause such injuries.

208.   The Wrights have been working with a private adoption agency, Your Loving Family, to find a sibling for their son, Abel. They have explained that they wish to adopt a healthy boy roughly Abel's age who has no known psychological or emotional difficulties. The agency suggests that David fits the bill, although the agency warns that he is somewhat quiet and withdrawn until he gets to know everyone.

The Wrights bring David into their home. David remains quiet and withdrawn, although the Wrights assume that he just needs more time. David continues to be quiet even after the adoption is finalized. However, one night when everyone is asleep, David tries to set the house on fire. The Wrights discover not only that David has severe psychological and emotional problems but that Your Loving Family knew about those problems all along. The Wrights sue for damages. What result?

(A) The Wrights are unlikely to recover any damages because no parent is guaranteed a perfect child.

(B) The Wrights are likely to recover the costs of raising David through adulthood because they would not have adopted him had they known of his difficulties.

(C) Because David may well not be able to provide for himself once he reaches adulthood and because the Wrights would then be responsible for him, Your Loving Family is likely to be held liable for the costs of raising and supporting David for the rest of his life.

(D) Your Loving Family is likely to be responsible for the extraordinary costs associated with raising David which might include counseling costs or even the costs of institutionalizing him if that is necessary.

209. Jordan and Kelly Anderson have decided that they wish to adopt a child. However, they have decided that they do not want to adopt a child with special needs, which they make eminently clear to the adoption agency, Your Heart's Content. They are told that the agency has just the child for them, Wanda. Jordan and Kelly again explain that it is very important to them that the child whom they adopt not be known to have special needs, and they are assured by Your Heart's Content that neither Wanda nor anyone in her family has any history of mental or emotional difficulties. While Wanda is very withdrawn, Jordan and Kelly are committed to making her feel like she belongs with them.

A year after the adoption is finalized, the Andersons learn not only that Wanda has severe emotional and mental difficulties but that Your Heart's Content knew about those difficulties and had specifically instructed all people dealing with the Andersons to deny that Wanda had any difficulties, precisely because the Andersons would then never have adopted her. The Andersons not only seek money damages but also seek to undo the adoption, What result?

(A) The adoption will not be vacated. Once an adoption is final, the child is viewed by the law as if the child had been born into the family. Just as one cannot pretend that a birth never occurred, one cannot pretend that an adoption never occurred.

(B) While the adoption cannot be undone, the agency might not only be forced to pay the costs incurred in raising Wanda, but may also be required to afford the Andersons the first opportunity to adopt another child who does not have special needs.

(C) The adoption can be undone because the Andersons made very clear that they were unwilling to raise a child with severe emotional or mental difficulties.

(D) While jurisdictions vary, some will permit adoptions to be abrogated if an agency affirmatively misleads parents about important facts rather than merely negligently fails to discover or disclose such facts.

210. Blair and Dana are divorced, with Blair having custody of their child, Margaret. Dana asks Blair if Margaret can come for a weekend celebration of Margaret's grandfather's seventieth birthday. Blair talks to Dana's father, Steve, and is told that there will be a weekend celebration and that they would love to have Margaret come. Blair permits Margaret to attend.

During the weekend, Blair tries to talk to Margaret but is always told that Margaret is out or asleep. When Margaret is not delivered back home the following Monday, she calls and is told that Dana left that morning to bring Margaret back. A few days pass and Margaret does not appear. Eventually, Blair discovers that Dana had taken Margaret to Canada and that there had never been a party. Instead, Dana and Steve conspired to remove Margaret from the country. Blair sues Dana and Steve for intentional interference with a parent's custodial relationship. What result?

   (A) While Dana is subject to suit for having taken Margaret out of the country, Steve did not do that and hence is not liable.

   (B) Both Dana and Steve may be liable on these facts, absent some legally valid justification or excuse.

   (C) While Steve is potentially liable, Dana (as one of Margaret's parents) is not.

   (D) Because such a suit might destroy Margaret's relationships with her family, the suit will be barred as a matter of public policy.

211. Samuel and Robert are divorced, with Samuel having custody of their child, Alice. Robert has overnight visitation on alternate weekends. On several occasions, Samuel and Alice were not where they were supposed to be when Robert went to pick up Alice for her overnight visits. Eventually, Robert sues Samuel for intentional interference with a parental relationship. What result?

   (A) Robert will likely be awarded damages, absent some justification or excuse for these missed connections.

   (B) Assuming the lack of a legal justification or excuse, Robert will likely be awarded damages as long as the jurisdiction recognizes a cause of action for intentional interference with a custodial relationship.

   (C) Even if the jurisdiction recognizes a cause of action for intentional interference with a custodial relationship, it may well not recognize an analogous cause of action for a non-custodial parent.

   (D) Even if there is no justification or excuse, the jurisdiction is unlikely to recognize this cause of action just as it is unlikely to recognize a cause of action for intentional interference with a custodial relationship.

212. Lynn and Dana, who live in the state of Alabippi, have been having marital problems and are now separated. Dana meets Casey and they start to date. Lynn learns of the relationship between Dana and Casey and sues for criminal conversation and alienation of affections. What result?

ANSWER:

213. Rory and Tate Willington live with their three-year-old, Abby, in the state of New Colorona. Abby loves playing with the neighbor's dog, Rex. One day, Rory and Tate were distracted for a few minutes, just enough time for Abby to slip out the front door. Abby saw Rex cross the street and she decided to follow. Delores Driver was driving down the street and was not paying attention. She hit Abby, causing severe injuries. When Rory and Tate sue Delores, Delores seeks contribution from Rory and Tate, claiming negligent supervision. What result?

ANSWER:

214. Thomas and Sarah Robertson have been married for 10 years in South Georgiana. They have two children, Alex and Bevan. The Robertsons have been arguing a great deal lately. After one particularly nasty exchange, Sarah says, "Haven't you ever wondered why the children look nothing like you? That's because you are not their father." She rushes out the door with the children and some previously packed bags in tow to go to her mother's house. Thomas and Sarah divorce. Thomas sues Sarah for intentional infliction of emotional distress. What result?

ANSWER:

215. Jordan and Kelly have lived together for years in the state of New Vermshire and are raising Kelly's two children from a previous relationship. However, Jordan and Kelly have never married, not believing in the institution. One day, Jordan was several steps ahead of Kelly as they walked toward their car. Ned Negligent was not looking where he was driving and ran into Jordan. Kelly was never in any physical danger but nonetheless saw the accident. Kelly sues Ned for negligent infliction of emotional distress. What result?

ANSWER:

Professional Responsibility

216. Tracy and Shannon Rowanton are having marital difficulties and they consult a lawyer, Alex Attorney. Alex talks to each of them individually, discussing a variety of private matters after assuring them that the matters would not be repeated to anyone. He then brings them back together. He believes that the marriage is salvageable and urges them to see a marriage counselor. He charges a fee. Eventually, Tracy files for divorce. Shannon comes to see Alex, explaining that Tracy has filed for divorce and asking Alex to represent him. During their discussion, Shannon admits having had an affair. Alex explains that he cannot represent anyone who has had an affair. After Shannon leaves, Alex calls Tracy, explaining that Shannon had been in Alex's office and that Alex could do a very good job for Tracy. Tracy hires Alex and does quite well in the distribution of marital assets. Alex would not have been subject to professional discipline if only:

    (A) He had acted exactly as he did, because he would not have been subject to professional discipline on these facts.

    (B) He had agreed to represent Shannon when asked.

    (C) He had refused to represent either of them after the initial consultation.

    (D) He had not called Tracy to offer his services.

217. Alice and Betty have agreed to divorce. They consult Laura Lawyer about representing them both. Laura explains that she would be representing both of them and that she would not be promoting the interests of one to the detriment of the other. Alice and Betty agree in writing to this arrangement and that they understand what Laura can and cannot do when representing both of them. They hire Laura and both are quite pleased. Nonetheless, Laura has been reported to the Office of Disciplinary Counsel. Is Laura subject to discipline?

    (A) Because both clients were satisfied, Laura cannot be sanctioned.

    (B) Because Laura has informed written consent from both parties, she is not subject to sanction.

    (C) Because there was a possibility that either Alice or Betty would be dissatisfied, Laura is subject to sanction.

    (D) As to whether dual representation in a divorce is permissible even with full disclosure and informed written consent, this is a matter of local law. Some jurisdictions have a per se bar against dual representation in a divorce, while others do not. Laura may be subject to sanction depending upon local law.

218. Dana is a stay-at-home parent who wants a divorce. Unfortunately, Dana is entirely dependent upon spouse Tory's income. Dana talks to Ann Attorney, who is willing to represent Dana on a contingency fee basis. Dana does very well in the distribution of property and in the amounts of spousal and child support awarded, but now believes that the agreed-upon one-third contingency fee arrangement is excessive. Ann sues Dana for the owed compensation. What result?

(A) States have long allowed contingency fee arrangements and the agreed-upon one-third does not seem exorbitant. Ann will likely be successful.

(B) Contingency fee arrangements in the domestic relations context violate public policy because they provide a disincentive for an attorney to encourage reconciliation. There is no jurisdiction in which Ann is likely to be successful.

(C) While contingency fee arrangements provide a disincentive for attorneys to promote reconciliation, Ann will nonetheless likely be successful if there was no realistic chance that Dana and Tory would reconcile.

(D) While some jurisdictions prohibit contingency fee arrangements in the divorce context, others permit them. The success of Ann's suit will depend upon local law.

219. Larry Lawyer has agreed to act as a scribe for Adrian and Bettina, who are divorcing. Larry has made quite clear that he will neither advise them nor look out for their interests. Instead, he will simply write up what they have agreed. While writing up their agreement, Larry realizes that Adrian is trying to defraud Bettina. What should Larry do?

ANSWER:

Federal-State Power Distribution

220. Casey and Dana are divorced, with Casey having custody of the couple's children. Casey lives in Illtucky and Dana lives in Old York. Casey, who is tired of Dana's late child support payments, pursues legal action to force Dana to pay in a timely fashion. Dana, who has a very bad relationship with Casey, decides to post some allegedly defamatory content on the Internet, which will be seen by many of Casey's friends, family, and business associates. Casey sues Dana in federal court, meeting the requirements for diversity of citizenship and the amount in controversy. Dana argues that the suit cannot be heard in federal court because of the domestic relations exception and so must be dismissed. What result?

    (A) Dana is likely to be successful because the domestic relations exception precludes individuals from suing current or former family members in federal court.

    (B) Dana is unlikely to be successful because the domestic relations exception only applies to individuals in intact families.

    (C) Dana is likely to be successful because the suit is obviously related to family matters, e.g., the relationship between the former spouses or the timing of the child support payments.

    (D) Dana is unlikely to be successful because the domestic relations exception only precludes federal courts from issuing divorce, spousal support, or child custody decrees.

221. The state of Virgiland has a law specifying that if an individual divorces and remarries but forgets to change the beneficiary designation on his or her insurance, the new spouse rather than the former spouse will be entitled to the insurance benefits. However, federal law permits federal employees to designate a beneficiary other than the current spouse on his or her insurance.

    Federal employee Drew Daniels (who lives in Virgiland) divorced former spouse, Tracy, and then married Riley. But Drew forgot to change the designated beneficiary from Tracy to Riley. Drew unexpectedly died and Tracy received the proceeds of Drew's policy. Riley sued, citing Virgiland law. What result?

    ANSWER:

Practice Final Exam

222. Simon and Horatio, both age 17 and living in Connachusetts, are going to Old York City for their class field trip. They tell their parents about the trip but neglect to mention that they plan to marry while there. During the trip, they go to a Justice of the Peace, lie about their respective ages, and marry. When they return home, they tell no one what they have done. By the time that they reach their eighteenth birthdays, they do not like each other and simply pretend that they never got married in the first place.

   On his eighteenth birthday, Simon inherits a great deal of money from his great uncle. Simon goes out to celebrate and dies in a terrible car accident. Horatio consults an attorney to find out whether he is entitled to an intestate share of the estate. What should the attorney say?

   (A) Because Simon and Horatio never ratified the marriage after each had attained majority, the marriage never came into being and Horatio is not entitled to anything.

   (B) Horatio is likely to be found entitled to a share of Simon's estate as long as Connachusetts treats minor marriages as voidable rather than void.

   (C) Horatio is unlikely to be entitled to anything because he and Simon told no one about their marriage.

   (D) Horatio is likely to be entitled to a share of Simon's estate because a marriage valid where celebrated is valid everywhere.

223. Reese and Sasha, both age 17, live in Delaland, which treats minor marriages as void. They cross the border and go to the neighboring state of Penntucky, which treats minor marriages as voidable. They go to a Justice of the Peace, lie about their ages, and marry. They go back to Delaland.

   When they each attain majority, Reese and Sasha move out of their respective parents' homes and into an apartment together. One year later, Reese and Sasha are driving home when their car is hit head-on by a drunk driver, who is driving the wrong way on a one-way street. Reese dies in the accident. Sasha survives and sues the drunk driver for wrongful death. What result?

   (A) Because Reese and Sasha ratified their marriage by living together once they each had attained majority, their marriage will be recognized and Sasha will likely be successful.

   (B) Because Penntucky treats minor marriages as voidable rather than void and because the marriage was never annulled by a court, the marriage will be recognized and Sasha will likely be successful.

(C) Because Penntucky treats minor marriages as voidable rather than permitted and because Sasha and Reese never formally renewed their vows once they were 18, their marriage will not be recognized and Sasha's suit will likely be dismissed.

(D) Because Reese and Sasha are and have been domiciled in Delaland, which treats minor marriages as void, their marriage will likely be viewed as never having existed and not capable of ratification. Sasha's suit will likely be dismissed because Sasha was not Reese's spouse.

224. Storm and Tate are 17-year-olds living in New Texaho, which treats minor marriages as voidable. They lie about their ages and are married by a Justice of the Peace. They live together over the garage that is adjacent to Tate's parents' home. A year and a half later, they find that they have fallen out of love with each other. They seek a declaratory judgment from a court that their marriage is a nullity because it was contracted while they each were minors. What result?

ANSWER:

225. Frances and Greer live in West Kantucky. They heard a lot about each other from other family members ever since Greer was adopted by Frances's mother, but had never met in person because Frances had already moved out of the house when Greer was adopted. They finally met at a family funeral when each was over age 18 and fell in love at first sight. They got to know each other much better after that and decided that they wanted to marry. They consult an attorney to find out their options. What should the attorney say?

(A) They will be permitted to marry as long as no one in the family objects.

(B) They will not be allowed to marry, assuming that West Kantucky, like most jurisdictions, does not permit siblings (including adoptive siblings) to marry.

(C) There is no bar to their marrying because each has attained majority and they are not related by blood.

(D) They will not be allowed to marry unless they are unable to have a child through their union.

226. Alex and Blair are first cousins who have been in love with each for as long as they can remember. They are vacationing in the state of Anythinggoesland and go to a Justice of the Peace on impulse. They marry and return to their home in the state of Traditionaland. It never occurred to them that their marriage might not be recognized but something that someone said to Blair worried them. They consult an attorney to find out whether their marriage will be recognized. What should the attorney say?

ANSWER:

227. Casey and Ellis live in Washtana. They have a lot in common, each having raised children as a single parent after having lost a spouse to cancer. They have decided to marry, much to the consternation of their respective children.

On their wedding day, both Casey and Ellis have too much to drink before the ceremony, possibly because they know that their respective children oppose the union. When it is time to exchange vows, both Casey and Ellis's statements are unintelligible. When they are pronounced married, they kiss.

That night, they are taking a cab to dinner when a drunk driver strikes the cab, killing Casey and severely injuring Ellis. To make a tragic situation even worse, Casey's children later challenge the validity of the marriage, claiming that neither Casey nor Ellis was competent to enter into the marriage, because of their advanced states of inebriation. Whether Ellis is entitled to a spousal share of Casey's estate depends upon whether the marriage is valid. What result?

(A) Ellis will likely be found entitled to a share of the estate as long as Ellis and Casey were not so drunk as not to know what they were doing when exchanging vows. Even if they were found not to have been competent to contract the marriage, the marriage might still be recognized as long as the state treats marriages contracted by temporarily incompetent individuals as voidable rather than void.

(B) Ellis will likely be found not to be entitled to a share of the estate because Ellis and Casey were too drunk to contract a marriage and there was no evidence of their having ratified the marriage while both were sober.

(C) Ellis is unlikely to be found to have contracted a marriage with Casey because there is no evidence that the marriage was ever consummated.

(D) Because Ellis and Casey seemed to exchange vows and were pronounced married, the marriage must be treated as valid and Ellis will likely be entitled to a share of the estate.

228. Dana and Phoenix have been married for several years. One day, Phoenix is very angry when coming home from work after having been told by an unnamed friend that Dana has been spending time during lunch hours with a former love interest. Phoenix threatens to seek a divorce unless Dana (1) agrees never to see this former flame again, and (2) makes their vacation cabin Phoenix's separate property. Dana agrees. Dana and Phoenix remain together for another two years but ultimately divorce, with Phoenix claiming that the vacation cabin is separate rather than marital property by virtue of the postnuptial agreement. Dana claims that the postnuptial agreement is invalid, arguing coercion and lack of consideration. What result?

(A) Because Phoenix did not give Dana anything in exchange for the vacation cabin, the postnuptial agreement is void for lack of consideration.

(B) Because Dana signed the agreement for fear that otherwise their divorce would be imminent, Dana's agreement was coerced rather than voluntary and thus the postnuptial agreement will be found unenforceable.

(C) The postnuptial agreement is unenforceable both because of a lack of consideration and because it was made after Phoenix had threatened divorce.

(D) The postnuptial agreement will likely be upheld. The consideration was Phoenix's remaining in the marriage and a threat to file for divorce does not constitute coercion in these circumstances.

229. Ellis and Finley have been married for several years. Regrettably, they have been drifting apart recently and Ellis announces that it is time for the couple to divorce. Finley, who had been thinking the same thing, agrees. Ellis gives Finley a list of their marital holdings and they agree about the distribution of assets. They divorce with the assets distributed in light of their agreement. Later, it becomes clear that some holdings had been omitted. Finley challenges the separation agreement that had been incorporated into the divorce decree, arguing fraud, whereas Ellis argues that because this was an honest mistake the agreement must stand, and they must simply divide the few omitted assets equitably. What result?

ANSWER:

230. Tracy and Sloan were already successful attorneys when they married. Because each had had a contentious divorce and each was already doing rather well, they signed a prenuptial agreement specifying that there would be no spousal support in the event of divorce. Now, when they are divorcing, Tracy is no longer able to work because undergoing aggressive chemotherapy. Tracy argues that the prenuptial agreement is unenforceable because it is unconscionable. What result?

(A) Because the agreement was not unconscionable when it was made, it is enforceable now.

(B) Because Tracy and Sloan both knew what they were doing when making the agreement and because there is no evidence of fraud, duress, misrepresentation, coercion, or overreaching, the prenuptial agreement cannot be declared unenforceable merely because of some unfortunate occurrences since then.

(C) Because Tracy would be receiving significant support but for the prenuptial agreement, it is obviously unfair to enforce that agreement and impose those significant opportunity costs on Tracy.

(D) According to the law of many states, premarital agreements are unenforceable if unconscionable at the time the agreements are made or enforced. If, for example, enforcement of the premarital agreement would result in Tracy having to receive public support, the agreement might well be found unenforceable, even it was not unconscionable when made.

231. Morgan and Pat, who have been married for five years, are divorcing in the state of Foreverland. Morgan argues that the prenuptial agreement is unenforceable because it was presented to Morgan two days before the wedding was to take place. By then, guests had come in from various parts of the country and, in any event, too many last-minute items had to be taken care of for Morgan to be able to find an attorney who could offer advice. Pat argues that the agreement is enforceable because Morgan could have consulted an attorney had that been a priority and, in any event, Morgan signed the agreement voluntarily. What result?

(A) Because Morgan signed the agreement voluntarily, the Foreverland court is likely to hold the agreement enforceable unless another defect can be established, e.g., that Morgan did not have the requisite information about the assets at stake.

(B) Because Morgan had two days to consult an attorney or could have delayed the wedding if more time were needed, the Foreverland court might find the prenuptial agreement enforceable, although the Foreverland court might instead find that Pat's having presented the agreement shortly before the wedding was enough to make it unenforceable.

(C) The prenuptial agreement will be held unenforceable only if it was substantively unfair.

(D) If Pat handed Morgan the prenuptial agreement two days before the wedding and insisted on its being signed before the wedding could take place, Foreverland, like all other jurisdictions, will treat this prenuptial agreement as unenforceable.

232. Angel and Blair are planning on marrying and they have started talking about whether to have a prenuptial agreement and, if so, what to include. Angel insists on having custody of any children born of the marriage, which is fine with Blair, who would not want custody anyway. Blair is quite willing to agree to the custody condition if Angel will agree that neither will have any spousal support obligations should the marriage end. They sign a prenuptial agreement incorporating those elements.

When Angel and Blair divorce 10 years later, they have two minor children, Matthew and Martha. Blair, who has been the stay-at-home parent for the past several years, wants the prenuptial agreement declared void in its entirety. What result?

ANSWER:

233. Erin and Dallas are married with two children. One day, Erin finds out that Dallas's ex-spouse is still living and was merely figuratively dead, i.e., in Dallas's eyes. Erin, who has strong religious beliefs about not marrying anyone with a living ex-spouse, seeks an annulment. What result?

(A) Because Erin and Dallas had children together, the marriage is unlikely to be annulled because otherwise the children will be illegitimate.

(B) The marriage is likely to be annulled if Dallas knew before the marriage that Erin would never willingly marry someone with a living ex-spouse.

(C) The marriage is unlikely to be annulled if Dallas believed in good faith that Erin would never find out that Dallas's ex-spouse was still alive.

(D) The marriage is unlikely to be annulled if the fact that Dallas's ex-spouse is still alive does not go to the essentials of marriage.

234. Alex and Brett live together in the state of New Delvania. New Delvania does not afford non-marital parents any rights beyond those protected under the federal Constitution. Further,

state law presumes that a child born into a marriage is a child of the marriage. That presumption can be rebutted only if a party to the marriage challenges that parental status within two years of the child's birth.

Brett announces that she is pregnant and Alex says that he wants her to get an abortion. Brett tries to convince Alex that it will be wonderful to have a child, but Alex is adamant. Brett moves out to live with her mother.

Three years later, Alex discovers that Brett gave birth to a baby boy, Caleb, shortly after marrying someone named Drew. Alex decides that he wants to establish parental rights after all and consults an attorney. What should the attorney say?

(A) Assuming that Alex is the biological father of Caleb, Alex should have no difficulty in establishing his parental rights.

(B) Assuming that there has been no final adoption of Caleb by Drew, Alex should have no difficulty in establishing his parental rights.

(C) Because Caleb was born into an existing marriage, he will likely be presumed a child of Brett and Drew. If Brett and Drew wish to bar Alex from establishing parental rights, Alex is very unlikely to be able to establish those rights.

(D) Alex is unlikely to be able to establish parental rights because he suggested that Brett obtain an abortion.

235. Gene and Greer are married and living in Minnigan, which recognizes equitable parent doctrine. They have been raising Georgette, who was born into their marriage six years ago. One day, Greer comes home from work and announces that she wants a divorce. She explains that Gene will not have to worry about paying child support because Georgette is not his child anyway. When they divorce, Gene argues that he should be recognized as Georgette's equitable parent. What result?

(A) Gene will not be able to use equitable parent doctrine to his advantage because that doctrine merely recognizes the parental status of the adult who has equitably adopted a child.

(B) Gene is likely to be successful because although not Georgette's biological parent, he was married to Georgette's mother, he has a parent-child relationship with Georgette that had been encouraged by Greer, and he is willing and able to have the rights and responsibilities of parenthood.

(C) Gene is likely to be successful because all he needs to show to be an equitable parent is that he has a parent-child relationship with Georgette and that it would be in Georgette's interest for that relationship to continue.

(D) Gene is unlikely to be successful because Greer, Georgette's legal and biological parent, opposes his having parental rights.

236. Harlow had always wanted to have a child but she had always wanted to wait until she and her soulmate could have a child together. Regrettably, Harlow has never found anyone

suitable and she is now afraid that she will not be able to have a child unless she acts soon. Harlow explains her predicament to her next-door neighbor, Robert, who seems sympathetic. On the spur of the moment, she asks Robert if he would be willing to provide sperm so that she can have a child via artificial insemination. He agrees and eventually Harlow has a child, William. To her surprise and consternation, Robert says that he wants to play a role in William's life. Harlow refuses and Robert seeks to establish his parental rights. What result?

(A) Because William was born via artificial insemination, Robert is unlikely to be recognized as William's legal parent.

(B) Whether Robert is recognized as William's legal parent will likely depend upon the explicit or implicit agreement between Robert and Harlow when Robert provided his sperm and upon whether local law required that donors provide the sperm to a doctor to avoid the imposition of parental rights or obligations.

(C) Because Robert is genetically related to William and Robert sought to establish his rights in a timely way, he will be recognized as William's father.

(D) Because Harlow wants to raise William without Robert's participation or interference, Robert is unlikely to be recognized as having parental rights.

237. Whitney and Vick live in Illowa, which does not recognize equitable parent doctrine. They were dating for a few months when Whitney announced that she was pregnant and that Vick was the father. Vick proposed and they went to a Justice of the Peace to marry.

Several months later, Whitney gave birth to a very healthy little girl, Sarah. All went well for several years. However, when Sarah was six years old child, Whitney announced that she was through with the marriage. When Vick started discussing custody and visitation, Whitney said that he could forget about seeing Sarah, who was not his child. Vick consulted an attorney to explore his options. What should the attorney have said?

ANSWER:

238. Alice and Bernard have been dating for two months when Alice announces that she is pregnant and that Bernard is the father. They have a quick wedding one month later because they want to be married before the baby arrives. Three months later, Alice gives birth to a bouncing baby boy, Tommy, who was born full term.

Alice and Bernard stay together for 10 years. However, they gradually drift apart and on their tenth anniversary Alice announces that she wants a divorce. When Bernard starts discussing custody and visitation, Alice tells him that Tommy is not his son. Bernard becomes very angry, at least in part because he suspected for a long time that he was not Tommy's biological father.

Bernard consults an attorney to find out whether the marriage could be annulled based on Alice's misrepresentation of parentage. What result?

ANSWER:

239. Ned and Pat are married, although each realizes that the marriage is irretrievably broken. They finally face facts and decide to end their marriage formally.

The day after they agree to divorce, Ned calls his employer and explains that he is ill and will not be able to come to work. He then goes to the bank and empties their joint savings account of $40,000. He goes to the local casino and has a wild day. That evening, he has no cash left in his wallet.

The only contested issue in the divorce is how to divide the marital property. Pat argues that $40,000 lost in the casino should be credited to Ned when the marital assets are divided, whereas Ned argues that the assets at the time of divorce should be divided equally. What result?

(A) Because the gambling losses cannot be recovered and because crediting all of those losses to Ned might mean that he would get relatively little of the remaining assets, Ned's approach to the division of assets will likely be adopted.

(B) Because Pat would have been entitled to some of the winnings had Ned's gambling adventure been more successful, Ned's approach will likely be adopted by the court.

(C) Because Ned's gambling adventure occurred after the marriage was over (at least as a practical matter), his action will be viewed as a paradigmatic example of waste or dissipation and Pat's approach to the distribution of assets will likely be adopted.

(D) Because gambling is by its very nature risky, anyone who loses money gambling will have those monies credited to him or her for purposes of the distribution of marital assets, as long as good records are kept. Pat's approach to the distribution of assets will likely be adopted.

240. Wanda and Sally are divorcing. They can agree about everything except the proper characterization of a necklace that Wanda gave Sally for their fifth anniversary, which was purchased using funds from her salary earned during the marriage. Wanda claims that the necklace is marital property subject to distribution, whereas Sally contends that the necklace is her separate property. What result?

(A) The necklace will be treated as marital property because it was received during the marriage.

(B) The necklace will be treated as marital property because it was purchased with marital funds.

(C) The necklace will be treated as Wanda's separate property because she bought it out of her own salary and obviously would not want Sally to keep it now that the marriage is over.

(D) The necklace will be treated as Sally's separate property or as marital property depending upon local law and Wanda's intent.

241. Taylor and Storm are divorcing. They can agree about everything except the appropriate characterization of two items of property. Taylor's car, which he alone drives, is worth $75,000

and was purchased during the marriage with monies coming out of his paycheck. Storm's painting, which she inherited during the marriage from an aunt, is also worth about $75,000. How should these be characterized?

(A) The painting is Storm's separate property and the car is Taylor's separate property.

(B) Because both items were acquired during the marriage, both are marital property.

(C) Because acquired during the marriage, Storm's painting is marital. However, because the car was purchased solely using funds from Taylor's paycheck, the car is Taylor's separate property.

(D) Because Storm's painting was inherited by Storm alone, it is separate property. Because Taylor's car was purchased using funds earned during the marriage, it is marital.

242. When Robin and Shannon married, they decided to move into the house that Robin had inherited years ago. Marital funds were used to pay for repairs to the house, but no improvements were made to the house during their 10 years of marriage. Robin and Shannon decide to divorce, and the sole point of contention is whether the appreciation in the house's value over the 10 years is marital property subject to distribution. What result?

(A) Because Robin's home became the marital domicile, the house itself is marital property so the increase in the house's value is of course marital property.

(B) Because the increase in the house's value occurred during the marriage, that increase in value is marital property subject to distribution.

(C) Because Shannon was never made a co-owner of the house, the house is separate property as is any increase in the house's value.

(D) Assuming that Robin never made a gift of the house to Shannon or to the marital estate, the house will likely be treated as separate and any increase in its value as separate property as long as no marital assets were used to increase the house's value.

243. Mary Morningstar, 42, lives in the state of Tortsylvania, which recognizes a cause of action for wrongful birth. Mary is pregnant and is worried that her child might have Down Syndrome. An amniocentesis is performed and Mary is quite relieved when told that there is no cause for concern.

Mary gives birth to a little boy, Bobby, with Down Syndrome. She later discovers that she was negligently given someone else's amniocentesis results. Mary sues for wrongful birth. What result?

(A) Mary will likely be successful as long as she can establish that she incurred extraordinary costs in raising Bobby.

(B) Mary will likely be successful if she can establish that her own emotional and financial harm was caused by the negligence at issue and that she would have secured an abortion if she had received the correct test results in a timely way.

(C) Mary will only be successful if she can establish that Bobby would have been better off never having been born.

(D) Mary will only be successful if she can establish that Bobby would not have had Down Syndrome if she had received the correct test results in a timely way.

244. Pat and Parker Padlington live in East Minnegan. They have been married for 10 years, although the last few years have not been happy ones. Finally, Pat decides that it is time to start a new life. Pat quickly packs some possessions and moves back home to West Kanowa. Pat's parents are very supportive because they had never thought much of Parker in the first place.

Pat gets a new job, finds an apartment, gets a driver's new license, and registers to vote. Once Pat has met the residency requirement, Pat files for divorce in West Kanowa, seeking a division of property located in East Minnegan. Parker, who has never set foot in West Kanowa, argues that the West Kanowa court can grant the divorce but does not have jurisdiction to divide up the property. What result?

ANSWER:

245. Casey and Dana Eddington have been married for 10 years and have three children. When they divorce, each seeks primary custody. Dana is awarded custody and Casey is ordered to pay $2,000/month in child support in addition to a spousal support obligation.

After several years of working extremely hard but seeing a significant part of the monthly paycheck disappear in support payments, Casey decides to take a demotion and a pay cut so as to have a better work-life balance. Casey then seeks to have the child support obligation reduced because of a material change in circumstances. Dana opposes the support modification, contending that Casey is voluntarily underemployed. What result?

ANSWER:

246. Juan and Roberto are married and living in Georgiana with their two children. When they divorce, Roberto is awarded primary custody and Juan is ordered to pay child support.

Juan moves to Calington to take advantage of a wonderful job opportunity, and he continues to be very punctual in meeting his support obligations. Regrettably, because of a downturn in the economy, Juan's employer is forced to lay off many workers, including Juan. Juan tries to get another job, but is only able to get a job that is much less remunerative. Eventually, he files in Calington to have his child support obligation reduced. Roberto opposes the reduction in support, making all of the appropriate arguments. What result?

(A) Juan is unlikely to be successful because he will likely get a much better paying job once the economy improves again.

(B) Juan is likely to be successful as long as he can establish that he was not fired for cause.

(C) Juan is unlikely to be successful assuming that the children's needs have remained constant.

(D) Juan is unlikely to be successful because the Calington court is unlikely to have jurisdiction under the Calington and Georgiana versions of the Uniform Family Interstate Support Act.

247. Beverly, who is six months pregnant, has been dating Cameron for two months. Beverly and Cameron marry before the child is born with Cameron knowing that he is not the father of the child that Beverly is carrying.

One year later, Beverly seeks a divorce. Cameron has never bonded with Beverly's child, Cassandra, and has never held her out as his daughter. Beverly seeks child support but Cameron argues that no support obligation should be imposed because Cassandra is not his child. What result?

(A) No child support obligation will be imposed, because such obligations can only be imposed on fathers who are genetically related to their children.

(B) Even if Cameron is not genetically related to Cassandra, he will still have a support obligation imposed because he married Beverly before Cassandra's birth, all the while knowing that he had not fathered Cassandra.

(C) Cameron may well not have a child support obligation imposed because the presumption of paternity is rebuttable and he never held out Cassandra as his child.

(D) Cameron will likely be ordered to pay support, because a child born into a marriage is presumed to be the child of the parties.

248. Emerson Ewington dies as a result of medical malpractice committed by Dr. Sloppy Surgeon in the state of Tortington. Emerson's adult child, Skyler, sues for loss of consortium. Dr. Surgeon argues that the suit must be dismissed because adult children cannot bring such a cause of action. What result?

(A) Because loss of consortium is a cause of action based on the lost opportunity to have sexual relations with a loved one, this cause of action is likely to be dismissed.

(B) Even if Tortington recognizes a loss of consortium action for minor children, it might not permit adult children to bring such an action. It is simply unclear whether this suit will be dismissed.

(C) Skyler is likely to succeed as long as Tortington permits minor children to bring a loss of consortium action against those negligently causing the death of a parent.

(D) As long as Skyler and Emerson had a close relationship and Skyler suffered harm attributable to Surgeon's negligence, Skyler is likely to be successful.

249. Darby and Ellis marry. Ellis moves into Darby's mortgage-free home, which is titled solely in Darby's name. Over the years, funds from Darby's paychecks are used to improve the home.

When Ellis and Darby divorce, the sole issues in contention involve whether the home is marital or separate and to what extent, if any, should Ellis receive some kind of credit for the improvements to the home.

(A) As long as the home is titled in Darby's name alone, it will remain separate property. Ellis is not entitled to any credit for improvements to the home, which came from Darby's paychecks.

(B) Because marital funds were used to improve the home, it will likely be treated as marital and Ellis will be entitled to half of its current fair market value.

(C) Absent evidence of Darby's intent to gift the home to the marriage, the home will likely be treated as Darby's separate property. However, because Darby's paychecks were marital funds, Ellis will likely be credited with a percentage of the value of the home's improvement or, perhaps, will likely be credited with a percentage of the costs of the improvement.

(D) As long as the home is titled in Darby's name alone, it will remain separate property. Ellis is not entitled to any credit for improvements to the home. Ellis's share of the marital funds used for improvement will likely be treated as a gift.

250. Robin and Tracy are first cousins living in East Vermshire, which treats first-cousin marriages as void rather than voidable. Because they want to marry, they move to West Massecticut, where they are permitted to marry. They marry in Massecticut and live their lives there.

Several years later, Tracy's brother dies in East Vermshire. Robin and Tracy go to the funeral. On the way to Tracy's parents' house after the funeral, they are in a terrible car accident. Tracy has severe injuries. The negligent driver argues that Robin cannot sue for loss of consortium because Robin does not qualify as one of Tracy's immediate family members. What result?

(A) Because Robin and Tracy left East Vermshire to evade the state's marriage laws, their marriage will not be recognized and Robin's suit will likely be dismissed.

(B) Because Robin and Tracy could not currently marry in East Vermshire, their marriage will not be recognized and Robin's suit will be dismissed.

(C) Even if East Vermshire treats first-cousin marriages as void, Robin and Tracy's marriage may nonetheless be recognized because validly celebrated in their domicile. Robin may well be successful when bringing suit.

(D) Assuming that first cousins are not immediate family members under East Vermshire law, Robin's suit will likely be dismissed.

Answers

Minor Marriages

1. **Answer (D) is the best answer.** Once the marriage has been ratified by cohabitation when both parties have reached the age of consent, the marriage is valid and no longer subject to annulment. *See Medlin v. Medlin*, 981 P.2d 1087 (Ariz. App. 1999) (minor marriage ratified when minor cohabited with spouse after reaching eighteenth birthday). *See also Matthes v. Matthes*, 198 Ill. App. 515, 523 (Ct. App. 1916) ("[I]f after arriving at the age of consent the parties should continue the marriage relation, then they must be considered to have ratified same and the marriage thereby becomes valid and binding.").

   Answer (A) is incorrect. If Bryan had been the minor and if he had not reached the age of consent, then his parents could seek to annul the action. *See Brewer v. Griggs*, 10 Tenn. App. 378, 389 (Ct. App. 1929) (suggesting that the "guardian could institute, prosecute, and control a suit to annul the marriage of his said ward"). But Bryan had already reached the age of consent.

   Answer (B) is incorrect. The marriage will not be treated as void merely because the parties intentionally deceived the Justice of the Peace. *See Samluk v. Gorecki*, 265 A.2d 46 (Del. Super. 1970) (court refused to annul marriage even though parent's consent was forged).

   Answer (C) is incorrect. While the Adamsons might have been able to have the marriage annulled while Ann was still a minor, *cf. Wolf v. Wolf*, 185 N.Y.S. 37 (App. Div. 1920) (discussing case in which a parent had his minor child's marriage annulled), they could no longer do so once she reached the age of consent and ratified the marriage. *See Medlin v. Medlin*, 981 P.2d 1087 (Ariz. App. 1999).

2. **Answer (D) is the best answer.** Once the marriage has been ended by the death of one of the parties, it will no longer be subject to annulment. *See Matter of Davis' Estate*, 640 P.2d 692, 693 (Or. App. 1982) ("a suit for annulment does not survive the death of one of the parties"); *Greene v. Williams*, 88 Cal. Rptr. 261, 264 (Ct. App. 1970) (nonconsenting parent cannot challenge the validity of the marriage of the deceased minor).

   Answer (A) is incorrect. A voidable marriage is valid until annulled by a court. *See In re J.M.N.*, 2008 WL 2415490, at *8 (Tenn. App. 2008).

   Answer (B) is incorrect. The marriage can be challenged by the party himself/herself once that party has attained majority. *See Greene v. Williams*, 88 Cal. Rptr. 261, 263 (Ct. App. 1970) (describing who may challenge a minor marriage).

   Answer (C) is incorrect. A minor's marriage without parental consent is voidable rather than void. *See Greene v. Williams*, 88 Cal. Rptr. 261, 262 (Ct. App. 1970) ("A marriage by an under-age child without parental consent is voidable only and remains in full force until dissolved.").

3.   **Answer (A) is the best answer.** While it might be better to have a declaration of invalidity to avoid possible future misunderstandings, *cf. Beyerle v. Bartsch*, 190 P. 239, 240 (Wash. 1920) ("The fact that actions of annulment are taken to declare bigamous marriages void does not have the effect of making such marriages voidable."), it is not necessary to do so. *See Campbell v. Thomas*, 897 N.Y.S.2d 460, 466 (App. Div. 2010) ("[T]he parties to a void marriage (and everyone else) are free to treat the marriage as a nullity without the involvement of a court.").

      Answer (B) is incorrect. If the marriage is void rather than voidable, then it cannot be ratified. *See In re Estate of Toutant*, 633 N.W.2d 692, 699 (Wis. App. 2001) ("In the void marriage, the relationship of the parties is an absolute nullity from the very beginning and cannot be ratified.").

      Answer (C) is incorrect. A void marriage need not be annulled by a court. *See Campbell v. Thomas*, 897 N.Y.S.2d 460, 466 (App. Div. 2010).

      Answer (D) is incorrect. David's agreement that the marriage was a mistake is not enough to obviate the need to have it annulled. If Marryvania had treated minor marriages as voidable rather than void, then it would have been necessary to have the marriage annulled, David's agreement that the marriage was a mistake notwithstanding. *See Peters v. Peters*, 214 N.W.2d 151, 155 (Iowa 1974) ("[W]hen a marriage is voidable it is legally valid for all civil purposes until it is judicially annulled.").

4.   **Answer (C) is the best answer.** Had Yolanda been older, the marriage might have immunized the relations. *See* Vt. Stat. Ann. tit. 13, § 3252 (c)(1) (West) ("No person shall engage in a sexual act with a child who is under the age of 16, except where the persons are married to each other and the sexual act is consensual"). However, such immunity may not be conferred where the child is very young. *See* Vt. Stat. Ann. tit. 13, § 3253 (a) (8) (West) ("A person commits the crime of aggravated sexual assault if the person commits sexual assault under . . . the following circumstances: The victim is under the age of 13 and the actor is at least 18 years of age.").

      Answer (A) is incorrect. Zeke could be charged if local law so specified. *See* Vt. Stat. Ann. tit. 13, § 3253 (a) (8) (West).

      Answer (B) is incorrect in that parental consent may not immunize Zeke from prosecution. *See* Vt. Stat. Ann. tit. 13, § 3253 (a) (8) (West).

      Answer (D) is incorrect. The age of the minor may be important. *See* Vt. Stat. Ann. tit. 13, § 3252 (c) (1) (West) and Vt. Stat. Ann. tit. 13, § 3253 (a) (8) (West).

5.   Many states permit individuals to marry even if they have not yet attained majority. For example, a state might permit a minor to marry as long as he or she has parental permission. *See*, for example, Mo. Ann. Stat. § 451.090 (West) (2) ("No recorder shall issue a license authorizing the marriage of any male under the age of eighteen years or of any female under the

age of eighteen years, except with the consent of his or her custodial parent or guardian, which consent shall be given at the time, in writing, stating the residence of the person giving such consent, signed and sworn to before an officer authorized to administer oaths."). Even if parental consent cannot be obtained, some states authorize a court to provide the necessary consent in particular circumstances including the pregnancy of the minor. *See*, for example, Fla. Stat. Ann. § 741.0405 (3) (b) (West) ("When the fact of pregnancy is verified by the written statement of a licensed physician, the county court judge of any county in the state may, in his or her discretion, issue a license to marry . . . [t]o any female under the age of 18 years and male over the age of 18 years upon the female's application sworn under oath that she is an expectant parent."). A separate issue involves whether the attorney should address the difference between void and voidable marriages. A void marriage never comes into being and cannot be ratified. *See Falk v. Falk*, 2005 WL 127077, at *3 (Tenn. App. 2005) ("Void marriages are void *ab initio* and are neither given recognition by the courts nor are such marriages capable of ratification by the parties."), whereas a voidable marriage is valid until annulled. *See In re Estate of Meek*, 2014 WL 2553469, at *4 (Tenn. App. 2014) ("A voidable marriage is a valid marriage until avoided by appropriate legal proceeding."). Nonetheless, there are a number of additional factors to consider when deciding whether to celebrate a voidable marriage, including the possibility that the marriage would be annulled and that contracting a voidable marriage might have very detrimental effects on other family relationships.

Bigamous Marriages

6.   **(C) is the best answer.** Jordan will not be subject to a bigamy charge when this amount of time has passed. *See In re Cassidy's Estate*, 178 N.Y.S. 366, 367 (Sur. Ct. 1919) ("After seven years McGuire would be presumed to be dead, and bigamy could not be predicated of any subsequent marriage of the administratrix."). Further, because Riley will be presumed dead after having been missing for seven years, the first marriage will be viewed as having ended. At that point, Jordan is free to marry again, assuming that there is no reason to believe that Riley continues to be alive. *See Cann v. Cann*, 632 A.2d 322, 324 (Pa. Super. 1993) ("[H]ere a spouse from a prior marriage has been missing for a period of seven years, she is presumed dead for the purposes of the validity of a prior marriage."). *See also Loera v. Loera*, 815 S.W.2d 910, 912 (Tex. App. 1991) ("The law provides that a person absent for seven consecutive years shall be presumed dead unless it is proved that he was alive during that period.").

Answer (A) is incorrect. Some states preclude a bigamy prosecution if an individual reasonably but mistakenly believes his or her spouse dead. *See State v. Stank*, 1883 WL 5040, at *1 (Ohio Com. Pl. 1883). Further, where an individual has been missing for a specified number of years, that person will be presumed dead and a subsequent marriage will be valid even if the person is in fact alive. *See Baxter v. Baxter*, 334 S.W.2d 714, 714 (Ark. 1960) ("A related section, also part of the Revised Statutes, provides that where any husband abandons his wife and resides beyond the limits of the State for five years, without being known to his wife to be living during that time, his death shall be presumed, and any subsequent marriage entered into by the wife after the end of the five years shall be valid.").

Answer (B) is incorrect. Jordan's lack of knowledge that Riley was alive will not prevent a bigamy prosecution. *Braun v. State*, 185 A.2d 905, 909 (Md. 1962) ("[W]e think that the appellant has failed to establish a bona fide and reasonable belief that he was divorced . . . . Such a belief is, we think, required to establish a successful defense even in those jurisdictions which recognize a genuine though mistaken belief as an excuse from liability under a bigamy statute, even where the mistake is one of fact.").

Answer (D) is not the best answer. Many states do not preclude a bigamy prosecution merely because the defendant reasonably believed a spouse dead. *See State v. Hendrickson*, 245 P. 375, 376 (Utah 1926) ("[T]he great majority of the cases in this country are opposed to the rule that honest belief in the death or divorce of the lawful spouse is a defense to a prosecution for bigamy."). The length of time that Riley has been missing (during which there was no reason to believe that Riley was alive) provides the basis for holding the second marriage valid and for Jordan's not being subject to a bigamy charge.

7.   **Answer (B) is the best answer.** Assuming that the lottery winnings are viewed as marital property, *see Ullah v. Ullah*, 555 N.Y.S.2d 834, 835 (App. Div. 1990) ("[A] lottery jackpot, including future payments, the right to which arose during the marriage by virtue of the efforts of one spouse, and upon a wager of marital funds, constitutes marital property subject to equitable distribution."), and a search of the relevant records reveals that neither Addison nor Bailey ever ended their marriage, *cf. Quinn v. Miles*, 124 So. 2d 883, 886 (Fla. App. 1960) ("It has been repeatedly held that if the records of the State Bureau of Vital Statistics fail to disclose any divorce by the decedent against his wife during the period of their separation, such evidence will be sufficient proof that no such divorce was ever procured, and likewise sufficient to rebut the presumption of validity attaching to the subsequent marriage of decedent"), Bailey may well be entitled to a share of the lottery winnings.

Answer (A) is incorrect. While Bailey might have provided a ground for ending the marriage by abandoning it, *see*, for example, *Gulati v. Gulati*, 876 N.Y.S.2d 430, 432 (App. Div. 2009) ("Pursuant to Domestic Relations Law § 170(2), an action for a divorce on the ground of abandonment may be maintained when the defendant abandons the plaintiff for a period of one or more years."), the marriage itself will only be ended if one of the parties to the marriage dies or if a court dissolves the marriage. *See Albrecht v. Albrecht*, 856 N.W.2d 755, 756 (N.D. 2014).

Answer (C) is incorrect. Addison's sincere belief will not suffice to establish the validity of the second marriage or the invalidity of the first. At the very least, Addison should have engaged in a search to find out if Bailey was still alive. *See Anonymous v. Anonymous*, 62 N.Y.S.2d 130, 133 (Sup. Ct. 1946) ("[T]hat statute authorizes the dissolution of a marriage on the ground of the absence of a spouse for five successive years then last past, without being known to the petitioner to be living during that time, where the petitioner believes the absent spouse to be dead, and proves that a diligent search has been made to discover evidence showing that such spouse is living and that no such evidence has been found.").

Answer (D) is incorrect. While states have a strong presumption that the last marriage is valid, that presumption is rebuttable. *See Mamo v. Estate of Mandeng*, 2015 WL 1721426, at *2 (N.J. Super. App. Div. 2015) (individual must provide clear and convincing evidence that the last marriage was not valid); *Cason v. Cason*, 2001 WL 1830006, at *5 (Va. Cir. Ct. 2001) ("[T]here is a rebuttable presumption in Virginia that when a party has been married twice, and both parties to the first marriage are living at the time of the second marriage, then the second marriage is presumed to be valid."); *Argo v. State*, 371 S.E.2d 922, 923 (Ga. App. 1988) ("As a general rule, the validity of a second marriage will be presumed 'until evidence is adduced that the spouse of the first marriage is living, and only then [is] the burden on the party contending that the second marriage is valid to go forward with the evidence and show that the first marriage was dissolved by divorce.'").

8.   **Answer (C) is the best answer.** While the marriage is void, local law may still permit spousal support or a division of property. *See Petty v. Blount-Petty*, 2017-Ohio-7035, ¶ 29-30 (Ct. App. 2017). Further, Jamie might be estopped from challenging the validity of his marriage to Emerson. *See Jessie v. Jessie*, 920 S.W.2d 874, 877 (Ark. App. 1996) ("[W]hile a legal marriage

cannot be created by estoppel, equity can require that parties be estopped from denying the validity of a marriage.").

Answer (A) is incorrect. While that marriage is void, it is nonetheless true that marital property can be divided and, where appropriate, spousal support ordered. *See Petty v. Blount-Petty*, 2017-Ohio-7035, ¶ 29-30 (Ct. App. 2017).

Answer (B) is incorrect because the marriage is invalid, notwithstanding Emerson's having married Jamie in good faith. *See Matter of Estate of Meetze*, 2017 WL 3027483, at *3 (N.C. App. 2017) ("Because . . . Decedent was still married to Petitioner at the time he married Respondent, we affirm the trial court's order . . . concluding that the marriage between Carol Meetze and John Timothy Meetze was void *ab initio*.").

Answer (D) is incorrect. The marriage can still be challenged. *Cf. Smith v. Smith*, 224 So. 3d 740, 747 (Fla. 2017) ("[T]he validity of a void marriage may be challenged at any time, including after the death of the alleged spouses."). *See also In re Estate of Everhart*, 783 N.W.2d 1, 6 (Neb. App. 2010) (upholding invalidity of marriage, notwithstanding that the marriage was not challenged until 16 years after its celebration).

9. **Answer (D) is the best answer.** *See D.L.H. v. J.D.H.*, 521 S.W.3d 324, 326–27 (Mo. App. 2017) (noting that under Texas law "a bigamous marriage may become valid under Texas law if . . . after the date of the dissolution, the parties have lived together as husband and wife and represented themselves to others as being married").

    Answer (A) is incorrect. A marriage that was void *ab initio* can be attacked even after one of the parties to the purported marriage had died. *See Smith v. Smith*, 224 So. 3d 740, 747 (Fla. 2017) ("[T]he validity of a void marriage may be challenged at any time, including after the death of the alleged spouses.").

    Answer (B) is incorrect. A void marriage can be challenged by interested parties who were not parties to the marriage. *See In re Estate of Everhart*, 783 N.W.2d 1, 7 (Neb. App. 2010) ("The marriage is void ab initio by statute, and its invalidity may be maintained in any proceeding in any court between any proper parties whether in the lifetime or after the death of the supposed husband and wife.").

    Answer (C) is incorrect. While it is true that the bigamous marriages are void *ab initio, see Petty v. Blount-Petty*, 2017-Ohio-7035, ¶ 18 (Ct. App. 2017) (a "bigamous marriage is void ab initio and of no legal purpose"), it is not clear that Madison will be viewed as a legal stranger to Paris. Some states offer protection for putative spouses. *See Ayala v. Valderas*, 2008 WL 4661846, at *4 (Tex. App. 2008) ("A putative marriage is one that was entered into in good faith by at least one of the parties, but which is invalid by reason of an existing impediment on the part of one or both parties. . . . The effect of a putative marriage is to give the putative spouse, who acted in good faith, rights to property acquired during the marital relationship that are analogous to those rights given to a lawful spouse.").

10. Even if it can be established that Miranda's marriage to Zeno did not formally end until Zeno's death, William might still be able to collect workmen's compensation benefits. First, if the

state in which William and Miranda lived recognized the putative spouse doctrine, then William might qualify for benefits as a putative spouse, *see Williams v. Fireman's Fund Ins. Co.*, 670 P.2d 453, 455 (Colo. App. 1983) ("As Randy's putative spouse, upon his death, Kathryn acquired the legal spouse's right to compensation."), because he had had no reason to believe that his marriage to Miranda was not valid. *Cf. Davis v. Davis*, 2014 WL 890899, at *9 (Tex. App. 2014) ("Carol was a putative spouse, based on her testimony that she did not understand her ceremonial marriage to Mohammad to have any legally-recognized import and, consequently, was unaware there was a legal impediment to her marriage to Frank."). Or, if the state in which they lived recognized common law marriage, then William and Miranda might have contracted a common law marriage once Zeno had died. *See Gillaspie v. E. W. Blair Const. Corp.*, 388 P.2d 647, 650 (Kan. 1964) ("While the marriage of Pearl and Gillaspie was of no legal effect in the first instance . . . , persistence of the relation after Pearl's disability was removed on November 28, 1961, made them husband and wife under the common law without further proof of a new express exchange of consent."). However, even if the state does recognize common law marriages, it might not recognize William and Miranda's marriage merely by virtue of their continuing to treat each other as spouses and holding themselves out to the community as married after Zeno's death. Some states require more than the removal of an impediment to the marriage. *See Byers v. Mount Vernon Mills, Inc.*, 231 S.E.2d 699, 700 (S.C. 1977) ("[T]he removal of an impediment to a marriage contract (the divorce in this case) does not convert an illegal bigamous marriage into a common law marriage."). In such states, the couple would have to do something different after the impediment had been removed to establish their marriage. *See id.* ("After the barrier to marriage has been removed, there must be a new mutual agreement, either by way of civil ceremony or by way of a recognition of the illicit relation and a new agreement to enter into a common law marriage arrangement.").

Incestuous Marriages

11.   **Answer (D) is the best answer.** If individuals marry in accord with the law of the state of celebration, their marriage may be valid in the domicile even though the domicile precludes their marrying locally. However, that decision is itself left up to the domicile. *Compare Mazzolini v. Mazzolini*, 155 N.E.2d 206 (Ohio 1958) (upholding validity of first cousin marriage celebrated elsewhere even though such a marriage could not be celebrated within the state) *with In re Stile's Estate*, 391 N.E.2d 1026 (Ohio 1979) (holding marriage between uncle and niece void, even though the marriage had been validly celebrated elsewhere).

   Answer (A) is incorrect. A domicile might refuse to recognize a marriage valid in the state of celebration. *See Cook v. Cook*, 104 P.3d 857, 867 (Ariz. App. 2005) (explaining that first-cousin marriages celebrated after 1996 will be void in Arizona even if they were valid in the state of celebration).

   Answer (B) is incorrect. A domicile might recognize a marriage valid in the state of celebration even if that marriage could not have been celebrated within the domicile. *See Mason v. Mason*, 775 N.E.2d 706 (Ind. App. 2002) (upholding validity of first cousin marriage celebrated in Tennessee, even though such a marriage would have been invalid if celebrated in Indiana).

   Answer (C) is incorrect. *See Cook v. Cook*, 104 P.3d 857, 867 (Ariz. App. 2005) (making clear that first-cousin marriages celebrated after a certain date would not be recognized in Arizona even if valid in the state of celebration).

12.   **Answer (D) is correct.** There are two issues to be considered: (1) whether the state treats individuals related by half in the same way as individuals related by whole, and (2) whether the state treats individuals who are adopted and have no blood relation in the same way as it treats individuals who are related by blood. A state might not prohibit a half-uncle and half-niece from marrying, even though it prohibited an uncle from marrying his niece. *See Nguyen v. Holder*, 21 N.E.3d 1023, 1024 (N.Y. 2014) ("A marriage where a husband is the half brother of the wife's mother is not void as incestuous under Domestic Relations Law § 5(3)."). Even if the state prohibits half-uncles and half-nieces from marrying as a general matter, it might nonetheless permit this marriage because Loren was adopted (and thus is not related by blood to Kevin). *See*, for example, *Bagnardi v. Hartnett*, 366 N.Y.S.2d 89, 91 (Sup. Ct. 1975) (holding no impediment exists to marriage between man and adoptive daughter); *Israel v. Allen*, 577 P.2d 762, 763 (Colo. 1978) (upholding marriage between brother and sister by adoption). *See also La. Civ. Code Ann.* art. 90 ("[P]ersons related by adoption, though not by blood, in

the collateral line within the fourth degree may marry each other if they obtain judicial authorization in writing to do so."); La. Civ. Code Ann. art. 90 Revision comments ("The phrase 'collaterals within the fourth degree' includes aunt and nephew, uncle and niece, siblings, and first cousins.").

Answer (A) is incorrect. A state might preclude marriages between uncles and nieces related by whole blood but not by half blood. *See* 18 Pa. Stat. and Cons. Stat. Ann. § 4302 (a) (West) ("[A] person is guilty of incest, a felony of the second degree, if that person knowingly marries or cohabits or has sexual intercourse with an ancestor or descendant, a brother or sister of the whole or half blood or an uncle, aunt, nephew or niece of the whole blood.").

Answer (B) is incorrect. Even if the statute does not specify that it applies to individuals related by half as well as by whole, it might nonetheless be so construed by a court. *See*, for example, *Singh v. Singh*, 569 A.2d 1112, 1121 (Conn. 1990) ("[A] marriage between persons related to one another as half-uncle and half-niece is void under General Statutes §§ 46b-21 and 53a-191 as incestuous.").

Answer (C) is incorrect. A state might permit marriages between individuals who would not otherwise be permitted to marry if one has been adopted and is not related by blood. *See Bagnardi v. Hartnett*, 366 N.Y.S.2d 89 (Sup. Ct. 1975); *Israel v. Allen*, 577 P.2d 762 (Colo. 1978). *See also* La. Civ. Code Ann. art. 90.

13.   **Answer (D) is the best answer.** The marriage would be valid if the stepparent-stepchild relationship ended when the relationship between the parent and stepparent ended. *See Back v. Back*, 125 N.W. 1009 (Iowa 1910). However, some states would interpret the ban as still being in existence even after the marriage between the parent and stepparent has ended. *See Rhodes v. McAfee*, 457 S.W.2d 522, 524 (Tenn. 1970).

Answer (A) is incorrect. Some states preclude a stepparent from marrying the child of his/her ex-spouse. *See Rhodes v. McAfee*, 457 S.W.2d 522, 524 (Tenn. 1970) ("The marriage of B. E. Plunk to his stepdaughter, Gladys Griggs, was void ab initio.").

Answer (B) is incorrect. Some states treat the stepparent-stepchild relationship as ending when the stepparent-parent relationship ends. In that event, the adult can marry the child of a former spouse, absent some other bar to the marriage. *See Back v. Back*, 125 N.W. 1009 (Iowa 1910) (recognizing the validity of a marriage between a man and his former stepchild).

Answer (C) is incorrect. Even if the statute expressly bars marriages between stepparent and stepchild, the marriage might nonetheless be recognized if the cessation of the marriage between parent and stepparent is viewed as ending the stepparent-stepchild relationship, too. *See Back v. Back*, 125 N.W. 1009 (Iowa 1910).

14.   Harper and Jesse's marriage will likely be viewed as valid. Even in states where stepparent/stepchild marriages are prohibited, the law may well be construed as not prohibiting a marriage between a stepparent and a *former* stepchild. *See People v. Parker*, 504 N.E.2d 1006, 1008 (Ill. App. 1987) ("[U]nder [Illinois law] . . . , a divorced or widowed stepparent may marry

his or her stepchild."). Here, Harper was not Jesse's stepparent, so that prohibition would likely not apply anyway. Even were the stepparent/stepchild prohibition construed as also prohibiting marriages between de facto parents and children in their care, *cf.* W. Va. Code Ann. §61-8D-5 (a) (West) (criminalizing sexual relations between a child and a person who had care, custody or control of that child), Jesse was not a child and the romantic relationship began after Jesse had moved out. The marriage would likely be viewed as valid.

Marriage and Sexual Relations

15.   **Answer (A) is the best answer.** Here, both parties knew beforehand that there would be no consummation, so this would not be a reason to grant an annulment. *See Kugel v. Kugel*, 1991 WL 270412 (Ohio App. 1991) (reversing annulment because both parties knew before the marriage that consummation would be impossible and thus no one was at fault for the nonconsummation).

   Answer (B) is incorrect. There may be an additional requirement that the inability to consummate the marriage was not known to the parties at the time of the marriage. *See* 750 Ill. Comp. Stat. Ann. 5/301 (2) ("The court shall enter its judgment declaring the invalidity of a marriage (formerly known as annulment) entered into under the following circumstances: . . . a party lacks the physical capacity to consummate the marriage by sexual intercourse and at the time the marriage was solemnized the other party did not know of the incapacity.").

   Answer (C) is incorrect. Annulments are not disfavored merely because they are other grounds upon which a marriage might be ended. *See Patel v. Patel*, 11 N.E.3d 800, 804 (Ohio App. 2014) (granting wife an annulment notwithstanding that husband instead sought a divorce).

   Answer (D) is not correct. Where both parties know prior to the marriage that there will be no consummation, many states would not permit the marriage to be annulled. *See* 750 Ill. Comp. Stat. Ann. 5/301 (2). Where this is not known by both parties beforehand, many states permit either party to assert nonconsummation. *See*, for example, Alaska Stat. Ann. § 25.05.031 (West) ("[I]f either party fails to consummate the marriage, the marriage is voidable but only at the suit of the party under the disability or upon whom the force or fraud is imposed.").

16.   **Answer (B) is the best answer.** Testimony establishing that "irreconcilable differences had arisen between the parties which caused an irremediable breakdown of the marriage" requires granting of a divorce. *See Flynn v. Flynn*, 388 A.2d 1170, 1171 (R.I. 1978). Further, impotence as a ground for annulment refers to the inability to consummate the marriage rather than the inability to father a child. *See Donati v. Church*, 80 A.2d 633, 633 (N.J. Super. App. Div. 1951) ("Impotence is not sterility or inability to beget or bear a child. It is inability to have sexual intercourse."). *See also Wilson v. Wilson*, 191 A. 666, 668 (Pa. Super. 1937) ("An examination of a host of decided cases in other jurisdictions has failed to disclose a single case where a court has granted a divorce upon the bare ground of sterility.").

   Answer (A) is incorrect. Although it may be correct that they would have had a child but for Nico's sterility, an annulment on the ground of impotence is met by a showing of nonconsummation rather than of sterility. *See T v. M*, 242 A.2d 670, 673 (N.J. Super. Ch. Div. 1968) (Impotency is the inability to have sexual intercourse; impotence is not sterility.).

Answer (C) is incorrect. The relative merits of adoption are beside the point. Even if Parker had legitimate reasons to oppose adoption, she still would be unable to have the marriage annulled on the basis of impotence. *See Donati v. Church*, 80 A.2d 633, 633 (N.J. Super. App. Div. 1951).

Answer (D) is incorrect. Regardless of why Nico is impotent, Parker will be unable to have the marriage annulled. *See Donati v. Church*, 80 A.2d 633, 633 (N.J. Super. App. Div. 1951). If Nico can establish that the marriage is irretrievably broken, then the divorce should be granted, *see Flynn v. Flynn*, 388 A.2d 1170, 1171 (R.I. 1978), regardless of how he came to be sterile.

17.   **Answer (C) is the best answer.** The annulment is likely to be granted because the parties have not consummated the marriage and because there seem to be no plans to bring about the formal welcoming so that the couple can engage in marital relations. *See Patel v. Patel*, 11 N.E.3d 800, 801 (Ohio App. 2014) (granting annulment due to nonconsummation when the couple was to remain chaste until a particular religious ceremony had been performed and there were no plans to undergo that ceremony, notwithstanding that the couple had already been married for a year).

Answer (A) is incorrect. It is not necessary for the parties to refuse to ever consummate the marriage in order for an annulment to be granted based on nonconsummation. *See Patel v. Patel*, 11 N.E.3d 800, 801 (Ohio App. 2014).

Answer (B) is incorrect. It is not necessary to establish impotency in order to satisfy the non-consummation ground for annulment. *See Lang v. Reetz-Lang*, 488 N.E.2d 929, 931 (Ohio App. 1985) ("[T]he pre-existence of a condition preventing consummation [like impotency] is not a requisite for annulment for nonconsummation.").

Answer (D) is incorrect. An annulment can be granted because of nonconsummation even if there is no other basis upon which to challenge the validity of the marriage. *See Lang v. Reetz-Lang*, 488 N.E.2d 929, 931–32 (Ohio App. 1985) ("Where one of the parties has willfully or knowingly refused or avoided consummation of the marriage, the other has a proper ground for annulment, although the marriage was valid.").

18.   The attorneys should suggest that Cameron is likely to be able to get the marriage annulled. Unless there is some good reason for the nonconsummation, *see Svenson v. Svenson*, 70 N.E. 120 (N.Y. 1904) (suggesting that nonconsummation was justified when marital partner had a venereal disease), there is no need for Dallas to affirm a settled intent to refrain from engaging in marital relations in order for an annulment to be granted. *See Patel v. Patel*, 11 N.E.3d 800, 801 (Ohio App. 2014) (granting annulment even though husband had not expressed a firm intention not to engage in marital relations).

Marriage and Competency

19.   **Answer (D) is the best answer.** If the marriage between Yuri and Zena is treated as voidable, then their having lived together once Yuri became competent would ratify the marriage. *See Com. ex rel. Johnson v. Johnson*, 124 A.2d 423, 426 (Pa. Super. 1956) ("[T]he fact that the parties lived together as man and wife in Florida, after appellant's disability had been removed, ratified the marriage."). Further, as a general matter, a voidable marriage cannot be challenged after the death of one of the parties. *See Arnelle v. Fisher*, 647 So. 2d 1047, 1048 (Fla. App. 1994) ("Upon the death of either party, the [voidable] marriage is good *ab initio*.").

   Answer (A) is not the best answer. Some states treat marriages involving incompetents as voidable rather than void. *See Coulter v. Hendricks*, 918 S.W.2d 424, 426 (Tenn. App. 1995) ("A marriage is voidable from the beginning (1) *when either party was insane*."). As a general matter, voidable marriages cannot be challenged after the death of one of the parties. *See Arnelle v. Fisher*, 647 So. 2d 1047, 1048 (Fla. App. 1994) ("[A] voidable marriage is good for every purpose and can only be attacked in a direct proceeding during the life of the parties.").

   Answer (B) is incorrect. While Zena's decision to go through with the wedding might have been reasonable, that reasonableness could not somehow make a void marriage valid. Void marriages cannot be made valid. *See In re Estate of Toutant*, 633 N.W.2d 692, 699 (Wis. App. 2001) ("In the void marriage, the relationship of the parties is an absolute nullity from the very beginning and cannot be ratified."). Further, while it was not Zena's fault that Yuri was temporarily insane, she nonetheless decided to go through the marriage knowing that he was not competent. *Cf. Parkinson v. Mills*, 159 So. 651, 655 (Miss. 1935) ("Where one of the parties to a marriage is incapable of entering into the marriage state because of insanity, and the other party, knowing of such insanity, fraudulently induces and brings about the marriage, in order to inherit the estate of the insane spouse in case the latter should die first, any member of the family of the insane spouse sufficiently interested could have a guardian appointed, and by a proper proceeding in court through such guardian have the marriage annulled in the lifetime of the parties.").

   Answer (C) is not the best answer. If the marriage is void, then Tatum could challenge it, notwithstanding his having waited so long. *Cf. In re Estate of Everhart*, 783 N.W.2d 1, 6 (Neb. App. 2010) ("Arlene argues . . . that the doctrine of laches precluded Charlotte from questioning the validity of the marriage approximately 16 years after the date of the marriage ceremony. Arlene's assertions have no merit. We affirm the order of the county court finding that the marriage between Paul and Arlene was void and that Arlene is not entitled to any statutory allowances as a surviving spouse.").

20. **Answer (A) is the best answer.** Bacchus will likely be unable to secure an annulment because he understood the nature of the ceremony, as evidenced by his having said, "I do," at the appropriate time. *See Levine v. Dumbra*, 604 N.Y.S.2d 207, 208 (App. Div. 1993) ("In order to obtain an annulment on the ground of lack of understanding, it must be shown that the party was incapable of understanding the nature, effect, and consequences of the marriage."). Modesta may well be successful, given that both parties seek to end the marriage. *Cf.* Ohio Rev. Code Ann. § 3105.01 (K) (West) ("The court of common pleas may grant divorces for the following causes: . . . Incompatibility, unless denied by either party."). She might have been able to end it based on her own reasonable assertion that the couple's differences were irreconcilable. *See Dunn v. Dunn*, 511 P.2d 427, 428–29 (Or. App. 1973) ("[O]nce the existence of a difference . . . claimed by the petitioner to be irreconcilable has been established, . . . the test our statute contemplates is: (1) whether or not such difference is one that reasonably appears to the court to be in the mind of the petitioner an irreconcilable one, and (2) . . . whether or not the court concludes that the breakdown of that particular marriage is irremediable.").

Answer (B) is incorrect. The question is not simply whether he was drunk, but whether he understood what he was doing. *See Levine v. Dumbra*, 604 N.Y.S.2d 207, 208 (App. Div. 1993).

Answer (C) is incorrect. The question is not whether he was faking his drunkenness, but whether he understood what was going on. *See Levine v. Dumbra*, 604 N.Y.S.2d 207, 208 (App. Div. 1993).

Answer (D) is not the best answer. While Bacchus will likely be unsuccessful in securing an annulment because he seemed to understand what was going on, *see Levine v. Dumbra*, 604 N.Y.S.2d 207, 208 (App. Div. 1993), this answer misrepresents the conditions for irreconcilable differences, instead conflating it with the different no-fault ground involving the parties living separate and apart. *See* N.C. Gen. Stat. Ann. § 50-6 ("Marriages may be dissolved and the parties thereto divorced from the bonds of matrimony on the application of either party, if and when the husband and wife have lived separate and apart for one year.").

21. **Answer (A) is the best answer.** According to the law of some states, a marriage involving an incompetent who remains incompetent through his or her death is void *ab initio* and subject to challenge even after the incompetent's demise. *See In re Estate of Santolino*, 895 A.2d 506, 514 (N. J. Super. Ch. Div. 2005) ("[I]f Mr. Santolino lacked the capacity to consent then his marriage will be rendered void ab initio. . . . [T]he civil disability of inability to consent to the marriage allows the court to render a posthumous judgment of nullity with regard to the marriage at issue because a void marriage is deemed not to have been a marriage at all."). However, not all states permit such an action under these circumstances. *See In re Estate of Randall*, 999 A.2d 51, 54 (D.C. 2010) (refusing to permit challenge to marriage involving alleged incompetent after the alleged incompetent had died).

Answer (B) is incorrect. The question is not what Jamie knows, but whether the state treats the marriage as void or voidable. *See In re Estate of Randall*, 999 A.2d 51, 52 (D.C. 2010). Suppose, for example, that Jamie knows that Hayden is not competent at the time of the wedding but believes that the marriage will be ratified later. If the voidable marriage is later ratified, then it will be considered valid. *Cf. Hunt v. Hunt*, 412 S.W.2d 7, 17 (Tenn. App. 1965) ("If it be conceded that Mr. Hunt might have been mentally incompetent from use of drugs or overpersuasion at the time of the saying of the ceremony unquestionably he had many, many lucid moments between July 18, 1958, and August 10, 1962, in which he ratified and confirmed the marriage ceremony.").

Answer (C) is incorrect. Some states would permit such a challenge. *See In re Estate of Santolino*, 895 A.2d 506, 514 (N. J. Ch. Div. 2005).

Answer (D) is incorrect. Even had the parties been closer in age, the marriage might have been challenged if the marriage of an incompetent who never becomes competent is treated as void *ab initio*. *See In re Estate of Santolino*, 895 A.2d 506, 514 (N. J. Ch. Div. 2005).

22.   **Answer (D) is the best answer.** He was so drunk that he did not know what he was doing. *See Levine v. Dumbra*, 604 N.Y.S.2d 207, 208 (App. Div. 1993) ("In order to obtain an annulment on the ground of lack of understanding, it must be shown that the party was incapable of understanding the nature, effect, and consequences of the marriage."). Further, there was no time after the marriage that the marriage was ratified. Had he been incompetent during the marriage ceremony but ratified it afterward, the marriage would have been valid. *Cf. Hunt v. Hunt*, 412 S.W.2d 7, 17 (Tenn. App. 1965) (discussing ratification of marriage after the ceremony).

Answer (A) is not the best answer. The question is not whether he at one time had wanted to marry Drew but whether he in fact consented to the marriage or, instead, was at the time incompetent to consent because he was so drunk that the did not know what he was doing. *See Levine v. Dumbra*, 604 N.Y.S.2d 207, 208 (App. Div. 1993).

Answer (B) is incorrect. Regardless of whether their having had sexual relations prior to the marriage would prevent either from seeking an annulment based on lack of consortium after the marriage, *cf. Woronzoff-Daschkoff v. Woronzoff-Daschkoff*, 104 N.E.2d 877, 881 (N.Y. 1952) (when rejecting that an annulment should be granted, the court noted among other factors that although the couple had not consummated the marriage after the wedding, they had had premarital relations), the ground here involves Casey's incompetency at the time of the marriage. *See Levine v. Dumbra*, 604 N.Y.S.2d 207, 208 (App. Div. 1993) (discussing degree of inebriation necessary for annulment).

Answer (C) is not the best answer, because it misstates the reason that the annulment should be granted. If he cannot stand but nonetheless understands what he is doing when taking marriage vows, then the marriage will be valid. *See Anderson v. Anderson*, 219 N.E.2d 317, 318 (Ohio Com. Pl. 1966) ("The evidence is not clear and convincing in this case that the plaintiff was intoxicated at the time of the marriage to such an extent that he did not know what he was doing.").

23.   The attorney should suggest that an annulment is very unlikely to be granted. First, Lynn would have to show more than that they had had a great deal to drink. Either Lynn or Finley

would have had to have been so drunk that there was no understanding of the nature or effect of the ceremony. *See Levine v. Dumbra*, 604 N.Y.S.2d 207, 208 (App. Div. 1993). Even were it possible to establish the necessary lack of understanding, Lynn and Finley ratified the marriage by staying together the next six months to try to make the marriage successful. *See Hunt v. Hunt*, 412 S.W.2d 7, 17 (Tenn. App. 1965) (discussing ratification). While an annulment is unlikely, Lynn and Finley can presumably divorce on a no-fault ground, e.g., irreconcilable differences, *see* N.D. Cent. Code Ann. § 14-05-09.1 (West) ("Irreconcilable differences are those grounds which are determined by the court to be substantial reasons for not continuing the marriage and which make it appear that the marriage should be dissolved.") or an irretrievable breakdown of the marriage. *See* Mont. Code Ann. § 40-4-107 (1) (West) ("If both of the parties by petition or otherwise have stated under oath or affirmation that the marriage is irretrievably broken or one of the parties has so stated and the other has not denied it, the court, after hearing, shall make a finding whether the marriage is irretrievably broken."). If that is not an option, then they might live separate and apart for the requisite period. *See* N.C. Gen. Stat. Ann. § 50-6 ("Marriages may be dissolved and the parties thereto divorced from the bonds of matrimony on the application of either party, if and when the husband and wife have lived separate and apart for one year.").

Cohabitation and Prenuptial and Postnuptial Agreements

24. **Answer (D) is the best answer.** Even states willing to enforce cohabitation agreements might be unwilling to do so where one of the parties is married to someone else. *See Norton v. Hoyt*, 278 F. Supp. 2d 214, 227 (D. R. I. 2003) (refusing to enforce cohabitation agreement); *Thomas v. LaRosa*, 400 S.E.2d 809, 814 (W. Va. 1990) (refusing to enforce cohabitation agreement at least in part because doing so might adversely affect the interests of the spouse and progeny of one of the parties). Some states require such agreements to be in writing. Minn. Stat. Ann. § 513.075 (West); N.J. Stat. Ann. § 25:1-5 (h) (West); Tex. Bus. & Com. Code Ann. § 26.01 (a) (b) (West); and in some states such agreements are simply unenforceable. *See Hewitt v. Hewitt*, 394 N.E.2d 1204 (Ill. 1979).

    Answer (A) is not the best answer. First, Chris's threat would likely not be viewed as subjecting Bobby to duress. In a marital context, if one spouse threatens to end the relationship unless the other spouse does something, e.g., stops seeing a paramour, that is unlikely to be viewed as constituting duress. *See Garner v. Garner*, 848 N.Y.S.2d 741, 743 (App. Div. 2007) ("While defendant claims that he was under duress when he signed the agreement because he feared losing his marriage and children, we note that the threat of a divorce action by plaintiff, which was her lawful right to commence, does not constitute duress."). Further, many states will not enforce cohabitation agreements even absent a showing of duress. *See Hewitt v. Hewitt*, 394 N.E.2d 1204 (Ill. 1979) (holding cohabitation agreements unenforceable as against public policy).

    Answer (B) is not the best answer. While meretricious agreements are likely to be viewed as unenforceable, *see Jones v. Daly*, 122 Cal. App. 3d 500, 509 (Ct. App. 1981) (holding cohabitation agreement unenforceable because based on meretricious considerations), many states will not enforce cohabitation agreements even if they are not based on meretricious considerations. *See*, for example, *Lauper v. Harold*, 492 N.E.2d 472, 474 (Ohio App. 1985) (refusing to enforce cohabitation agreements as a general matter).

    Answer (C) is not correct. Many states do enforce cohabitation agreements. *See*, for example, *Marvin v. Marvin*, 557 P.2d 106 (Cal. 1976); *Posik v. Layton*, 695 So. 2d 759, 761 (Fla. App. 1997); *Boland v. Catalno*, 151 A.2d 142 (Conn. 1987).

25. **Answer (D) is the best answer,** because the provision regarding the frequency of sexual relations might make the whole agreement unenforceable. *See Jones v. Daly*, 122 Cal. App. 3d 500, 509 (Ct. App. 1981) (striking cohabitation agreement as unenforceable because based on the

provision of sexual services). *But see Whorton v. Dillingham*, 248 Cal. Rptr. 405, 408 (Ct. App. 1988) (suggesting that the meretricious aspect of the agreement might be severable, leaving the rest of the agreement enforceable).

Answer (A) is incorrect. Even if the parties are thought sophisticated, the state might nonetheless refuse to enforce such agreements as a matter of public policy. *See Hewitt v. Hewitt*, 394 N.E.2d 1204, 1208 (Ill. 1979).

Answer (B) is not the best answer. While certain provisions involving who takes out the trash during the relationship might be thought unenforceable because it would involve courts in the day-to-day operations of the relationship, a separate question would be whether such a provision was severable so that the rest of the contract could be enforced. *Cf. In re Marriage of Iqbal & Khan*, 11 N.E.3d 1, 13 (Ill. App. 2014) (holding that unenforceable provision regarding child custody was not severable so that the entire agreement was unenforceable).

Answer (C) is incorrect. Some states would enforce a cohabitation agreement specifying support. *See*, for example, *Posik v. Layton*, 695 So. 2d 759, 762 (Fla. App. 1997).

26.   **Answer (D) is the best answer.** A court might find that there was an implied agreement to distribute the property acquired during the relationship. *See Beal v. Beal*, 577 P.2d 507, 510 (Or. 1978) ("[A]bsent an express agreement, courts should closely examine the facts in evidence to determine what the parties implicitly agreed upon."). Or, property acquired during a "meretricious" relationship might be subject to distribution even absent an express or implied agreement to do so. *See Matter of Marriage of Lindsey*, 678 P.2d 328 (Wash. 1984).

Answer (A) is incorrect. In some states, property acquired during a meretricious relationship is subject to distribution when the relationship ends. *See Matter of Marriage of Lindsey*, 678 P.2d 328, 331 (Wash. 1984).

Answer (B) is incorrect. Some states might find an implied agreement to distribute the property. *See Beal v. Beal*, 577 P.2d 507, 510 (Or. 1978).

Answer (C) is incorrect. States may refuse to distribute property even when there is an express cohabitation agreement because the enforcement of such agreements is viewed as contrary to good public policy. *See*, for example, *Lauper v. Harold*, 492 N.E.2d 472, 474 (Ohio App. 1985) (refusing to enforce cohabitation agreements as a general matter).

27.   **Answer (C) is the best answer.** Certain provisions like those specifying the faith in which a child will be raised are unenforceable. *See In re Marriage of Bonds*, 5 P.3d 815, 830 (Cal. 2000) ("[A] premarital agreement to raise children in a particular religion is not enforceable."). However, provisions involving property may well be enforceable if not unconscionable. *Sanford v. Sanford*, 694 N.W.2d 283, 291 (S.D. 2005) ("[P]roperty rights are a proper subject matter for a prenuptial agreement."). *See also Colon v. Colon*, 2006 WL 2318250, at *9 (N.J. Super. App. Div. 2006) ("Prenuptial agreements are enforceable assuming full disclosure and absent unconscionability.").

Answer (A) is incorrect. As a general matter, prenuptial agreements are not viewed as contrary to public policy. *See Van Kipnis v. Van Kipnis*, 900 N.E.2d 977, 979 (N.Y. 2008) ("It is well settled that duly executed prenuptial agreements are generally valid and enforceable.").

Answer (B) is incorrect. The same reliance argument might be made about any provision, and a provision deemed contrary to public policy would be unenforceable even if one of the parties had relied on it. *See*, for example, *Sanford v. Sanford*, 694 N.W.2d 283, 293 (S.D. 2005) ("Provisions in a prenuptial agreement purporting to limit or waive spousal support are void and unenforceable as they are contrary to public policy.").

Answer (D) is incorrect. A prenuptial agreement specifying the religion in which a child will be raised is unenforceable regardless of whether one of the parents has undergone a religious awakening. *See In re Marriage of Bonds*, 5 P.3d 815, 830 (Cal. 2000) ("[A] premarital agreement to raise children in a particular religion is not enforceable.").

28.   **Answer (B) is the best answer.** The guiding consideration in custody decisions is the best interests of the children. *In re A.A.*, 2016 WL 4611248, at *3 (W. Va. 2016) ("[The guiding principle in all matters concerning child custody is the best interests of the child.").

Answer (A) is incorrect. Such a provision is unenforceable if not in the best interests of the children, even assuming that Parker is a fit parent. *See McKee v. Flynt*, 630 So. 2d 44, 51 (Miss. 1993) ("With regard to child custody, the paramount issue is that of the best interest and welfare of the child. In Mississippi, the chancery courts are charged with the duty and responsibility to make this determination. Parents of minor children cannot, by entering into private contracts, subordinate the authority of the chancery court.").

Answer (C) is not the best answer. The relevant question is not which parent envisioned having custody years before the children were born but, instead, which parent's having custody would promote the children's best interests (assuming that custody will not be shared). *See Moak v. Moak*, 631 So. 2d 196, 198 (Miss. 1994) ("The best interests of the children remain the polestar consideration of the courts.").

Answer (D) is incorrect. First, the marriage itself is viewed as consideration for the prenuptial agreement. *Dove v. Dove*, 680 S.E.2d 839, 841 (Ga. 2009) ("The agreement was upheld as valid on the grounds that it was an inducement to marriage and that marriage is a valuable consideration."). Notwithstanding the existence of consideration, the agreement is not enforceable because custody is to be determined in light of the children's best interests rather than in light of a private agreement made prior to the marriage. *See McKee v. Flynt*, 630 So. 2d 44, 51 (Miss. 1993).

29.   **Answer (A) is the best answer.** Here, there was no indication of fraud, unconscionability, or lack of disclosure. *See Scherer v. Scherer*, 292 S.E.2d 662, 666 (Ga. 1982) ("[T]he trial judge should employ basically three criteria in determining whether to enforce such an agreement in a particular case: (1) was the agreement obtained through fraud, duress, or mistake, or through misrepresentation or nondisclosure of material facts? (2) Is the agreement unconscionable? (3) Have the facts and circumstances changed since the agreement was executed, so as to

make its enforcement unfair and unreasonable?"). Two weeks would likely be viewed as sufficient. *See Sanderson v. Sanderson*, 170 So. 3d 430, 432 (Miss. 2014) (suggesting that presentation of prenuptial agreement two weeks prior to the wedding did not constitute duress).

Answer (B) is incorrect. The presentation of such an agreement a very short time before the wedding without any prior notice that such an agreement would have to be signed might provide the basis for non-enforcement later. *See Fletcher v. Fletcher*, 628 N.E.2d 1343, 1348 (Ohio 1994) ("The presentation of an agreement a very short time before the wedding ceremony will create a presumption of overreaching or coercion if, in contrast to this case, the postponement of the wedding would cause significant hardship, embarrassment or emotional stress."). But the agreement was presented two weeks before the wedding, and there was prior notice that a prenuptial agreement would be presented.

Answer (C) is not the best answer. While the prior notice militates in favor of enforcement, *see Simeone v. Simeone*, 581 A.2d 162, 167 (Pa. 1990) (upholding the validity of a prenuptial agreement presented the evening before the wedding when it had been discussed several times prior to the wedding), two weeks is probably enough time to consult an attorney and decide what to do. *Cf. Sanford v. Sanford*, 694 N.W.2d 283, 295 (S.D. 2005) (refusing to invalidate most of a prenuptial agreement because among other reasons there was sufficient time to consult an attorney).

Answer (D) is incorrect. Prenuptial agreements will be held unenforceable if they are procured fraudulently, are unconscionable, or if there is a lack of full disclosure. *See Scherer v. Scherer*, 292 S.E.2d 662, 666 (Ga. 1982).

30.   **Answer (D) is the best answer.** Some jurisdictions do not permit support to be waived. *See Sanford v. Sanford*, 694 N.W.2d 283, 293 (S.D. 2005) ("Provisions in a prenuptial agreement purporting to limit or waive spousal support are void and unenforceable as they are contrary to public policy."). While many jurisdictions do permit such waivers, those waivers may well not be enforced if their enforcement would be unconscionable, e.g., if their enforcement would leave the challenging spouse without any means of support. *See O'Daniel v. O'Daniel*, 419 S.W.3d 280, 286 (Tenn. App. 2013) ("[W]here circumstances have changed over the course of the marriage such that enforcement of the agreement would be unconscionable or unfair because enforcement would likely result in a disadvantaged spouse being unable to provide for his or her reasonable needs, the courts will set aside the relevant portions of the agreement and award alimony.").

Answer (A) is not the best answer. While the agreement might have been reasonable when it was made, many states require that enforcement at the time of divorce not be unconscionable. *See Kelcourse v. Kelcourse*, 23 N.E.3d 124, 126 (Mass. App. 2015) ("An antenuptial agreement is enforceable if it was valid when executed, and is conscionable at the time of divorce.").

Answer (B) is incorrect. While there had been no diagnosis at that time, the knowledge required to make the agreement enforceable only speaks to knowledge of the other party's finances, not to what the future may bring. *See Randolph v. Randolph*, 937 S.W.2d 815, 817 (Tenn. 1996) (discussing the knowledge requirement as requiring that the challenging spouse have been offered "a full and fair disclosure of the nature, extent and value of his or her holdings" or that the challenging spouse had come to have the requisite knowledge in another way).

Answer (C) is incorrect. Some provisions of a prenuptial agreement might be found unenforceable while other provisions might still be enforced. *See Rogers v. Yourshaw*, 448 S.E.2d 884, 887 (Va. App. 1994) (enforcing some provisions of a prenuptial agreement but not others).

31.   **Answer (D) is the best answer.** Provisions in prenuptial agreements eliminating child support are unenforceable. *See Huck v. Huck*, 734 P.2d 417, 419 (Utah 1986) ("[P]rovisions eliminating the payment of child support or alimony in prenuptial agreements are not binding on the court."). *See also* Iowa Code Ann. § 596.5 (2) (West) ("The right of a . . . child to support shall not be adversely affected by a premarital agreement.").

Answer (A) is incorrect. Even if the agreement was enforceable as a general matter, it would not be enforceable insofar as it precluded child support. *See*, for example, N.H. Rev. Stat. Ann. § 460:2-a ("A man and woman in contemplation of marriage may enter into a written interspousal contract and the courts of this state shall give the same effect to such contracts entered in other jurisdictions as would the courts of that other jurisdiction. However, no contract otherwise enforceable under this section may contain any term which attempts to abrogate the statutory or common law rights of minor children of the contemplated marriage.").

Answer (B) is not the best answer. The reason that such agreements are not enforceable is not due to the lack of knowledge about whether they would have a child together. Even if they knew that they would have a child together because they had already had a child or because they were already expecting a child, child support still could not be precluded in the prenuptial agreement. *See* Utah Code Ann. § 30-8-4 (2) (West) ("The right of a child to support, health and medical provider expenses, medical insurance, and child care coverage may not be affected by a premarital agreement.").

Answer (C) is incorrect because such agreements are not enforceable. *See* N.C. Gen. Stat. Ann. § 52B-4 (b) ("The right of a child to support may not be adversely affected by a premarital agreement."). It may be that some will be less willing to agree to a custody arrangement if they are not assured that they can avoid child support. However, it is also true that were such agreements enforceable, many children might thereby be denied the support that they need.

32.   **Answer (C) is the best answer.** The validity of the marriage will likely be upheld, private writing suggesting that it is a sham notwithstanding. *See Lester v. Lester*, 87 N.Y.S.2d 517, 520 (Dom. Rel. Ct. 1949). Lottery winnings are marital property if won during the marriage and marital funds were used to purchase the ticket. *See In re Marriage of Mahaffey*, 564 N.E.2d 1300, 1306 (Ill. App. 1990) ("[T]he lottery winnings, the irrevocable right to which was acquired during the marriage, are fruit of the shared enterprise of marriage and should be divided as marital property."); *Smith v. Smith*, 557 N.Y.S.2d 22, 23 (App. Div. 1990) ("The lottery winnings are marital property even though they were acquired by the efforts of defendant.").

Answer (A) is incorrect. Private writing notwithstanding, they married in accord with local law and their marriage will likely be treated as valid, especially because they lived together. *See Lester v. Lester*, 87 N.Y.S.2d 517, 520 (Dom. Rel. Ct. 1949). *See also Steines v. Steines*, 89 S.W.2d 520, 522 (Mo. 1936) (discussing sham marriage where parties had no intention to live together).

Answer (B) is incorrect. The validity of the marriage is likely to be upheld. Contracts that undermine marriage are likely to be held unenforceable because against public policy. *See Grant v. Butt*, 17 S.E.2d 689, 694 (S.C. 1941) ("[C]ontracts in restraint of marriage are nonenforceable.").

Answer (D) is incorrect. The reason that he will likely be unable to have the marriage annulled is not because of when he sought to annul it but because they formally wed and continued living together after the marriage. *See Lester v. Lester*, 87 N.Y.S.2d 517, 520 (Dom. Rel. Ct. 1949). *See also Steines v. Steines*, 89 S.W.2d 520, 522 (Mo. 1936). It might be thought that Jordan and Kelly would grow to love each other even if love did not exist at the time of the marriage. *Cf. Anonymous v. Anonymous*, 85 A.2d 706, 718 (Del. Super. Ct. 1951) ("[F]alse vows of love and affection, in and of themselves, do not amount to fraud under our annulment law where the marriage has been consummated and marital duties and obligations have been performed."); *Feynman v. Feynman*, 4 N.Y.S.2d 787, 788 (Sup. Ct. 1938) ("The fact that the defendant never loved the plaintiff would not entitle her to an annulment. Law does not recognize the necessity of love in the marriage relationship.").

33.   **Answer (D) is the best answer.** *Bratton v. Bratton*, 136 S.W.3d 595, 597 (Tenn. 2004) ("Postnuptial agreements will be enforceable if knowing and voluntary, where there has been no duress or coercion and there is consideration. Postnuptial agreements are not contrary to public policy so long as there is consideration for the agreement, it is knowledgeably entered into, and there is no evidence of fraud, coercion or duress."); *see also Petracca v. Petracca*, 956 N.Y.S.2d 77, 79 (App. Div. 2012) (such agreements also require good faith).

Answer (A) is incorrect. Alex's refraining from filing for divorce is consideration. *See In re Marriage of Tabassum & Younis*, 881 N.E.2d 396, 407 (Ill. App. 2007) ("Forbearance of bringing or prosecuting a divorce action has been directly recognized as consideration in other states, and we find no compelling reason to deviate from these authorities.").

Answer (B) is incorrect. The postnuptial agreement is unlikely to be treated as having been made under duress merely because Cassidy feared that otherwise Alex would file for divorce. *See In re Marriage of Labuz*, 54 N.E.3d 886, 898 (Ill. App. 2016) (rejecting that the postnuptial agreement was signed under duress because the spouse had threatened to leave otherwise).

Answer (C) is not the best answer. While a necessary condition of enforcement is that the parties understand the agreement, the agreement in addition must not be unconscionable at the time of enforcement. *Cf. Bedrick v. Bedrick*, 17 A.3d 17, 29 (Conn. 2011) (upholding unenforceability of prenuptial agreement because "as a matter of law, enforcement of the agreement would be unconscionable").

34.   **Answer (B) is the best answer.** Even if the agreement is valid because knowing and voluntary and even if its enforcement would not be unconscionable, its not having been made in good faith might make it fraudulent and therefore unenforceable. *See Fogg v. Fogg*, 567 N.E.2d 921, 924 (Mass. 1991) ("The husband signed the agreement as a result of the wife's fraudulent and deceptive promise to attempt to maintain the marriage. Therefore, the agreement is unenforceable.").

Answer (A) is incorrect. The postnuptial agreement might well be unenforceable even if made knowingly and voluntarily if enforcing the agreement at the time of divorce would be unconscionable. *See Bedrick v. Bedrick*, 17 A.3d 17, 29 (Conn. 2011) (refusing to enforce postnuptial agreement because "enforcement of the agreement would be unconscionable").

Answer (C) is not the best answer. Even if enforcement would not be unconscionable, Mickey's having made the agreement when he had no intention of trying to save the marriage might itself suffice to make the agreement unenforceable. *See Fogg v. Fogg*, 567 N.E.2d 921, 924 (Mass. 1991).

Answer (D) is incorrect. Montana's gifting separate property to Mickey in a postnuptial agreement would be enforceable assuming that the agreement was knowing, voluntary, not a product of fraud or duress, and not unconscionable at the time of enforcement. *Bratton v. Bratton*, 136 S.W.3d 595, 597 (Tenn. 2004) ("Postnuptial agreements will be enforceable if knowing and voluntary, where there has been no duress or coercion and there is consideration. Postnuptial agreements are not contrary to public policy so long as there is consideration for the agreement, it is knowledgeably entered into, and there is no evidence of fraud, coercion or duress."). *See also Rice v. Rice*, 2004 WL 362289, at *2 (Ky. App. 2004) (discussing "whether changed circumstances at the time when enforcement is sought render the enforcement of the agreement unfair").

35.   **Answer (D) is the best answer.** The agreement will be enforceable, assuming that there are no independent reasons that its enforcement would be contrary to public policy. *See D'Aston v. D'Aston*, 808 P.2d 111, 113 (Utah App. 1990) ("[A] postnuptial agreement is enforceable . . . absent fraud, coercion, or material nondisclosure.").

Answer (A) is incorrect. This agreement treats different parties differently in light of their past actions. *See*, for example, *Gilley v. Gilley*, 778 S.W.2d 862, 864 (Tenn. App. 1989) ("As we see the agreement, its purpose was to encourage marital fidelity on the part of the husband by setting forth, prior to reconciliation, the outcome of a divorce should one occur after the reconciliation.").

Answer (B) is incorrect. The consideration was Luella's not seeking a divorce when Phil had strayed before the postnuptial agreement had been signed. *See Gilley v. Gilley*, 778 S.W.2d 862, 864 (Tenn. App. 1989) ("Wife had several grounds upon which to prosecute a divorce, which she did not do at the husband's request, receiving promises of faithfulness secured by a property distribution, in the event of divorce, satisfactory to wife.").

Answer (C) is incorrect. The issue here is not whether Phil was making the agreement in good faith, *cf. Fogg v. Fogg*, 567 N.E.2d 921, 924 (Mass. 1991) (discussing "the wife's fraudulent and deceptive promise to attempt to maintain the marriage"), but instead whether he would in future be faithful to his spouse. *See Gilley v. Gilley*, 778 S.W.2d 862, 864 (Tenn. App. 1989) (the agreement's "purpose was to encourage marital fidelity on the part of the husband").

36.   **Answer (D) is the best answer.** Some jurisdictions do not permit support to be waived. *See Sanford v. Sanford*, 694 N.W.2d 283, 293 (S.D. 2005) ("Provisions in a prenuptial agreement purporting to limit or waive spousal support are void and unenforceable as they are contrary to public policy."). While many jurisdictions do permit such waivers, those waivers will not be enforced if their enforcement would be unconscionable, e.g., if their enforcement would leave the challenging spouse without any means of support. *See O'Daniel v. O'Daniel*, 419 S.W.3d 280, 286 (Tenn. App. 2013) ("[W]here circumstances have changed over the course of the marriage such that enforcement of the agreement would be unconscionable or unfair because enforcement would likely result in a disadvantaged spouse being unable to provide for his or her reasonable needs, the courts will set aside the relevant portions of the agreement and award alimony."). Here, enforcement of that provision would likely not be held unconscionable. The provisions regarding custody and religious training are unenforceable. *See McKee v. Flynt*, 630 So. 2d 44, 51 (Miss. 1993) ("With regard to child custody, the paramount issue is that of the best interest and welfare of the child. In Mississippi, the chancery courts are charged with the duty and responsibility to make this determination. Parents of minor children cannot, by entering into private contracts, subordinate the authority of the chancery court."); *In re Marriage of Bonds*, 5 P.3d 815, 830 (Cal. 2000) ("[A] premarital agreement to raise children in a particular religion is not enforceable.").

Answer (A) is incorrect. The provisions regarding custody and religious training are unenforceable. *See McKee v. Flynt*, 630 So. 2d 44, 51 (Miss. 1993); *In re Marriage of Bonds*, 5 P.3d 815, 830 (Cal. 2000).

Answer (B) is not the best answer. While the prenuptial specification of custody with respect to not-yet-born children is unenforceable, *see McKee v. Flynt*, 630 So. 2d 44, 51 (Miss. 1993), the specification regarding religious upbringing is also unenforceable. *See In re Marriage of Bonds*, 5 P.3d 815, 830 (Cal. 2000).

Answer (C) is not the best answer. While the provision regarding religious training is unenforceable, *see In re Marriage of Bonds*, 5 P.3d 815, 830 (Cal. 2000), the provision regarding custody is also unenforceable. *See McKee v. Flynt*, 630 So. 2d 44, 51 (Miss. 1993).

37.   The provision most likely to be enforced is the one about which there does not seem to be a conflict. Many, but not all, states permit spousal support to be waived as long as enforcement of that provision would not be unconscionable. *See Hardee v. Hardee*, 558 S.E.2d 264, 269 (S.C. App. 2001) ("Generally, a waiver of spousal support in a premarital agreement will

be enforced unless the court finds the waiver unconscionable."). Alice will receive custody if her having custody would promote the best interests of the children, but the provision specifying that she will have custody is not enforceable. *See* N.M. Stat. Ann. § 40-3A-4 (B) (West) ("A premarital agreement may not adversely affect . . . a party's right to child custody or visitation."). So, too, the provision regarding religious training of the children is unenforceable. *See In re Marriage of Wolfert*, 598 P.2d 524, 526 (Colo. App. 1979) ("[P]remarital agreements concerning the religious training of unborn children are unenforceable in the courts.").

Marriage and Fraud

38.   **Answer (C) is the best answer.** An annulment will likely not be granted merely because one party was misled into believing that the other party was wealthier. *See Cervone v. Cervone*, 280 N.Y.S. 159, 165 (Sup. Ct. 1935) ("[T]he courts have not yet gone so far as to recognize marriage as a mere matter of bargain and sale or to annul it because one of the parties is disappointed in the material wealth of the other.").

   Answer (A) is not the best answer. It is not necessary to state a falsehood to provide the basis for an annulment. *See Douglass v. Douglass*, 307 P.2d 674, 675 (Cal. App. 1957) (concealment of criminal record sufficed for annulment).

   Answer (B) is not the best answer. That something is subjectively important to one of the parties will not alone suffice to make a misrepresentation about that issue a basis for annulment. *See Cervone v. Cervone*, 280 N.Y.S. 159, 165 (Sup. Ct. 1935).

   Answer (D) is not the best answer. While misrepresentations can lead to a loss of trust and trust is an important element of marriage, most jurisdictions require that the fraud reach the essentials of marriage. *See Ur-Rehman v. Qamar*, 2012 WL 3889129, at *5 (N.J. Super. App. Div. 2012) ("In order to nullify a marriage on this ground, a court must determine that the party seeking the annulment showed fraud as to one of the essentials of marriage by clear and convincing evidence.").

39.   **Answer (A) is the best answer.** Attitudes about having children go to the essentials of marriage and the misrepresentation of these attitudes can be the basis of an annulment. *See Tobon v. Sanchez*, 517 A.2d 885, 886 (N.J. Super. Ch. Div. 1986) ("[P]remarital, fraudulent intent not to have a child is grounds for annulment of a marriage.").

   Answer (B) is not the best answer. While opening the floodgates would be a concern, that concern does not seem implicated because many jurisdictions limit annulments on the basis of fraud to matters involving the essentials of marriage. *See Ur-Rehman v. Qamar*, 2012 WL 3889129, at *5 (N.J. Super. App. Div. 2012) ("In order to nullify a marriage on this ground, a court must determine that the party seeking the annulment showed fraud as to one of the essentials of marriage by clear and convincing evidence.").

   Answer (C) is not the best answer. One party's making clear that a particular issue is important will not suffice to make the other party's knowing misrepresentation about that issue the basis for an annulment. In addition, the matter at issue must be viewed as involving one of the essentials of marriage. *See Ur-Rehman v. Qamar*, 2012 WL 3889129, at *5 (N.J. Super. App. Div. 2012).

Answer (D) is not the best answer. While Adriana and Bevan might not have been able to have children even if they had tried, the basis for an annulment is that Adrian knowingly misrepresented his position on something viewed as very important to the marriage. *See Ur-Rehman v. Qamar*, 2012 WL 3889129, at *5 (N.J. Super. App. Div. 2012).

40.   **Answer (D) is the best answer.** In most states, the basis of the fraud must involve the essentials of marriage. While that test is met here because marital relations are viewed as an essential of marriage, an additional element that must be shown is that there was a misrepresentation prior to the marriage. Here, Dana allegedly changed his mind after the marriage about his interest in having sexual relations. *Cf. Tobon v. Sanchez*, 517 A.2d 885, 886 (N.J. Super. Ch. Div. 1986) ("[T]he evidence here does not establish clearly and convincingly that the defendant's intention not to father children with plaintiff was fixed prior to the marriage.").

Answer (A) is not the best answer. While Dana knew beforehand that Cassidy wished to have a healthy sexual relationship, Dana allegedly did not know beforehand that he was uninterested in having sexual relations. *Cf. Tobon v. Sanchez*, 517 A.2d 885, 886 (N.J. Super. Ch. Div. 1986).

Answer (B) is incorrect. Consummation occurs once the parties have sexual relations. *See Sharon v. Sharon*, 16 P. 345, 351 (Cal. 1888) ("The word 'consummation,' whenever used as something different from the mere consent or formal solemnization of marriage, had always been held to mean 'simply sexual intercourse, copulation, nothing more nor less.'"). But at issue here is an alleged misrepresentation about having a healthy sexual relationship within the marriage, and one act of coitus will not satisfy that condition.

Answer (C) is not the answer. While the willingness to have sexual relations does involve one of the essentials of marriage, *see Ngo v. Lee*, 2016 WL 7444006, at *2 (Conn. Super. 2016) (explaining that the "doctrine of essentials . . . requires the misrepresentations claimed by the party seeking an annulment to be related to the sexual obligations of the marriage, that is, the ability or willingness to have sexual relations"), more must be shown. Here, it was not clear that Dana was misrepresenting his own views about sexual relations before the marriage. *Cf. Tobon v. Sanchez*, 517 A.2d 885, 886 (N.J. Super. Ch. Div. 1986).

41.   Quinn is not likely to be successful unless there is an existing statute that would permit an annulment on these grounds. *See Shaffer v. Shaffer*, 185 N.Y.S.2d 67, 68 (Sup. Ct. 1959) (granting annulment of a marriage where husband had falsely claimed that he had never before married, although this annulment was based on a statute). Absent such a statute, it would be unlikely that the existence of a prior marriage would be held to go to the essentials of marriage. *See Saunders v. Saunders*, 120 A.2d 160, 163 (Del. Super. 1956) ("Fraud as to a prior marriage and divorce does not go to the essentials of the marriage relationship."); *Charley v. Fant*, 892 S.W.2d 811, 813 (Mo. App. 1995) ("The general rule in American jurisdictions is that misrepresentation or concealment of prior marital status is not ground for annulment of marriage.").

Common Law Marriage

42.   **Answer (C) is the best answer.** Once a common law marriage is established, it must be ended formally or through the death of one of the parties. *See Dibble v. Dibble*, 100 N.E.2d 451, 461 (Ohio App. 1950) ("[W]hen a valid marriage is proven it continues until legally dissolved by death or divorce and this is so whether it be a ceremonial or a common-law marriage."). The record search is necessary to show that Addison never divorced Bobby. *See Powell v. Estate of Fletcher*, 128 P.3d 670, 673 (Wyo. 2006) ("Evidence that the spouse asserting the validity of the prior marriage thoroughly searched records in any jurisdiction where the unavailable spouse lived and may have legally sought a divorce will normally be sufficient.").

       Answer (A) is incorrect. While Bobby's abandonment may constitute a ground for ending the marriage, *see* Tex. Fam. Code Ann. §6.005 (West) ("The court may grant a divorce in favor of one spouse if the other spouse: (1) left the complaining spouse with the intention of abandonment; and (2) remained away for at least one year."), the existence of a ground will not suffice to end the marriage. In addition, the aggrieved party must seek the divorce.

       Answer (B) is incorrect. While a common law marriage is informal, *see Small v. McMaster*, 352 S.W.3d 280, 282 (Tex. App. 2011) ("An informal or common-law marriage exists in Texas if the parties (1) agreed to be married, (2) lived together in Texas as husband and wife after the agreement, and (3) there presented to others that they were married."), such a marriage, once established, will continue to exist until its dissolution or the death of one of the parties. *See Dibble v. Dibble*, 100 N.E.2d 451, 461 (Ohio App. 1950).

       Answer (D) is incorrect. While a settled and firm intention not to return to the marriage might establish the ground of abandonment, *see Sheehan v. Sheehan*, 145 A. 180, 181 (Md. 1929) ("Abandonment or desertion, as a marital offense . . . must be the deliberate act of the party complained of, with the intent that the marriage relation no longer exist."), the existence of a ground does not end the marriage. Further, even if there had been no settled and firm intention to end the marriage, it nonetheless would have ended if, for example, Addison had secured a divorce on a different basis. *See*, for example, N.C. Gen. Stat. Ann. §50-6 ("Marriages may be dissolved and the parties thereto divorced from the bonds of matrimony on the application of either party, if and when the husband and wife have lived separate and apart for one year, and the plaintiff or defendant in the suit for divorce has resided in the State for a period of six months.").

43.   **Answer (B) is the best answer.** Because they met the conditions for a common law marriage and they were free to marry once Reese died, the state might well recognize their marriage as valid. *See Jennings v. Jennings*, 315 A.2d 816, 824 (Md. App. 1974) ("If, therefore, they

cohabitated as husband and wife in the District of Columbia after the impediment to the marriage was removed, their relationship would ripen into a valid common-law marriage.").

Answer (A) is not the best answer because it does not address whether Sloan and Tate have contracted a common law marriage. While Sloan and Tate do not have a valid marriage by virtue of the ceremony, *see Hill v. Bert Bell/Pete Rozelle NFL Player Ret. Plan*, 747 S.E.2d 791 (S.C. 2013) (second marriage void because man still had spouse living from whom he had not been divorced), they might still have a valid common law marriage. *See Jennings v. Jennings*, 315 A.2d 816, 824 (Md. App. 1974) ("If, therefore, they cohabitated as husband and wife in the District of Columbia after the impediment to the marriage was removed, their relationship would ripen into a valid common-law marriage.").

Answer (C) is incorrect. Even if Tate did not know of Sloan's first marriage, that would not make Tate and Sloan's marriage valid. *See Hill v. Bert Bell/Pete Rozelle NFL Player Ret. Plan*, 747 S.E.2d 791 (S.C. 2013) (second marriage void even though purported wife did not know that purported husband had never divorced his first wife). A separate question would be whether the jurisdiction recognized putative spouses so that Tate would be entitled to some benefits. *Compare Hill v. Bert Bell/Pete Rozelle NFL Player Ret. Plan*, 747 S.E.2d 791, 792 (S.C. 2013) ("We decline to adopt the putative spouse doctrine.") *with Ceja v. Rudolph & Sletten, Inc.*, 302 P.3d 211, 221 (Cal. 2013) ("[S]ection 377.60(b) defines a putative spouse as 'the surviving spouse of a void or voidable marriage who is found by the court to have believed in good faith that the marriage to the decedent was valid.' The good faith inquiry is a subjective one that focuses on the actual state of mind of the alleged putative spouse.").

Answer (D) is incorrect. A void marriage can be challenged after the death of one of the parties to it. *See In re Estate of Everhart*, 783 N.W.2d 1, 7 (Neb. App. 2010) ("Because the marriage was void, it was proper to challenge the validity of the marriage after Paul's death and during the probate proceedings.").

44.   **Answer (D) is the best answer.** Piper and Quinn treated each other as spouses, held themselves out to the community as spouses and, further, recognized that their relationship was different once the impediment to the marriage no longer existed. *See Callen v. Callen*, 620 S.E.2d 59, 62 (S.C. 2005) ("For the relationship to become marital, ... there must be a new mutual agreement either by way of civil ceremony or by way of recognition of the illicit relation and a new agreement to enter into a common law marriage.").

Answer (A) is incorrect. While Piper and Quinn could not have contracted a common law marriage while Piper had a spouse living, *see Blackwood v. Kilpatrick*, 294 So. 2d 753, 755 (Ala. Civ. App. 1974) ("This file clearly reveals that Les Davis had a living spouse in the fall of 1967 and was not divorced from this spouse until the 23rd day of July, 1969. In view of the above, this court is clear to the conclusion that there could not have been a common law marriage between appellant's ward and Les Davis in the fall of 1967."), they could contract one once the impediment had been removed. *See Jennings v. Jennings*, 315 A.2d 816, 824 (Md. App. 1974).

Answer (B) is incorrect in that it misstates the test. In some states recognizing common law marriage, such a marriage will not be established merely because an impediment to the marriage has been removed. *Callen v. Callen*, 620 S.E.2d 59, 62 (S.C. 2005) ("[A]fter the impediment is removed, the relationship is not automatically transformed into a common-law marriage. Instead, it is presumed that relationship remains non-marital.").

Answer (C) is not the best answer. States recognizing common law marriage may recognize the illicit nature of the former relationship by requiring that the couple do something different once an impediment has been removed to indicate their understanding that the formerly illicit relationship has now changed. That way, the rebuttable presumption that the illicit relationship continued would be rebutted. *See Kirby v. Kirby*, 241 S.E.2d 415, 416 (S.C. 1978) ("[T]he presumption . . . is that the illicit relationship continued after the impediment to marriage was removed."). *See also id.* at 417 ("After appellant's divorce the parties agreed to marry and then lived together without separation for sixteen years, all the while treating each other in every respect as husband and wife. In our view the preponderance of the evidence demonstrates the parties' new mutual agreement to enter into a common law marriage.").

45.   State law determines whether a marriage celebrated by someone not authorized to officiate will be void, voidable, or merely prohibited. Some states will recognize such a marriage as long as at least one of the parties believed that the officiant was official. *See Donlann v. Macgurn*, 55 P.3d 74, 76 (Ariz. App. 2002) ("Judge Araneta . . . decided that 'Arizona also recognizes the solemnization and validity of a marriage as long as the only defect is in the person performing the ceremony and as long as one spouse believes in good faith that the person is authorized to perform the ceremony.'"). *See also* Va. Code Ann. § 20-31 (West) ("No marriage solemnized under a license issued in this Commonwealth by any person professing to be authorized to solemnize the same shall be deemed or adjudged to be void, nor shall the validity thereof be in any way affected on account of any want of authority in such person, or any defect, omission or imperfection in such license, if the marriage be in all other respects lawful, and be consummated with a full belief on the part of the persons so married, or either of them, that they have been lawfully joined in marriage."). *But see Mussa v. Palmer-Mussa*, 731 S.E.2d 404, 411 (N.C. 2012) (suggesting that marriage performed by individual not authorized to officiate was not valid).

Even were the marriage not recognized as valid, a separate question would involve whether the state recognized common law marriages. Here, the difficulty was not that there was an impediment to the marriage but that it had not been celebrated in accord with local law. If the state recognized common law marriages, then Aubrey and Bailey would likely be recognized as having contracted a common law marriage, even if their ceremonial marriage was not recognized by the state.

46.   **Answer (D) is the best answer.** One of the important issues is whether Taylor and Scout met the conditions under Texarkana law to establish a common law marriage. If Texarkana will recognize a common law marriage between individuals who spend several weeks in the state even if they are not domiciled in the state, then Taylor and Scout might have established a common law marriage in Texarkana. *See*, for example, *Oklahoma Dep't of Mental Health & Substance Abuse v. Pierce*, 283 P.3d 894, 898–99 (Okla. Civ. App. 2012) ("Some evidence of consent to enter into a common law marriage are cohabitation, actions consistent with the

relationship of spouses, recognition by the community of the marital relationship, and declarations by the parties."). Even if they have met the requirements of Texarkana law, a separate issue is whether Marryvania will recognize common law marriages when the parties were not domiciled in the state recognizing such marriages. *Compare In re Singer's Estate*, 138 N.Y.S.2d 740, 742–43 (Sur. Ct. 1955) ("The evidence clearly supports a finding that the requirements of a common-law marriage in New Jersey were satisfied; namely, that there was cohabitation accompanied by matrimonial intent and repute. . . . [D]ecedent and respondent honeymooned in New Jersey. On many subsequent occasions they stayed in New Jersey resort hotels, at all times registering and referring to themselves as husband and wife.") *with Standridge v. Standridge*, 769 S.W.2d 12, 15 (Ark. 1989) ("[M]ere visits or sojourns of parties to a common law marriage state are insufficient to create a common law marriage recognized in Arkansas."). Otherwise, Taylor will be successful only if Marryvania relaxes the conditions under which individuals can successfully sue for loss of consortium. *See Lozoya v. Sanchez*, 66 P.3d 948, 957 (N.M. 2003) ("Claimants must prove an 'intimate familial relationship' with the victim in order to recover for loss of consortium."). *But see Laws v. Griep*, 332 N.W.2d 339, 340 (Iowa 1983) ("This right has not been recognized in Iowa for unmarried cohabiting persons who live together as if they were married.").

Answer (A) is not the best answer. Because Marryvania will recognize a common law marriage validly contracted elsewhere, the question at hand will be whether Taylor and Scout contracted such a marriage elsewhere. *Cf. Delaney v. Delaney*, 405 A.2d 91, 92 (Conn. Super. 1979) (recognizing common law marriage contracted in Rhode Island even though such marriages cannot be contracted in Connecticut).

Answer (B) is not the best answer. Marryvania law only recognizes common law marriages that have been validly contracted in other states. If Taylor and Scout have not in fact contracted a common law marriage in another state, then they will not be recognized as married in Marryvania. *See Abramson v. Abramson*, 74 N.W.2d 919, 926 (Neb. 1956) (refusing to recognize a common law marriage because the couple had not met the conditions for contracting such a marriage in Iowa while the couple was there).

Answer (C) is not the best answer. The question at hand will be whether Scout and Taylor met the conditions for contracting a common law marriage while they were in Texarkana for several weeks each year. If so and if Marryvania will recognize a common law marriage contracted elsewhere in accord with local law even when the parties were not domiciled in the state recognizing common law marriage, then Marryvania might recognize that Taylor and Scout are married. *See In re Singer's Estate*, 138 N.Y.S.2d 740, 742–43 (Sur. Ct. 1955). It is of course true that if the conditions for bringing a loss of consortium claim are relaxed, then Taylor might be successful in his suit. *See Lozoya v. Sanchez*, 66 P.3d 948, 957 (N.M. 2003) ("Claimants must prove an 'intimate familial relationship' with the victim in order to recover for loss of consortium."). *But see Laws v. Griep*, 332 N.W.2d 339, 340 (Iowa 1983) ("This right has not been recognized in Iowa for unmarried cohabiting persons who live together as if they were married.").

47.   **Answer (D) is the best answer.** In some states recognizing common law marriage, the removal of an impediment validates a formally invalid marriage. The claim was not that the ceremonial

marriage became valid by virtue of the impediment's removal, but that the couple established a common law marriage once they were able to marry. *See Dacunzo v. Edgye*, 111 A.2d 88, 94 (N.J. Super. App. Div. 1955) ("The doctrine that cohabitation continued after the removal of the impediment to an invalid marriage validates the marriage is not based on a theory of ratification of the earlier marriage, but on the theory that a new common-law marriage is contracted after the removal of the impediment to the marriage of the parties."). Or, the state may have a statute that validates a marriage once the impediment has been removed. *See* Mass. Gen. Laws Ann. ch. 207, §6 (West) ("If a person, during the lifetime of a husband or wife with whom the marriage is in force, enters into a subsequent marriage contract with due legal ceremony and the parties thereto live together thereafter as husband and wife, and such subsequent marriage contract was entered into by one of the parties in good faith, in the full belief that the former husband or wife was dead, that the former marriage had been annulled by a divorce, or without knowledge of such former marriage, they shall, after the impediment to their marriage has been removed by the death or divorce of the other party to the former marriage, if they continue to live together as husband and wife in good faith on the part of one of them, be held to have been legally married from and after the removal of such impediment, and the issue of such subsequent marriage shall be considered as the legitimate issue of both parents.").

Answer (A) is incorrect. In a state permitting common law marriages to be contracted, three conditions must be met. The individuals must treat each other as spouses, they must be viewed by the community as spouses, and there must be no bar to their marrying. *See*, for example, *Stringer v. Stringer*, 689 So. 2d 194, 195 (Ala. Civ. App. 1997) ("A valid common-law marriage exists in Alabama when the following elements are present: 1) capacity; 2) present, mutual agreement to permanently enter the marriage relationship to the exclusion of all other relationships; and 3) public recognition of the relationship as a marriage and public assumption of marital duties and cohabitation."). There of course is no requirement for a wedding.

Answer (B) is not the best answer. While Jean and Harlow could not have had a valid common law marriage while Greer was alive, a separate issue is whether they contracted one after Greer's death when there was no longer a bar to their marrying. *See*, for example, *Dowd v. Dowd*, 418 A.2d 1387, 1389 (Pa. Super. 1980) ("[W]henever one or both parties enter a matrimonial relationship in good faith, ignorant of an impediment to a valid marriage, continued cohabitation after the impediment has been removed results in a valid marriage.").

Answer (C) is not the best answer. While there is a presumption that the last-in-time marriage is valid, *see Matter of Estate of Warner*, 687 S.W.2d 686, 688 (Mo. App. 1985) ("The presumption of the validity of the last marriage may be repelled only by the most cogent and satisfactory evidence."), that presumption can be overcome if there was no filing for divorce in any of the relevant counties while the first spouse was alive. *See Roberts v. Roberts*, 167 So. 808, 810 (Fla. 1936) ("[B]ut if she shows the counties that William Roberts lived in during the thirty years that elapsed from his desertion of Laura Cheval Roberts to his marriage to Lucille Roberts and that no divorce was issued in any of these counties and that he had no ground on which to seek a divorce, the presumption in favor of the validity of the second marriage will be overcome.").

Civil Unions

48. **Answer (B) is the best answer.** Because Ryan would have been able to elect against the will had they entered into a marriage that had never formally been dissolved, *see* Vt. Stat. Ann. tit. 14, § 319 (a) (West) ("A surviving spouse may waive the provisions of the decedent's will and in lieu thereof elect to take one-half of the balance of the estate, after the payment of claims and expenses."), he would also be able to elect against the will because part of a civil union that had never been formally dissolved. *Cf. In re Van Schaick's Estate*, 40 N.W.2d 588, 589 (Wis. 1949) ("[T]he petitioner could only be relieved from the legal impediment created by her first marriage by a divorce."). *See also* Vt. Stat. Ann. tit. 15, § 1204 (a) (West) ("Parties to a civil union shall have all the same benefits, protections, and responsibilities under law, whether they derive from statute, administrative or court rule, policy, common law, or any other source of civil law, as are granted to spouses in a civil marriage.").

    Answer (A) is incorrect. Just as a public renunciation would not end a marriage, such a renunciation would not end a civil union. *See* Vt. Stat. Ann. tit. 15, § 1204 (d) (West) ("The law of domestic relations, including annulment, separation and divorce, child custody and support, and property division and maintenance shall apply to parties to a civil union.").

    Answer (C) is incorrect. Just as a spouse to a marriage could claim the right to elect against a will, *see* Ind. Code Ann. § 29-1-3-1 (West) ("The surviving spouse, upon electing to take against the will, is entitled to one-half (½) of the net personal and real estate of the testator."), Ryan would be able to do so as well. *See* Vt. Stat. Ann. tit. 15, § 1204 (a) (West).

    Answer D) is incorrect. Ryan will be allowed to elect against the will. *See* Vt. Stat. Ann. tit. 14, § 319 (a) (West); Vt. Stat. Ann. tit. 15, § 1204 (a) (West). If Rory had entered into a civil union with Skylar and Skylar had been unaware that Rory had never ended the civil union with Ryan, then Skylar might have been treated as a putative spouse if Vermington law recognized putative spouses. *See*, for example, Mont. Code Ann. § 40-1-404 (West) ("A person who has cohabited with another to whom the person is not legally married in the good faith belief that the person was married to that person is a putative spouse until knowledge of the fact that the person is not legally married terminates that status and prevents acquisition of further rights. A putative spouse acquires the rights conferred upon a legal spouse, including the right to maintenance following termination of that status, whether or not the marriage is prohibited . . . . If there is a legal spouse or putative spouses, rights acquired by a putative spouse do not supersede the rights of the legal spouse or those acquired by other putative spouses."). In this case, Skylar would neither qualify for nor have any need of putative spouse doctrine. He would not qualify because he and Rory did not contract a civil union or marriage and he would not need to invoke the doctrine because he was expressly provided for in Rory's will.

49. Civil unions and domestic partnerships are creatures of state law, and Traditionaland would have the option of refusing to recognize that status. *See*, for example, *Langan v. St. Vincent's Hosp. of New York*, 802 N.Y.S.2d 476 (App. Div. 2005) (refusing to recognize civil union for purposes of wrongful death action). However, Traditionaland might decide to give effect to civil unions. *See Elia-Warnken v. Elia*, 972 N.E.2d 17, 21 Mass. (2012) ("It also would be inconsistent for us to refuse to recognize Vermont civil unions, which *extended* the right of same-sex couples to enter into a legal, spousal relationship."), so the Traditionaland attorney should try to determine through relevant statutes and case law whether the state would give effect to a New Vermshire civil union. The attorney might point out in addition that even if the state did not recognize civil unions, the prospective employers might recognize domestic partnership benefits, which would mitigate some of the opportunity cost associated with Traditionaland's refusal to give effect to civil union status.

Divorce

50. **Answer (B) is the best answer.** Some states expressly provide that where an individual threatens a spouse's health and safety thereby forcing that spouse to flee, the person posing the threat will be construed as having abandoned or deserted the marriage or the marital home. *See* S.D. Codified Laws § 25-4-10 ("Departure or absence of one party from the family dwelling place caused by cruelty or by threats of bodily harm from which danger would be reasonably apprehended from the other is not desertion by the absent party, but it is desertion by the other party.").

Still other states treat the threatening spouse as having constructively abandoned or deserted the home. *See Edwards v. Edwards*, 356 A.2d 633, 637 (D.C. 1976) ("[A] divorce on the ground of constructive desertion may be granted only upon a showing that by reason of the cruelty of one spouse the other spouse was compelled for his or her own safety to leave the family home and make a home elsewhere."); *Blair v. Blair*, 121 N.Y.S.2d 30, 36 (Dom. Rel. Ct. 1953) ("To entitle a wife who has left her husband to support on ground of 'constructive abandonment,' court must find as a matter of fact that it is impossible or unsafe for the wife to continue to live with her husband.").

Answer (A) is not the best answer. Although many states recognize abandonment or desertion as a ground for divorce when one of the parties has left the marital domicile for a year, *see* Md. Code Ann., Fam. Law § 7-103 (2) (i)-(iii) (West); Idaho Code Ann. § 32-609 (West), they tend to require that the desertion or abandonment not be justified. *See* 23 Pa. Stat. and Cons. Stat. Ann. § 3301 (a) (1) (West) ("The court may grant a divorce to the innocent and injured spouse whenever it is judged that the other spouse has: Committed willful and malicious desertion, and absence from the habitation of the injured and innocent spouse, without a reasonable cause, for the period of one or more years.").

Answer (C) is not the best answer. Here, there have been several incidents and Alexander has promised each time not to hit her again. As long as her decision to leave is reasonable, he is unlikely to be successful in his claim that she deserted or abandoned him.

Answer (D) is not the best answer. Many states do not bar a divorce even when both parties are at fault. *See* Iowa Code Ann. § 598.18 (West) ("If, upon the trial of an action for dissolution of marriage, both of the parties are found to have committed an act or acts which would support or justify a decree of dissolution of marriage, such dissolution may be decreed, and the acts of one party shall not negate the acts of the other, nor serve to bar the dissolution decree in any way."). Here, though, he is the only one at fault.

51.   **Answer (D) is the best answer.** It is necessary to show both opportunity and an inclination to engage in adultery. *See Stuckey v. Waid*, 195 So. 3d 872, 875 (Miss. App. 2016) ("To prove adultery by circumstantial evidence, the plaintiff must provide clear and convincing evidence supporting a finding of: (1) an adulterous inclination, and (2) a reasonable opportunity to satisfy that inclination."). Further, the facts presented must be such that they are not plausibly construed as compatible with an innocent explanation. *See Pool v. Pool*, 989 So. 2d 920, 925 (Miss. App. 2008) ("If circumstantial evidence is offered, the party asserting adultery as a ground must bear the following burden: If there are two or more reasonable theories which may be drawn from the facts proven, the proof will be insufficient because, to invest mere circumstances with the force of truth, the conclusion must not only be logical, and tend to prove the facts charged, but must be inconsistent with a reasonable theory of innocence.").

        Answer (A) is not the best answer. One must show opportunity and an adulterous inclination, *see Stuckey v. Waid*, 195 So. 3d 872, 875 (Miss. Ct. App. 2016). However, here, there is no showing of an adulterous inclination beyond James's suspicion. *See Boldon v. Boldon*, 354 So. 2d 275, 276 (Ala. Civ. App. 1978) ("[T]he proof to support the charge of adultery must be such as to create more than a suspicion.").

        Answer (B) is incorrect. While eyewitness testimony may suffice, it is not necessary to establish adultery. *See Billington v. Billington*, 531 So.2d 924, 924 (Ala. Civ. App. 1988) ("While it is difficult and somewhat rare to prove adultery by direct means, the charge of adultery in a divorce case may be proven by circumstantial evidence which creates more than a mere suspicion.").

        Answer (C) is not the best answer. Adultery can be established through circumstantial evidence. *See Aguilera v. Aguilera*, 2014 WL 1614282, at *6 (Tex. App. 2014) ("Adultery can be shown by direct or circumstantial evidence.").

52.   **Answer (C) is the best answer.** While much discretion is given to the trier of fact who is in the best position to assess witness credibility, *see Gorecki v. Gorecki*, 693 S.E.2d 419, 424 (S.C. App. 2010) ("[T]he family court found Husband and his witnesses' testimony to be less credible than that of Wife, which merits our deference based on the family court's ability to observe witnesses and assess their credibility."), the evidence of the past relationship plus the opportunities for adultery plus Peter's lying about his whereabouts would likely suffice as a basis for a court to find adultery. *See Stuckey v. Waid*, 195 So. 3d 872, 875 (Miss. App. 2016).

        Answer (A) is incorrect. To establish adultery, it is not necessary to catch the parties in the act. While eyewitness testimony may suffice, it is not necessary to establish adultery. *See Billington v. Billington*, 531 So. 2d 924, 924 (Ala. Civ. App.1988) ("While it is difficult and somewhat rare to prove adultery by direct means, the charge of adultery in a divorce case may be proven by circumstantial evidence which creates more than a mere suspicion.").

        Answer (B) is not the best answer. The alternative explanation of the relevant facts must not only be possible but reasonable. *See Pool v. Pool*, 989 So. 2d 920, 925 (Miss. App. 2008). Given his admitted, allegedly past, infatuation, and the several opportunities to commit adultery, a court might well find adultery on these facts. *See Holden v. Frasher-Holden*, 680 So. 2d 795,

796 (Miss. 1996) ("Finding that there is sufficient evidence of infatuation and the opportunity to satisfy that infatuation, we affirm the decision of the chancery court.").

Answer (D) is incorrect. Mary forgave his past acts but not his committing the same act in the future. *See Young v. Young*, 154 N.E. 405, 407 (Ill. 1926) ("Condonation, in the law of divorce, is the forgiveness of an antecedent matrimonial offense on condition that it shall not be repeated.").

53.   **Answer (D) is the best answer.** Their admitting their attraction and the sexual nature of some of their activities would suffice to establish the necessary inclination, and their numerous meetings in a car would suffice to establish the necessary opportunity. *See Brown v. Brown*, 665 S.E.2d 174, 179–80 (S.C. App. 2008) (concluding that these elements justified the inference that the couple had engaged in intercourse, their denial notwithstanding).

Answer (A) is incorrect. It is not necessary for there to have been an eyewitness, *see Billington v. Billington*, 531 So. 2d 924, 924 (Ala. Civ. App. 1988), and it is not necessary for them to have been in a house or hotel room for them to be inferred to have had sexual relations. *See Brown v. Brown*, 665 S.E.2d 174, 179–80 (S.C. App. 2008) ("[W]e disagree with the family court's finding that Wife and Craft's continued and secretive meetings in various parking lots did not provide sufficient evidence to establish an opportunity to commit adultery.").

Answer (B) is incorrect. It is necessary to do more than merely show that William and Zelda wanted to have sexual relations with each other. It is necessary to provide evidence that provides the basis for inferring that they did have such relations. *See Stuckey v. Waid*, 195 So. 3d 872, 875 (Miss. App. 2016) ("[T]o commit adultery, a married person must have sexual intercourse with a person other than his or her spouse.").

Answer (C) is not the best answer. To establish an adulterous inclination, one merely needs to show an infatuation with the alleged love interest. *See Stuckey v. Waid*, 195 So. 3d 872, 876 (Miss. App. 2016). The admissions of sexual attraction and their having engaged in activities of a sexual nature will likely suffice to establish the requisite inclination. *See Brown v. Brown*, 665 S.E.2d 174, 179 (S.C. App. 2008).

54.   **Answer (C) is the best answer.** Many jurisdictions do not require that the couple live in separate residences if their lives are sufficiently independent. *See Teodorski v. Teodorski*, 857 A.2d 194, 197 (Pa. Super. 2004) ("[T]he gravamen of the phrase 'separate and apart' becomes the existence of separate lives not separate roofs."); *In re Marriage of Uhls*, 549 S.W.2d 107, 112 (Mo. App. 1977) ("Our interpretation of the phrase 'living separate and apart' . . . does not necessarily mean separate roofs but rather means separate lives."); *In re Marriage of Tomlins & Glenn*, 983 N.E.2d 118, 123 (Ill. App. 2013) ("Parties can be said to be living 'separate and apart' even if they reside in the same house."); *Boyce v. Boyce*, 153 F.2d 229, 230 (D.C. Cir. 1946) ("The essential thing is not separate roofs, but separate lives.").

Answer (A) is incorrect. Many jurisdictions would permit this couple to divorce on this ground, notwithstanding their living in the same apartment. *See Teodorski v. Teodorski*,

857 A.2d 194, 197 (Pa. Super. 2004); *In re Marriage of Uhls*, 549 S.W.2d 107, 112 (Mo. App. 1977).

Answer (B) is incorrect. Some states require separate residences. *See Rogers v. Rogers*, 63 So. 2d 807, 808 (Ala. 1953) ("Living in separate rooms within the same matrimonial abode is not living 'separate and apart' within the meaning of the statute.").

Answer (D) is not the best answer. The important question is not whether they occasionally talk to each other, but whether the marriage is "irretrievably broken." *See Tardino v. Tardino*, 31 Pa. D. & C.3d 563, 567 (Com. Pl. 1984). *See also In re Marriage of Kenik*, 536 N.E.2d 982, 987 (Ill. App. 1989) ("Under the no-fault provisions of section 401(a)(2), dissolution is predicated upon a finding of 'irretrievable breakdown' of the marriage due to 'irreconcilable differences.' . . . In our opinion, this is a state which can be realized without physical distance between the parties.").

55.   **Answer (B) is the best answer.** Living separate and apart requires the couple to be living separate lives. *See Ballard v. Ballard*, 307 A.2d 637, 638 (N.J. Super. Ch. Div. 1973) ("The essential thing is separate lives, not separate roofs."). A couple that regularly engages in sexual relations will not be considered to be living separate lives. *See Mackey v. Mackey*, 545 A.2d 362, 365 (Pa. Super. 1988) (When finding that the couple had been living separate and apart, the court noted the significance of the parties' stipulation that "they have not engaged in sexual relations with each other since June of 1983.").

Answer (A) is incorrect. While one of the conditions of living separate and apart can be met if the parties live in separate residences, they must also refrain from having marital relations. *See Bergeris v. Bergeris*, 90 A.3d 553, 558 (Md. App. 2014) ("[A] couple purporting to live apart but engaging in physical sexual relations cannot be said to be living separate and apart.").

Answer (C) is incorrect. Even if the marriage is irretrievably broken in other respects, the court may well refuse to grant a divorce based on this ground if they continue to have sexual relations. *See Britton v. Britton*, 582 A.2d 1335, 1337 (Pa. Super. 1990) (refusing to grant divorce on the ground of living separate and apart because, *inter alia*, the couple had had marital relations during the period of separation).

Answer (D) is incorrect. A couple's living in the same apartment house will not preclude their being granted a divorce based on their living separate and apart. *See In re Marriage of Tomlins & Glenn*, 983 N.E.2d 118, 123 (Ill. App. 2013) ("Parties can be said to be living 'separate and apart' even if they reside in the same house."); *Ballard v. Ballard*, 307 A.2d 637, 638 (N.J. Super. Ch. Div. 1973) (noting that a couple might be living separate and apart even if living in the same apartment building).

56.   **Answer (C) is the best answer.** Individuals seeking a divorce on this ground must live separate lives, *see Ballard v. Ballard*, 307 A.2d 637, 638 (N.J. Super. Ch. Div. 1973) ("The essential thing is separate lives."), which includes their not having marital relations regularly. *See Bergeris v. Bergeris*, 90 A.3d 553, 558 (Md. App. 2014) ("[A] couple purporting to live apart but engaging in physical sexual relations cannot be said to be living separate and apart.").

However, various states will not treat an isolated instance of sexual relations as requiring that the clock begin again. *Osborn v. Osborn*, 25 Pa. D. & C.3d 709, 717 (Com. Pl. 1983) ("Isolated instances of sexual intercourse, sporadic visits together, and trips together does not establish cohabitation prohibiting a divorce under Section 201(d) of the Divorce Code requiring the parties live separate and apart for three years prior to divorce."). For example, Delaware expressly provides that a couple will not be forced to restart the clock just because they unsuccessfully tried to resume their marriage, although that state requires that the instance of relations not have occurred within one month of the court's hearing the petition for divorce. *See* Del. Code Ann. tit. 13, § 1505 (e) (West) ("Bona fide efforts to achieve reconciliation prior to divorce, even those that include, temporarily, sleeping in the same bedroom and resumption of sexual relations, shall not interrupt any period of living separate and apart, provided that the parties have not occupied the same bedroom or had sexual relations with each other within the 30-day period immediately preceding the day the Court hears the petition for divorce.").

Answer (A) is not the best answer. While it is true that the ground requires that the members of the couple live separate lives, *see Ballard v. Ballard*, 307 A.2d 637, 638 (N.J. Super. Ch. Div. 1973), and that the couple not be engaging in marital relations regularly, *see Bergeris v. Bergeris*, 90 A.3d 553, 558 (Md. App. 2014), that does not end the discussion. Some states will not start the clock over for purposes of this ground merely because the couple has had an isolated fling. *Osborn v. Osborn*, 25 Pa. D. & C.3d 709, 717 (Com. Pl. 1983).

Answer (B) is incorrect. While the ground does require that the members of the couple live separate lives, *see Ballard v. Ballard*, 307 A.2d 637, 638 (N.J. Super. Ch. Div. 1973), that factor is not established merely because the members of the couple have separate residences. *See Orihuela v. Orihuela*, 184 So. 3d 182, 186 (La. App. 2015) (rejecting that the couple lived separate and apart because "they went to lunch and dinner regularly, went on a couple of brief trips together, engaged in sexual relations, and spent nights at each other's houses").

Answer (D) is incorrect. Merely because the states might not permit a couple to be divorced on this ground when they regularly have sexual relations does not speak to whether their having had relations once during the relevant period would require them to begin the clock again. Several states permit divorces on this ground even if there has been one instance of sexual relations during the relevant period. *See Millon v. Millon*, 352 So. 2d 325, 327 (La. Ct. App. 1977) ("While sexual intercourse constitutes strong evidence that the relationship has been resumed, proof of one act or of several isolated acts of sexual intercourse is not necessarily conclusive of the issue of reconciliation."); *Osborn v. Osborn*, 25 Pa. D. & C.3d 709, 717 (Com. Pl. 1983); *In re Marriage of A.J.H., Jr.*, 2002 WL 31454020, at *1 n.1 (Del. Fam. Ct. 2002) (noting that one instance of sexual relations in testing whether the couple can resume their marriage will not require a clock reset with respect to the ground of living separate and apart).

57.   **Answer (C) is the best answer.** Tate will have to establish both the severity of the conduct and the harm that the conduct caused. *See Jones v. Jones*, 43 So. 3d 465, 470 (Miss. App. 2009) ("Since the conduct's effect on the suffering spouse determines whether a divorce on the ground of habitual cruel and inhuman treatment is warranted, the chancellor has a dual focus: the conduct of the offending spouse and the impact of that conduct on the offended spouse.").

Answer (A) is not the best answer. Merely because one spouse has been willing to put up with the other spouse's cruel and inhuman treatment for a long time does not forever bar securing a divorce on that ground. *See Melnick v. Melnick*, 496 N.Y.S.2d 221, 221 (App. Div. 1985) (suggesting that one spouse could be awarded a divorce from the other based on cruel and inhuman treatment for almost 20 years).

Answer (B) is not the best answer. While the length of time that they have been together will not bar securing a divorce on this ground, *see Melnick v. Melnick*, 496 N.Y.S.2d 221, 221 (App. Div. 1985), there is still the question whether this kind of abuse rises to what is necessary to be awarded a divorce on this ground. *See*, for example, *McMahon v. McMahon*, 840 N.Y.S.2d 826, 828 (App. Div. 2007) (upholding lower court finding that insufficient evidence had been established to justify granting divorce based on cruel and inhuman treatment). *See also Reed v. Reed*, 839 So. 2d 565, 570 (Miss. App. 2003) ("The conduct may be in the form of emotional abuse; however, it must be more than mere unkindness, rudeness, or incompatibility.").

Answer (D) is not the best answer. While the marriage may be irretrievably broken, that is a different ground and so would not justify granting the divorce on cruel and inhuman treatment. *Compare* N.Y. Dom. Rel. Law § 170 (1) (McKinney) ("An action for divorce may be maintained by a husband or wife to procure a judgment divorcing the parties and dissolving the marriage on any of the following grounds: . . . the cruel and inhuman treatment of the plaintiff by the defendant such that the conduct of the defendant so endangers the physical or mental well being of the plaintiff as renders it unsafe or improper for the plaintiff to cohabit with the defendant.") *with* N.Y. Dom. Rel. Law § 170 (7) (McKinney) ("An action for divorce may be maintained by a husband or wife to procure a judgment divorcing the parties and dissolving the marriage on any of the following grounds: . . . The relationship between husband and wife has broken down irretrievably for a period of at least six months, provided that one party has so stated under oath.").

58.   **Answer (D) is the best answer.** Physical violence is a prime example of the kind of behavior that might provide the basis for securing a divorce on this ground. *See Richard v. Richard*, 711 So. 2d 884, 889 (Miss. 1998) ("[D]ivorce granted on the grounds of cruel and inhuman treatment is usually due to acts of physical violence or such acts that result in apprehension thereof.").

Answer (A) is not the best answer. Habitual drunkenness and abuse are different grounds, so this response misstates the basis upon which Finley seeks the divorce. *Compare* Miss. Code. Ann. § 93-5-1 (West) ("Divorces from the bonds of matrimony may be decreed to the injured party for any one or more of the following twelve (12) causes: . . . Fifth. Habitual drunkenness.") *with* Miss. Code. Ann. § 93-5-1 (West) ("Divorces from the bonds of matrimony may be decreed to the injured party for any one or more of the following twelve (12) causes: . . . Seventh. Habitual Cruel and inhuman treatment, including spousal domestic abuse.").

Answer (B) is incorrect. Drew might sincerely claim and believe that Finley provoked the violence, but that simply is not the relevant question. *See In re Marriage of Smith*, 2002 WL 31188736, at *3 (Tex. App. Oct. 3, 2002) ("[P]rovocation is not relevant to determining whether there was physical abuse or a history or pattern of domestic violence.").

Answer (C) is incorrect. A pattern of physical abuse would support granting a divorce on this ground even if the incidents of violence did not differ in type or degree. *See Bernholc v. Bornstein*, 898 N.Y.S.2d 228, 230 (App. Div. 2010) ("A party seeking a divorce on the ground of cruel and inhuman treatment must generally show a course of conduct by the defendant spouse which is harmful to the physical or mental health of the plaintiff and makes cohabitation unsafe or improper . . . A pattern of conduct which includes verbal abuse and physical harassment is sufficient.").

59. **Answer (A) is the best answer.** While Alice and Brian will be able to secure a divorce, they may have to spend a period during which they will remain married but will be living apart before the divorce will be granted. *See*, for example, Vt. Stat. Ann. tit. 15, § 551 (7) (West) ("A divorce from the bond of matrimony may be decreed: . . . when a married person has lived apart from his or her spouse for six consecutive months and the Court finds that the resumption of marital relations is not reasonably probable.").

    Answer (B) is incorrect. No-fault divorce is also open to married couples with children. *See Joy v. Joy*, 423 A.2d 895, 896 (Conn. 1979) (granting divorce based on irretrievable breakdown of marriage and awarding custody of children to wife). However, some states might make it more difficult to secure the divorce if there are children of the marriage. *See* La. Civ. Code Ann. art. 103 (1) ("[A] divorce shall be granted on the petition of a spouse upon proof that: . . . The spouses have been living separate and apart continuously for the requisite period of time, in accordance with Article 103.1, or more on the date the petition is filed.") and (proposed legislation) La. Civ. Code Ann. art. 103.1 ("The requisite periods of time, in accordance with Articles 102 and 103 shall be as follows: (1) One hundred eighty days where there are no minor children of the marriage. (2) Three hundred sixty-five days when there are minor children of the marriage . . .").

    Answer (C) is incorrect. Some states might require a waiting period before the irretrievably broken marriage can be dissolved. *See*, for example, Vt. Stat. Ann. tit. 15, § 551 (7) (West).

    Answer (D) is incorrect. Securing a divorce on this ground does not preclude one spouse from receiving spousal support. *See Jayne v. Jayne*, 663 A.2d 169, 175 (Pa. Super. 1995) (granting divorce on ground of irretrievable breakdown of the marriage and awarding wife rehabilitative spousal support).

60. **Answer (C) is the best answer.** States differ about the proper approach where one of the parties denies that the marriage cannot be saved. *Compare Palermo v. Palermo*, 950 N.Y.S.2d 724 (Sup. Ct. 2011) (discussing the "wisdom of the state legislature's determination to permit divorce on the subjective sworn testimony of one of the marriage's partners") *with* Ohio Rev. Code Ann. § 3105.01 (K) (West) ("The court of common pleas may grant divorces for the following causes: . . . Incompatibility, unless denied by either party.").

    Answer (A) is not the best answer. Some states do distinguish depending upon whether both spouses agree that the marriage cannot be saved. *See*, for example, Ohio Rev. Code Ann. § 3105.01 (K) (West) ("The court of common pleas may grant divorces for the following causes: . . . Incompatibility, unless denied by either party."); Colo. Rev. Stat. Ann. § 14-10-110

(1)-(2) (West) (distinguishing between what the court should do when no party denies that the marriage is irretrievably broken and when one of the parties does deny that the marriage is irretrievably broken).

Answer (B) is incorrect. A divorce can still be granted on this basis even if one of the parties denies that the marriage is irretrievably broken. *See* Colo. Rev. Stat. Ann. § 14-10-110 (2) (West).

Answer (D) is not the best answer. In many jurisdictions, a divorce can still be granted on this ground even if one of the spouses disagrees. *See,* for example, Colo. Rev. Stat. Ann. § 14-10-110 (2) (West); Mont. Code Ann. § 40-4-107 (2) (West); N.J. Stat. Ann. § 2A:34-2 (i) (West) ("Divorce from the bond of matrimony may be adjudged for the following causes heretofore or hereafter arising: . . . Irreconcilable differences which have caused the breakdown of the marriage for a period of six months and which make it appear that the marriage should be dissolved and that there is no reasonable prospect of reconciliation."); Ala. Code § 30-2-1 (a) (7) ("[W]hen the court is satisfied from all the testimony in the case that there exists such a complete incompatibility of temperament that the parties can no longer live together.").

61.   **Answer (D) is the best answer.** Absent some kind of local law to the contrary, the domicile and residency requirement can be met by either of the parties. *See* W. Va. Code Ann. § 48-5-105 (2) (West) ("If the marriage was not entered into within this state, an action for divorce is maintainable if: (A) One of the parties was an actual bona fide resident of this state at the time the cause of action arose, or has become a resident since that time; and (B) The residency has continued uninterrupted through the one-year period immediately preceding the filing of the action.") Then, local law will be applied to determine if the relevant ground has been met. *See Sinha v. Sinha*, 834 A.2d 600, 605 (Pa. Super. 2003).

Answer (A) is incorrect. She may be able to file in Penntucky because John is domiciled there and has been a resident there for the requisite period. *See* W. Va. Code Ann. § 48-5-105 (2) (West) ("If the marriage was not entered into within this state, an action for divorce is maintainable if: (A) One of the parties was an actual bona fide resident of this state at the time the cause of action arose, or has become a resident since that time; and (B) The residency has continued uninterrupted through the one-year period immediately preceding the filing of the action.").

Answer (B) is incorrect. As a general matter, the law of the domicile where the divorce is filed will be applicable. *See Sinha v. Sinha*, 834 A.2d 600, 605 (Pa. Super. 2003).

Answer (C) is inaccurate in that more than mere personal jurisdiction is required. In addition, the court must have jurisdiction over the marriage, which would be conferred by virtue of one of the parties being domiciled there. *See Lewis v. Lewis*, 930 S.W.2d 475, 477 (Mo. Ct. App. 1996) ("A dissolution of marriage decree is void for lack of subject matter jurisdiction if it is entered in a state in which neither of the parties to the action are domiciled at the commencement of the action.").

62.   **Answer (B) is the best answer.** Zelda knew where Alexander was staying and could easily have given him actual notice of her filing for divorce. Her failure to give actual notice when that could easily have been done can result in the divorce being declared invalid. *See Keating v. Keating*, 855 A.2d 80, 85 (Pa. Super. 2004) (lack of proper notice made divorce invalid).

   Answer (A) is incorrect. A failure to meet notice requirements can render a divorce void and of no legal effect. *See Clark v. Clark*, 43 So. 3d 496, 498 (Miss. App. 2010) (failure to meet notice requirements rendered divorce void).

   Answer (C) is incorrect. Constructive notice will not suffice when actual notice can easily be given. *See M.T.L. v. T.P.L.*, 414 A.2d 510, 514 (Del. 1980) ("The concept that constructive notice may continue to serve as legal notice is no longer viable as to a divorce respondent having a known out-of-state mailing address.").

   Answer (D) is incorrect. Local law can be applied to determine how long they must live separate and apart in order for the relevant ground to have been met. *See Sinha v. Sinha*, 834 A.2d 600, 605 (Pa. Super. 2003).

63.   **Answer (D) is the best answer.** A party's having an affair during the marriage might speak to the moral fitness of the parent, which in some states is a factor to be considered in custody. *See White v. White*, 166 So. 3d 574, 586–87 (Miss. App. 2015) ("[A]dultery is a factor to be considered in evaluating moral fitness."). It may be considered when a court is allocating marital property. *See Brown v. Brown*, 771 S.E.2d 649, 655 (S.C. App. 2015) (noting that one of the factors affecting the distribution of marital property involves marital misconduct or fault). Marital fault might be considered when deciding how much or even whether spousal support should be awarded. *See Burgess v. Burgess*, 753 S.E.2d 566, 570 (S.C. App. 2014) (listing marital fault as one of the factors to be considered when determining spousal support). *See also Dukelow v. Dukelow*, 341 S.E.2d 208, 210 (Va. App. 1986) ("The determination of spousal support is a two-step process: first, the court must determine whether either of the parties is barred from receiving support due to the existence of a marital fault amounting to a statutory ground for divorce; and, second, if no fault ground exists, then the court must weigh the relative needs and abilities of the parties in accordance with the statutory factors.").

   Answer (A) is incorrect. Ellis's having a serious relationship with Robin might affect spousal support, *see* Fla. Stat. Ann. § 61.08 (West) ("[T]he court may consider the adultery of either spouse and the circumstances thereof in determining the amount of alimony, if any, to be awarded."), the distribution of property, *see Erickson v. Erickson*, 384 N.W.2d 659, 661 (N.D. 1986) ("It is well settled that fault is a factor the court may consider when dividing property."), or custody. *See Smith v. Smith*, 599 So. 2d 1182, 1186 (Ala. Civ. App. 1991) ("[A]dultery by a parent may enter a court's decision concerning custody.").

   Answer (B) is incorrect. Post-separation adultery might be the ground upon which a divorce is based and, further, might preclude an award of permanent spousal support. *See Billingsley v. Billingsley*, 618 So. 2d 562, 565 (La. Ct. App. 1993) ("[I]n order to preclude an award of permanent alimony, the post-separation fault must be of the magnitude that it would, if standing alone, constitute grounds for divorce. . . . Post-separation adultery has uniformly been held to be fault of such magnitude that it would preclude permanent alimony.").

Answer (C) is incorrect. Merely announcing this to Drew will not preclude Drew from using evidence of adulterous relations to affect custody, division of property, or spousal support in a jurisdiction in which adultery is permitted to play such a role. *See* Fla. Stat. Ann. § 61.08 (West). *See also Erickson v. Erickson*, 384 N.W.2d 659, 661 (N.D. 1986) and *Smith v. Smith*, 599 So. 2d 1182, 1186 (Ala. Civ. App. 1991).

64.   **Answer (A) is the best answer.** If Kennedy and Lee had an adulterous relationship during the separation, that might result in the court awarding a divorce on the basis of adultery and in some states might preclude spousal support. *See Morris v. Morris*, 367 S.E.2d 24, 26 (S.C. 1988) ("[A]n adulterous spouse is absolutely barred from alimony."); *Billingsley v. Billingsley*, 618 So. 2d 562, 565 (La. Ct. App. 1993) ("Post-separation adultery has uniformly been held to be fault of such magnitude that it would preclude permanent alimony."). However, merely because they had some dates will not establish that Kennedy and Lee committed adultery. *Cf. Noce v. Noce*, 2006 WL 908062, at *2 (Va. App. 2006) ("The evidence presented by husband simply did not rise above the level of speculation and suspicion. We find no error in the trial court's conclusion that husband failed to establish wife committed adultery by clear and convincing evidence.").

Answer (B) is incorrect. *See Morris v. Morris*, 367 S.E.2d 24, 26 (S.C. 1988). Further, that post-separation adultery might provide the ground upon which the divorce will be granted. *See Legat v. Legat*, 1999 WL 1133312, at *1 (Va. App. 1999) (upholding trial court granting divorce on the basis of post-separation adultery).

Answer (C) is incorrect. Even if they met post-separation, their relationship might be thought to have contributed to the irretrievable breakdown of the marriage. *See Derby v. Derby*, 378 S.E.2d 74, 76 (Va. App. 1989) ("The fact that the adultery occurred after the parties separated does not lead inexorably to the conclusion that the adultery had nothing to do with the breakdown of the marriage."). Further, if they committed adultery, Kennedy might be barred from receiving spousal support. *See Morris v. Morris*, 367 S.E.2d 24, 26 (S.C. 1988).

Answer (D) is incorrect. Support might be barred even if the marriage was already unsalvageable. *See Morris v. Morris*, 367 S.E.2d 24, 26 (S.C. 1988).

65.   **Answer (D) is the best answer.** If transgender status itself is thought to be one of the essentials of marriage, then the marriage might be annulled. *See Woy v. Woy*, 737 S.W.2d 769, 776 (Mo. App. 1987) ("The fraud must be something essential to the marriage relation, making its performance impossible or its continuance dangerous to health or life."). Concealing a firm commitment never to have children can provide the basis for annulling a marriage. *See Williams v. Witt*, 235 A.2d 902 (N.J. Super. App. Div. 1967). Here, however, there had been an agreement not to have children, so that would not provide the basis for the annulment. If the status does not go to one of the essentials of marriage, then the marriage might be dissolved based on irreconcilable differences, *see* Or. Rev. Stat. Ann. § 107.025 (1) (West) ("A judgment

for the dissolution of a marriage or a permanent or unlimited separation may be rendered when irreconcilable differences between the parties have caused the irremediable breakdown of the marriage.") or, perhaps, on the parties living separate and apart for the requisite period. *See* La. Civ. Code Ann. art. 103 (1) ("[A] divorce shall be granted on the petition of a spouse upon proof that [t]he spouses have been living separate and apart for the requisite period of time.").

Answer (A) is not the best answer. The issue here is whether the failure to divulge her transgender status constituted a fraud involving an essential of marriage such that there was a positive duty to divulge this. *Compare Svenson v. Svenson*, 70 N.E. 120, 121 (N.Y. 1904) (holding that concealing venereal disease provided a basis for annulling a marriage) *with Wier v. Still*, 31 Iowa 107 (1871) (concealing prison record did not provide a basis for annulling the marriage).

Answer (B) is not the best answer. In most states, the issue is not merely whether one of the parties believed the matter important, but in addition whether the matter at issue went to an essential of the marriage. *See Woy v. Woy*, 737 S.W.2d 769, 776 (Mo. App. 1987) ("The fraud must be something essential to the marriage relation, making its performance impossible or its continuance dangerous to health or life.").

Answer (C) is not the best answer. In many states, the issue is not merely whether both parties knew that a particular issue was important to the uninformed party but whether, in addition, that issue went to one of the essentials of marriage. *See Woy v. Woy*, 737 S.W.2d 769, 776 (Mo. App. 1987).

Divorce Defenses

66.   **Answer (D) is the best answer.** If neither party was domiciled in Divorca, then the Divorca court would not have jurisdiction to grant the divorce. *See Hileman v. Hileman*, 2016 WL 538334, at *1 (Ariz. App. 2016) ("[N]o state has jurisdiction to grant a divorce unless one of the spouses is a domiciliary of the state, for without such domicile there is no sufficient nexus between the state and the marriage relationship or status to entitle that state to put an end to the marriage.").

   Answer (A) is incorrect. If the Divorca court had jurisdiction to grant the divorce, then the decree is not subject to challenge merely because the Divorca court applied local law to grant the divorce. *See Rowley v. Lampe*, 331 S.W.2d 887, 890 (Ky. 1960) (suggesting that local law should be applied).

   Answer (B) is incorrect. Addison does not get to challenge the Divorca decision on the merits in a collateral attack. *See Richer v. Richer*, 2014 WL 5462721, at *6 (Mich. App. 2014) ("[T]he defendant's failure to appeal the original divorce judgment precluded a collateral attack on the merits of the judgment.").

   Answer (C) is incorrect. Irreconcilable differences is a no-fault ground. *See Clementi v. Clementi*, 85 A.3d 425, 427 (N.J. Super. Ch. Div. 2013) (discussing "the no-fault ground of irreconcilable differences"). Further, Addison would not be permitted to base his challenge on the merits in any event. *See Richer v. Richer*, 2014 WL 5462721, at *6 (Mich. App. 2014).

67.   While Cameron is likely correct that Casey never established domicile in Divorca and that the Divorca court did not have jurisdiction over the marriage if neither Cameron nor Casey was domiciled there, Cameron will nonetheless be unable to challenge the divorce decree collaterally. Cameron already sought to establish that Casey was not domiciled in Divorca, but the Divorca trial court rejected that claim. Cameron could have appealed the trial court decision in the Divorca courts. *See Sherrer v. Sherrer*, 334 U.S. 343, 356 (1948) ("[S]uch litigation should end in the courts of the State in which the judgment was rendered."). An individual who has fully litigated an issue in one state will not be permitted to get a second bite at the apple by collaterally attacking the decision in another state merely because he did not agree with the initial result. *See id.* at 355-56.

68.   **Answer (A) is the best answer.** If she did not commit adultery and there was no other ground upon which the divorce could be granted, then the trial court would likely not grant the divorce. *See Graham v. Graham*, 419 P.2d 419, 420 (Or. 1966) (affirming trial court finding

that insufficient evidence was presented to justify granting divorce). Even in a state where collusion was not a bar to granting a divorce, *see* Wis. Stat. Ann. § 767.317 (West) ("Previously existing defenses to divorce and legal separation, including but not limited to condonation, connivance, collusion, recrimination, insanity, and lapse of time, are abolished."), evidence would still have to be presented to meet one of the grounds. Some states still bar granting a divorce if collusion can be established. *See* Idaho Code Ann. § 32-611 (West) ("Divorces must be denied upon showing: 1. Collusion; 2. Condonation; 3. Recrimination; or, 4. Limitation and lapse of time.").

Answer (B) is incorrect. Many states do not bar granting a divorce even if there has been collusion. *See*, for example, Minn. Stat. Ann. § 518.06 (West) ("Defenses to divorce, dissolution and legal separation, including but not limited to condonation, connivance, collusion, recrimination, insanity, and lapse of time, are abolished.").

Answer (C) is incorrect. Even if Gillian is not believed that she and Gene colluded, the divorce still could not be granted if no adultery took place and there was no other ground upon which the divorce could be granted. *See Dzierwa v. Cerda*, 2014 WL 3843950, at *3 (Tex. App. 2014) (remanding case to see whether there was the basis for granting a divorce on a different ground because the evidence of adultery was insufficient to grant a divorce on that basis).

Answer (D) is incorrect. Recrimination involves a charge that the other spouse also committed a marital fault. *See Jenkins v. Jenkins*, 55 So. 3d 1094, 1095 (Miss. App. 2010) ("Under the common-law doctrine of recrimination, if each party to a marriage proved a fault-based ground for divorce, then neither party was entitled to a divorce."). Even if Gillian is not believed, she still would not have committed a marital fault. Further, where recrimination was established, that was thought to bar rather than require granting a divorce. *See id.* ("Under the common-law doctrine of recrimination, . . . neither party was entitled to a divorce.").

69.   **Answer (D) is the best answer.** Angel might be granted the divorce on a no-fault ground and thus might not be subject to the penalty that the jurisdiction might associate with a fault-based ground. *See Krause v. Krause*, 1990 WL 751283, at *3 (Va. Cir. Ct. 1990) ("[B]ecause the doctrine of recrimination bars Mr. Krause from obtaining a divorce based on fault, his obligation to pay spousal support continues. The right to spousal support is not affected by an award of no-fault divorce.").

Answer (A) is not the best answer. While Angel has committed adultery, so has Erin. There is no reason for Angel to be forced to accept a smaller share of the marital assets on these facts. He can offer a defense of recrimination and still be granted a divorce on a no-fault ground. *See Krause v. Krause*, 1990 WL 751283, at *3 (Va. Cir. Ct. 1990).

Answer (B) is not the best answer. Angel can argue recrimination and then secure a no-fault divorce. *See Krause v. Krause*, 1990 WL 751283, at *3 (Va. Cir. Ct. 1990).

Answer (C) is not the best answer. In many states, recrimination does not bar a divorce. *See*, for example, Tex. Fam. Code Ann. § 6.008 (West) (a) ("The defenses to a suit for divorce of recrimination and adultery are abolished.").

70.   **Answer (D) is the best answer.** One act of conjugal relations may not be viewed as condonation. *See Stewart v. Stewart*, 175 So. 2d 692, 695 (La. App. 1965). Even if Brian is viewed as having condoned the adultery, he may be able to secure a divorce on a no-fault ground of irreconcilable differences or irretrievable breakdown of the marriage. *See*, for example, Or. Rev. Stat. Ann. § 107.025 (1) (West) ("A judgment for the dissolution of a marriage or a permanent or unlimited separation may be rendered when irreconcilable differences between the parties have caused the irremediable breakdown of the marriage.").

        Answer (A) is not correct. Where one spouse commits adultery but the other spouse forgives the transgression, the latter spouse will not be able to assert the adultery as a ground for obtaining a divorce. *See Vinson v. Vinson*, 880 So. 2d 469, 475 (Ala. Civ. App. 2003) ("Here, the mother committed adultery; however, in light of the evidence regarding condonation, we conclude that the trial court erred in finding adultery as a ground for divorce.").

        Answer (B) is incorrect. Condonation is forgiveness of a past act with the understanding that it will not be repeated. *See Srivastava v. Srivastava*, 769 S.E.2d 442, 448 (S.C. App. 2015).

        Answer (C) is not the best answer. Having sexual relations after a marital fault has been revealed will not always be construed as condonation. *See Ware v. Ware*, 7 So. 3d 271, 274 (Miss. App. 2008) (refusing to construe husband's having sexual relations with wife after her adultery was revealed as condonation).

71.   **Answer (B) is the best answer.** Both because Dallas waited so long to assert the rights, *see Weiner v. Weiner*, 216 N.Y.S.2d 788, 789 (App. Div. 1961) (laches barred challenge when ex-wife waited eight and a half years to challenge divorce) and because Dallas acted in a way that presumed the validity of the divorce when she remarried, *see Haiman v. Haiman*, 803 N.Y.S.2d 18 (Sup. Ct. 2005) ("[H]aving accepted the benefits of her agreement to litigate her divorce dispute in Puerto Rico, the wife is now barred by estoppel and/or laches from seeking to claim that the judgment of divorce entered by the Puerto Rican court must be set aside."), Dallas will likely be denied a share of the winnings.

        Answer (A) is not the best answer. While procedural due process rights were not met when Devon gave Dallas constructive rather than actual notice of the divorce proceeding, *see M.T.L. v. T.P.L.*, 414 A.2d 510, 514 (Del. 1980) ("The concept that constructive notice may continue to serve as legal notice is no longer viable as to a divorce respondent having a known out-of-state mailing address."), that is not dispositive. A separate question is whether Dallas has sat on her rights for a long enough period that she should not be permitted to assert them now. *Cf. Weiner v. Weiner*, 216 N.Y.S.2d 788, 789 (App. Div. 1961).

        Answer (C) is incorrect. Recrimination involves the claim that the party seeking a divorce has also committed a marital fault. *See Jenkins v. Jenkins*, 55 So. 3d 1094, 1095 (Miss. App. 2010) ("Under the common-law doctrine of recrimination, if each party to a marriage proved a fault-based ground for divorce, then neither party was entitled to a divorce."). Here, Devon is being accused of having not given Dallas adequate notice; he is not being accused of having committed a marital fault.

Answer (D) is incorrect. Dallas's knowledge does not somehow indicate forgiveness, which is what condonation involves. *See In re Dube*, 44 A.3d 556, 559 (N.H. 2012) ("The affirmative defense of condonation is the forgiveness of an antecedent matrimonial offense on condition that it shall not be repeated.").

72.   **Answer (A) is the best answer.** John acted to bring about his wife's committing a marital fault and then sought to benefit from her having committed that fault. *See Greene v. Greene*, 190 S.E.2d 258, 260 (N.C. App. 1972) ("Connivance, or procurement, denotes direction, influence, personal exertion, or other action with knowledge and belief that such action would produce certain results and which results are produced."). *See also Hollis v. Hollis*, 427 S.E.2d 233, 235 (Va. App. 1993) ("The trial court found that the husband's adultery resulted from the wife's 'connivance and procurement' and granted the husband a divorce on no-fault grounds.").

Answer (B) is incorrect. Recrimination involves the claim that the party accusing the marital partner of committing a marital fault has also committed a marital fault. *See Jenkins v. Jenkins*, 55 So. 3d 1094, 1095 (Miss. App. 2010). Here, John has not committed a marital fault, although he has acted to bring about his wife's doing so.

Answer (C) is incorrect. While John and Brennan are colluding, the defense of collusion involves an agreement between the spouses for one to commit or appear to commit a marital fault. *See Lundy v. Lundy*, 445 S.W.3d 518, 520 (Ark. App. 2014) ("The purpose of this rule is to prevent the *parties* from obtaining a divorce through collusion.") (emphasis added).

Answer (D) is not the best answer. Condonation involves forgiveness of a marital partner's wrong. *See Hollis v. Hollis*, 427 S.E.2d 233, 235 (Va. App. 1993) ("Condonation, on the other hand, is one spouse's forgiveness of the other spouse's adulterous misconduct, usually evidenced by resumption and continuation of apparently normal matrimonial relations."). But that means as a general matter that the condonation occurs after the marital fault has occurred. *See id.* ("Condonation, it follows, may only occur after the occurrence of the misconduct and differs from connivance in when the act of consent or, in the case of connivance, influence occurs. While condonation occurs after the misconduct, connivance occurs before the misconduct.").

73.   **Answer (D) is the best answer.** While Bernard might well be estopped from challenging the decree, *see Rodriguez v. Rodriguez*, 1976 WL 191010, at *3 (Ohio App. 1976) ("[W]e agree with the trial court's finding that appellee was estopped to assail the validity of his *divorce* because of his subsequent remarriage."), a court might nonetheless permit the challenge and hold the divorce void. *Cf. Colarusso v. Teachers' Ret. Bd.*, 392 N.E.2d 844, 846 (Mass. 1979) ("Since Marie did not appear or participate in the divorce proceedings in any way, she is not estopped from attacking the validity of the divorce decree.").

Answer (A) is not the best answer. While Alice was not domiciled in Eezeebreak and the divorce is not entitled to full faith and credit, *see Kushnick v. Kushnick*, 763 N.Y.S.2d 889, 892 (Sup. Ct. 2003) ("A divorce granted by a sister state will be afforded full faith and credit with regard to the termination of the marital relationship only when at least one of the parties was a domiciliary of that state."), a separate question is whether Bernard can challenge the divorce's validity when he implicitly accepted its validity by remarrying. *Cf. McDougall v. McDougall*, 961 P.2d 382, 385 (Wyo. 1998) ("In this case, both parties have since remarried. By taking their vows of remarriage, both relied upon the validity of the divorce decree.").

Answer (B) is incorrect. Courts are not *required* to recognize foreign decrees out of comity, although they may choose to do so. *See Lima-St. Denis v. St. Denis*, 2017 WL 3011605, at *2 (Conn. Super. 2017) ("[W]hile the rules of comity do not require the courts of this state to recognize or enforce every decree of a foreign nation, in particular, in the area of divorce, but they will generally do so where, as here, both parties submitted to the jurisdiction of the court in Brazil, had a fair opportunity to be heard, and the basic principles of due process were applied.").

Answer (C) is incorrect. While states must give full faith and credit to divorce decrees issued in sister states when the issuing court had jurisdiction to issue that decree, states need not give full faith and credit to a decree if the decree-granting court lacked jurisdiction to grant the divorce. *See Atassi v. Atassi*, 451 S.E.2d 371, 374 (N.C. App. 1995) ("Under the United States Constitution, North Carolina is required by Article IV, Section 1, the 'full faith and credit clause,' to recognize divorce judgments from sister-states . . . . However, this recognition is not absolute, and may be withheld from a sister-state divorce decree when there is an insufficient jurisdictional basis for granting the divorce.").

74. The attorney might explain that even if Evelyn has had an affair, that might not mean that she would be barred from receiving an equitable division of property. *See Blickstein v. Blickstein*, 472 N.Y.S.2d 110, 111 (App. Div 1984) ("[M]arital fault is not generally a relevant consideration in the equitable distribution of marital property of divorcing spouses."). Even if marital fault is considered, that would not make the factor dispositive. *See Brusach v. Brusach*, 2017 WL 4654979, at *4 (Mich. App. 2017) ("Fault is merely one of the factors to consider and is not dispositive."). Even where marital fault might be dispositive, Evelyn can offer the defense of recrimination, assuming that Donald's abuse would provide a ground for divorce. If so, then the divorce might be awarded on a no-fault basis like irreconcilable differences or irremediable breakdown of the marriage. In that event, Evelyn would not be adversely affected in the awarding of support or in the distribution of marital property. *See Chabot v. Chabot*, 497 A.2d 851, 852 (N.H. 1985) ("[I]f the plaintiff does not prove fault on which divorce can be granted and the court grants a divorce on the ground of irreconcilable differences, fault would not be considered on the questions of property division or alimony.").

Recognition of Foreign Marriages and Divorces

75.   **Answer (D) is the best answer.** Even though such marriages are considered incestuous because the parties are too closely related by blood, the marriage (if validly celebrated elsewhere) might nonetheless be recognized because not violating a very important policy of the state. *See Ghassemi v. Ghassemi*, 998 So. 2d 731, 749–50 (La. App. 2008) ("[A]lthough Louisiana law expressly prohibits the marriages of first cousins, such marriages are not so 'odious' as to violate a strong public policy of this state. Accordingly, a marriage between first cousins, if valid in the state or country where it was contracted, will be recognized as valid.").

   Answer (A) is incorrect. Marriages that may not be celebrated within the state may nonetheless be recognized if validly celebrated elsewhere. *See Appling v. Doyle*, 826 N.W.2d 666, 673 (Wis. App. 2013) ("[W]e follow the general rule that '[marriages valid where celebrated are valid everywhere.'").

   Answer (B) is incorrect. A marriage that violates an important public policy might not be recognized even if it was valid in the state of celebration. *See Seabold v. Seabold*, 84 N.E.2d 521, 521 (Ohio App. 1948) ("The law of the state in which a marriage is celebrated, including the law with respect to the capacity of the parties to enter into the contract of marriage, governs the validity of a marriage of persons domiciled in this state except when the statutes of this state declare such marriage void or when its celebration offends a strong public policy of this state.").

   Answer (C) is not the best answer. While the first cousin restriction falls within the state incest restrictions, it might nonetheless not be thought sufficiently offensive to public policy to justify its non-recognition. *Compare In re Stiles Estate*, 391 N.E.2d 1026, 1027 (Ohio 1979) (refusing to recognize an uncle-niece marriage validly celebrated elsewhere) *with Mazzolini v. Mazzolini*, 155 N.E.2d 206, 208 (Ohio 1958) (recognizing first-cousin marriage validly celebrated elsewhere).

76.   **Answer (D) is the best answer.** If they established a common law marriage in their domicile, then other states would be likely to recognize it. *See Netecke v. State Through Dep't of Transp. & Dev.*, 715 So. 2d 449, 450 (La. App. 1998) ("The law of the domicile of the alleged married couple is to be applied to determine whether the marriage is valid."). *See also Smith v. Anderson*, 821 So. 2d 323, 326 (Fla. App. 2002) ("Other states that do not recognize common-law marriages have refused to recognize such marriages when they have been contracted in other states by their own citizens.").

   Answer (A) is incorrect. Merely because common law marriages may not be contracted within Limitania does not in addition mean that the state will not recognize such marriages if validly celebrated elsewhere. *See D.L.H. v. J.D.H.*, 521 S.W.3d 324, 327 (Mo. App. 2017) (recognizing common law marriage contracted in Texas).

Answer (B) is not the best answer. The members of a couple might treat each other as spouses and hold themselves out as married in a state in which they are vacationing and not thereby establish a common law marriage. *See Walker v. Hildenbrand*, 410 P.2d 244, 244 (Or. 1966) (holding that a common law marriage had not been established even though "[o]n four different occasions they went on vacation fishing trips to a resort in Idaho where they registered as husband and wife, held themselves out as such, and lived together during their stay").

Answer (C) is not the best answer because it incorrectly implies that the only way for the couple to have their marriage recognized would be for them to have formally married. *See D.L.H. v. J.D.H.*, 521 S.W.3d 324, 327 (Mo. App. 2017) (recognizing common law marriage contracted in Texas).

77.   The Libertania divorce is not entitled to full faith and credit because neither Monty nor Madeline was domiciled in Libertania. *See Kushnick v. Kushnick*, 763 N.Y.S.2d 889, 892 (Sup. Ct. 2003) ("A divorce granted by a sister state will be afforded full faith and credit with regard to the termination of the marital relationship only when at least one of the parties was a domiciliary of that state."). A separate question, though, is whether Monty's adultery will provide the basis for Madeline's preferential treatment. According to the law of some states, adultery committed after divorce papers have been filed will not provide a ground for divorce. *See Turner v. Turner*, 210 So. 3d 603, 606 (Ala. Civ. App. 2016) ("[A] trial court may divorce parties only for adulterous conduct preceding the filing of the divorce complaint."). Here, however, the date of filing may not be viewed as the relevant consideration because Monty filed in a state that did not have jurisdiction to grant the divorce. If Monty argues in the alternative that he and Madeline had already been living separate and apart for the statutorily required period before he began a relationship with Agatha, then the question would be whether adultery post-separation but prior to a (legitimate) filing could provide the basis for divorce. Some states permit post-separation, pre-filing adultery to provide a ground for divorce. *See Matthew H. v. Heather H.*, 2016 WL 6312069, at *5 (W. Va. 2016).

In this case, the divorce will likely be granted either because of their having lived separate and apart for the requisite period or because of the adultery. If adultery is the ground, then a separate question is whether it should affect support or the division of property. In some jurisdictions, adultery that is not the cause of the breakup of the marriage will not affect support or the distribution of property. *Compare Bradle v. Bradle*, 293 N.W.2d 183 (Wis. App. 1980) (noting that "the adultery was not so much a cause as a symptom of the breakup of this marriage" and thus should not affect the distribution of property) *with Tampira v. Tampira*, 539 So. 2d 981, 983 (La. App. 1989) ("The wife against whom a judgment of divorce has been rendered on the grounds of adultery cannot claim permanent alimony even if the adultery occurred subsequent to the couple's separation.").

78.   While no state permits siblings related by blood to marry, a separate question is whether the state's incest law would preclude a sibling from marrying a sibling by adoption. *See Israel v.*

Allen, 577 P.2d 762, 764 (Colo. 1978) (permitting sibling to marry sibling by adoption). Even if Tradington does not permit such marriages to be contracted, a separate question would be whether the state viewed such marriages as so offensive to public policy that they could not be recognized even if validly celebrated elsewhere.

In addition, a further issue would be whether Sarah and Max are in violation of criminal incest laws. *Compare Beam v. State*, 1 So. 3d 331 (Fla. App. 2009) (individual could not be convicted of incest with victim because they were not related by blood) *with Howard v. Commonwealth*, 484 S.W.3d 295, 298 (Ky. 2016) (incest statute applied even when parties were not related by blood). Some states expressly preclude sexual relations between siblings when related by whole or half blood, *see* 18 Pa. Stat. and Cons. Stat. Ann. § 4302 (a) (West), which might suggest that there is not a strong public policy against a marriage between individuals who are not related by blood.

Property

79. **Answer (D) is the best answer.** Here, the loss of the funds was not intentional. Further, John was not spending it on a non-marital purpose (notwithstanding that he might have enjoyed the painting more than she) and, in any event, the purchase was not made in anticipation of the breakup of the marriage. *See Nichols v. Nichols*, 2003 WL 1343212, at *1 (Ky. App. 2003) ("A spouse can be charged with the dissipation of marital assets only under clearly-defined circumstances. Kentucky courts have found dissipation of assets only where one party to the marriage has intentionally misappropriated or disposed of marital assets for non-marital purposes after separation or during a period when separation is clearly contemplated—but before entry of a decree.").

    Answer (A) is not the best answer. While the purchase of the painting was a bad investment, there was no indication that he anticipated that loss in value or that he anticipated the breakdown of the marriage. *See Morehead v. Morehead*, 2012 WL 1432311, at *5 (Neb. App. 2012) ("'Dissipation of marital assets' is defined as one spouse's use of marital property for a selfish purpose unrelated to the marriage at the time when the marriage is undergoing an irretrievable breakdown.").

    Answer (B) is incorrect. Had the painting increased in value, there would have been no temptation to think of this as dissipation, even though Mary still would not have liked the painting. He might well have been thinking of this as an investment to benefit the marriage rather than only himself, and there was no indication that he thought that the success of the marriage was in jeopardy. *Cf. In re Marriage of Drummond*, 509 N.E.2d 707, 715 (Ill. App. 1987) ("There was no evidence of intent to wilfully dissipate marital assets. . . . [T]he investments were made . . . when there was no indication whatsoever of marital discord. Since the investments were not made in contemplation of dissolution, the acts of husband do not constitute dissipation of marital assets.").

    Answer (C) is not the best answer. While even experts may make mistakes about whether a particular work of art is a good investment, that is not the relevant test. Rather, the question is whether the wasting was intentional and was in contemplation of the end of the relationship. *See In re Marriage of Drummond*, 509 N.E.2d 707, 715 (Ill. App. 1987).

80. **Answer (C) is the best answer.** Because Alex was not attempting to spend the monies on himself and because he was not acting in anticipation of the end of the marriage, he is unlikely to be found to have dissipated the funds. *See Reed v. Reed*, 763 N.W.2d 686, 695 (Neb. 2009). ("We have explained that 'dissipation of marital assets' is defined as one spouse's use of

marital property for a selfish purpose unrelated to the marriage at the time when the marriage is undergoing an irretrievable breakdown.").

Answer (A) is not the best answer. While Alex has indeed lost the marital assets, leaving Beatrice in the same financial position as she would have been had he spent those assets on himself, the test is not simply whether the assets were lost but whether the assets were spent on Alex himself in anticipation of the end of the marriage. *See Reed v. Reed*, 763 N.W.2d 686, 695 (Neb. 2009).

Answer (B) is not the best answer. While Alex may have been negligent, that is not the test for dissipation. *See Reed v. Reed*, 763 N.W.2d 686, 695 (Neb. 2009). *See also Mikhail v. Mikhail*, 2005-Ohio-322 (Ct. App.) (rejecting that poor investment strategy resulting in substantial losses qualifies for dissipation).

Answer (D) is incorrect. Dissipation of assets occurs before the marriage has been dissolved. *See Morehead v. Morehead*, 2012 WL 1432311, at *5 (Neb. App. 2012) ("Dissipation of marital assets is defined as one spouse's use of marital property for a selfish purpose unrelated to the marriage at the time when the marriage is undergoing an irretrievable breakdown."). Where dissipation has occurred, the dissipated funds will be attributed to the party guilty of the dissipation. *See Reed v. Reed*, 763 N.W.2d 686, 695 (Neb. 2009) ("As a remedy, we have held that marital assets dissipated by a spouse for purposes unrelated to the marriage should be included in the marital estate in dissolution actions.").

81.   **Answer (B) is the best answer.** Gambling when a marriage is irretrievably broken is a paradigmatic example of an activity that qualifies as dissipation. *See Gershman v. Gershman*, 943 A.2d 1091, 1094 (Conn. 2008) ("[C]ourts have traditionally recognized dissipation in the following paradigmatic contexts: gambling, support of a paramour, or the transfer of an asset to a third party for little or no consideration."). *See also Morehead v. Morehead*, 2012 WL 1432311, at *5 (Neb. App. 2012) ("'Dissipation of marital assets' is defined as one spouse's use of marital property for a selfish purpose unrelated to the marriage at the time when the marriage is undergoing an irretrievable breakdown.").

Answer (A) is incorrect. Where dissipation occurs, the lost funds can be attributed to the party who spent those funds. *See Romano v. Romano*, 632 So. 2d 207, 210 (Fla. App. 1994) ("Where marital misconduct results in a depletion or dissipation of marital assets, such misconduct can serve as a basis for an unequal division of marital property, or can be assigned to the spending spouse as part of that spouse's equitable distribution.").

Answer (C) is not the best answer. While it is true that there was some possibility that Mickey would have won money gambling and, further, that those winnings (if publicly acknowledged) would have been marital, gambling losses are nonetheless paradigmatic of those losses that might qualify as involving dissipation. *See Gershman v. Gershman*, 943 A.2d 1091, 1094 (Conn. 2008).

Answer (D) is not the best answer because overbroad. Individuals can act in ways that substantially decrease marital assets without being guilty of dissipation. *See Morehead v.*

Morehead, 2012 WL 1432311, at *5 (Neb. App. 2012) ("Dissipation of marital assets is defined as one spouse's use of marital property for a selfish purpose unrelated to the marriage at the time when the marriage is undergoing an irretrievable breakdown.").

82. **Answer (C) is the best answer.** A court can distribute separate property where the dissipation of marital property precludes an equitable distribution. *See Haslem v. Haslem*, 727 N.E.2d 928, 930 (Ohio App. 1999) ("Because the magistrate found that Mr. Haslem engaged in the dissipation and concealment of marital property, a distributive award of his separate assets or a greater award of marital property to Mrs. Haslem is warranted in this case.").

   Answer (A) is incorrect. While marital property should be divided equitably, there is no requirement that it be divided evenly, especially when one of the parties has dissipated the assets. *See Romano v. Romano*, 632 So. 2d 207, 210 (Fla. App. 1994) ("Where marital misconduct results in a depletion or dissipation of marital assets, such misconduct can serve as a basis for an unequal division of marital property, or can be assigned to the spending spouse as part of that spouse's equitable distribution.").

   Answer (B) is incorrect. In many jurisdictions, separate property can be reached to offset the effects of the dissipation of marital funds. *See Haslem v. Haslem*, 727 N.E.2d 928, 930 (Ohio App. 1999).

   Answer (D) is incorrect. A disproportionate share can be awarded even if the divorce is based on a no-fault ground. *Cf. Nowzaradan v. Nowzaradan*, 2007 WL 441709, at *7 (Tex. App. 2007) ("The trial court may . . . take into consideration that a spouse unfairly depleted or dissipated community assets and may . . . award the aggrieved party a judgment for the value of those assets as a means of equalizing the community estate.").

83. **Answer (B) is the best answer.** While the court could not itself transfer title to the property, *see Johnson v. Johnson*, 891 N.Y.S.2d 848, 850 (App. Div. 2009) (a divorce court cannot transfer title of real property located in another state), the court could order Pat to transfer title or could order Pat to sell the property. *See Buchanan v. Weber*, 567 S.E.2d 413, 416 (N.C. App. 2002) ("The Kansas court, having *in personam* jurisdiction, could . . . require defendant to execute a conveyance or sale of real property in North Carolina.").

   Answer (A) is incorrect. While the court would not have the power to transfer title, *see Johnson v. Johnson*, 891 N.Y.S.2d 848, 850 (App. Div. 2009), the court would be able to order Pat to sell the property and split the proceeds. *See Buchanan v. Weber*, 567 S.E.2d 413, 416 (N.C. 2002).

   Answer (C) is incorrect. The court would not have the power to perform that transfer. *See Johnson v. Johnson*, 891 N.Y.S.2d 848, 850 (App. Div. 2009).

   Answer (D) is incorrect. Custody decisions should not be made to punish parents, *see Black v. Black*, 456 S.W.3d 773, 778 (Ark. App. 2015) ("Custody awards are not made to punish or reward either parent."). Instead, they should be made in light of what would promote the best interests of the children. *See Baxter v. Borden*, 998 N.Y.S.2d 541, 542 (App. Div. 2014) ("[A]n award of custody must be based on the best interests of the children.").

84.   **Answer (D) is the best answer.** Property inherited by one party during a marriage is separate property and, absent extenuating circumstances, is unlikely to be subject to distribution. *See Sampson v. Sampson*, 14 P.3d 272, 276 (Alaska 2000) ("There is a strong presumption that inherited property is separate property not to be included in the disposition of property during a divorce.").

      Answer (A) is incorrect. As a general matter, property inherited by an individual during that person's marriage is separate property. *See Sampson v. Sampson*, 14 P.3d 272, 276 (Alaska 2000) ("Inherited property is separate, even if received during marriage.").

      Answer (B) is not the best answer. Merely because a vacation home that is separate property is used during a marriage need not change the character of that property into marital property. *See Rubin v. Rubin*, 767 N.Y.S.2d 96, 97 (App. Div. 2003) (suggesting that use of vacation home owned as separate property did not transmute it into marital property).

      Answer (C) is not correct. Property that is inherited by one party during a marriage is separate property. *See Sampson v. Sampson*, 14 P.3d 272, 276 (Alaska 2000). The non-inheriting party does not own that property and thus would not be able to make it a gift.

85.   **Answer (A) is the best answer.** Absent a statute specifying otherwise, the winnings will likely be treated as marital property subject to distribution because the ticket was purchased with marital assets during the marriage. *See Damon v. Damon*, 823 N.Y.S.2d 540, 541 (App. Div. 2006) ("[T]he proceeds of a winning lottery ticket acquired by a spouse during the marriage constitute marital property.").

      Answer (B) is not the best answer. Absent case law or statutory language to the contrary, the lottery winnings would likely be viewed as marital. *See In re Marriage of Morris*, 640 N.E.2d 344, 347 (Ill. App. 1994) (lottery winnings deemed marital even though lottery ticket was purchased while the husband and wife were living separately).

      Answer (C) is not the best answer. Even those winnings that would be distributed after the divorce was final would likely be considered marital and subject to distribution. *See In re Marriage of Morris*, 640 N.E.2d 344, 347 (Ill. App. 1994) ("The fact that the payments are made solely in petitioner's name and that the majority of the lottery payments would not be received until after entry of the judgment of dissolution of marriage does not change the fact that the winnings are marital property.").

      Answer (D) is not the best answer. The court is unlikely to characterize the winnings as marital or separate based solely on the reporting of the subjective views of the parties with respect to when the marriage was irretrievably broken. *See Damon v. Damon*, 823 N.Y.S.2d 540, 541 (App. Div. 2006); *In re Marriage of Morris*, 640 N.E.2d 344, 347 (Ill. App. 1994).

86.   **Answer (B) is the best answer.** The Corvette is marital because it was purchased using marital assets (Yvette's salary). *See Hobbs v. Hobbs*, 2017 WL 603555, at *1 (Mich. App. 2017) ("Any income earned during the marriage from employment, including wages, salaries, commissions, royalties, overtime, and similar payments, and including income from sources such as self-employment, partnerships, close corporations, and independent contracts, shall

be deemed marital property of the parties."). The painting is separate property because it was inherited by Wyatt alone. *See In re Marriage of Rigdon*, 896 N.W.2d 785 (Iowa App. 2017) (property inherited by either party during the marriage is separate property).

Answer (A) is incorrect. The Corvette is marital because it was purchased with marital funds. *See Hobbs v. Hobbs*, 2017 WL 603555, at *1 (Mich. App. 2017). The painting is separate because inherited solely by Wyatt. *See In re Marriage of Rigdon*, 896 N.W.2d 785 (Iowa App. 2017).

Answer (C) is incorrect. While Wyatt's property is separate, *see In re Marriage of Rigdon*, 896 N.W.2d 785 (Iowa App. 2017), Yvette's is not because it was purchased with marital funds (her salary). *See Hobbs v. Hobbs*, 2017 WL 603555, at *1 (Mich. App. 2017).

Answer (D) is incorrect. Property inherited by a single party during a marriage is separate rather than marital. *See In re Marriage of Rigdon*, 896 N.W.2d 785 (Iowa App. 2017).

87. **Answer (D) is the best answer.** Some states have a presumption regarding intent when interspousal gifts are made. *See Pearson v. Pearson*, 2016 WL 240683, at *6 (Tex. App. 2016) ("Interspousal transfers are presumed to be a gift and, thus, the separate property of the recipient spouse."). However, absent such a presumption or sufficient evidence of intent to make a gift of the painting as separate property, *see McCreery v. McCreery*, 2005 WL 2249594, at *2 (Va. Cir. Ct. 2005) ("The jewelry was simply a gift between the parties as spouses, and, as a result, the jewelry cannot be considered Wife's separate property."), the painting is likely to be treated as marital property and subject to distribution. *See Marshall-Beasley v. Beasley*, 77 So. 3d 751, 758 (Fla. App. 2011) ("Any gift of jewelry from Former Husband to Former Wife bought with marital assets remains a marital asset.").

Answer (A) is not the best answer. Merely because an individual gives his or her spouse a gift does not establish that the individual in addition wants that gift to be classified as separate property. *See Marshall-Beasley v. Beasley*, 77 So. 3d 751, 758 (Fla. App. 2011).

Answer (B) is incorrect. If the intent was to make this gift Miguel's separate property, then it would retain that classification even after the break-up of the marriage. *See Kelln v. Kelln*, 515 S.E.2d 789, 793–94 (Va. App. 1999) ("Where the facts clearly and unambiguously support the conclusion that one of the parties has relinquished all right and interest in marital property and has transferred those rights unconditionally to the other, to the exclusion of the donor's continuing claim upon the property as a marital asset . . . , a separate property right will be found to exist.").

Answer (C) is incorrect. If the intent to make the painting separate property is clear and unambiguous, it will likely be treated as separate property. *See Kelln v. Kelln*, 515 S.E.2d 789, 793–94 (Va. App. 1999).

88. **Answer (B) is the best answer.** The house was Whitney's separate property because she alone inherited it. It was titled solely in her name, so there was no presumption triggered that she made a gift to the marital estate by titling it in both of their names. *See Sandford v. McKee*, 2012 WL 4474177, at *5 (Tenn. App. 2012) (placing title in both names can create a presumption of a gift to the marital estate). Further, she maintained the house using separate funds, so the

194 ANSWERS · TOPIC 13: PROPERTY

house would remain her separate property and any increases in its value would also be separate. *See Stephens v. Stephens*, 899 N.W.2d 582, 593 (Neb. 2017) ("[A]ppreciation or income of separate property is marital property to the extent that it was caused by marital funds or marital efforts.").

Answer (A) is not the best answer. According to the law of most states, a house that was separate property will not become marital property solely because that house has been the marital domicile. *See Worden v. Worden*, 2017-Ohio-8019 (Ct. App.) (house that was separate property did not become marital merely because the parties to the marriage lived in it).

Answer (C) is incorrect. Separate funds retain their separate character as long as they are not commingled with marital (or community) funds. *See Kite v. Kite*, 2010 WL 1053014, at *3 (Tex. App. 2010).

Answer (D) is incorrect. Separate property can become partially marital if marital funds are used to improve it or to reduce a mortgage. *See Moran v. Moran*, 512 S.E.2d 834, 835 (Va. App. 1999).

89. **Answer (D) is the best answer.** Because Casey's apartment building was kept separate and no marital time, energy, or funds were invested in it, that apartment building is likely to be characterized as separate property. *See Bricker v. Bricker*, 877 P.2d 747, 751 (Wyo. 1994) ("The district court did not abuse its discretion in determining that the Pennsylvania farm was Carol's separate property. The record discloses that James made absolutely no contribution, by way of capital or effort, to the appreciation of that property. Carol did not invest any of her marital time or energies to increasing the value of the Pennsylvania farm."). Because Emerson invested marital time and energy in his building, the building may well be characterized as partly marital or, in the alternative, Casey might be thought owed some compensation for the marital investment in that building. *See Courembis v. Courembis*, 595 S.E.2d 505, 512 (Va. App. 2004) ("[T]he increase in value to separate property attributable to the significant personal contributions of *either* party renders that increase marital property.").

Answer (A) is incorrect. Merely because the apartment building was acquired before the marriage does not preclude it from becoming marital property at least in part if marital funds or marital time and effort are invested in it. *See Johnson v. Johnson*, 378 S.W.3d 889, 895 (Ark. App. 2011) ("When one spouse makes significant contributions of time, effort and skill that are directly attributable to the increase in value of nonmarital property, the presumption arises that such increase belongs to the marital estate.").

Answer (B) is incorrect. Separate property that is kept separate and does not have marital time, energy, or funds invested in it will remain separate property. *See Bricker v. Bricker*, 877 P.2d 747, 751 (Wyo. 1994).

Answer (C) is incorrect. If the apartment buildings are relevantly dissimilar in that marital time, energy, or funds were invested in one but not the other, then the characterization of the two need not be the same. *Compare Courembis v. Courembis*, 595 S.E.2d 505, 512 (Va. App. 2004) *with Bricker v. Bricker*, 877 P.2d 747, 751 (Wyo. 1994).

90.   **Answer (D) is the best answer.** Many states will provide some way to benefit the spouse when the other spouse earned a professional degree during the marriage, although not by treating the degree as marital property subject to distribution. *See Downs v. Downs*, 574 A.2d 156, 158 (Vt. 1990) ("The majority of courts . . . hold that a professional degree is not an asset subject to property distribution upon divorce, but, in the interest of justice and equity, fashion a maintenance award using the increased earning potential of the spouse with the degree as a relevant factor in determining an appropriate award."). However, relatively few courts do this by calling the degree property subject to distribution. *See Washburn v. Washburn*, 677 P.2d 152, 155 (Wash. 1984) ("A few appellate courts adopt the view that the professional degree (or the enhanced earning potential which it represents) is property which must be valued and distributed upon dissolution of the marriage.").

       Answer (A) is not the best answer. Many states deny that a professional degree constitutes marital property and is subject to division. *See Archer v. Archer*, 493 A.2d 1074, 1080 (Md. 1985) ("The latter is but an intellectual attainment; it is not a present property interest. It is personal to the holder; it cannot be sold, transferred, pledged or inherited."). *But see Lapham v. Ruflin*, 661 N.Y.S.2d 373, 374 (App. Div. 1997) ("It is well settled that a degree or professional license earned during the marriage is marital property subject to equitable distribution."). However, those states not treating professional degrees as property may try to account for the value of such a degree in other ways. *See*, for example, *Stevens v. Stevens*, 492 N.E.2d 131, 134 (Ohio 1986) ("[T]he future value of a medical degree acquired by one of the parties during the marriage was not subject to division or transfer upon divorce, but should be considered an element in reaching an equitable award of alimony.").

       Answer (B) is not the best answer. While the spouse may benefit when the other spouse acquired a professional degree during the marriage, that benefit is less likely to be calculated in terms of the opportunity cost and more likely to be calculated in terms of the enhanced earning power. *See Haspel v. Haspel*, 911 N.Y.S.2d 408, 410 (App. Div. 2010) ("Enhanced earnings from degrees and professional licenses attained during a marriage are subject to equitable distribution."); *Stevens v. Stevens*, 492 N.E.2d 131, 134 (Ohio 1986) ("the professional degree [is] relevant to the parties' earning abilities").

       Answer (C) is not the best answer. There may be difficulties in assessing the value of a professional degree. *See Downs v. Downs*, 574 A.2d 156, 158 (Vt. 1990) ("[A] professional degree, unlike a vested pension whose value can be readily computed, provides nothing more than the possibility of enhanced earnings that may never be realized."). Nonetheless, courts are not precluded from awarding the non-degree-earning spouse something. *See id.* ("The majority of courts . . . hold that a professional degree is not an asset subject to property distribution upon divorce, but, in the interest of justice and equity, fashion a maintenance award using the increased earning potential of the spouse with the degree as a relevant factor in determining an appropriate award.").

91.   **Answer (D) is the best answer.** The pension benefits earned during the marriage are marital and subject to distribution. Because John was married to Matthew for one-half of the years that John worked at Forever Corporation, one-half of the pension benefits are marital and

subject to distribution, which would mean that Matthew would be entitled to one-quarter of the benefits. *See In re Marriage of Hunt*, 909 P.2d 525, 531 (Colo. 1995) ("The 'time rule' formula includes a marital fraction, sometimes referred to as a 'coverture fraction,' which determines the marital interest in the pensions. The marital fraction consists of the numerator which is the number of years (or months if more accurate) that the employee spouse has earned towards the pension during the marriage, over the denominator, which is the number of years (or months if more accurate) of total service towards the pension.").

Answer (A) is incorrect. John earned about one-half of those benefits while he was married, making those benefits marital property. *See In re Marriage of Richardson*, 884 N.E.2d 1246, 1251 (Ill. App. 2008) ("[P]ension benefits earned during the marriage are considered marital property and, upon dissolution, are subject to division like any other property.").

Answer (B) is incorrect. While some of the pension benefits are marital property subject to distribution, those benefits earned before the marriage are separate property. *See Hutson v. Hutson*, 1993 WL 278457, at *3 (Tenn. App. 1993) ("The portion of a spouse's pension or other retirement benefits attributable to credible service prior to the marriage is separate property.").

Answer (C) is incorrect. Each spouse will have an interest in the pension benefits earned by the other spouse during the marriage. *See Carranza v. Gonzales*, 2016 WL 3101784, at *3 (Ariz. App. 2016) ("[E]ach spouse is entitled to one-half of the 'community's interest' in the other's pension.").

92.   **Answer (D) is the best answer.** The New Arizico court likely had jurisdiction to grant the divorce, assuming that William can establish that he is domiciled there in light of his new job, his new apartment, his registering to vote, his opening a bank account, and his getting a new driver's license. Nonetheless, Wanda can challenge the court's jurisdiction to divide property located in Wardaho, given Wanda's lack of connection to New Arizico. *See Ferrari v. Ferrari*, 585 S.W.2d 546 (Mo. App. 1979) (upholding court's having jurisdiction to grant a divorce because one of the parties is domiciled there but denying that the court has jurisdiction to divide property located elsewhere because the other party has no connections to the state).

Answer (A) is incorrect. Wanda can challenge the property division even if the court had jurisdiction to grant the divorce. *See In re Marriage of Berry*, 155 S.W.3d 838 (Mo. App. 2005).

Answer (B) is incorrect. Merely because a court has jurisdiction to grant a divorce does not establish that the court has jurisdiction to divide marital property. *See In re Marriage of Berry*, 155 S.W.3d 838 (Mo. App. 2005).

Answer (C) is incorrect. Wanda is not required to travel to another state more than 1,000 miles away to protect her property interests. *See In re Marriage of Berry*, 155 S.W.3d 838 (Mo. App. 2005) (wife was not subject to jurisdiction of Missouri court granting divorce and thus property division was void).

93.   **Answer (B) is the best answer.** While the court would have the power to grant the divorce, courts are split with respect to whether, in addition, the court would have the power to divide

property within the state. *Compare Fox v. Fox*, 559 S.W.2d 407, 410 (Tex. Civ. App. 1977) ("a Texas court may grant an ex parte divorce . . . [and] may even divide property within its jurisdiction") *with Singh v. Gomar*, 1994 WL 1031093, at *1 (Va. Cir. Ct. 1994) ("Based on the domicile of the plaintiff, and lacking personal jurisdiction over the defendant, this Court is limited to an in rem proceeding addressing only the marriage itself, not any property or support issues arising from it.").

Answer (A) is incorrect. Even though the New Arizico court did not have jurisdiction over Wanda, that would not preclude the court from granting the divorce. *See Ferrari v. Ferrari*, 585 S.W.2d 546 (Mo. App. 1979) (upholding court's having jurisdiction to grant a divorce because one of the parties was domiciled there, had met the residency requirement, and had given the other party notice).

Answer (C) is not the best answer. As a general matter, Wanda is not required to travel to another state more than 1,000 miles away to protect her property interests, and the court would not have had jurisdiction to divide property not located in that jurisdiction. *See In re Marriage of Berry*, 155 S.W.3d 838 (Mo. Ct. App. 2005) (wife was not subject to jurisdiction of Missouri court granting divorce and thus property division was void).

Answer (D) is not the best answer, in that courts are split with respect to whether a court would have jurisdiction to divide property located in the state under these circumstances. *Compare Fox v. Fox*, 559 S.W.2d 407, 410 (Tex. Civ. App. 1977) *with Singh v. Gomar*, 1994 WL 1031093, at *1 (Va. Cir. Ct. 1994).

94.   **Answer (D) is the best answer.** The painting would have been characterized as marital property had they been divorcing in New Vermshire. *See Miller v. Miller*, 2007 WL 2592465, at *6 (Va. App. 2007) ("[P]roperty acquired during the marriage is not the 'sole' property of one spouse, so neither spouse can 'keep or retain sole ownership,' even if all purchases are financed with the salary of one spouse."). However, because they are divorcing in Orington, the property will be classified as quasi-community property, because it would have been classified as community property had it been acquired in a community property state. *See* Cal. Fam. Code § 125 ("'Quasi–community property' means all real or personal property, wherever situated, acquired before or after the operative date of this code in any of the following ways: (a) By either spouse while domiciled elsewhere which would have been community property if the spouse who acquired the property had been domiciled in this state at the time of its acquisition. (b) In exchange for real or personal property, wherever situated, which would have been community property if the spouse who acquired the property so exchanged had been domiciled in this state at the time of its acquisition.").

Answer (A) is incorrect. Because it was purchased with salary earned during the marriage, it was purchased with marital funds and thus would not be separate property. *See Miller v. Miller*, 2007 WL 2592465, at *6 (Va. App. 2007).

Answer (B) is not the best answer. While property purchased from a salary earned during the marriage would be community property if this occurred in a community property state, *see Zemke v. Zemke*, 860 P.2d 756, 760 (N.M. App. 1993), ("the stock he purchased with salary bonuses and adjustments during the marriage was community property"), New Vermshire is not a community property state, so the painting would not be community property but instead marital property. *See Hopper v. Hopper*, 171 P.3d 124, 131 (Alaska 2007) ("Assets acquired during marriage as compensation for marital services—most commonly salaries earned by either spouse during marriage—are considered marital assets.").

Answer (C) is not the best answer. While it is true that this would be characterized as marital property if Orington were a common law state, *see Miller v. Miller*, 2007 WL 2592465, at *6 (Va. App. 2007), Orington is a community property state and Orington rather than New Vermshire will be the state characterizing the property.

95.   The appropriate characterizations of the watch and car depend upon donor intent, so more information may well be required. In many states, designating something as a gift will not suffice to establish that the individual giving the gift intended to relinquish all interest in that gift. *See Cameron v. Cameron*, 715 P.2d 1246, 1247 (Ariz. App. 1985). Nonetheless, an individual can make a gift of a car to a spouse and thereby make that gift the separate property of the spouse. *See In re Marriage of Mason*, 155 Cal. Rptr. 350, 355 (Ct. App. 1979).

Some states assume that interspousal gifts, whether cars or jewelry, are marital property subject to distribution. *See Ruiz v. Ruiz*, 548 So. 2d 699, 700 (Fla. App. 1989) ("[I]t is uncontroverted that the jewelry was purchased during the marriage and with marital funds. As such, it became subject to equitable distribution."). However, other states will treat an interspousal gift as separate property if there is sufficient evidence that the individual intended to relinquish all interest in it. *See Errington v. Errington*, 2002-Ohio-1419, at *3 (Ct. App.) ("We view all of the foregoing to be clear and convincing evidence that this jewelry was given as a gift.").

96.   Depending upon state law, the marital estate may well be owed monies because marital assets were used to reduce the mortgage debt. The increased equity resulting from the payments would be subject to distribution. *See Adkins v. Adkins*, 650 So. 2d 61, 66 (Fla. App. 1994). However, the credit or reimbursement would not be for all of the payments made (because that would include payments for interest), but merely be for the increase in equity in the house. *See Longo v. Longo*, 474 So. 2d 500, 503 (La. App. 1985).

Some states would not credit the marital estate at all, notwithstanding that the mortgage payments were made with marital funds. *See Vail-Beserini v. Beserini*, 654 N.Y.S.2d 471, 473 (App. Div. 1997) ("Marital funds used to pay off the debt on separate property are to be credited to the marital estate only where the indebtedness was the result of expenditures for improvements or renovations to the separate property.").

Custody/Visitation

97.   **Answer (C) is the best answer.** John is likely to be awarded custody as long as he is a fit parent and his having custody would not be detrimental to the children. *See Smith v. Smith*, 97 So. 3d 43, 46 (Miss. 2012) ("The natural-parent presumption can be rebutted by a clear showing that (1) the parent has abandoned the child; (2) the parent has deserted the child; (3) the parent's conduct is so immoral as to be detrimental to the child; or (4) the parent is unfit, mentally or otherwise, to have custody.").

   Answer (A) is not the best answer because it understates the preference given to legally recognized parents. *See Davis v. Vaughn*, 126 So. 3d 33, 37 (Miss. 2013) ("Giving preference to natural parents, even against those who have stood in their place, honors and protects the fundamental right of natural parents to rear their children.").

   Answer (B) is not the best answer. As a general matter, the stepparent must do more than establish that awarding the children to him or her would promote the children's best interests. *See Olvera v. Superior Court In & For Cty. of Yuma*, 815 P.2d 925, 926 (Ariz. App. 1991) (holding that stepparent could not be awarded custody of child).

   Answer (D) is not the best answer. The children are not old enough for their preference to be given significant weight. *See JR v. TLW*, 371 P.3d 570, 575 (Wyo. 2016) ("[T]heir ages — eight and nine at the time of trial — do not provide significant weight."). Further, this would not give adequate weight to the presumption in favor of the natural parent. *See Smith v. Smith*, 97 So. 3d 43, 46 (Miss. 2012).

98.   **Answer (C) is the best answer.** The tender years presumption, where recognized, is a rebuttable presumption that it is better to award custody of young children to the mother. This presumption is only one of many factors to consider in a custody decision. *See Gillespie v. Gillespie*, 590 S.W.2d 420, 423 (Mo. App. 1979) ("[I]t is merely a rebuttable presumption and, therefore, not conclusive on the issue of child custody."). While the failure to consider the presumption might be the basis for a remand, that failure might also be considered harmless error where there is other evidence in the record to support the trial court's determination. *See Webb v. Webb*, 974 So. 2d 274, 277 (Miss. App. 2008) ("We cannot find that the chancellor's conclusion on this issue rises to the level of manifest error, and certainly does not warrant reversal, since the tender years doctrine is only a presumption to be considered along with the other . . . factors.").

   Answer (A) is incorrect. The presumption does not involve the age of the parent but the age of the children. *See Gooding v. Gooding*, 477 S.W.3d 774, 777 n.1 (Tenn. App. 2015) ("The tender years doctrine is a presumption that young children should remain in their mother's custody.").

Answer (B) is incorrect. The presumption is not about when children's preferences should be given weight, but when children are rebuttably presumed to be better off if the mother has custody. *See Gooding v. Gooding*, 477 S.W.3d 774, 777 n.1 (Tenn. App. 2015).

Answer (D) is incorrect. Assuming that the tender years presumption is employed and not held unconstitutional, *see Ex parte Devine*, 398 So. 2d 686, 696 (Ala. 1981) (striking down tender years presumption as a violation of equal protection guarantees), it is still only a rebuttable presumption. *See Harper v. Harper*, 229 S.E.2d 875, 877 (Va. 1976) (suggesting that the presumption is "no more than a permissible and rebuttable inference, that when the mother is fit, and other things are equal, she, as the natural custodian, should have custody of a child of tender years").

99.   **Answer (C) is the best answer.** The most important consideration is promoting the best interest of the child. *See Albright v. Albright*, 437 So. 2d 1003, 1004 (Miss. 1983) ("[T]he cardinal principle to be applied to custody decisions is that which is in the best interests and welfare of the minor child."). The child's expressed preference is not determinative. *See Phillips v. Phillips*, 45 So. 3d 684, 694 (Miss. App. 2010) ("The child's preference is not outcome determinative."), and a court's decision to reject a stated preference may be upheld if reasonable. *See Phillips v. Phillips*, 45 So. 3d 684 (Miss. App. 2010) (awarding joint custody rather than placing child in father's custody in accord with her stated preference). For example, a court might reject a stated preference because the child is choosing the parent who exercises no control over the child. *See Brown v. Brown*, 606 S.E.2d 785, 789 (S.C. App. 2004) ("The child's preference will be given little weight where the wishes of the child are influenced by the permissive attitude of the preferred parent.").

Answer (A) is incorrect. The expressed preferences of a mature child are but one factor and are not themselves dispositive. *See McKay v. Mitzel*, 137 N.W.2d 792, 794–95 (N.D. 1965) ("In determining an award of custody, the court may consider the wishes of the children where such children have reached the age of discretion, although such preference is not controlling on the court.").

Answer (B) is incorrect. A mature child's express preference should be given legal weight. *See Mosbrucker v. Mosbrucker*, 562 N.W.2d 390, 393 (N.D. 1997) ("In determining the child's best interests, the preference of the child is a factor the trial court should consider.").

Answer (D) is incorrect. A trial court's refusal to consider a child's preference can be the basis for reversing the decision. *See Holiday v. Holiday*, 247 P.3d 29, 30 (Wyo. 2011) ("We conclude the district court erred in not considering the oldest son's preference and reverse.").

100. **Answer (C) is the best answer.** The ability to promote a relationship with the other parent is considered, but it is only one factor among many when determining custody. *See Maska v. Maska*, 742 N.W.2d 492, 496–97 (Neb. 2007) ("While the promotion and facilitation of a relationship with the noncustodial parent is a factor that may be considered, it is not the only factor nor is it a completely determinative factor.").

Answer (A) is incorrect. The ability to promote a relationship with the other parent is one of the factors considered in determining which parent's having custody would promote the child's best interests. *See Koch v. Koch*, 993 N.Y.S.2d 794, 795 (App. Div. 2014) (discussing relevant factors, including the parent's "willingness to foster a positive relationship between the child and the other parent").

Answer (B) is incorrect. While the ability to promote a relationship with the other parent is a factor to be considered, it is only one factor among many and is not itself dispositive. *See Plowman v. Plowman*, 597 A.2d 701, 704 (Pa. Super. 1991) ("[O]ne parent's ability to promote a continuing relationship with the other is only one factor to be considered.").

Answer (D) is incorrect. The ability to foster a relationship with the other parent is a factor and is not merely a tiebreaker. *See Koch v. Koch*, 993 N.Y.S.2d 794, 795 (App. Div. 2014).

101.   **Answer (B) is the best answer.** This is not the kind of material change that would justify a modification of custody, especially because Robert might benefit from Oscar's increase in salary in other ways — the court might increase Oscar's support obligation rather than modify custody. *See Powell v. Powell*, 976 So. 2d 358, 361 (Miss. Ct. App. 2008) ("A modification of custody requires the noncustodial parent to prove: (1) that a material change of circumstances has occurred in the custodial home since the most recent custody decree, (2) that the change adversely affects the child, and (3) that modification is in the best interest of the child.").

Answer (A) is incorrect. For purposes of modifying custody, the material or significant change must be one that adversely affects the child. *See Powell v. Powell*, 976 So. 2d 358, 361 (Miss. App. 2008). Oscar's salary increase might simply result in a change in child support, which means that Robert will presumably benefit even if the custodial arrangement remains the same.

Answer (C) is incorrect. If the noncustodial parent's subjective belief were the test, then the test would be met whenever that parent sincerely believed that there had been a substantial change. But such a standard would result in much litigation and would be very destabilizing for the child. *See Geren Williams v. Geren*, 458 S.W.3d 759, 766 (Ark. App. 2015) ("[C]ourts impose more stringent standards for modifications in custody than they do for initial determinations of custody in order to promote stability and continuity in the life of the child and to discourage repeated litigation of the same issues.").

Answer (D) is incorrect. Merely because a child believes a change significant does not establish that there has been a change that significantly affects the child's well-being. *See Boyer v. Heimermann*, 238 S.W.3d 249, 256 (Tenn. App. 2007) (discussing "whether the change is one that affects the child's well-being in a meaningful way").

102.   **Answer (D) is the best answer.** A parent's trying to alienate the child from the other parent can in extreme cases result in a modification of custody. *See F.S.-P. v. A.H.R.*, 844 N.Y.S.2d 644, 645 (Fam. Ct. 2007) (defining "parental alienation as the 'extreme denigration by one parent of the other parent, or the indoctrination and brainwashing' of the child to turn him against the parent . . ."). When parental alienation is extreme, it can be the basis for a

modification of custody. *See*, for example, *Hanson v. Spolnik*, 685 N.E.2d 71, 78 (Ind. App. 1997) (modifying custody after noting that "Marianne made numerous disparaging comments about, and allegations against, Edward in front of M.S. and others, including comments that M.S. would have to be decontaminated after wearing Edward's hat and that her father hired a hit man").

Answer (A) is not the best answer. Parental alienation in this context does not involve one parent being alienated from the other parent but, instead, one parent trying to alienate the child from the other parent. *See McClain v. McClain*, 539 S.W.3d 170, 175 (Tenn. App. 2017) (discussing "a case of severe parental alienation in which the father had actively supported the children's alienation from the mother without reasonable cause").

Answer (B) is incorrect. Parental alienation does not involve one of the parents becoming temporarily alienated from parenting but, instead, one of the parents trying to alienate the child from the other parent. *See*, for example, *F.S.-P. v. A.H.R.*, 844 N.Y.S.2d 644, 645 (Fam. Ct. 2007).

Answer (C) is incorrect. Parental alienation does not involve one parent's refusing to act like a parent but instead one parent's seeking to alienate the child from the other parent. *See F.S.-P. v. A.H.R.*, 844 N.Y.S.2d 644, 645 (Fam. Ct. 2007).

103.   **Answer (D) is the best answer.** The original decree was made in New Caledonia, where Charlie, Anne, and Devon continue to reside. New Caledonia would continue to have jurisdiction for a custody modification so Skyler should have filed there when he sought to modify custody. *See Gorup v. Brady*, 46 N.E.3d 832, 839 (Ill. App. 2015) ("[T]he UCCJEA requires a finding that the initial state has either ceded jurisdiction or that no party presently resides in that state (thus ending exclusive, continuing jurisdiction).").

Answer (A) is not the best answer. Skyler filed in the wrong place, so the Old Jersey court should not address the merits. *See Gorup v. Brady*, 46 N.E.3d 832, 839 (Ill. App. 2015). Even had Skyler filed in the correct jurisdiction, he does not seem to have met his burden to show that there has been a material change in circumstances adversely affecting Ann and Devon. He would likely be unsuccessful even if Charlie had not remarried. *See Hall v. Hall*, 134 So. 3d 822, 825 (Miss. App. 2014) ("To successfully move to modify custody of a child, a noncustodial parent must prove (1) that a substantial change in circumstances has transpired since issuance of the custody decree, (2) that this change adversely affects the child's welfare, and (3) that the child's best interests mandate a change of custody.").

Answer (B) is not the best answer. Skyler has filed in the wrong place. *See Gorup v. Brady*, 46 N.E.3d 832, 839 (Ill. App. 2015). Even had he filed with the correct court, his showing that he could now provide a good home for the children would not suffice to show that there had been a material change in circumstances adversely affecting the children. *See Hall v. Hall*, 134 So. 3d 822, 825 (Miss. App. 2014).

Answer (C) is not the best answer. Skyler has filed in the wrong jurisdiction. *See Gorup v. Brady*, 46 N.E.3d 832, 839 (Ill. App. 2015). Even had this been the correct jurisdiction, Skyler would have had to do more to show that there had been a material change in the circumstances adversely affecting the children. *Cf. Hall v. Hall*, 134 So. 3d 822, 825 (Miss. App. 2014). Had there been such a change, then a factor in the analysis would be whether Ann and Devon got along with their new stepparent. *See Looney v. Looney*, 536 So. 2d 728, 732 (La. App. 1988) (justifying the change in custody by looking at a variety of considerations, including that the children had a strong relationship with their stepmother).

104. **Answer (D) is the best answer.** Skyler will have to show that there has been a material change in circumstances adversely affecting Ann and Devon, and that his having custody would promote their best interests. *See Hall v. Hall*, 134 So. 3d 822, 825 (Miss. App. 2014) ("To successfully move to modify custody of a child, a noncustodial parent must prove (1) that a substantial change in circumstances has transpired since issuance of the custody decree, (2) that this change adversely affects the child's welfare, and (3) that the child's best interests mandate a change of custody.").

 Answer (A) is not the best answer. Merely because Skyler has remarried and gotten a new job does not establish that there has been a material change in circumstances adversely affecting the children. *See*, for example, *McDonald v. McDonald*, 840 N.W.2d 573, 582 (Neb. App. 2013) (ex-husband's new job did not qualify as a material change in circumstances); *McEvoy v. Brewer*, 2003 WL 22794521, at *4 (Tenn. App. 2003) ("Remarriage, by itself, is not the sort of change in circumstances that triggers a re-examination of an existing custody arrangement because remarriage is such a common occurrence in contemporary society that it can reasonably be anticipated when parties divorce."). Further, even if Charlie had remarried and advanced professionally, this would not establish that the children would be better off there. For example, if Ann and Devon felt endangered by Charlie's new spouse or stepchildren, that might provide the basis for a custody modification. *See Graves v. Stockigt*, 911 N.Y.S.2d 705, 706 (App. Div. 2010) (granting request for custody modification for several reasons, including that the stepfather was abusive).

 Answer (B) is not the best answer. Merely because Skyler can provide a good home for the children does not establish that there has been a material change in circumstances adversely affecting the children. *See Hall v. Hall*, 134 So. 3d 822, 825 (Miss. App. 2014).

 Answer (C) is not the best answer because the determination of custody will not be determined solely by looking at Ann and Devon's relationship with Casey. Skylar will have to establish that there has been a material change in circumstances adversely affecting Ann and Devon. *See Hall v. Hall*, 134 So. 3d 822, 825 (Miss. App. 2014). Were he able to establish the material change in circumstances, then one of the factors to be considered would involve the relationship between Casey and the children. *See Looney v. Looney*, 536 So. 2d 728, 732 (La. App. 1988).

105. **Answer (D) is the best answer.** Assuming that no emergency exists that might justify the Florabama courts having jurisdiction, *see Bradfield v. Urias*, 2018 WL 560406, at *3 (Kan. App. 2018) ("[T]he Kansas court lacked subject matter jurisdiction unless there was an emergency."), the West Delolina court had continuing and exclusive jurisdiction to decide

whether custody should be modified because Dakota still lives there and because the children would visit Dakota there. *See In re Forlenza*, 140 S.W.3d 373, 377 (Tex. 2004) (state initially granting decree has continuing exclusive jurisdiction to decide modification of custody if noncustodial parent continues to live there and the state has sufficient contacts with children, e.g., because they visit the noncustodial parent there). The West Delolina court could decline to exercise jurisdiction, but that would be a decision for the West Delolina court rather than the Floramaba court. *See White v. Harrison-White*, 760 N.W.2d 691, 696 (Mich. App. 2008) (under the UCCJEA, a court with continuing exclusive jurisdiction can decline to exercise that jurisdiction, e.g., because it is an inconvenient forum).

Answer (A) is not the best answer. The Florabama court would not have jurisdiction to decide this matter, *see In re Forlenza*, 140 S.W.3d 373, 377 (Tex. 2004), and it is simply false that children will never be believed because they contradicted what an adult has said. *Cf. State v. Hebert*, 480 A.2d 742 (Me. 1984) (jury believed child's accusation of sexual abuse rather than father's denial).

Answer (B) is not the best answer because the Florabama court would not have had jurisdiction. *See In re Forlenza*, 140 S.W.3d 373, 377 (Tex. 2004). A separate issue would have involved whether the allegations were in fact true. *Compare State v. Hebert*, 480 A.2d 742 (Me. 1984) (jury believed child's accusation of sexual abuse rather than father's denial) *with In re A.N.F.*, 2008 WL 4334712, at *2 (Tenn. App. 2008) (suggesting that allegations of sexual abuse were fabricated).

Answer (C) is not the best answer. The Florabama court will not have jurisdiction simply because Florabama is the children's home state. Because Dakota still lives in West Delolina and because the children have visited Dakota there, the West Delolina court would continue to have jurisdiction. *See In re Forlenza*, 140 S.W.3d 373, 377 (Tex. 2004).

106.   **Answer (D) is the best answer.** Paris will likely be permitted to relocate with the children as long as she can establish that doing so would promote their best interests. *See Wheeler v. Wheeler*, 591 S.E.2d 698, 703 (Va. App. 2004) (affirming granting custodial parent permission to relocate because "it was in the children's best interests to move to Florida").

Answer (A) is not the best answer. While relocation requests are sometimes denied out of a concern that the relocation would impair the relationship with the noncustodial parent, *see C.M.K. v. K.E.M.*, 45 A.3d 417, 429 (Pa. Super. 2012), the relationship between Pat and the children does not seem very strong and it is not at all clear that relocation would significantly affect the visitation that actually occurs. *See In re Custody of Curtis L.S.*, 824 N.Y.S.2d 768 (Fam. Ct. 2006) ("This Court further finds that Respondent Mother's visitation has been so inconsistent and sporadic that it is not clear that relocation would substantially interfere with her rights as a practical matter.").

Answer (B) is incorrect. The court would not be denying Paris the right to travel but merely denying Paris the right to relocate with the children, presumably because such a move would not promote the children's interests. *See Fredman v. Fredman*, 960 So. 2d 52, 59 (Fla. App. 2007) ("[T]he relocation statute requires the court to consider the competing interests, with an appropriate focus on the parents' rights, along with the best interest of the child. There-fore, the statute does not violate the Mother's right to travel.").

Answer (C) is not the best answer. While Paris might be prevented from relocating if the relocation would benefit her but harm the children, she would not be prevented from relo-cating if her doing so would both help her career and promote the best interests of the children. *See Petry v. Petry*, 589 S.E.2d 458, 465 (Va. App. 2003) ("A trial court may consider a benefit to the custodial parent from relocation so long as the move independently benefits the children.").

107.   **Answer (B) is the best answer.** As a general matter, states require that a relocation request be in good faith and for a legitimate reason. One parent attempting to interfere with the other parent's relationship with the children will not be viewed as legitimate, *see Harrison v. Mor-gan*, 191 P.3d 617, 624–25 (Okla. Civ. App. 2008) ("[T]his best interest test or balancing of the relocation factors need not occur unless the trial court has determined the relocating par-ent has carried his or her burden to prove that 'the proposed relocation is made in good faith.' If not, nothing further is required."), absent some reason to believe that the latter parent's having contact with the children would be detrimental to them. *See Watkins v. Lee*, 227 So. 3d 84, 86 (Ala. Civ. App. 2017) ("A noncustodial parent generally enjoys 'reasonable rights of visitation' with his or her children. . . . However, those rights may be restricted in order to protect children from conduct, conditions, or circumstances surrounding their non-custodial parent that endanger the children's health, safety, or well-being.").

Answer (A) is not the best answer if Sarah is correct that Robert's primary motivation is to undermine the relationship between Sarah and the children. *See Perez v. Perez*, 85 So. 3d 273, 280 (La. App. 2012) ("Relocation is a two-prong test, requiring that the relocating par-ent prove that the proposed relocation is made in good faith and that it is in the best interest of the child.").

Answer (C) is not the best answer if Sarah is able to demonstrate that the relocation request is being made in bad faith. *See Perez v. Perez*, 85 So. 3d 273, 280 (La. App. 2012).

Answer (D) is not the best answer. While Sarah's inability to see the children as frequently would be a factor that would be considered, it would not be dispositive. There might be other ways to assure that the children spend a significant amount of time with their mother, e.g., by lengthening the visits when the children are with her. *See In re Marriage of Burgess*, 913 P.2d 473, 484 (Cal. 1996) ("[T]he trial court has broad discretion to modify orders concern-ing contact and visitation to minimize the minor children's loss of contact and visitation with the noncustodial parent in the event of a move, e.g., by increasing the amount of visitation with the noncustodial parent during vacations from school, allocating transportation expenses to the custodial parent, or requiring the custodial parent to provide transportation of the children to the noncustodial parent's home.").

108.   **Answer (D) is the best answer.** Here, where the move would likely undermine the children's relationship with their mother and move them far from extended family and take them out of a school and home environment where they were thriving, a court might well modify

custody rather than permit the children to move. *See H.H. v. A.A.*, 3 N.E.3d 30, 38 (Ind. Ct. App. 2014) (refusing to permit relocation of child when child was thriving where she was and the move would take her far from extended family).

Answer (A) is not the best answer. Jurisdictions differ as to whether a proposed relocation amounts to a material change in circumstances. *See Gerot v. Gerot*, 61 S.W.3d 890, 895 (Ark. App. 2001) ("A custodial parent's move that is made in order to better his or her financial ability to provide for a child is not, in and of itself, a material change in circumstances to be used to the detriment of that parent."). In any event, a proposed relocation in combination with other factors might well suffice to establish the requisite change in circumstances. Here, not only would it be more difficult for the children to have frequent contact with Ursula, but they would move far from extended family and would have to leave their current schools. *See Arnott v. Arnott*, 293 P.3d 440, 458 (Wyo. 2012) ("[A] relocation by the primary physical custodian, as well as 'factors that are derivative of the relocation'—including 'the inherent difficulties that the increase in geographical distance between parents imposes'—may constitute a material change in circumstances sufficient to warrant consideration of the best interests of the children.").

Answer (B) is not the best answer. While Ulysses' desire to live with his new spouse is understandable, he would likely have to show that the move would not only benefit him, but would also benefit his children and would not severely undermine the children's relationship with their mother. *See Russenberger v. Russenberger*, 654 So. 2d 207, 212 (Fla. App. 1995) ("In these cases, the court not only must weigh the interests of the children, the primary interest to be considered, but also the interests of the custodial parent, who many times see a substantial advantage in relocation, and the interests of the noncustodial parent, who, as a result of a relocation, may effectively lose visitation rights and certainly may have greatly reduced contact with the children.").

Answer (C) is not the best answer. While the relocation might benefit the parent, it might harm the children, especially because a move might undermine their relationship with the noncustodial parent. *See In re Marriage of Melville*, 18 Cal. Rptr. 3d 685, 693 (Ct. App. 2004) ("[T]he noncustodial parent bears the initial burden of showing that the proposed relocation of the children's residence would cause detriment to the children, requiring a reevaluation of the children's custody. The likely impact of the proposed move on the noncustodial parent's relationship with the children is a relevant factor in determining whether the move would cause detriment to the children and, when considered in light of all the relevant factors, may be sufficient to justify a change in custody.").

109.   When deciding which parent's having custody would best promote Brian's interests, the court should consider a number of factors. Some jurisdictions only consider a parent's having committed adultery a negative factor if the adultery has a negative impact on the child. *See Smith v. Smith*, 39 So. 3d 458, 461 (Fla. App. 2010) ("[W]hen a parent's alleged adultery is at issue, as in the case here, the act of adultery should not be taken into consideration in determining custody if the trial court finds that the spouse's adultery does not have any bearing on the children's welfare."). However, other jurisdictions might consider a parent's having

committed adultery as a negative factor because it speaks to that parent's moral fitness. *See Burge v. Burge*, 223 So. 3d 888, 898 (Miss. App. 2017) ("Moral fitness favored Craig, as Kelly admitted to post-separation adultery and had a pre-separation infatuation with Burke."). In addition, it is important for the custodial parent to support the relationship with the noncustodial parent, *see Schutz v. Schutz*, 581 So. 2d 1290, 1292 (Fla. 1991) ("[A] custodial parent has an affirmative obligation to encourage and nurture the relationship between the child and the noncustodial parent."), and the court will have to assess whether both Reese and Robin can do that. In appropriate circumstances, a court might order a shared parenting arrangement. *See Clouse v. Clouse*, 2009-Ohio-1301 (Ct. App. 2009) (affirming adoption of shared parenting arrangement), although successful shared parenting requires that the parents cooperate with each other. *See Seng v. Seng*, 2008-Ohio-6758, ¶ 21 (Ct. App. 2008) ("Successful shared parenting requires . . . a strong commitment to cooperate [and] . . . a capacity to engage in the cooperation required."). The trial court will have to decide whether shared parenting would be a realistic option in this case.

110. A parent petitioning for a modification of custody must establish that there has been a material change in circumstances and that the children's best interests would be promoted by granting that petition. *See Curtiss v. Curtiss*, 891 N.W.2d 358, 361 (N.D. 2017) ("To modify parenting time, the moving party must demonstrate a material change in circumstances has occurred since entry of the previous parenting time order and that the modification is in the best interests of the child."). While Alfred and Beatrice are old enough and may well be mature enough to express a preference regarding the parent with whom they wish to live, that alone may not satisfy the requirement that a material change in circumstances have occurred. *See Mulkey-Yelverton v. Blevins*, 884 P.2d 41, 43 (Wyo. 1994) (14-year-old's express preference to live with other parent did not establish that a material change in circumstances had occurred). *But see Parkerson v. Parkerson*, 306 S.E.2d 97, 98 (Ga. App. 1983) ("A child's selection of the parent with whom he desires to live, where the child has reached 14 years of age, is controlling absent a finding that such parent is unfit."). Here, however, the children have not merely stated a preference. They have discussed their fear of their stepfather. This new living situation might well suffice to establish that there has been a material change in circumstances. *See Wilson v. Phillips*, 2017 WL 5495402, at *25 (Tenn. App. 2017) ("The presence of the stepfather in the home and the consequent change in the home environment to one of strained relations and apprehension satisfies the requirement of changed circumstances."). Assuming that there was good reason to fear their stepfather, these changed circumstances would likely justify a modification of custody. *See Overturf v. Leverett*, 702 So. 2d 469, 470 (Ala. Civ. App. 1997) (upholding custody modification because of child's fear of stepfather).

111. A parent seeking to modify custody must establish that there has been a material change in circumstances adversely affecting the child. *See Curtiss v. Curtiss*, 891 N.W.2d 358, 361 (N.D. 2017). Mere disapproval of an ex-spouse's marital partner does not establish that there has been a material change in circumstances adversely affecting the child. *See In re Marriage of Collins*, 51 P.3d 691, 693 (Or. App. 2002) ("The fact that mother's companion was of the same sex may have been significant to father; he frankly testified that he disapproved of mother's 'lifestyle.' But it is not and cannot be significant to this court."). If Barbara can show that the

new living arrangement would somehow pose a serious risk of harm to Ronald, then she might be successful when seeking to modify custody.

112.   As a general matter, states consider both the biological and the adoptive parent as each having parental rights. *See In re Lilly S. v. Kenny S.*, 903 N.W.2d 651, 662 (Neb. 2017) ("Unless it has been affirmatively shown that a biological or adoptive parent is unfit or has forfeited his or her right to custody, the U.S. Constitution and sound public policy protect a parent's right to custody of his or her child."); *In re D.B.J.*, 286 P.3d 1201, 1206 (Mont. 2012) ("Under Montana law, the legal 'parent-child relationship' only encompasses natural or adoptive parents."). In this kind of case, the court would award custody to the parent whose having custody would promote the best interests of the child. *See Matter of Guardianship of Williams*, 869 P.2d 661, 665 (Kan. 1994) ("The Kansas courts have long applied the best interests of the child test in resolving custody disputes between two fit parents.").

113.   Some jurisdictions will treat a natural or adoptive parent on the one hand and a stepparent on the other as on a par in a custody dispute, as long as the stepparent has a parent-child relationship with the child whose custody is in dispute. *See In re Marriage of Sleeper*, 982 P.2d 1126, 1130 (Or. 1999) ("[T]he legislature intended that courts shall use the 'best interests of the child' standard in determining custody of minor children in custody disputes between a biological parent and a stepparent with a child-parent relationship with the subject minor child."). However, other jurisdictions do not treat the parent and stepparent as on the same level in a custody dispute. *See Kinnard v. Kinnard*, 43 P.3d 150, 154 (Alaska 2002) ("The child's biological parent must be awarded custody unless the trial court determines that the parent is unfit, has abandoned the child, or that the welfare of the child requires that a non-parent receive custody. Even in custody disputes between parents and stepparents, the best interests standard is rejected in favor of the . . . parental preference."). It will be a matter of New Arizico law as to whether Ramsey would have to establish that Sidney's being awarded custody of Nancy would actually be detrimental or whether, instead, Ramsey would merely have to establish that Sidney's being awarded custody would not promote Nancy's best interests.

114.   As a general matter, custody decisions are based on what would promote the children's best interests. *See In re Guardianship of BJO*, 165 P.3d 442, 446 (Wyo. 2007) ("[A]ll jurisdictions we reviewed agree that the paramount focus in determining who should be given custody of a child is what outcome would optimally serve the best interest of each child."). However, jurisdictions as a general matter disfavor splitting siblings. *See Harris v. Harris*, 647 A.2d 309, 313 (Vt. 1994) ("[T]he family court should avoid separating siblings in custody or divorce proceedings unless the evidence indicates that the best interests of the children favor split custody."). Some jurisdictions require "exceptional circumstances," *see Leppert v. Leppert*, 519 N.W.2d 287, 291 (N.D. 1994), or "compelling reasons," *see Mitzel v. Black Cloud-Walberg*, 511 N.W.2d 816, 818 (S.D. 1994), to justify splitting siblings. In any event, keeping the siblings together might itself be a reason to favor one custody award over another. While the particular standard would be a matter of Idoming law, *compare In re Guardianship of BJO*, 165 P.3d 442, 446 (Wyo. 2007) ("some jurisdictions recognize that sufficient circumstances, looking at the

totality of the situation with the best interest of the child being the paramount concern, must exist before siblings are separated") *with Fuerstenberg v. Fuerstenberg*, 591 N.W.2d 798, 809 (S.D. 1999) ("Siblings should not be separated absent compelling circumstances.") and there would have to be a developed discussion as to why Finley was seeking custody of one child rather than both, all else being equal, Dominique's seeking custody of both children would itself be a factor weighing in her favor. *Cf. Hathaway v. Bergheim*, 648 N.W.2d 349, 352 (S.D. 2002) ("[E]ven though it might have been in the best interests of Christian, individually, to be with his father, when all things are considered, it was in his best interests to be with his brother and his mother, and not his father.").

115. Here, Salem is not Nathaniel's biological or adoptive parent and the question is whether her having functioned as a parent will allow her to compete with Leslie for custody and even be accorded visitation (contrary to Leslie's wishes). Even if Salem could establish that she had been acting as a parent, a separate question is whether Massecticut law recognizes a special status for functional, de facto, or psychological parents. *See*, for example, *Jones v. Barlow*, 154 P.3d 808, 819 (Utah 2007) ("[W]e decline to adopt a de facto parent doctrine."). Other states recognize a special status for a de facto parent but only allow such an individual to compete for custody if that individual can show that the biological/adoptive parent was unfit or had abandoned or deserted the child. *See Davis v. Vaughn*, 126 So. 3d 33, 39 (Miss. 2013). However, some jurisdictions will allow a de facto parent to be awarded custody or visitation even if the biological/adoptive parent is not unfit and has not abandoned or deserted the child. *See C.E.W. v. D.E.W.*, 845 A.2d 1146, 1151 (Me. 2004).

116. A surrogacy arrangement involving artificial insemination of a surrogate who agrees to surrender the child corresponds to traditional or genetic surrogacy. Or, the arrangement might involve gestational surrogacy where embryos are implanted in the surrogate's womb and the surrogate agrees to relinquish the child. In the former but not the latter scenario, the surrogate is genetically related to the child.

Jurisdictions differ about whether traditional surrogacy contracts are enforceable. *See*, for example, *In re Baby*, 447 S.W.3d 807, 826 (Tenn. 2014) ("Although sections 36-1-108 and -109 do not preclude the enforcement of traditional surrogacy contracts, they do impose certain limitations."). It will thus be important to consider Minnegan's law in particular. It may be that local law makes the agreement unenforceable, *see R.R. v. M.H.*, 689 N.E.2d 790, 797 (Mass. 1998) ("the surrogacy agreement is not enforceable") or, perhaps, that the contract is voidable. *See In re Marriage of Moschetta*, 30 Cal. Rptr. 2d 893 (Ct. App. 1994) (traditional surrogacy contract not enforceable against the surrogate).

117. Jurisdictions differ about whether surrogacy contracts are enforceable, so it will be important to consider East Monaho law. However, an important element of this case is that it involves gestational rather than genetic (traditional) surrogacy. Some jurisdictions distinguish between the two types of surrogacy and make gestational surrogacy contracts in particular enforceable. *See J.F. v. D.B.*, 879 N.E.2d 740, 741 (Ohio 2007); Johnson v. Calvert, 851 P.2d 776 (Cal. 1993).

118.   While the tender years presumption is no longer employed in some states because of equal protection guarantees, *see Ex parte Devine*, 398 So. 2d 686, 695 (Ala. 1981) ("[T]he tender years presumption represents an unconstitutional gender-based classification which discriminates between fathers and mothers in child custody proceedings solely on the basis of sex."), and has been weakened in other states, *see Albright v. Albright*, 437 So. 2d 1003, 1005 (Miss. 1983) ("[T]he 'tender years' doctrine has undergone a weakening process in many jurisdictions as well as in this state."), that presumption facially discriminates on the basis of sex because it accords a presumption in favor of mothers over fathers. Mere disproportionate impact without some evidence of invidious purpose would be unlikely to be held sufficient to justify striking down a practice. *See Personnel Administrator of Massachusetts v. Feeney*, 442 U.S. 256 (1979). Maxwell Mallington's appeal is unlikely to be successful unless Alice Attorney can establish more than disproportionate impact, e.g., establish an invidious purpose to discriminate on the basis of sex.

Support

119.   **Answer (A) is the best answer.** Jurisdictions differ about whether they will reinstate spousal support if the recipient spouse attempts to remarry, but the subsequent marriage is void *ab initio*. *See DeWall v. Rhoderick*, 138 N.W.2d 124, 128 (Iowa 1965) ("Appellant-defendant's status was not changed by the void marriage to Rhoderick. A void marriage is no marriage under our statute.").

   Answer (B) is not the best answer. Some jurisdictions would reinstate the payments. *See DeWall v. Rhoderick*, 138 N.W.2d 124, 128 (Iowa 1965).

   Answer (C) is not the best answer. There was no suggestion here that Nancy waited too long. *See Sullivan v. Mandigo*, 332 NYS.2d 200 (App. Div. 1972) (challenge to validity of divorce after six years not barred by laches). Had Nancy waited too long, then her challenge to the validity of the divorce would not have been successful. *See Matter of Guido*, 438 N.Y.S.2d 9, 10 (App. Div. 1981) (challenge to divorce barred because wife waited too long).

   Answer (D) is not the best answer. Norman would be unlikely to be viewed as responsible especially because he was quite honest about what he had done. Had he lied, he *might* have been sued for misrepresentation. *Boren v. Windham*, 425 So. 2d 1353, 1356 (Miss. 1983) ("The loss of alimony may give rise to a separate cause of action against Boren for his alleged misrepresentations which caused appellant to forfeit her right to receive alimony.").

120.   **Answer (B) is the best answer because the refusal to have sexual relations without using contraception would likely be viewed as going to the essentials of marriage and be the basis for an annulment.** *See Heup v. Heup*, 172 N.W.2d 334, 337 (Wis. 1969). However, some jurisdictions distinguish between void and voidable marriages and would only reinstate spousal support if the second marriage was void rather than voidable. *See Darling v. Darling*, 335 N.E.2d 708 (Ohio App. 1975); *Watts v. Watts*, 547 N.W.2d 466 (Neb. 1996).

   Answer (A) is not the best answer. The basis for the annulment would be that Tania had made a misrepresentation about something going to the essentials of the marriage. *See Stegienko v. Stegienko*, 295 N.W. 252 (Mich. 1940) (granting annulment on wife's misrepresentation about her wanting to have children).

   Answer (C) is not the best answer. Seth would not have to have explicitly expressed his desire to have a big family in order for this to be held a fraud going to the essentials of marriage. *See Stegienko v. Stegienko*, 295 N.W. 252 (Mich. 1940).

   Answer (D) is not the best answer. While Rhonda's having taken on additional responsibilities might play a role in some analyses, *see Boren v. Windham*, 425 So.2d 1353, 1355 (Miss.

1983) ("Regardless of whether the subsequent marriage is void or voidable the revival of alimony from a wife's first husband upon annulment of the second marriage will depend upon the facts and circumstances of each case."), some jurisdictions will not reinstate support obligations when a voidable marriage has been annulled. *See Darling v. Darling*, 335 N.E.2d 708 (Ohio App. 1975).

121. **Answer (C) is the best answer.** The ages of the children are not relevant with respect to whether permanent support should be ordered if only because as a general matter the children will reach majority and will no longer need support. The other factors are all relevant to consider. *See Pearson v. Pearson*, 771 N.W.2d 288, 291 (N.D. 2009).

      Answer (A) is incorrect because the ability of the spouse (possibly with retraining) to enter the job market is one of the factors to consider. *See Beal v. Beal*, 300 P.3d 769, 772 (Utah App. 2013) (listing as one of the factors as "the recipient's earning capacity or ability to produce income").

      Answer (B) is incorrect because the length of the marriage is one of the factors to consider when awarding permanent support. *See Beal v. Beal*, 300 P.3d 769, 772 (Utah App. 2013) (listing this as one of the factors).

      Answer (D) is incorrect because the standard of living (coupled with the earning ability of each of the parties) is a factor to consider. *See Zeigler v. Zeigler*, 635 So. 2d 50, 54 (Fla. App. 1994) ("In situations where the superior earning power of one spouse is achieved during a period when the other spouse is out of the job market as a result of an agreement that the nonworking spouse will care for the children, the courts of this state have reversed awards of temporary support in lieu of permanent alimony.").

122. **Answer (C) is the best answer.** Rehabilitative support is designed to get the recipient spouse back into the workforce. *See Pearson v. Pearson*, 771 N.W.2d 288, 292 (N.D. 2009) ("Rehabilitative spousal support should be awarded when 'it is possible to restore an economically disadvantaged spouse to independent economic status,' or when the burden of the divorce can be equalized by increasing the disadvantaged spouse's earning capacity."). Where rehabilitative support would not enable the spouse to become self-sufficient, permanent support may instead be appropriate. *See id.* ("Permanent spousal support may be appropriate when there is substantial disparity between the spouse's incomes that cannot be readily adjusted by property division or rehabilitative support.").

      Answer (A) is not the best answer. While testimony regarding abuse may be helpful in determining appropriate maintenance, *see Soutiere v. Soutiere*, 657 A.2d 206, 208 (Vt. 1995) ("[P]laintiff testified to numerous instances of physical and psychological abuse she suffered during her marriage to defendant.") and *id.* ("Plaintiff argued that the testimony was relevant and helpful on the property and maintenance issues before the court."), rehabilitative support is designed to make an individual ready to go back into the workforce. *See Pearson v. Pearson*, 771 N.W.2d 288, 292 (N.D. 2009).

      Answer (B) is not the best answer. While there are instances in which spouses need therapy to recover from the physical abuse of a current or former spouse, *see Kent v. Green*, 701 So.

2d 4, 8 (Ala. Civ. App. 1996) ("[T]he husband committed serious violence against the wife that required her to undergo extensive hospitalization and caused her to suffer severe emotional trauma."), rehabilitative support specifically refers to the support designed to enable a former spouse to get back into the workforce. *See Pearson v. Pearson*, 771 N.W.2d 288, 292 (N.D. 2009).

Answer (D) is not the best answer. While establishing which spouse was at fault may affect support or a property division, *see Cotton v. Cotton*, 2017 WL 6523098, at *4 (Tex. App. 2017) ("a trial court's finding of adultery can support the disproportionate division of the community property"), rehabilitative support refers to the support that will enable a spouse to get back into the workforce. *See Pearson v. Pearson*, 771 N.W.2d 288, 292 (N.D. 2009).

123.	**Answer (D) is the best answer.** Parents cannot waive child support. *See Eynon v. Gillis*, 2017 WL 6520875, *2 (Miss. App. 2017) ("[A] parent's willingness to forgo child support cannot operate to waive her children's right to appropriate child support from the other parent."). However, many jurisdictions permit a spouse to waive his or her right to spousal support. *See Silverman v. Spitzer*, 2014 WL 7157419, at *12 (Mich. App. 2014) ("The parties to a divorce may waive their statutory right to receive spousal support.").

Answer (A) is not the best answer. While a parent can seek custody of a child in a divorce, *see Troyer v. Troyer*, 987 N.E.2d 1130, 1133 (Ind. App. 2013) ("[A]bsent evidence to the contrary, there is an established presumption that each parent is a fit and proper person to have the care, custody, and control of [a child]."), a separate question is whether a parent can bargain away a child's right to support. *See Eynon v. Gillis*, 2017 WL 6520875, *2 (Miss. App. 2017).

Answer (B) is not the best answer. While parents cannot, as a general matter, waive child support, *see Eynon v. Gillis*, 2017 WL 6520875, *2 (Miss. App. 2017), many jurisdictions permit parents to waive spousal support. *See*, for example, *Silverman v. Spitzer*, 2014 WL 7157419, at *12 (Mich. App. 2014).

Answer (C) is not the best answer. As a general matter, the parent cannot waive child support. *See Eynon v. Gillis*, 2017 WL 6520875, *2 (Miss. App. 2017).

124.	**Answer (B) is the best answer.** Some jurisdictions require divorced parents to pay some of their children's college education costs even if the divorcing parents did not have an agreement to that effect, where such an obligation would be reasonable to impose. *See In re Gilmore*, 803 A.2d 601, 603 (N.H. 2002) ("Both this court and the legislature, however, have recognized the superior court's jurisdiction to order divorced parents, consistent with their means, to contribute toward the educational expenses of their adult children.").

Answer (A) is not the best answer. While parents can include within their divorce agreement that they will contribute to their children's college educations, *see Avelino-Catabran v. Catabran*, 139 A.3d 1202, 1211 (N.J. Super. App. Div. 2016) ("[W]here parties to a divorce have reached an agreement regarding children attending college and how those college expenses should be divided, and no showing has been made that the agreement should be vacated or modified, . . . the court should enforce the agreement as written."), such support can be ordered even absent such an agreement. *See In re Gilmore*, 803 A.2d 601, 603 (N.H. 2002).

Answer (C) is not the best answer. While some states require divorced parents to contribute to college education costs where reasonable to do so, *see In re Gilmore*, 803 A.2d 601, 603 (N.H. 2002), not all states do. *See Grapin v. Grapin*, 450 So. 2d 853, 854 (Fla. 1984) ("[A] trial court may not order post-majority support simply because the child is in college and the divorced parent can afford to pay.").

Answer (D) is not the best answer. Courts can order parents to pay some college costs when doing so would not impose an unreasonable burden, even though the children have attained majority. *See Newburgh v. Arrigo*, 443 A.2d 1031, 1038 (N.J. 1982) ("[I]n appropriate circumstances, the privilege of parenthood carries with it the duty to assure a necessary education for children. In those cases [where children seek contribution from the noncustodial parent for college expenses], courts have treated 'necessary education' as a flexible concept that can vary in different circumstances.").

125.   **Answer (D) is the best answer.** While his failure to specify that he would only contribute to state schools means that he might be responsible for sharing the reasonable costs of a private school, the quality of the flagship state university plus his having conditioned his support on his having a say in the matter might limit how much he would have to pay. *See In re Paternity of Pickett*, 44 N.E.3d 756, 767–68 (Ind. Ct. App. 2015) ("In determining whether educational support should be limited to the cost of in-state, state-supported colleges, the trial court should balance the advantages of the more expensive college in relation to the needs and abilities of the child with the increased hardship of the parent.").

Answer (A) is not the best answer. Merely because Sidney was permitted to have his say will not be the end of the matter. A separate question will involve the costs and benefits associated with the different universities in addition to the burdens that would be imposed on the parents that would be associated with footing some of those costs. *See Saliba v. Saliba*, 753 So. 2d 1095, 1103 (Miss. 2000) ("David is a man of considerable means. Therefore, he is able and should be required to contribute to the college education at an institution of his daughter's choice, commensurate with her parents' station in life.").

Answer (B) is not the best answer. A divorce agreement specifying that the parents will contribute to their children's college education is enforceable. *See Avelino-Catabran v. Catabran*, 139 A.3d 1202, 1211 (N.J. Super. App. Div. 2016) ("A court's obligation to enforce marital settlement agreements applies to provisions regarding the parents' obligation to pay for their children's college expenses.").

Answer (C) is not the best answer. Sometimes, states require individuals to help pay their children's college education expenses where that burden would not be unreasonable. However, that obligation is linked to in-state tuition rather than tuition at a public school located in another state. *See* 750 Ill. Comp. Stat. Ann. 5/513 (d) (1) ("Educational expenses may include, but shall not be limited to, the following: except for good cause shown, the actual cost of the child's post-secondary expenses, including tuition and fees, provided that the cost for tuition and fees does not exceed the amount of in-state tuition and fees paid by a student at the University of Illinois at Urbana-Champaign for the same academic year.").

126. **Answer (B) is the best answer.** When John as Melinda's husband consented to the artificial insemination, he was also accepting responsibility for the child that might thereby be born. *See In re Marriage of A.C.H. & D.R.H.,* 210 P.3d 929, 933 (Or. App. 2009) ("[F]or purposes of determining the legal relationship between the mother's husband and the child conceived through artificial insemination, we conclude that the only inquiry is whether the husband 'consented to the performance of artificial insemination.'").

   Answer (A) is not the best answer. By consenting to the artificial insemination, he was accepting responsibility even while knowing that he would not have a genetic connection to the child. *See Levin v. Levin,* 645 N.E.2d 601, 604 (Ind. 1994) ("This consent constituted Donald's promise to become the father of the resulting child and to assume his support."). Further, there is nothing suggesting that Oscar is somehow responsible for his nonexistent relationship with John. *See Collins v. Mississippi Dep't of Human Servs.,* 2017 WL 2559801, at *3 (Miss. App. 2017) ("[A] child generally will not forfeit support from a noncustodial parent unless his or her actions toward the parent are clear and extreme.").

   Answer (C) is incorrect. If, for example, the child had been the result of an extramarital affair, John might not be responsible for support. *See Miller v. Miller,* 314 N.Y.S.2d 855, 857 (Fam. Ct. 1970) ("To hold the respondent financially liable for child born while his wife was engaged in an extra-marital affair would be eminently unfair.").

   Answer (D) is not the best answer. Merely because John tried in good faith to have a relationship with the child does not justify terminating child support that the child might well need. *See Collins v. Mississippi Dep't of Human Servs.,* 2017 WL 2559801, at *3 (Miss. App. 2017).

127. **Answer (D) is the best answer.** Norman is unlikely to be ordered to pay support if Sarah's conception resulted from Penelope and Thomas having coital relations. *See In re Marriage of Adams,* 701 N.E.2d 1131, 1133 (Ill. App. 1998) (husband not responsible for children born as a result of extramarital relations, notwithstanding that husband had agreed to artificial insemination). However, the result might have been different had artificial insemination been used. *See id.* ("A child born as a result of artificial insemination is considered the natural child of the husband and wife who requested and consented to the procedure.").

   Answer (A) is not the best answer. Norman might well be responsible for a child resulting from consented-to artificial insemination. *See In re Marriage of Adams,* 701 N.E.2d 1131, 1133 (Ill. App. 1998).

   Answer (B) is not the best answer. Merely because Norman agreed to artificial insemination does not mean that he would be responsible for children born as a result of his wife's having coital relations with another man. *See In re Marriage of Adams,* 701 N.E.2d 1131, 1133 (Ill. App. 1998).

Answer (C) is not the best answer. While Sarah might benefit from receiving support from Norman, that nonetheless might be thought not to justify imposing that burden on Norman when Sarah's conception had resulted from Penelope's having had sexual relations with another man. *See Miller v. Miller*, 314 N.Y.S.2d 855, 857 (Fam. Ct. 1970).

128.   **Answer (D) is the best answer.** Jurisdictions differ about whether individuals can be ordered to pay support notwithstanding the discovery that the children had been conceived in extramarital liaisons. *Compare Fischer v. Zollino*, 35 A.3d 270 (Conn. 2012) (husband not estopped from denying paternity when DNA testing revealed that he was not the father of a daughter born during the marriage) *with S.R.D. v. T.L.B.*, 174 S.W.3d 502, 510 (Ky. App. 2005) (ex-husband estopped from denying paternity of child, DNA test revealing that he was not genetically related to child notwithstanding).

Answer (A) is not the best answer. There is no suggestion here that the biological father(s) of the children would be unable to pay support. *See B.E.B. v. R.L.B.*, 979 P.2d 514, 520 (Alaska 1999) ("[T]o support a finding of estoppel, the evidence must show financial prejudice."). If the biological father(s) can pay, then the children will still be receiving needed support.

Answer (B) is not the best answer. A husband can be required to support a child that is not genetically related to him when he took on that obligation knowing the identity of the child's biological father. *See Sheetz v. Sheetz*, 63 N.E.3d 1077, 1078 (Ind. App. 2016) ("Husband told Wife not to tell the biological father, not to seek support from him, and not to file a paternity action, and Wife relied on Husband's representations in not establishing paternity in the biological father, we find that Husband is equitably estopped from rebutting the presumption that he is the child's biological father.").

Answer (C) is not the best answer. The relevant issue would not be how much Dominique was making, but who should be helping Dominique support the children. *See*, for example, *Perkins v. Simmonds*, 227 So. 3d 646, 650 (Fla. App. 2017) (best interests of child justified permitting biological father to establish his paternity and take on the legal obligation of support).

129.   **Answer (B) is the best answer.** Beatrice will likely be estopped from denying Apollo's paternity. She actively encouraged him to believe that he was the children's father and to act as their father, so she likely will be prevented from seeking to undermine his parentage now. *See DeFinis v. DeFinis*, 41 Pa. D. & C.3d 409, 415 (Com. Pl. 1984).

Answer (A) is not the best answer. Beatrice will likely be estopped from denying Apollo's paternity, *see DeFinis v. DeFinis*, 41 Pa. D. & C.3d 409, 415 (Com. Pl. 1984), so he might well be awarded custody or visitation. *See Jean Maby H. v. Joseph H.*, 676 N.Y.S.2d 677, 682 (App. Div. 1998) (husband permitted to assert estoppel so that he could seek custody of or visitation with child born during the marriage, even though he had no biological connection to the child).

Answer (C) is not the best answer. First, Apollo might be estopped from denying paternity. *See S.R.D. v. T.L.B.*, 174 S.W.3d 502, 505 (Ky. App. 2005) (husband estopped from denying paternity because such a denial was not in the best interests of the child). Even were Apollo permitted to deny paternity, he and Beatrice stand in different positions because Beatrice had known that he was not the children's father and thus might be thought to have been acting fraudulently when encouraging him to believe that he was the children's biological father. *Cf, Sekol v. Delsantro*, 763 A.2d 405, 411 (Pa. Super. 2000) ("[T]he trial court shall conduct a full and complete evidentiary hearing giving due consideration to the claims of estoppel and the interplay of the alleged fraud/misrepresentation, and shall then determine whether under the facts of this case, any fraud/misrepresentation [on the part of the wife] so found precludes the application of estoppel [against the husband] in the instant case.").

Answer (D) is not the best answer. Apollo can be required to pay support and under other circumstances might be estopped from denying his paternity, lack of genetic connection notwithstanding. *See S.R.D. v. T.L.B.*, 174 S.W.3d 502, 505 (Ky. App. 2005).

130. **Answer (B) is the best answer.** Grant will likely be required to pay child support, notwithstanding his having made clear that he would only have protected sex and his having been told that contraception was being used. *See Wallis v. Smith*, 22 P.3d 682, 687 (N.M. App. 2001).

Answer (A) is not the best answer. Grant can be held financially responsible for the child he fathered, even if he had been misled into believing that contraception was being used. *See Wallis v. Smith*, 22 P.3d 682, 687 (N.M. App. 2001).

Answer (C) is not the best answer. Both parents are financially responsible for their children, even if either one would be able to provide adequate support for the child. *See In re Bruce R.*, 662 A.2d 107, 117 (Conn. 1995) (discussing "the overwhelming public policy in support of requiring that parents be held financially responsible for their children's support").

Answer (D) is not the best answer. Grant will likely be held responsible, even if Hermione had that actual notice and even if she expressly lied about using contraception. *See Wallis v. Smith*, 22 P.3d 682, 687 (N.M. App. 2001).

131. **Answer (A) is the best answer.** John may well be permitted to disestablish his paternity based on the DNA evidence and Karen's having admitted that he was not the father. *See Dep't of Revenue v. M.J.M.*, 217 So. 3d 1148, 1154 (Fla. App. 2017).

Answer (B) is not the best answer. States permit individuals under certain circumstances to disestablish their paternity. *See Dep't of Revenue v. M.J.M.*, 217 So. 3d 1148, 1154 (Fla. App. 2017).

Answer (C) is not the best answer. Where there is good reason to believe that an individual is not in fact the father of a child, it may not be necessary to establish that the mother knew all along that he was not the father. *See Sidney W. v. Chanta J.*, 978 N.Y.S.2d 274, 277 (App. Div. 2013) (individual permitted to challenge when mother had been sexually intimate with more than one individual around the time of conception and it was not clear whether she knew who the father was).

Answer (D) is incorrect. He may well be able to disestablish paternity even if he does not know who the father was. *See Dep't of Revenue v. M.J.M.*, 217 So. 3d 1148, 1154 (Fla. App. 2017).

132.   **Answer (D) is the best answer.** Where an individual voluntarily quits his job without adequate justification, he may be found to be shirking his support obligation, which might mean that the court would refuse to modify the child support owed. *See Kanka v. Kanka*, 2018 WL 565841, at *5 (Tenn. App. 2018) ("When a party with child support obligations voluntarily leaves their employment and chooses to accept a job which provides significantly less income, courts are more inclined to find willful and voluntary underemployment."); *Kabasan v. Kabasan*, 2018 WL 414074, at *19 (N.C. App. 2018). If the court finds that the parent's voluntary unemployment or underemployment is the result of the parent's bad faith or deliberate suppression of income to avoid or minimize his or her child support obligation, child support may be calculated based on the parent's potential, rather than actual, income.

   Answer (A) is not the best answer. An important issue is whether his voluntary loss of income was due to his attempting to evade his support obligation. *In re Marriage of Sorokin*, 83 N.E.3d 556, 562 (Ill. App. 2017) ("[T]o have his support obligation decreased, based on a voluntary change in employment, the supporting parent must prove that he made the change in good faith and not to evade his financial responsibility to his children.").

   Answer (B) is not the best answer. Merely because he no longer has his previous job and is looking for another does not establish that his quitting was in good faith and that his support obligation should be suspended. *See In re Marriage of Sorokin*, 83 N.E.3d 556, 562 (Ill. App. 2017).

   Answer (C) is not the best answer. Under some circumstances, the support obligation will be reduced even if the children's needs have not changed. *See Fuller v. Fuller*, 783 N.Y.S.2d 671, 674 (App. Div. 2004) ("[B]ecause the evidence shows that petitioner lost his old job through no fault of his own and was compelled to take a new one for less pay, we find that he has shown a 'sufficient and involuntary change in financial circumstances' warranting a downward modification of his child support obligation.").

133.   **Answer (B) is the best answer.** The court is likely to consider whether the retirement is voluntary rather than mandated or, perhaps, forced because of existing medical conditions, and whether his decision to retire now was made in good faith. *Cf. Longtin v. Longtin*, 2009 WL 2226110, at *1 (Minn. App. 2009) ("Because the evidence supports the district court's finding that appellant's retirement was voluntary and in bad faith, appellant failed to meet his burden of proving a substantial change of circumstances that justifies modification.").

   Answer (A) is not the best answer. Because many of those retiring at age 65 do not still have minor children to support, it is not clear that the general approach to retirement should be used in this case. *See Lissner v. Marburger*, 926 A.2d 890, 896 (N.J. Super. Ch. Div. 2007) ("[I]t is generally expected that by age sixty-five, a parent's children will have reached the age of majority. It is reasonable to conclude that a person who decides to become a parent late in life voluntarily takes on the responsibility of working and saving for that child beyond the age that would otherwise be expected.").

   Answer (C) is not the best answer. While it is true that the children's needs may not decrease, the court might nonetheless use the retirement income as the basis. *See In re N.T.P.*, 402 S.W.3d

13, 17 (Tex. App. 2012) (upholding reduction in support obligation because of father's retirement).

Answer (D) is not the best answer. The same reasoning might be used to show that Methuselah should not have his support obligation reduced in that he also knew when taking on the responsibility of having children that he would reach retirement age before the children reached majority. *See Lissner v. Marburger*, 926 A.2d 890, 896 (N.J. Super. Ch. Div. 2007).

134. **Answer (C) is the best answer.** Because Robin has a legal duty to support the twins, that obligation may well be considered when Casey seeks a support increase. *See TSR v. State ex rel. Dep't of Family Servs., Child Support Enf't Div.*, 406 P.3d 729, 731 (Wyo. 2017) ("[A]lthough the court must initially base the support amount only on the number of minor children on whose behalf the modification proceeding is brought, the court may subsequently take into consideration a party's support obligation to later-born minor children from subsequent marriages.").

Answer (A) is incorrect. Many states permit consideration of later-acquired obligations to support children when a court is determining whether to modify a previous support order. *See Ameen v. Ameen*, 84 P.3d 802, 804 (Okla. Civ. App. 2004) ("[W]hen one of the parties seeks to modify a prior order, the trial court must consider all of the facts and circumstances in existence at the time of the requested modification. If the payor party has incurred and is paying additional child support obligations, then § 118(E)(5) requires that they be considered.").

Answer (C) is not the best answer. While Casey's decrease in income will be one factor to consider, Robin's additional responsibilities will also be important to consider. *See Pohlmann v. Pohlmann*, 703 So. 2d 1121, 1124 (Fla. App. 1997) ("The issue of subsequent children may only be raised in a proceeding for an upward modification of an existing award and may not be applied to justify a decrease in an existing award."); *State ex rel. Jarvela v. Burke*, 678 N.W.2d 68, 71 (Minn. App. 2004) ("[W]hen a party moves to increase child support, the circumstances change and the adjudicator is obligated to consider the needs of after-born children.").

Answer (D) is not the best answer. Many states permit consideration of children born into a subsequent marriage when there is a request for an increase in child support. *See Pohlmann v. Pohlmann*, 703 So. 2d 1121, 1124 (Fla. App. 1997); *State ex rel. Jarvela v. Burke*, 678 N.W.2d 68, 71 (Minn. App. 2004).

135. This is a matter of state law. Some states employ the nurturing parent doctrine, which permits a parent in appropriate cases to stay home with a young child without having the foregone income imputed to that parent for child support purposes. *See Reinert v. Reinert*, 926 A.2d 539, 543 (Pa. Super. 2007) ("[T]he nurturing parent doctrine applied in Mother's situation and, accordingly, suspended her support obligation."). However, even in states where the doctrine is recognized, that doctrine will not be applicable in all cases. *See Doherty v. Doherty*, 859 A.2d 811, 813 (Pa. Super. 2004) (affirming trial court's decision not to apply the nurturing parent doctrine in the particular case). Further, many states do not recognize the doctrine. *See Snader v. Dudley*, 741 A.2d 17 (Del. 1999) ("Delaware has not adopted the nurturing parent doctrine and we decline to do so on the facts of this case.").

136.   **Answer (D) is the best answer.** Under UIFSA, a Washifornia court would not have jurisdiction to modify the support obligation. Instead, Skyler would have to file in New Mexizona. *See Hamilton v. Hamilton*, 914 N.E.2d 747, 751–52 (Ind. 2009) ("UIFSA's cornerstone provision is: 'As long as one of the individual parties or the child continues to reside in the issuing State [in this case Florida], and as long as the parties do not agree to the contrary, the issuing tribunal has continuing, exclusive jurisdiction over its [child-support] order—which in practical terms means that it may modify its order.' . . . As a corollary, a responding state, in this case Indiana, 'shall recognize and enforce, but may not modify, a registered order if the issuing tribunal had jurisdiction.'").

   Answer (A) is not the best answer. A Washifornia court would not even have jurisdiction to modify support. *See Hamilton v. Hamilton*, 914 N.E.2d 747, 751–52 (Ind. 2009). Once the merits were addressed, it would be very helpful for Skyler to establish that she was not at fault for her job loss. *See Meyer v. Meyer*, 614 N.Y.S.2d 42, 43 (App. Div. 1994) ("We agree with the Family Court that the father's loss of employment constituted a change of circumstances which warranted a downward modification of his child support obligation. . . . The evidence in the record supports the Hearing Examiner's finding that the father lost his job through no fault of his own and had diligently sought reemployment in his field.").

   Answer (B) is not the best answer. A Washifornia court would not even have jurisdiction to modify support. *See Hamilton v. Hamilton*, 914 N.E.2d 747, 751–52 (Ind. 2009). While it is true that William's needs would not have been diminished merely because Skyler had lost her job, Skyler's ability to pay would have been significantly altered. That would justify a downward modification in her support obligation as long as she continued to look for a job commensurate with her abilities and experience. *See Baffi v. Baffi*, 807 N.Y.S.2d 388, 390 (App. Div. 2005) ("Loss of employment can constitute a change of circumstances warranting a downward modification of support obligations where a parent has diligently sought re-employment commensurate with his or her qualifications and experience.").

   Answer (C) is not the best answer. Charlie's appearing notwithstanding, the Washifornia court would still lack jurisdiction to hear the case. *See Hamilton v. Hamilton*, 914 N.E.2d 747, 751–52 (Ind. 2009).

137.   **Answer (D) is the best answer.** Under UIFSA, the issuing state continues to have exclusive jurisdiction as long as one of the parties continues to live there, absent party agreement to the contrary. *See Sootin v. Sootin*, 41 So. 3d 993, 994 (Fla. App. 2010) ("Under UIFSA, the Miami-Dade court has 'continuing *exclusive* jurisdiction over a spousal support order throughout the existence of the support obligation.' . . . The correct procedure under UIFSA is to register the spousal support judgment in another state for enforcement there. § 88.3011 (2) (c). Even after registration, however, the foreign court must send the case back to the Florida court to consider any modification of the order.").

   Answer (A) is not the best answer. The Old York court would not have jurisdiction to decide the matter. *See Sootin v. Sootin*, 41 So. 3d 993, 994 (Fla. App. 2010).

Answer (B) is not the best answer. The Old York court would not have jurisdiction to decide whether the modification was appropriate. *See Sootin v. Sootin*, 41 So. 3d 993, 994 (Fla. App. 2010). Even if the court had jurisdiction to decide whether a modification was warranted, the court would have to consider a number of factors rather than one such as the needs of the supported spouse. *See McLeod v. Macul*, 139 A.3d 920, 924 (Me. 2016) ("[I]f the court determines that a substantial change in circumstances has been established and a modification is warranted, it must then consider the statutory factors governing spousal support in arriving at a modified award.").

Answer (C) is not the best answer. Old York would not have jurisdiction to consider the matter. *See Sootin v. Sootin*, 41 So. 3d 993, 994 (Fla. App. 2010).

138. **Answer (D) is the best answer.** Assuming that Phoenix is now domiciled in West Pennio and has met the residency requirement, the West Pennio court can grant the divorce. *See Phelps v. Phelps*, 246 S.W.2d 838, 844 (Mo. App. 1952) ("To create a domicile or residence, two elements are essential; Actual bodily presence in the place combined with a freely exercised intention to remain there permanently, or at least for an indefinite time."). Further, the West Pennio court would likely be able to assert jurisdiction over Parker via the state's long-arm statute because Phoenix and Parker had married in West Pennio and had lived in West Pennio both before and after their marriage. *Cf. Bradley v. Bradley*, 806 S.E.2d 58, 74 (N.C. App. 2017) ("[B]ased on our consideration of the relevant factors, we are satisfied that Joshua has sufficient minimum contacts with North Carolina such that the exercise of personal jurisdiction over him would not offend traditional notions of fair play and substantial justice.").

Answer (A) is not the best answer. It is true that the state does not have to have jurisdiction over both parties to the marriage in order to grant a divorce. *See Jiminez v. De La Cruz*, 2017 WL 4653025, at *2 (Conn. Super. 2017) (discussing "[t]he rule that a [domicile] of at least one of the spouses is essential to give the court jurisdiction to grant a divorce applies to decrees of foreign nations as well as to decrees entered within the United States, even though a [domicile] is not required by the laws of the jurisdiction which grants the divorce"). However, the West Pennio court could have jurisdiction to order spousal support via its long-arm statute. *See Bradley v. Bradley*, 806 S.E.2d 58, 74 (N.C. App. 2017).

Answer (B) is incorrect. It is not necessary for both parties to a marriage to be domiciled in a state in order for a court in that state to have jurisdiction to grant a divorce. *See Jiminez v. De La Cruz*, 2017 WL 4653025, at *2 (Conn. Super. 2017).

Answer (C) is incorrect. Merely because a court has jurisdiction to grant a divorce does not mean in addition that the court will have jurisdiction to grant spousal support. *See Latta v. Latta*, 654 So. 2d 1043, 1044 (Fla. App. 1995) ("In the instant case, it is undisputed that the wife is a Florida resident, and the court thus had jurisdiction to dissolve the marriage. Under Florida law, however, a court cannot adjudicate alimony and property rights unless the court has *in personam* jurisdiction over the parties.").

139. **Answer (C) is the best answer.** Because a child's station in life should not be tied to the child's station in life at the time of divorce, a substantial increase in salary may justify an increase in support even if the children's needs have not changed. *See Eglinton v. Eglinton*, 2003 WL 22390115, at *2 (Conn. Super. 2003) ("[T]he same criteria that determine an initial award of alimony and support are relevant to the question of modification. These require the court to consider, without limitation, the needs and financial resources of each of the parties [and their children] as well as such factors as health, age and station in life.").

  Answer (A) is not the best answer. The children's needs are relevant but are but one factor among many that should be considered when deciding upon the appropriate amount of support. *See Eglinton v. Eglinton*, 2003 WL 22390115, at *2 (Conn. Super. 2003).

  Answer (B) is not the best answer. Just because Tatum's salary has also increased does not establish that no support obligation increase is appropriate. One of the goals is to have the children enjoy the kind of lifestyle that they might have enjoyed had the parents stayed together, so the custodial parent's increase in income would not justify preventing the children from also benefiting from the noncustodial parent's increased income. *See McKeon v. Lennon*, 138 A.3d 242, 253 (Conn. 2016) ("[T]he determination of a parent's child support obligation must account for *all* of the income that would have been available to support the children had the family remained together.").

  Answer (D) is not the best answer. Because both parents have the duty to support their children, *see Dull v. Dull*, 392 N.E.2d 421, 424 (Ill. App. 1979) ("[B]oth parents share an equal duty to support their children."), and because one of the goals is to help the children have the kind of lifestyle that they would have had if the parents had stayed together, *see McKeon v. Lennon*, 138 A.3d 242, 253 (Conn. 2016), the fact that the custodial parent's salary increase was greater than the noncustodial parent's salary increase would not alone justify refusing to increase the noncustodial parent's support obligation. *Cf. Smith v. Freeman*, 814 A.2d 65, 75 (Md. App. 2002) (noting that "[t]he guidelines are premised on the concept that a child should receive the same proportion of parental income, and thereby enjoy the same standard of living, he or she would have experienced had the child's parents remained together").

140. **Answer (D) is the best answer.** Although David has become a father and has responsibility for his child, he nonetheless will likely not be found emancipated if he is still living at home and dependent upon his parents. *See Clapper v. Clapper*, 2017 WL 2291580, at *4 (N.J. Super. App. Div. 2017) ("Emancipation of a child is reached when the fundamental dependent relationship between parent and child is concluded.").

  Answer (A) is incorrect. Joining the military is a basis for emancipation. *See Hays v. Alexander*, 114 So. 3d 704, 712 (Miss. 2013) ("noting that *[u]nless otherwise provided for in the underlying child support judgment*, emancipation shall occur when the child: . . . [j]oins the military and serves on a full-time basis").

  Answer (B) is incorrect. *See Hays v. Alexander*, 114 So. 3d 704, 712 (Miss. 2013) ("*[u]nless otherwise provided for in the underlying child support judgment*, emancipation shall occur when the child . . . [m]arries").

Answer (C) is not the best answer. Carl might well be found emancipated. *See Monti v. DiBedendetto*, 56 N.Y.S.3d 544, 547 (App. Div. 2017) (noting that "[c]hildren of employable age are emancipated if they become economically independent of their parents through employment, and are self-supporting").

141.   **Answer (B) is the best answer.** Baylor and Emery's marriage was valid until annulled, which means that Emery was emancipated while married. However, once that marriage was annulled, Emery's emancipated status might itself change, which would provide the basis for a reinstatement of Thomas's support obligation. *See In re Marriage of Fetters*, 584 P.2d 104, 106 (Colo. App. 1978) ("Because her marriage was no longer recognized as valid, and because she was but 16 and living with and dependent upon her mother for support, the daughter's emancipated status terminated at that time. . . . Consequently, respondent's support obligations were revived."). *See also Fernandez v. Fernandez*, 717 S.W.2d 781, 783 (Tex. App. 1986) ("[T]he annulment of the Appellee's minor daughter reinstated her minority and, also, reinstated Appellee's duty of support as provided in the previous court orders.").

Answer (A) is not the best answer. The marriage not only did not work out but was annulled, which made it nonexistent in the eyes of the law. *See In re Marriage of Fetters*, 584 P.2d 104, 106 (Colo. App. 1978) ("[T]his relationship was declared void. Because her marriage was no longer recognized as valid, and because she was but 16 and living with and dependent upon her mother for support, the daughter's emancipated status terminated at that time.").

Answer (C) is not the best answer. Assuming that the minor marriage was voidable rather than void, that marriage would be legally recognized until annulled by a court, which would justify ending the father's support obligation at least while the marriage was still legally recognized. *See In re Marriage of Fetters*, 584 P.2d 104, 106 (Colo. App. 1978) ("[T]his marriage was voidable, not [v]oid ab initio, [a]nd a legal status attached to the marriage until set aside by the annulment action.").

Answer (D) is not the best answer because the marriage was annulled, making it void in the eyes of the law. *See In re Marriage of Fetters*, 584 P.2d 104, 106 (Colo. App. 1978). If the marriage had not been annulled and Baylor and Emery nonetheless came to live with Trudy, then Emery might still be viewed as emancipated and Thomas's support obligation would not be reinstated. *See Guzman v. Guzman*, 854 P.2d 1169, 1174 (Ariz. App. 1993) (refusing to reinstate support obligation even though the mother "provided continued support to their son and to his wife and baby").

142.   **Answer (B) is the best answer.** States differ about the conditions under which a support obligation can be reinstated after the second marriage of the recipient spouse has been declared void. Some jurisdictions distinguish between void and voidable marriages, only reinstating the support obligation if the second marriage was void. The courts in those states may reason that the void marriage was never valid in the eyes of the law, while the voidable marriage was valid until declared void by a court. *See Broadus v. Broadus*, 361 So. 2d 582, 585 (Ala. Civ. App. 1978) ("[T]he status of the wife under the terms of the original divorce decree is not changed by the void marriage to the second husband and her right to receive alimony

from her first husband is deemed to have been revived."); *Ballew v. Ballew*, 191 N.W.2d 462, 464 (Neb. 1971) ("We hold that under a divorce decree providing that alimony payments shall terminate upon remarriage of the wife, the right of the divorced wife to receive such payments is terminated upon remarriage and is not revived by an annulment of her remarriage on grounds which rendered the remarriage voidable."); *Watts v. Watts*, 547 N.W.2d 466, 469 (Neb. 1996) (reinstating support obligation when ex-wife's second marriage was void). *But see Glass v. Glass*, 546 S.W.2d 738, 742 (Mo. App. 1977) ("[R]emarriage within § 452.075 refers to the ceremony of marriage and not to the status or relationship — valid, voidable or void — which actually results. The public policy which our enactment establishes rests on the same considerations of fairness which the California and New Jersey courts discern for their statutory counterparts: the right of the husband to rely on the apparent remarital status of the former wife, the lack of standing of the husband to challenge the validity of the remarriage, and the justness that — as between them — the former wife should bear the consequences of events she brought on.")

Answer (A) is not the best answer. Many courts have refused to reinstate the obligation if the second marriage was voidable rather than void. They sometimes reason that they do not want to give the former spouse the option of ending the second marriage via divorce or an annulment depending upon which option might yield more support. *See Flaxman v. Flaxman*, 273 A.2d 567, 570 (N.J. 1971) ("[I]n many cases the wife has the option of obtaining an annulment or a divorce from the second husband. If alimony could be revived by annulling the second marriage, the wife could choose between two sources of support. A divorce could lead to alimony from the second husband while an annulment could reinstate alimony from the first.").

Answer (C) is not the best answer. Courts may well consider that those paying support might take on additional responsibilities once their support obligations have ended, *see Flaxman v. Flaxman*, 273 A.2d 567, 570 (N.J. 1971) ("[H]usband whose wife enters into a voidable second marriage is no less likely to rely on the validity of that marriage than is one whose former wife enters into a valid second marriage."). However, many courts refusing to reinstate the support obligation have not required a showing that the obligor spouse had taken on new obligations. For example, in *Flaxman*, the court reasoned that the first husband was entitled to reorder his affairs based on the assumption that the obligation had ended — the court said nothing about the husband actually having done so. *See id.* at 569 ("When she enters into a second marriage ceremony, she holds herself out as having remarried. And her first husband is entitled to rely upon her new marital status. He may assume that his financial obligations to her have ceased and reorder his own affairs accordingly.").

Answer (D) is incorrect. Possibly reasonable expectations of the payor (first) spouse notwithstanding, many jurisdictions do distinguish between voidable and void second marriages in this kind of scenario. *See Broadus v. Broadus*, 361 So. 2d 582, 585 (Ala. Civ. App. 1978); *Ballew v. Ballew*, 191 N.W.2d 462, 464 (Neb. 1971); *Watts v. Watts*, 547 N.W.2d 466, 469 (Neb. 1996); *Flaxman v. Flaxman*, 273 A.2d 567, 570 (N.J. 1971).

143. **Answer (D) is the best answer.** While many jurisdictions will permit a modification or termination of spousal support where cohabitation and economic benefit can be shown, *see Gilman v. Gilman*, 956 P.2d 761, 764 (Nev. 1998) ("The current majority rule regarding the effect of post-divorce cohabitation on spousal support, at least in jurisdictions where no specific statute covers that situation, appears to be that the right to receive spousal support becomes subject to modification or termination only if the recipient spouse's need for the support decreases as a result of the cohabitation."), some do not. *See Cermak v. Cermak*, 569 N.W.2d 280, 285 (N.D. 1997) ("[C]ohabitation cannot be the sole basis for termination of spousal support at least where cohabitation is not included as a condition for termination in the divorce decree.").

     Answer (A) is incorrect. Many jurisdictions permit a reduction or elimination of spousal support due to cohabitation even where there is no agreement to that effect in the separation agreement. However, it may be necessary to show that the recipient spouse is benefiting economically from the cohabitation. *See Gilman v. Gilman*, 956 P.2d 761, 764 (Nev. 1998).

     Answer (B) is incorrect. Cohabitation is not the equivalent of marriage in the eyes of the law. *Bristol Hosp., Inc. v. Smith*, 2007 WL 1470326, at *3 (Conn. Super. 2007) ("[A]lthough two persons cohabit and conduct themselves as a married couple, our law neither grants to nor imposes upon them marital status."). A separate question involves under what conditions, if any, local law permits the reduction or termination of spousal support when the recipient ex-spouse is cohabiting with someone else. *See Gilman v. Gilman*, 956 P.2d 761, 764 (Nev. 1998).

     Answer (C) is incorrect. Cohabitation is not marriage. *See Cermak v. Cermak*, 569 N.W.2d 280, 286 (N.D. 1997) ("[R]ecipient spouse's unmarried cohabitation is not a remarriage."). A state that does not recognize common law marriage, *see* Ohio Rev. Code Ann. § 3105.12 (B) (1) (West) ("On and after October 10, 1991, except as provided in divisions (B)(2) and (3) of this section, common law marriages are prohibited in this state"), may reduce or terminate a spousal support obligation because of cohabitation. *See Perri v. Perri*, 608 N.E.2d 790, 795 (Ohio App. 1992) ("[T]he obligation to pay sustenance alimony can be properly terminated even if the relationship between the sustenance alimony recipient and the paramour comes to an end prior to the end of the period within which the other former spouse is required to pay sustenance alimony under the terms of the divorce decree."). By the same token, a state that does recognize common law marriage, *see Murphy v. Murphy*, 324 P.3d 1154 (Kan. Ct. App. 2014), might reduce or terminate spousal support because of cohabitation. *See Matter of Marriage of Knoll*, 381 P.3d 490 (Kan. App. 2016) (sufficient evidence to establish cohabitation and thus justifying termination of spousal support).

144. Where a parent becomes underemployed to avoid paying child support, the parent's potential rather than actual earnings will be used as the basis for determining support. *See Yeun-Hee Juhnn v. Do-Bum Juhnn*, 775 S.E.2d 310, 314 (N.C. App. 2015) ("[U]nchallenged findings are more than sufficient to support the trial court's conclusion that defendant acted in bad faith, and that the imputation of income to defendant would be appropriate."). However,

jurisdictions differ about whether to impute income when the individual is not seeking to avoid support but instead is seeking to pursue a legitimate lifestyle choice. *Compare In re Marriage of Otuonye*, 2015 WL 4879089, at *7 (Kan. App. 2015) (suggesting that a parent who in good faith is pursuing a legitimate lifestyle choice should not have income imputed to her) *with Robinson v. Tyson*, 461 S.E.2d 397, 399 (S.C. App. 1995) ("While we applaud the husband's law firm's charitable resolve to provide legal services to those in poverty, he is required to be responsible to his children before he is charitable to others. We find no abuse of discretion by the family court in imputing an income of $30,000 per year to the husband and, therefore, affirm the child support award.").

145. Dakota might be successful if the divorce decree included a provision specifying that spousal support could be increased if Frankie's earnings increased. *See McHugh v. Slomka*, 531 S.W.3d 588, 596 (Mo. App. 2017) ("[T]he parties bargained for a lesser amount of maintenance initially, but established a modification procedure where, upon Husband's employment, either party could initiate a modification proceeding to increase *or decrease* the maintenance amount, depending on Husband's 'future' salary."). However, absent such a stipulation, many jurisdictions will not modify the award merely because the obligor spouse is doing much better after the divorce. *See*, for example, *Talley v. Talley*, 2016-Ohio-3533, ¶ 17 (Ct. App.) ("A trial court lacks jurisdiction to modify a prior order of spousal support unless the decree of the court expressly reserved jurisdiction to make the modification and unless the court finds (1) that a substantial change in circumstances has occurred and (2) that the change was not contemplated at the time of the original decree."). The goal is to permit the ex-spouse to maintain the standard of living enjoyed at the time of divorce rather than to permit the ex-spouse to enjoy an increased standard of living because the obligor ex-spouse's standard of living has improved. *See Crews v. Crews*, 751 A.2d 524, 526–27 (N.J. 2000) ("[T]he goal of a proper alimony award is to assist the supported spouse in achieving a lifestyle that is reasonably comparable to the one enjoyed while living with the supporting spouse during the marriage.").

146. As a general matter, jurisdictions do not tie the appropriate level of child support to the standard of living existing at the time of divorce. Rather, the goal is to have the children enjoy the standard of living that would have been enjoyed had the parents stayed together. *See McKeon v. Lennon*, 138 A.3d 242, 249 (Conn. 2016) ("[T]he trial court may consider a substantial increase in the supporting spouse's income, standing alone, as sufficient justification for granting a motion to modify a child support order to ensure that the child receives the same proportion of parental income that he or she would have received if the parents had remained together."). All else equal, Justice will likely be successful. *See Brooks v. Piela*, 814 N.E.2d 365, 369 (Mass. App. 2004) ("[C]hildren's needs are to be defined, at least in part, by their parents' standard of living and that children are entitled to participate in the noncustodial parent's higher standard of living when available resources permit.").

147. If Alex is correct that Danielle is the product of coital relations between Beverly and Carl, then he is unlikely to be held responsible for child support. Even had he been married to Beverly, he would have been unlikely to be held responsible for child support, agreement to

artificial insemination notwithstanding, if the child was born through coital relations with a paramour. *See Dews v. Dews*, 632 A.2d 1160, 1169 (D.C. 1993). If Carl had not been in the picture, Alex would likely have been held responsible for support if Danielle's conception was the result of artificial insemination. *See In re Parentage of M.J.*, 787 N.E.2d 144, 152 (Ill. 2003) ("[I]f an unmarried man who biologically causes conception through sexual relations without the premeditated intent of birth is legally obligated to support a child, then the equivalent resulting birth of a child caused by the deliberate conduct of artificial insemination should receive the same treatment in the eyes of the law."). Assuming that Danielle was the product of artificial insemination, a separate issue that might have to be resolved would be whether the artificial insemination occurred after Beverly and Alex had ended their relationship or, perhaps, after Alex had withdrawn his consent to future artificial insemination. *Cf. Jackson v. Jackson*, 739 N.E.2d 1203 (Ohio App. 2000) (ex-husband responsible for support because he had not withdrawn consent to artificial insemination prior to the pregnancy).

148. Lottery winnings are appropriate to consider when determining child support. *See K.J.Y. v. B.L.*, 2017 WL 4930884, at *2 (Pa. Super. 2017). That said, it is important for both parents to contribute to support their child. *See Bogdon v. Bogdon*, 2018 WL 700823, at *6 (Pa. Super. 2018) ("Because child support is a shared responsibility, both parents are obligated to support their children in accordance with their relative incomes and ability to pay."). Assuming that the winnings constitute a material change in circumstances, *see McKinney v. Hamp*, 2018 WL 793995, at *4 (Miss. 2018) ("Parties may seek a child-support modification when there are substantial and material changes in circumstances."), the new support order will be made in light of the applicable guidelines. *Cf. Morales v. Morales*, 984 N.E.2d 748, 752 (Mass. 2013) ("[M]odification is presumptively required whenever there is an inconsistency between the amount of child support that is to be paid under the existing support order and the amount that would be paid under the guidelines.").

149. **Answer (B) is the best answer.** The doctrine of necessaries applied in a gender-neutral fashion provides the basis upon which an individual can be required to pay for a spouse's needed medical services. *See Wesley Long Nursing Ctr., Inc. v. Harper*, 2007 WL 4233643, at *1 (N.C. App. 2007) ("It is well settled that [the] 'doctrine of necessaries' applies to necessary medical expenses.").

Answer (A) is incorrect. The doctrine of necessaries requires the spouse to pay for needed medical expenses. *See Trident Reg'l Med. Ctr. v. Evans*, 454 S.E.2d 343, 344 (S.C. App. 1995) ("[U]nder the modern incarnation of the necessaries doctrine, both husbands and wives have an obligation to support their spouses, and both spouses are liable for the cost of necessaries supplied to one of the spouses, even if only one spouse is contractually liable for the necessaries.").

Answer (C) is incorrect. The doctrine of necessaries includes more than food, clothing, and housing. *See Wesley Long Nursing Ctr., Inc. v. Harper*, 2007 WL 4233643, at *1 (N.C. App. 2007).

Answer (D) is incorrect. The important issue is not whether Robin approved of this procedure or medical practitioner. Rather, the important issues are whether needed medical services were provided and whether the bills for those services were ever paid. *See Moses H. Cone Mem'l Hosp. Operating Corp. v. Hawley*, 672 S.E.2d 742, 744 (N.C. App. 2009) ("To establish a *prima facie* case 'for the recovery of expenses incurred in providing necessary medical services to the other spouse,' the party seeking to apply the doctrine must show: (1) medical services were provided to the spouse; (2) the medical services were necessary for the health and well-being of the receiving spouse; (3) the person against whom the action is brought was married to the person to whom the medical services were provided at the time such services were provided; and (4) the payment for the necessaries has not been made.").

150.   First, it will be important to consider the settlement agreement, which might itself have specified what will happen when Jody retires. *See*, for example, *Bohr v. Bohr*, 1997 WL 149198, at *1 (Wis. App. 1997) ("In their agreement, Steven agreed to pay Conchita $850 per month as maintenance 'until he retires from his present place of employment, or upon his death . . . [or] upon the marriage or death of [Conchita].'"). If the agreement does not say anything about retirement, then the question will be whether Jody is seeking to become voluntarily unemployed or, instead, is simply retiring when one might normally be expected to retire. *See Ebach v. Ebach*, 700 N.W.2d 684, 687 (N.D. 2005) ("refusing to modify support when individual sought to retire at 62 rather than 'at the customary retirement age of 65'"). Assuming that Jody is seeking to retire at a reasonable age, the retirement will likely constitute a substantial change in circumstances justifying a reduction in in support. *See Bogan v. Bogan*, 60 S.W.3d 721, 729 (Tenn. 2001) ("[W]e hold that when an obligor's retirement is objectively reasonable, it does constitute a substantial and material change in circumstances—irrespective of whether the retirement was foreseeable or voluntary—so as to permit modification of the support obligation.").

Family Privacy and the Constitution

151. **Answer (D) is the best answer.** Because the United States Constitution would not offer protection in this kind of case, *see In re Adoption of S.D.W.*, 758 S.E.2d 374, 375 (N.C. 2014) ("[O]btaining notice of the pregnancy and birth was not beyond John's control and . . . he had sufficient opportunity to acknowledge paternity and establish himself as a responsible parent within the time set by statute. Because he failed to do so, he falls outside the class of responsible biological fathers who enjoy a constitutionally protected relationship with their natural children."), Daniel would have to base his claim on available statutory or state constitutional protections. *See*, for example, *In re J.W.T.*, 872 S.W.2d 189 (Tex. 1994) (recognizing that the Texas Constitution offers biological fathers more robust protection than does the federal Constitution).

   Answer (A) is not the best answer. At this point, Daniel will be unlikely to be able to have the adoption annulled. *See In re Adoption of S.D.W.*, 758 S.E.2d 374, 375 (N.C. 2014).

   Answer (B) is not the best answer. At this point, he is unlikely to be able to have the adoption annulled. *See In re Adoption of S.D.W.*, 758 S.E.2d 374, 375 (N.C. 2014).

   Answer (C) is not the best answer. Because Daniel refused to return any of Ellen's calls or texts, he acted in a way that prevented him from availing himself of the opportunity to have a relationship with his child. *See Lehr v. Robertson*, 463 U.S. 248, 262 (1983) ("The significance of the biological connection is that it offers the natural father an opportunity . . . to develop a relationship with his offspring. If he grasps that opportunity and accepts some measure of responsibility for the child's future, he may enjoy the blessings of the parent-child relationship and make uniquely valuable contributions to the child's development. If he fails to do so, the Federal Constitution will not automatically compel a state to listen to his opinion of where the child's best interests lie.").

152. **Answer (D) is the best answer.** Because Kevin has never established a relationship with Melissa, he is unlikely to be able to block the adoption. *See Adoption of Michael H.*, 898 P.2d 891, 903 (Cal. 1995) ("Once the father knows or reasonably should know of the pregnancy, he must promptly attempt to assume his parental responsibilities as fully as the mother will allow and his circumstances permit. In particular, the father must demonstrate 'a willingness himself to assume full custody of the child—not merely to block adoption by others.'"). *See also In re J.M.D.*, 260 P.3d 1196, 1206–07 (Kan. 2011) ("[W]e hold that a natural parent's unfitness will not obviate the need for his or her consent to a stepparent adoption, unless the district court finds that the unfitness has prevented the natural parent from assuming the duties of a parent for 2 consecutive years next preceding the filing of the petition for

adoption.""). Assuming that the adoption would be in Melissa's best interest, *see D.P.H. v. J.L.B.*, 260 P.3d 320, 323 (Colo. 2011) ("The proceeding commences when a stepparent files for adoption. In order to approve the adoption, the court must first determine whether the adoption is in the best interests of the child."), the adoption will likely be permitted.

Answer (A) is not the best answer. Kevin is unlikely to be able to block the adoption. *See In re J.M.D.*, 260 P.3d 1196, 1206–07 (Kan. 2011).

Answer (B) is not the best answer. Merely because the custodial parent believes that adoption would be best is not dispositive if the noncustodial parent retains parental rights. *See Leger v. Coccaro*, 714 So. 2d 770, 772 ("An adoption may not be granted without the consent of both parents, except in situations in which parental consent has been dispensed with by law.").

Answer (C) is incorrect. Kevin's parental rights would likely be terminated prior to Samuel's being awarded parental rights. *See*, for example, *In re Diamonds M.*, 2006 WL 328586, at *3 (Conn. Super. 2006) ("[T]he Court finds by clear and convincing evidence that the child's best interest calls for termination of parental rights. Accordingly, the alleged ground of abandonment and the child's best interest both having been proven by clear and convincing evidence, the Court terminates the parental rights of the father, D.M., in and to his daughter, D.M; Mother is the sole parent and guardian of the child. The court approves a plan calling for stepparent adoption by mother's husband.").

153.   Paul is unlikely to be awarded custody of or visitation with Veronica because Paul does not have protected parental rights under the United States Constitution in this case. *See Michael H. v. Gerald D.*, 491 U.S. 110 (1989). Any protections would be provided by the state constitution, *see In re J.W.T.*, 872 S.W.2d 189 (Tex. 1994) (Texas Constitution affords non-marital biological fathers more robust rights than does the United States Constitution) or local law. *See Smith v. Jones*, 566 So. 2d 408 (La. Ct. App. 1990) (local law permits biological father to seek visitation with a child born into a marriage between the father's former paramour and her husband). Here, though, Famland law does not afford Paul any of those increased protections.

154.   **Answer (D) is the best answer.** The United States Constitution affords the pregnant woman the right to make the ultimate decisions regarding whether to have an abortion. *Planned Parenthood of Cent. Missouri v. Danforth*, 428 U.S. 52, 71 (1976) ("The obvious fact is that when the wife and the husband disagree on this decision, the view of only one of the two marriage partners can prevail. Inasmuch as it is the woman who physically bears the child and who is the more directly and immediately affected by the pregnancy, as between the two, the balance weighs in her favor."). Assuming that the fetus is not yet viable, the state cannot place an undue burden on a woman's right to abort. *See Planned Parenthood of Se. Pennsylvania v. Casey*, 505 U.S. 833, 878 (1992) ("An undue burden exists, and therefore a provision of law is invalid, if its purpose or effect is to place a substantial obstacle in the path of a woman seeking an abortion before the fetus attains viability.").

Answer (A) is incorrect. A spouse does not have the legal right to veto the pregnant spouse's obtaining an abortion. *Planned Parenthood of Cent. Missouri v. Danforth*, 428 U.S. 52, 71 (1976).

Answer (B) is incorrect. The state can impose a variety of restrictions on abortion once the fetus has attained viability. *See Roe v. Wade*, 410 U.S. 113, 163–64 (1973) ("State regulation protective of fetal life after viability thus has both logical and biological justifications. If the State is interested in protecting fetal life after viability, it may go so far as to proscribe abortion during that period, except when it is necessary to preserve the life or health of the mother.").

Answer (C) is not the best answer. It is not necessary for Kelsey to try to justify her decision to obtain an abortion of her pre-viable fetus. The state cannot impose an undue burden on her obtaining an abortion, *see Planned Parenthood of Se. Pennsylvania v. Casey*, 505 U.S. 833, 878 (1992), and Jesse does not have the right to veto Kelsey's obtaining an abortion. *See Planned Parenthood of Cent. Missouri v. Danforth*, 428 U.S. 52, 71 (1976). Once the fetus has attained viability, however, Kelsey might well have to provide a reason such as medical necessity. *See Roe v. Wade*, 410 U.S. 113, 163–64 (1973).

155. **Answer (D) is the best answer.** The Constitution requires that minors be given the opportunity to seek a judicial bypass so that parents will not need to be consulted in appropriate cases. *See Bellotti v. Baird*, 443 U.S. 622, 647 (1979) ("[E]very minor must have the opportunity—if she so desires—to go directly to a court without first consulting or notifying her parents. If she satisfies the court that she is mature and well enough informed to make intelligently the abortion decision on her own, the court must authorize her to act without parental consultation or consent.").

Answer (A) is incorrect. States do require parental consent for minor marriages and are not required to offer a judicial bypass option in that context. *See Moe v. Dinkins*, 533 F. Supp. 623 (S.D. N.Y. 1981) (upholding consent requirement for minor marriages and rejecting that a judicial bypass option must be afforded). However, a case involving a minor considering marriage and a case involving a minor considering abortion are distinguishable. *See id.* at 630 ("Giving birth to an unwanted child involves an irretrievable change in position for a minor as well as for an adult, whereas the temporary denial of the right to marry does not.").

Answer (B) is not the best answer. While both minors and adults have constitutional rights, the rights of minors are not always as robust as the rights of adults. *See Bellotti v. Baird*, 443 U.S. 622, 634 (1979) (recognizing "three reasons justifying the conclusion that the constitutional rights of children cannot be equated with those of adults: the peculiar vulnerability of children; their inability to make critical decisions in an informed, mature manner; and the importance of the parental role in child rearing").

Answer (C) is not the best answer. Parents are presumed to act in the best interests of their children. *See Parham v. J.R.*, 442 U.S. 584, 602 (1979) ("[H]istorically it has recognized that natural bonds of affection lead parents to act in the best interests of their children."). Further, parents have a fundamental interest in the care and custody of their children. *Troxel v. Granville*, 530 U.S. 57, 65 (2000) ("The liberty interest at issue in this case—the interest of parents in the care, custody, and control of their children—is perhaps the oldest of the fundamental liberty interests recognized by this Court."). Nonetheless, a judicial bypass option must also be afforded. *See Bellotti v. Baird*, 443 U.S. 622, 647 (1979).

156. **Answer (C) is the best answer.** The court is unlikely to award the embryos to Donald absent an agreement to that effect or some reason that he would never be able to father other children. *See Szafranski v. Dunston*, 34 N.E.3d 1132 (Ill. App. 2015) (awarding frozen embryos to woman who wanted to use them both because of the previous agreement and because she was no longer able to produce eggs). *See also In re Marriage of Witten*, 672 N.W.2d 708 (Iowa 2003) (maintaining status quo until parties could agree about the disposition of the frozen embryos).

Answer (A) is not the best answer. The court is unlikely to adopt this approach precisely because the embryos are not mere property. Absent agreement to the contrary or some compelling reason that the person wishing to use them needs these embryos in particular, the court is either more likely to preserve the status quo, *see In re Marriage of Witten*, 672 N.W.2d 708 (Iowa 2003), or to award them to the party who would not implant them. *See Davis v. Davis*, 842 S.W.2d 588, 604 (Tenn. 1992) ("Ordinarily, the party wishing to avoid procreation should prevail, assuming that the other party has a reasonable possibility of achieving parenthood by means other than use of the preembryos in question.").

Answer (B) is not the best answer. The pregnant woman is permitted to make the ultimate decision about her pregnancy, at least in part, because she is the one who must carry the pregnancy to term. *See Planned Parenthood of Cent. Missouri v. Danforth*, 428 U.S. 52, 71 (1976) ("The obvious fact is that when the wife and the husband disagree on this decision, the view of only one of the two marriage partners can prevail. Inasmuch as it is the woman who physically bears the child and who is the more directly and immediately affected by the pregnancy, as between the two, the balance weighs in her favor."). But bodily integrity is not implicated in the same way in this case, since she will not be carrying the child to term regardless of who is awarded the embryos. The court might instead favor the party whom the prior agreement specified could make the decision. *See Szafranski v. Dunston*, 34 N.E.3d 1132 (Ill. App. 2015). Or, the court might wait until the parties could agree. *See In re Marriage of Witten*, 672 N.W.2d 708 (Iowa 2003). Or, perhaps the court might lean against forcing someone to be a parent against his or her will. *See J.B. v. M.B.*, 783 A.2d 707 (N.J. 2001).

Answer (D) is not the best answer. The court is less likely to award them to the individual who wants to use them, absent agreement or some compelling need. *See Szafranski v. Dunston*, 34 N.E.3d 1132 (Ill. App. 2015). The court might well lean toward the individual who does not want to use them because that way no one would be forced to be a parent against his or her will. *See Davis v. Davis*, 842 S.W.2d 588, 604 (Tenn. 1992).

157. **Answer (D) is the best answer.** The statute is likely to be upheld because the state is seeking to prevent fetal exposure to harmful substances at a time when the fetus has already attained viability, *see Whitner v. State*, 492 S.E.2d 777 (S.C. 1997) (upholding law criminalizing exposure of fetus to drugs when the fetus has already attained viability), and when the state is already permitted to limit abortions as long as the limitation does not endanger the life or health of the pregnant woman. *See Planned Parenthood of Southeastern Pennsylvania v. Casey*, 505 U.S. 833, 834 (1992) (affirming "the State's power to restrict abortions after viability, if the law contains exceptions for pregnancies endangering a woman's life or health").

Answer (A) is not the best answer. This law will likely be found not to implicate the right to privacy. *See Whitner v. State*, 492 S.E.2d 777, 786 (S.C. 1997) ("It strains belief for Whitner to argue that using . . . cocaine during pregnancy is encompassed within the constitutionally recognized right of privacy.").

Answer (B) is not the best answer. First, the state might argue that it has a compelling interest in protecting the viable fetus. *See Whitner v. State*, 492 S.E.2d 777, 785 (S.C. 1997) ("[T]he State's interest in protecting the life and health of the viable fetus is not merely legitimate. It is compelling."). But even if the means chosen is not viewed as sufficiently narrowly tailored, that would likely not result in the invalidation of the law. Because this law does not limit the right to abortion, it will likely not be viewed as triggering strict scrutiny. *See id.* at 786 (holding that the law "does not burden [the] right to carry her pregnancy to term or any other privacy right").

Answer (C) is not the best answer. The state has the power to limit abortions of viable fetuses as long as the life and health of the pregnant woman are not thereby endangered. *See Planned Parenthood of Southeastern Pennsylvania v. Casey*, 505 U.S. 833, 834 (1992).

158. The United States Supreme Court has struck down a state statute criminalizing partial birth abortion in *Stenberg v. Carhart*, 530 U.S. 914 (2000). However, the Court upheld a federal statute prohibiting partial birth abortion in *Gonzales v. Carhart*, 550 U.S. 124 (2007). While the statutes differed somewhat in their wording, *see id.* at 152 ("the Act departs in material ways from the statute in *Stenberg*"), neither had an exception protecting the woman's heath. *See id.* at 170 (Ginsburg, J., dissenting) ("[T]he Court held the Nebraska statute unconstitutional in part because it lacked the requisite protection for the preservation of a woman's health."); *id.* (Ginsburg, J., dissenting) ("Retreating from prior rulings that abortion restrictions cannot be imposed absent an exception safeguarding a woman's health, the Court upholds an Act that surely would not survive under the close scrutiny that previously attended state-decreed limitations on a woman's reproductive choices."). It may be that the federal act was upheld because of the differences in statutory language, *see id.* at 133 ("Compared to the state statute at issue in *Stenberg*, the Act is more specific concerning the instances to which it applies and in this respect more precise in its coverage."), which would make the wording of the challenged Texarkana statute very important to consider.

159. **Answer (D) is the best answer.** The Court has suggested that the state can protect marriage without violating federal constitutional guarantees. *See Lawrence v. Texas*, 539 U.S. 558, 567 (2003) (cautioning states against setting boundaries to relationships "absent injury to a person or abuse of an institution the law protects"). *See also Lowe v. Swanson*, 639 F. Supp. 2d 857, 871 (N.D. Ohio 2009) ("If a choice needs to be made, then it would be more correct to narrowly construe *Lawrence,* so as not to unnecessarily disturb the prohibitions which were not before the Supreme Court in *Lawrence,* such as adultery . . ."). State constitutions sometimes offer more robust protections of the right to privacy than does the federal Constitution. *See In re J.W.T.*, 872 S.W.2d 189 (Tex. 1994) (recognizing that the Texas Constitution has more robust privacy protections than does the federal Constitution), so the challenge might be successful if state constitutional guarantees were so construed. However, it seems

unlikely that the federal Constitution would be interpreted to protect adultery, at least in part, because such a holding might impact many state laws. *See,* for example, *Cotton v. Cotton,* 2017 WL 6523098, at *4 (Tex. App. Dec. 21, 2017) ("[A] trial court's finding of adultery can support the disproportionate division of the community property.").

Answer (A) is not the best answer. The Court has suggested that some rights are enjoyed alike by the married and unmarried. *See Eisenstadt v. Baird,* 405 U.S. 438, 453 (1972) ("If the right of privacy means anything, it is the right of the individual, married or single, to be free from unwarranted governmental intrusion into matters so fundamentally affecting a person as the decision whether to bear or beget a child."). However, that does not mean that all distinctions between the married and the unmarried are impermissible. *See,* for example, *Mueller v. C.I.R.,* 2001 WL 522388, at *1 (7th Cir. 2001) ("[T]axing married couples and singles differently does not violate the Constitution.").

Answer (B) is incorrect. States do not have plenary power over marriage and divorce. *See Loving v. Virginia,* 388 U.S. 1 (1967) (striking down state anti-miscegenation law); *Zablocki v. Redhail,* 434 U.S. 374 (1978) (striking down law making it very difficult for indigent non-custodial parents to marry).

Answer (C) is not the best answer. As a general matter, the married have a right to engage in consensual relations with their spouses. *See Griswold v. Connecticut,* 381 U.S. 479, 485 (1965) (discussing "the sacred precincts of marital bedrooms"). Unmarried individuals also have the right to engage in consensual relations with adults. *See Witt v. Dep't of Air Force,* 527 F.3d 806, 823 (9th Cir. 2008) ("[T]he right to choose to engage in private, consensual sexual relations with another adult is a human right of the first order and, second, that right is firmly protected by the substantive guarantee of privacy—autonomy of the Due Process Clause."). Nonetheless, adult, consensual relations with a close family member are prohibited. *See Raines v. Com.,* 379 S.W.3d 152, 154 (Ky. App. 2012) ("[T]he plain meaning of the statute does not include the victim's age as an element of the crime of incest; our interpretation of the statute is that the primary element for incest is the relationship of the parties. Undoubtedly, the legislative intent is to prohibit sexual intercourse between persons with such relationships, including stepparents and stepchildren.").

160.   **Answer (D) is the best answer.** The United States Supreme Court has struck down a law prohibiting a group of persons all related by blood from living together, *see Moore v. City of East Cleveland,* 431 U.S. 494 (1977), and has upheld a zoning ordinance as applied to individuals who were unrelated. *See Village of Belle Terre v. Borass,* 416 U.S. 1 (1974). Here, the association of individuals seems to be more of a family than a collection of roommates even if they do not share the blood relation that was present in *Moore,* so it is not clear what the United States Supreme Court would say were this case to come before the Court.

Answer (A) is not the best answer. While the United States Supreme Court did strike down a zoning ordinance in *Moore v. City of East Cleveland,* 431 U.S. 494 (1977), the collection of individuals in that case were all related by blood, which is not true in this case, so *Moore* might be thought distinguishable.

Answer (B) is not the best answer. While the United States Supreme Court upheld a zoning ordinance in *Village of Belle Terre v. Borass*, 416 U.S. 1 (1974), the group of individuals at issue here seems closer to a functional family than does a group of college students, so *Borass* might seem distinguishable. *See id.* at 2–3 ("These six are students at nearby State University at Stony Brook and none is related to the other by blood, adoption, or marriage.").

Answer (C) is not the best answer. The United States Supreme Court has been unwilling to strike down zoning ordinances as burdening association rights where family ties were not implicated. *See Vill. of Belle Terre v. Boraas*, 416 U.S. 1, 7 (1974) ("It involves no 'fundamental' right guaranteed by the Constitution, such as . . . the right of association . . .").

161. **Answer (D) is the best answer.** The state's desire to minimize fraud coupled with the residency requirement merely delaying rather than precluding divorce were held to justify a one-year residency requirement. *See Sosna v. Iowa*, 419 U.S. 393, 408-10 (1975). The *Sosna* Court noted that some states have two-year residency requirements, *see id.* at 405, and nowhere suggested that such a requirement was any more problematic than the one-year requirement at issue before the Court.

Answer (A) is not the best answer. While the right to marry is fundamental, *see Loving v. Virginia*, 388 U.S. 1, 12 (1967) ("Marriage is one of the 'basic civil rights of man,' fundamental to our very existence and survival."), the Court would likely suggest that a residency requirement merely delays when the divorce will be granted. *See Sosna v. Iowa*, 419 U.S. 393, 410 (1975) ("No similar total deprivation is present in appellant's case, and the delay which attends the enforcement of the one-year durational residency requirement is, for the reasons previously stated, consistent with the provisions of the United States Constitution.").

Answer (B) is not the best answer. The Court would likely reject that such a requirement abridges the right to travel, at least in part, because such important individual interests are implicated in marriage and divorce including property rights and the care and support of children. *See Sosna v. Iowa*, 419 U.S. 393, 406–07 (1975).

Answer (C) is incorrect. States do not have plenary power over marriage and divorce. *See Loving v. Virginia*, 388 U.S. 1 (1967) (striking down anti-miscegenation laws); *Zablocki v. Redhail*, 434 U.S. 374 (1978) (striking down law making it very difficult for indigent noncustodial parents to marry); *Obergefell v. Hodges*, 135 S. Ct. 2584, 2594 (2015) (striking down same-sex marriage bans).

162. **Answer (A) is the best answer.** Because she is competent and the procedure quite invasive, her refusal will likely be respected. *See In re Baby Doe*, 632 N.E.2d 326, 330 (Ill. App. 1994) ("[A] woman's competent choice in refusing medical treatment as invasive as a caesarean section during her pregnancy must be honored, even in circumstances where the choice may be harmful to her fetus.").

Answer (B) is incorrect. Once the fetus has reached viability, the woman's right to make reproductive decisions is not unfettered. *See Planned Parenthood of Southeastern Pennsylvania v. Casey*, 505 U.S. 833, 846 (1992) (confirming "the State's power to restrict abortions after fetal viability, if the law contains exceptions for pregnancies which endanger the woman's life or health"). However, the state's power to restrict abortion does not mean that the state can order a woman to undergo invasive procedures, competent refusal notwithstanding. *See In re Baby Doe*, 632 N.E.2d 326, 330 (Ill. App. 1994).

Answer (C) is not the best answer. Even though it might be better for both Zena herself and her child if she undergoes the caesarian, this nonetheless is her decision to make. *See In re Baby Doe*, 632 N.E.2d 326, 330 (Ill. App. 1994).

Answer (D) is not the best answer. While the state is afforded much more flexibility once the fetus has attained viability, *see Planned Parenthood of Southeastern Pennsylvania v. Casey*, 505 U.S. 833, 846 (1992), that does not mean that the state can force a woman to undergo an invasive procedure, competent refusal notwithstanding. *See In re Baby Doe*, 632 N.E.2d 326, 330 (Ill. App. 1994).

163.   **Answer (B) is the best answer.** The United States Constitution does not immunize parents who have caused their children great harm merely because the parents are acting in accord with sincere religious beliefs. *See Prince v. Massachusetts*, 321 U.S. 158, 170 (1944) ("Parents may be free to become martyrs themselves. But it does not follow they are free, in identical circumstances, to make martyrs of their children before they have reached the age of full and legal discretion when they can make that choice for themselves.").

Answer (A) is not the best answer. The First Amendment to the United States Constitution has not been interpreted to protect parents in this kind of case. *See Prince v. Massachusetts*, 321 U.S. 158, 170 (1944).

Answer (C) is not the best answer. The parent cannot impose their own beliefs on the child and the child is not yet competent to make this decision for herself. *See Prince v. Massachusetts*, 321 U.S. 158, 170 (1944).

Answer (D) is not correct. Parents are entitled to some deference with respect to the decisions they make for their children. *See Troxel v. Granville*, 530 U.S. 57, 70 (2000) ("[I]f a fit parent's decision . . . becomes subject to judicial review, the court must accord at least some special weight to the parent's own determination."). However, that deference does not require the state to permit the parents to sacrifice their children. *See Prince v. Massachusetts*, 321 U.S. 158, 170 (1944).

164.   **Answer (D) is the best answer.** In some jurisdictions, courts will permit such sterilizations if it can be shown that such a procedure would be in the best interest of the incompetent herself. *See In re Penny N.*, 414 A.2d 541, 543 (N.H. 1980) ("[A] probate judge may permit a sterilization after making specific written findings from clear and convincing evidence, that it is in the best interests of the incapacitated ward, rather than the parents' or the public's convenience, to do so."). Other jurisdictions will approve such a procedure if the individual herself would have chosen it, had she been competent. *See Matter of Moe*, 432 N.E.2d 712, 721 (Mass. 1982) ("[T]he court is to determine whether to authorize sterilization when requested by the parents or guardian by finding the incompetent would so choose if competent. No

sterilization is to be compelled on the basis of any State or parental interest."). If both conditions are met, i.e., it would be in the individual's interests and it would be something that the individual would have chosen if competent, then it would likely be approved no matter which of the two standards was used in the jurisdiction.

Answer (A) is not the best answer. While the implicated right is fundamental, *see Estate of C.W.*, 640 A.2d 427, 428 (Pa. Super. 1994) ("[A] decision that an incompetent should undergo a sterilization procedure impinges on that person's fundamental right to procreate and involves an invasion of that person's bodily integrity."), courts have reasoned that incompetents should also be able to exercise the right to be sterilized where that procedure would be in that person's best interests. *See id.* ("[T]he crucial question to be answered in such cases [i]s whether the sterilization [i]s in the *best interest* of the incompetent.").

Answer (B) is not the best answer. While the sterilization might be permitted, that would be because it was in Alice's best interests or because she would have chosen such a procedure rather than because of the state's or parents' interests. *See Matter of Moe*, 432 N.E.2d 712, 721 (Mass. 1982) ("No sterilization is to be compelled on the basis of any State or parental interest.").

Answer (C) is not the best answer. Precisely because Alice, herself, would not be able to consent, some jurisdictions use substituted judgment, *see Matter of Moe*, 432 N.E.2d 712, 721 (Mass. 1982), whereas others use a best interests test. *See In re Penny N.*, 414 A.2d 541, 543 (N.H. 1980).

165. **Answer (D) is the best answer.** If it can be shown that Betty is sufficiently mature and informed to make a decision for herself, then a guardian would be unlikely to be appointed to make a decision for her, assuming that the state recognizes the mature minor doctrine. *See In re E.G.*, 549 N.E.2d 322, 326 (Ill. 1989) ("[M]ature minors may possess and exercise rights regarding medical care that are rooted in this State's common law.").

Answer (A) is not the best answer. While it is true that Betty has a very low chance of survival without treatment, she also has a relatively poor chance of survival even with treatment. Further, if Massecticut recognizes mature minor doctrine, then Betty might well be allowed to make this decision, assuming that the relevant degree of maturity and understanding can be established. *See In re E.G.*, 549 N.E.2d 322, 326 (Ill. 1989).

Answer (B) is not the best answer. If Betty is not found to be a mature minor, then a guardian might well be appointed, agreement between child and parents about the inappropriateness of treatment notwithstanding. *See In re Cassandra C.*, 112 A.3d 158, 159 (Conn. 2015) (upholding trial court rejection of minor's refusal of treatment, parental support of the minor's decision notwithstanding).

Answer (C) is not the best answer. While parents will not be permitted to sacrifice their children, *see Prince v. Massachusetts*, 321 U.S. 158, 170 (1944) ("Parents may be free to become martyrs themselves. But it does not follow they are free, in identical circumstances, to make martyrs of their children before they have reached the age of full and legal discretion when they can make that choice for themselves."), children, if sufficiently mature and informed, may be permitted to make such decisions for themselves. *See In re E.G.*, 549 N.E.2d 322, 326 (Ill. 1989).

166.   **Answer (D) is the best answer.** Surrogacy agreements are unenforceable in some jurisdictions. *See,* for example, N.Y. Dom. Rel. Law § 122 (McKinney) ("Surrogate parenting contracts are hereby declared contrary to the public policy of this state, and are void and unenforceable."); Mich. Comp. Laws Ann. § 722.855 (West) ("A surrogate parentage contract is void and unenforceable as contrary to public policy."); and enforceable in others. *See P.M. v. T.B.*, 2018 WL 911210 (Iowa 2018); *Johnson v. Calvert*, 851 P.2d 776 (Cal. 1993) (gestational surrogacy contract enforceable). The enforceability of the contract at issue will depend on Nebradaho law. However, it should not be assumed that a traditional surrogacy contract would be wholly unenforceable. *See In re Baby*, 447 S.W.3d 807 (Tenn. 2014); *In re F.T.R.*, 833 N.W.2d 634 (Wis. 2013).

   Answer (A) is not the best answer. While it is true that Daniella would not have become pregnant but for the agreement, that would also be true had she been a traditional surrogate and some jurisdictions permit the traditional surrogate to void the surrogacy agreement. *See In re Marriage of Moschetta*, 30 Cal. Rptr. 2d 893 (Ct. App. 1994).

   Answer (B) is not the best answer. While gestational surrogacy agreements are often enforced, *see P.M. v. T.B.*, 2018 WL 911210 (Iowa 2018); *C.M. v. M.C.*, 213 Cal. Rptr. 3d 351 (Ct. App.); *In re Baby S.*, 128 A.3d 296 (Pa. Super. 2015); *Raftopol v. Ramey*, 12 A.3d 783 (Conn. 2011), traditional surrogacy agreements are also sometimes enforced, at least in part. *See In re Baby*, 447 S.W.3d 807 (Tenn. 2014); *In re F.T.R.*, 833 N.W.2d 634 (Wis. 2013).

   Answer (C) is not the best answer. Many jurisdictions will enforce gestational surrogacy contracts. *See P.M. v. T.B.*, 2018 WL 911210 (Iowa 2018); *C.M. v. M.C.*, 213 Cal. Rptr. 3d 351 (Ct. App. 2017); *In re Baby S.*, 128 A.3d 296 (Pa. Super. 2015); *Raftopol v. Ramey*, 12 A.3d 783 (Conn. 2011).

167.   Brian is unlikely to prevail in this suit, at least in part, because the state did not play any role in causing Beatrice to be abused. *See DeShaney v. Winnebago Cty. Dep't of Soc. Servs.*, 489 U.S. 189, 202 (1989) ("Because . . . the State had no constitutional duty to protect Joshua against his father's violence, its failure to do so—though calamitous in hindsight—simply does not constitute a violation of the Due Process Clause."). In this case, the state never even had custody of Beatrice, much less did the state somehow put Beatrice in a more dangerous position than she would have been had the state never acted. *See id.* at 201 ("While the State may have been aware of the dangers that Joshua faced in the free world, it played no part in their creation, nor did it do anything to render him any more vulnerable to them."). A separate question would be whether state law afforded any relief. *Cf. id.* at 203 ("The people of Wisconsin may well prefer a system of liability which would place upon the State and its officials the responsibility for failure to act in situations such as the present one. They may create such a system, if they do not have it already, by changing the tort law of the State in accordance with the regular lawmaking process.").

168. While *Griswold* has been read to protect marital privacy, *see Washington v. Glucksberg*, 521 U.S. 702, 720 (1997) ("[T]he 'liberty' specially protected by the Due Process Clause includes the rights ... to marital privacy, *Griswold v. Connecticut*, 381 U.S. 479 (1965)"), that right has not been interpreted to include the right to have forced relations with a spouse. *See People v. Liberta*, 474 N.E.2d 567, 574 (N.Y. 1984) ("The marital exemption simply does not further marital privacy because this right of privacy protects consensual acts, not violent sexual assaults."). Peter is incorrect that he is immune from prosecution. That said, however, states sometimes limit what will count as rape if a spouse is involved. *Compare* Okla. Stat. Ann. tit. 21, § 1111 (B) (West) ("Rape is an act of sexual intercourse accomplished with a male or female who is the spouse of the perpetrator if force or violence is used or threatened, accompanied by apparent power of execution to the victim or to another person.") *with* Okla. Stat. Ann. tit. 21, § 1111 (5) (West) ("Rape is an act of sexual intercourse involving vaginal or anal penetration accomplished with a male or female who is not the spouse of the perpetrator and who may be of the same or the opposite sex as the perpetrator under any of the following circumstances: ... Where the victim is at the time unconscious of the nature of the act and this fact is known to the accused.").

169. States have differing laws about who owns the privilege that prevents an individual from being forced to testify against his or her spouse. *See*, for example, Vt. R. Evid. 504 (b) ("Any person has a privilege to refuse to disclose and to prevent his spouse or any other person from disclosing any confidential statement, conversation, letter, or other confidential communication between such person and his spouse occurring while they were lawfully married, and to refuse to testify and prevent his spouse from testifying in any case as to any matter which in the opinion of the court would lead to a violation of marital confidence. This privilege exists whether or not the person and spouse are still lawfully married at the time at which the spouse's testimony is to be given."). However, precisely because the exercise of such a privilege might prevent one spouse from testifying about certain matters when the parties' interests diverge, states often have created exceptions that will allow a spouse to offer testimony when the parties' interests conflict. *See* Vt. R. Evid. 504 (d) ("There is no privilege under this rule in a proceeding in which one spouse is charged with a crime, or alleged to have committed a tort, against the person or property of (1) the other, (2) a child of either, (3) a person residing in the household of either, or (4) a third person in the course of committing a crime against any of them. There is also no privilege under this rule in any other civil proceeding in which the spouses are adverse parties; or, in the discretion of the court, in any other proceeding where the interests of a child of either are involved.").

170. **Answer (D) is the best answer.** That marriage implicates a fundamental interest does not entail that all marriage regulations violate constitutional guarantees. The Court has rejected "that every state regulation which relates in any way to the incidents of or prerequisites for marriage must be subjected to rigorous scrutiny." *See Zablocki v. Redhail*, 434 U.S. 374, 386 (1978). Nonetheless, those marital restrictions that significantly impact the ability of individuals to marry must serve significant interests and must be closely tailored to the promotion of those interests. *See Zablocki v. Redhail*, 434 U.S. 374, 388 (1978) ("When a statutory classification significantly interferes with the exercise of a fundamental right, it cannot be

upheld unless it is supported by sufficiently important state interests and is closely tailored to effectuate only those interests.").

Answer (A) is not the best answer. While states are barred from prohibiting interracial marriage, *see Loving v. Virginia*, 388 U.S. 1 (1967), or same-sex marriage, *see Obergefell v. Hodges*, 135 S. Ct. 2584 (2015), they may impose some limitations on marriage. *See Reynolds v. United States*, 98 U.S. 145 (1878) (upholding polygamy restriction).

Answer (B) is not the best answer. Traditionally, an individual who marries in one state is not entitled to have that marriage recognized by all the states if the marriage violates an important public policy of the individual's domicile at the time of the marriage. *See Pesina v. Anderson*, 1995 WL 387752, at *1 (Minn. App. 1995) ("The validity of a marriage normally is determined by the law of the place where the marriage was contracted and if valid by that law, the marriage is valid everywhere unless it violates a strong public policy of the domicile of the parties.").

Answer (C) is not the best answer. A state is not required to permit individuals to divorce whenever they want to do so, *see Sosna v. Iowa*, 419 U.S. 393 (1975) (upholding residency requirement for divorce), even though individuals might thereby be delayed in when they can exercise their right to marry (again).

171. Frank is unlikely to be successful. As a general matter, children are not to be donors unless they themselves would benefit from the donation. *See Curran v. Bosze*, 566 N.E.2d 1319, 1331 (Ill. 1990) ("We hold that a parent or guardian may give consent on behalf of a minor daughter or son for the child to donate bone marrow to a sibling, only when to do so would be in the minor's best interest."). Here, there is no indication that John and Monica have a close relationship such that John would benefit from helping Monica (beyond the kind of benefit that might accrue from helping anyone in need). Usually, some kind of showing about the good relationship between the donor and done is required. *See id.* ("The primary benefit to the donor in these cases arises from the relationship existing between the donor and recipient."). Whether or not Frank is correct that Samantha still harbors resentment over their divorce, this does not seem to be the kind of case where Samantha would be justified in authorizing John's being a donor even if he were a suitable match. *See Curran v. Bosze*, 566 N.E.2d 1319, 1331 (Ill. 1990).

172. While parents are free to believe as they will, *see McDaniel v. Paty*, 435 U.S. 618, 626 (1978) ("The Free Exercise Clause categorically prohibits government from regulating, prohibiting, or rewarding religious beliefs as such."), they are not permitted to make martyrs of their children. *See Prince v. Massachusetts*, 321 U.S. 158, 170 (1944) ("Parents may be free to become martyrs themselves. But it does not follow they are free, in identical circumstances, to make martyrs of their children before they have reached the age of full and legal discretion when they can make that choice for themselves."). Here, Melissa is being harmed because of her diet, notwithstanding that her mother is acting according to sincere religious belief. *See Pankratz v. Pankratz*, 2017 WL 4842400, at *7 (Tenn. App. 2017) ("[T]he welfare and best interest of the child are always the court's paramount concerns, and a court may interfere when

there is a *clear and affirmative* showing that one parent's religious beliefs and practices threaten the health and well-being of the child."). The state's action will likely be upheld.

173.   **Answer (D) is the best answer.** The court is likely to uphold the law, *see State v. Holm*, 137 P.3d 726, 745 (Utah 2006) (upholding state polygamy law against constitutional challenge), notwithstanding that other marital restrictions have been struck down. *See Loving v. Virginia*, 388 U.S. 1 (1967) (striking down anti-miscegenation laws); *Zablocki v. Redhail*, 434 U.S. 374 (1978) (striking down law making it very difficult for indigent noncustodial parents to marry); *Obergefell v. Hodges*, 135 S. Ct. 2584 (2015) (striking down same-sex marriage bans).

    Answer (A) is not the best answer, because the court is not likely to strike down the law as a violation of the fundamental right to marry. *See State v. Holm*, 137 P.3d 726, 745 (Utah 2006).

    Answer (B) is not the best answer, because the court is unlikely to strike down the law on free exercise grounds. *See Reynolds v. United States*, 98 U.S. 145 (1878) (upholding polygamy restriction).

    Answer (C) is not the best answer. While the federal Constitution nowhere mentions the right to marry, *see Zablocki v. Redhail*, 434 U.S. 374, 392 (1978) ("The Constitution does not specifically mention freedom to marry."), it has nonetheless been interpreted to limit the power of states to restrict marriage on certain bases. *See Loving v. Virginia*, 388 U.S. 1 (1967); *Zablocki v. Redhail*, 434 U.S. 374 (1978); *Obergefell v. Hodges*, 135 S. Ct. 2584 (2015).

174.   Sarah's challenge is likely to be successful. While states should try to be good stewards of public funds, *see C & A Carbone, Inc. v. Town of Clarkstown, N.Y.*, 511 U.S. 383, 429 (1994) ("Protection of the public fisc is . . . legitimate"), that does not mean that such a goal will justify infringing the fundamental right to marry. Rather, for such an infringement to be upheld will require that a more important interest be at stake and that the statute be more closely tailored to the promotion of that interest. *See Zablocki v. Redhail*, 434 U.S. 374, 388 (1978) ("When a statutory classification significantly interferes with the exercise of a fundamental right, it cannot be upheld unless it is supported by sufficiently important state interests and is closely tailored to effectuate only those interests.").

Parenting Relationships

175. **Answer (B) is the best answer.** Depending upon state law, Norman might be precluded from having parenting time with Rachel. *See Lake v. Putnam*, 894 N.W.2d 62, 67 (Mich. App. 2016) ("[T]he equitable-parent doctrine does not extend to unmarried couples. . . . This is true whether the couple involved is a heterosexual or a same-sex couple. Consequently, because the equitable-parent doctrine does not apply, plaintiff lacks standing to seek parenting time in this case.").

   Answer (A) is incorrect. An unmarried man might be recognized as being a child's father even though the child was born through artificial insemination. *See In re T.P.S.*, 978 N.E.2d 1070, 1075 (Ill. App. 2012) ("The central issue before us in this appeal concerns whether Illinois recognizes a common law action for child custody and visitation where an unmarried couple agrees to conceive a child by artificial insemination, and the couple subsequently begins raising the child as coequal parents. We hold that, with respect to children born of artificial insemination, under the facts of this case, the Illinois legislature has not barred common law contract and promissory estoppel causes of action for custody and visitation brought by the nonbiological parent.").

   Answer (C) is not the best answer. Even if Rachel views Norman as her father, local law might preclude Norman from seeking parenting time. *See Lake v. Putnam*, 894 N.W.2d 62, 67 (Mich. App. 2016).

   Answer (D) is nor the best answer. The court's finding that awarding visitation privileges to Norman would be in Rachel's best interests would not suffice to justify rejecting Penelope's decision to preclude Norman from seeing Rachel, assuming that Norman does not have parental status. *Cf. Troxel v. Granville*, 530 U.S. 57, 72 (2000) ("[T]he visitation order in this case was an unconstitutional infringement on Granville's fundamental right to make decisions concerning the care, custody, and control of her two daughters.").

176. **Answer (B) is the best answer.** Assuming that Alex's consent was in writing, he will likely be required to pay support. If his consent was oral, he might not be required to pay support. *See K.B. v. N.B.*, 811 S.W.2d 634, 638 (Tex. App. 1991) ("We are not willing to hold that oral consent will estop a husband from asserting § 12.03, or estop him from denying paternity or avoiding child support."), unless he ratified the parent-child relationship, *see id.* at 639 ("Under the unique facts of this case, he has ratified the parent-child relationship."), or he is estopped from denying that he gave consent. *See R.S. v. R.S.*, 670 P.2d 923, 928 (Kan. App. 1983) ("[A] husband who with his wife orally consents to the treating physician that his wife be heterologously inseminated for the purpose of producing a child of their own is estopped to deny

that he is the father of the child, and he has impliedly agreed to support the child and act as its father.").

Answer (A) is not the best answer. A husband who consents to artificial insemination of his wife in accord with statutory requirements will likely be held responsible for child support. *See In re Marriage of A.C.H. & D.R.H.*, 210 P.3d 929, 933 (Or. App. 2009) (holding husband responsible for child support whose consent was in accord with the state's requirements).

Answer (C) is not the best answer. A husband who did not consent to the artificial insemination would likely not be required to support a child born through the artificial insemination, *see In re Marriage of Witbeck-Wildhagen*, 667 N.E.2d 122, 123 (Ill. App. 1996) (husband not required to support child born of unconsented to artificial insemination), absent later ratification. *K.B. v. N.B.*, 811 S.W.2d 634, 639 (Tex. App. 1991).

Answer (D) is not the best answer. The court would likely be unwilling to relieve Alex of a support obligation merely because he was willing not to have any part in the child's life, because approving such an approach would harm the child in multiple ways. *Cf. Perkinson v. Perkinson*, 989 N.E.2d 758, 762 (Ind. 2013) ("It is incomprehensible to this Court to imagine that either parent would ever stipulate to give up parenting time in lieu of not paying child support.").

177. **Answer (D) is the best answer.** If Alfred and Benita agreed that he would have parental rights, then he might well be recognized as having such rights, as long as he would not be considered a sperm donor in light of the relevant statute. *See C.O. v. W.S.*, 639 N.E.2d 523, 525 (Ohio Com. Pl. 1994) (recognizing donor as child's father where requirements for his being a sperm donor without rights were not met).

Answer (A) is not the best answer. Assuming that local law does not bar his having rights, *see A.A.B. v. B.O.C.*, 112 So. 3d 761, 764 (Fla. App. 2013), he might well be thought to have parental rights, especially if that was the agreement that he and Benita had made. *See In Interest of R.C.*, 775 P.2d 27, 35 (Colo. 1989).

Answer (B) is not the best answer. Mere genetic connection will not establish Alfred's paternity if according to local law he is a sperm donor with no parental rights. *See A.A.B. v. B.O.C.*, 112 So. 3d 761, 764 (Fla. App. 2013).

Answer (C) is not the best answer. Merely because she will have custody does not negate his having parental rights if that was their agreement. *See In Interest of R.C.*, 775 P.2d 27, 35 (Colo. 1989) ("Where, however, the unmarried recipient and the known donor at the time of insemination agree that the donor will be the natural father and act accordingly based on an express understanding that he will be treated as the father of any child so conceived, . . . that agreement and subsequent conduct are relevant to preserving the donor's parental rights.").

178. **Answer (A) is the best answer.** Oral consent might suffice in light of state law, *see In re Marriage of A.C.H. & D.R.H.*, 210 P.3d 929, 933 (Or. App. 2009) or the presumption that a child born into a marriage is a product of the marriage might apply. *See Wendy G-M. v. Erin G-M.*, 985 N.Y.S.2d 845, 858 (Sup. Ct. 2014) ("The presumption of parental status for children born

into a marriage should not be so easily discarded because the married couple, who planned for the child and celebrated its arrival, then encounter marital troubles.") Or, Nancy might be estopped from denying Mary's parental status. *See Estrellita A. v. Jennifer D.*, 963 N.Y.S.2d 843, 847 (Fam. Ct. 2013) ("[R]espondent is judicially estopped in this custody/visitation proceeding from asserting that petitioner is not a parent.").

Answer (B) is not the best answer. She might be recognized as a parent because of presumptions regarding a child born into a marriage. *See Wendy G-M. v. Erin G-M.*, 985 N.Y.S.2d 845, 858 (Sup. Ct. 2014).

Answer (C) is not correct. Presumptions about parentage might also be applied to mothers. *See Wendy G-M. v. Erin G-M.*, 985 N.Y.S.2d 845, 858 (Sup. Ct. 2014). Further, some states do not require written consent to artificial insemination. *See In re Marriage of A.C.H. & D.R.H.*, 210 P.3d 929, 933 (Or. App. 2009).

Answer (D) is not correct. An existing parent-child relationship might not suffice. *See Jones v. Barlow*, 154 P.3d 808, 819 (Utah 2007) ("[W]e decline to create such perpetual rights by adopting a doctrine similar to that of 'psychological parent' or 'de facto parent.'"). Further, a robust parent-child relationship might not be necessary. *See Wendy G-M. v. Erin G-M.*, 985 N.Y.S.2d 845, 858 (Sup. Ct. 2014) (presumed parent status recognized notwithstanding that couple separated a week after the child's birth).

179. **Answer (D) is the best answer.** It would have been better for the rights termination and the granting of the adoption to have occurred in different proceedings to avoid the possibility that the court's judgment concerning Zena's fitness was informed by its very favorable view of the Monroes' parenting skills. *See Kingsley v. Kingsley*, 623 So. 2d 780, 788 (Fla. App. 1993) ("Trying these two matters separately avoids an impermissible comparison between the natural parent's parenting skills and those of the prospective parents, a comparison which could impact greatly the outcome of any termination proceeding where the focus must remain on issues such as abandonment, neglect, or abuse.").

Answer (A) is not the best answer. While a child's wishes will be considered if he or she can express a meaningful preference, *see Lane v. Lane*, 446 A.2d 418, 419 (Me. 1982), that does not mean that adoption should be deferred until the child can express such a preference. Such a policy would prevent children from being able to benefit from early placement in stable, loving homes. *See In re Adoption of K.S.P.*, 804 N.E.2d 1253, 1255–56 (Ind. Ct. App. 2004) ("[E]arly, permanent placement of children with adoptive families furthers the interests of both the child and the state.").

Answer (B) is not the best answer. If this were a voluntary placement, then the biological parent's wishes would be given weight. *See Matter of Welfare of R.S.P.*, 2018 WL 414375, at *3 (Minn. App. 2018) ("When a parent has consented to adoption, 'only the person identified by the parent and agreed to by the agency as the prospective adoptive parent qualifies for adoptive placement of the child.'"). Here, however, the parental rights are being terminated involuntarily, which means that Zena is not in the position to require that her wishes be respected. *See In re B. E.*, 377 A.2d 153, 156 (Pa. 1977) ("[T]he purpose of involuntary termination of parental rights is to dispense with the need for parental consent to an adoption when, by choice or neglect, a parent has failed to meet the continuing needs of the child.").

Answer (C) is not the best answer. The Monroes would appropriately be preferred as adoptive parents if Thomas has bonded with them. *See Div. of Youth & Family Servs. v. S.S.*, 2011 WL 1405005, at *8 (N.J. Super. App. Div. 2011) (discussing the harm that might occur were the child not placed with the foster parents with whom he had bonded).

180. **Answer (B) is the best answer.** In some states, open adoptions do not afford the biological parent any rights that are enforceable. *Compare Fredericksen v. Olsen*, 2016 WL 5930432, at *7 (Iowa Ct. App. 2016) ("[O]pen adoptions are not enforceable.") *with Michaud v. Wawruck*, 551 A.2d 738 (Conn. 1988) (upholding agreement permitting post-adoption visitation provided that the continued visitation would be in the best interests of the child).

Answer (A) is incorrect. An open adoption involves an agreement permitting some kind of contact between the biological parent and the child after the adoption has been finalized. *See Michaud v. Wawruck*, 551 A.2d 738, 740–41 (Conn. 1988) ("The plaintiff's rights are not premised on an ongoing genetic relationship that somehow survives a termination of parental rights and an adoption. Instead, the plaintiff is asking us to decide whether, as an adult who has had an ongoing personal relationship with the child, she may contract with the adopting parents, prior to adoption, for the continued right to visit with the child, so long as that visitation continues to be in the best interest of the child.").

Answer (C) is incorrect. An open adoption is not an agreement to permit the child to have access to family medical history. Rather, it is an agreement to permit the biological parent to continue to have some sort of contact with the child post-adoption. *See Michaud v. Wawruck*, 551 A.2d 738, 740–41 (Conn. 1988).

Answer (D) is not the best answer. The biological parent does not retain parental rights, but may retain a right to contact (contingent on that contact being in the best interest of the child). *See Michaud v. Wawruck*, 551 A.2d 738, 740–41 (Conn. 1988).

181. **Answer (C) is the best answer.** The stepparent exception permits an individual to adopt his or her spouse's children without that spouse being forced to have his or her own parental rights terminated. *See In re M.M.D.*, 662 A.2d 837, 859–60 (D.C. 1995) ("The specified exception reflects the typical stepparent situation . . . [W]hen a natural parent remarries and plans to live with his or her children and new spouse as a family unit, the statutory 'cut off' requirement—terminating the birth parent's rights so that the adopting parent and child can begin a new family without interference by the birth parent—does not apply.").

Answer (A) is not the best answer. As a general matter, stepparents will not be forced to support stepchildren once the adults' relationship ends, *see Drawbaugh v. Drawbaugh*, 647 A.2d 240, 242 (Pa. Super. 1994) ("[N]o appellate case in Pennsylvania has imposed a duty of support on a stepparent . . . following the dissolution of the parties' marriage, absent a written agreement to assume such obligation."). That would also be true after the relationship of a cohabiting couple had ended, i.e., the adult with no legal or biological relationship to the children would not be required to support those children absent some kind of agreement to do so. *Cf. Elisa B. v. Superior Court*, 117 P.3d 660 (Cal. 2005) (individual responsible for child support after consenting to artificial insemination of former non-marital partner).

Answer (B) is not the best answer. A stepparent may well have legal responsibility for a child living in the home. *See In re R.R.N.*, 775 S.E.2d 656, 659 (N.C. 2015) ("The 'caretaker' statute protects children from abuse and neglect inflicted by people with significant, parental-type responsibility for the daily care of a child in the child's residential setting. Stepparents, foster parents, and adult members of the juvenile's household, for example, live with the child in the child's home.").

Answer (D) is not the best answer. While an individual may have parental obligations if he or she voluntarily assumes such obligations with respect to children living in the home, *see DeNomme v. DeNomme*, 544 A.2d 63, 65 (Pa. Super. 1988) ("The general rule is that a stepparent has no legal obligation to support stepchildren. ... It is the natural parent's absolute duty to do so. ... The courts of this Commonwealth have found an exception where the stepparent voluntarily assumes parental status and assumes parental duties; in this, known as the *in loco parentis* status."), that is not what the stepparent exception involves. *See In re M.M.D.*, 662 A.2d 837, 859–60 (D.C. 1995).

182. **Answer (C) is the best answer.** States permit a variety of reasonable fees and costs to be paid. *See In re Adoption of Baby Boy A*, 236 P.3d 116, 123 (Okla. 2010) ("The fees, costs, and expenses for which the prospective adoptive parents may pay money, property, or other thing of value, are listed . . . : a. reasonable attorney fees and court costs, b. reasonable medical expenses for birth mother and minor to be adopted, c. reasonable adoption counseling expenses for birth parents before and after the birth of the minor, not to exceed six (6) months from placement of the minor, d. reasonable fees of a licensed child-placement agency, e. reasonable living expenses for housing, food, clothing, utilities, and other necessities of the birth mother that are incurred during the adoption planning process or during the pregnancy . . . , f. reasonable costs for travel or transportation of the birth mother or minor as same is incurred for medical or adoption placement needs, g. reasonable expenses for a home study, and h. reasonable expenses legally required by any governmental entity related to the adoption of a minor.").

Answer (A) is not the best answer because the reimbursement for some reasonable costs is permissible. *See In re Adoption of Baby Boy A*, 236 P.3d 116, 123 (Okla. 2010).

Answer (B) is incorrect. Even if in fact those buying a child would be wonderful parents, buying or selling a child is nonetheless a crime. *See State v. Runkles*, 605 A.2d 111, 119 (Md. 1992) ("[W]hen the Legislature declared that a person may not sell, or offer to sell, a child for anything of value, it intended that the prohibition have a broad reach.").

Answer (D) is incorrect. There are limitations on how much attorneys may charge when helping to arrange adoptions. *See In re Adoption of Baby C*, 47 Pa. D. & C.3d 47, 48 (Orph. Ct. 1987) ("[T]his court has disallowed attorney fees beyond those which are reasonable and directly related to the expertise required, the time and effort expended in the preparation and presentation of the petition, and the representative of the client. The court's rationale is that excessive fees would permit the attorney to impermissibly profit from the placement and adoption of newborn infants.").

183. **Answer (D) is the best answer.** Some states recognize equitable adoptions, while others do not. Those that recognize such adoptions often require an agreement to adopt. *See Nguyen v. Boynes*, 396 P.3d 774, 777 (Nev. 2017) ("[E]quitable adoption as an equitable remedy to enforce an adoption agreement under circumstances where there is a promise to adopt, and in reasonable, foreseeable reliance on that promise a child is placed in a position where harm will result if repudiation is permitted."). Some states in addition require that the child have had a familial relationship with the would-be adopters. *See DeHart v. DeHart*, 986 N.E.2d 85, 103 (Ill. 2013) ("[A] plaintiff bringing an equitable adoption claim must prove an intent to adopt . . . and, additionally, must show that the decedent acted consistently with that intent by forming with the plaintiff a close and enduring familial relationship.").

Answer (A) is not the best answer. An equitable adoption is not merely one that meets some notion of fairness but instead involves certain conditions having been met such as agreement to adopt and the child having lived with the would-be adopters. *See Nguyen v. Boynes*, 396 P.3d 774, 777 (Nev. 2017); *DeHart v. DeHart*, 986 N.E.2d 85, 103 (Ill. 2013).

Answer (B) is not the best answer because an equitable adoption is not merely one that meets some notion of fairness but instead involves certain conditions having been met such as agreement to adopt and the child having lived with the would-be adopters. *See Nguyen v. Boynes*, 396 P.3d 774, 777 (Nev. 2017); *DeHart v. DeHart*, 986 N.E.2d 85, 103 (Ill. 2013).

Answer (C) is not the best answer. Foster parents may have an edge in adopting the children whom they have been fostering if only because they and the child might have a strong bond. *Cf. Div. of Youth & Family Servs. v. S.S.*, 2011 WL 1405005, at *8 (N.J. Super. App. Div. 2011) (discussing the harm that might occur were the child not placed with the foster parents with whom he had bonded). However, that is not what an equitable adoption involves. *See Nguyen v. Boynes*, 396 P.3d 774, 777 (Nev. 2017); *DeHart v. DeHart*, 986 N.E.2d 85, 103 (Ill. 2013).

184. An equitable adoption does not alter the status of the child, although it does allow an individual to inherit from his or her would-be adopters. *See Bd. of Educ. of Montgomery Cty. v. Browning*, 635 A.2d 373, 376 (Md. 1994) ("Under the doctrine of equitable adoption, however, no relationship of parent and child is created and consequently, an equitably adopted child does not attain the status of a statutorily adopted child."). *See also In re Adoption of A.R.*, 387 P.3d 1285, 1288 (Ariz. App. 2016) ("[T]he doctrine of equitable adoption . . . only enforces in equity the benefits of adoption in the context of inheritance."). But that means that Monica would still be Carl's child and thus might inherit from him. *See Gardner v. Hancock*, 924 S.W.2d 857, 859 (Mo. App. 1996) ("[A]n equitably adopted child [can] inherit from both the adoptive parents and from the natural parents because the doctrine of equitable adoption does not change the child's status to that of a legally adopted person.").

185. Some states recognize second-parent adoptions whereby an individual who is not married to the parent is nonetheless permitted to adopt that parent's child without that parent being

forced to give up his or her parental rights. If New Vermshire permits such adoptions, then Shannon and Tory will likely be permitted to establish the desired parent-child relationships. *See Matter of Jacob*, 660 N.E.2d 397, 398 (N.Y. 1995) (holding that state law permits "the unmarried partner of a child's biological mother, whether heterosexual or homosexual, who is raising the child together with the biological parent, to become the child's second parent by means of adoption"). However, some jurisdictions do not recognize second-parent adoptions. *See In re Adoption of Luke*, 640 N.W.2d 374 (Neb. 2002) (holding that Nebraska does not permit second-parent adoptions). If New Vermshire does not recognize second-parent adoptions, then Shannon and Tory will have to make other arrangements if they wish to protect the non-legally recognized parenting relationships. *See St. Mary v. Damon*, 309 P.3d 1027, 1029 (Nev. 2013) (upholding validity of co-parenting agreement between non-marital partners).

186. The conditions under which one adult can adopt another adult vary by state. Some states have relatively forgiving statutes. *See*, for example, Okla. Stat. Ann. tit. 10, § 7507-1.1 (West) ("An adult person may be adopted by any other adult person, with the consent of the person to be adopted or his guardian, if the court shall approve, and with the consent of the spouse, if any, of an adoptive parent, filed in writing with the court. . . . After a hearing on the petition and after such investigation as the court deems advisable, if the court finds that it is to the best interests of the people involved, a decree of adoption may be entered."). *See also* Minn. Stat. Ann. § 259.241 (West). However, other states restrict the circumstances under which adult adoptions can take place. *See* Ohio Rev. Code Ann. § 3107.02 (B) (West). Nonetheless, this is exactly the kind of adult adoption that at least some of the statutes contemplate. *See*, for example, Ohio Rev. Code Ann. § 3107.02 (B) (West) ("An adult may be adopted under any of the following conditions: . . . (3) If the adult had established a child-foster caregiver, kinship caregiver, or child-stepparent relationship with the petitioners as a minor, and the adult consents to the adoption; . . . (5) If the adult is the child of the spouse of the petitioner, and the adult consents to the adoption.").

187. **Answer (B) is the best answer.** Bob may well be found to have abandoned the children after having paid support occasionally and having spoken to the children once or twice a year. *Cf. In re J.W.*, 11 S.W.3d 699, 704 (Mo. App. 1999) (finding abandonment when "[t]he evidence shows that over a period of two years, Mother visited the children only ten times, failed to communicate regularly with them, and failed to contribute to their support financially").

Answer (A) is incorrect. A parent can be found to have abandoned his children if having very little contact with them and only paying support sporadically. *See In re Adoption of H.G.C.*, 761 N.W.2d 565, 570 (N.D. 2009) (affirming where "the district court found N.P. had abandoned the child because he has not had any significant meaningful contact with the child since March 2006, he has not had a substantial relationship with the child since 2004, [and] he did not provide any financial support for the child for two years and support was otherwise sporadic").

Answer (C) is incorrect. It is not necessary to establish that the parent had a firm intent never again to support or have contact with the children. *See Michael J. v. Arizona Dep't of Econ. Sec.*, 995 P.2d 682, 685–86 (Ariz. 2000) ("[A]bandonment is measured not by a parent's subjective intent, but by the parent's conduct: the statute asks whether a parent has provided reasonable support, maintained regular contact, made more than minimal efforts to support and communicate with the child, and maintained a normal parental relationship.").

Answer (D) is not the best answer. Occasional support and sporadic contact may not be enough to avoid a finding of abandonment. *See In re Adoption of H.G.C.*, 761 N.W.2d 565, 570 (N.D. 2009).

188.   **Answer (C) is the best answer.** Robert is likely to be awarded custody, *see Tyrrell v. Tyrrell*, 415 N.Y.S.2d 723, 724 (App. Div. 1979) ("[A] parent has a right to rear its child, and the child has a right to be reared by its parent. The right is not absolute, however, and it will not be enforced inexorably, contrary to the best interest of the child where extraordinary circumstances are present."). The case might be different if there were a statute to the contrary, see Del. Code Ann. tit. 13, § 733 (West) ("Notwithstanding that there is a surviving natural parent, upon the death or disability of the custodial or primary placement parent, the Court, at the request of the stepparent shall continue the placement of the child or children with the stepparent pending a hearing on the merits, provided the child has or children have resided with the stepparent immediately prior to the death or disability of the custodial or primary placement parent. Where the child has or children have so resided with the stepparent the Court shall apply the provisions of § 722 of this title and may grant permanent custody or primary physical placement to the stepparent. If the Court grants custody or primary placement of the child or children to the stepparent, the stepparent shall have all of the rights and obligations of a parent until such time as the stepparent no longer has custody or primary placement of the child or children.").

Even if Robert is awarded custody, Norman might be awarded visitation either because of a statute, *see In re K.P.R.*, 966 N.E.2d 952, 956 (Ohio App. 2011) (stepparent awarded visitation privileges in accordance with statute) or because it would be in the interests of the children, given the past parent-child relationship with Norman. *See In re Custody of Banning*, 541 N.E.2d 283 (Ind. App. 1989) (upholding granting of visitation privileges to stepparent following death of custodial parent).

Answer (A) is not the best answer. Robert would be unlikely to be awarded custody if the failure to award custody to Norman would be positively harmful to the children. *See Edwards v. Edwards*, 777 N.W.2d 606, 609 (N.D. 2010) ("[C]ustody may be awarded to a third party in exceptional circumstances in order to prevent serious harm or detriment to a child.").

Answer (B) is not the best answer. Because Robert is the legal parent and Norman is not, it is unlikely that the court would award custody to Norman merely because his having custody would better promote their interests. *See In re A.R.A.*, 919 P.2d 388, 392 (Mont. 1996) ("[T]he District Court erred in awarding custody of A.R.A. to Patrick based on the best interest of the child test in view of the fact there were no allegations of abuse and neglect or dependency."). Instead, a tougher standard would have to be met to justify not awarding custody to the legal parent, *see Tyrrell v. Tyrrell*, 415 N.Y.S.2d 723, 724 (App. Div. 1979), absent statutory authorization to the contrary. *See Del. Code Ann. tit. 13, § 733 (West).*

Answer (D) is not the best answer. It is more likely that Robert would be awarded custody, assuming no extraordinary circumstances exist. *See Tyrrell v. Tyrrell*, 415 N.Y.S.2d 723, 724 (App. Div. 1979). Further, shared parenting is not likely to be successful if the adults cannot cooperate with each other. *See Brandt v. Brandt*, 2012-Ohio-5932, ¶ 23 (Ct. App. 2012) (upholding trial court refusal to order shared parenting where parties could not cooperate with each other).

189. **Answer (C) is the best answer.** As a psychological parent, Jody is likely to be awarded visitation. *See McAllister v. McAllister*, 779 N.W.2d 652, 660 (N.D. 2010) (psychological parent status justifies award of custody to prevent harm to children or award of visitation). However, a separate question is whether such a status will permit an award of custody absent harm or special circumstances. *Compare Conover v. Conover*, 146 A.3d 433, 453 (Md. 2016) ("We hold that *de facto* parents have standing to contest custody or visitation and need not show parental unfitness or exceptional circumstances before a trial court can apply a best interests of the child analysis.") *with V.C. v. M.J.B.*, 748 A.2d 539, 554 (N.J. 2000) ("[U]nder ordinary circumstances when the evidence concerning the child's best interests (as between a legal parent and psychological parent) is in equipoise, custody will be awarded to the legal parent.").

Answer (A) is not the best answer. Absent a statute to the contrary, many jurisdictions will only award custody to a de facto or psychological parent if special circumstances exist. *See McAllister v. McAllister*, 779 N.W.2d 652, 660 (2010).

Answer (B) is not the best answer. While Kendall may be more likely to be awarded custody, Jody as a psychological or de facto parent is likely to be awarded visitation rather than have that decision left up to Kendall. *See McAllister v. McAllister*, 779 N.W.2d 652, 660 (N.D. 2010).

Answer (D) is not the best answer. Even if Jody's being awarded custody would promote the children's best interests, many jurisdictions would not award custody to a de facto parent rather than a legal parent, absent special circumstances. *See McAllister v. McAllister*, 779 N.W.2d 652, 655 (N.D. 2010). Even were Jody awarded custody, that would not justify failing to award visitation to Kendall, absent a showing of unfitness. *Cf. In re Adoption of Douglas*, 45 N.E.3d 595, 600 (Mass. 2016) ("Once a biological parent has been found unfit to care for a child, termination denies him or her physical custody, as well as the rights ever to visit, communicate with, or regain custody of the child.").

190. **Answer (C) is the best answer.** In this scenario, Lee will likely be treated as a third party. Because New Udaho does not recognize de facto, functional, or psychological parent status, Lee will likely be treated as any other third party seeking visitation against the fit parent's wishes. *See Jones v. Barlow*, 154 P.3d 808, 818 (Utah 2007) ("To the extent that there are guiding principles within the common law, they militate against a common law right of visitation for nonparents."). Absent some sort of statute or showing of unusual circumstances, Lee is unlikely to be awarded visitation. *Meeks v. Garner*, 598 So. 2d 261, 262 (Fla. App. 1992) ("Visitation rights are, with regard to a non-parent, statutory, and the court has no inherent authority to award visitation.").

Answer (A) is not the best answer. Because he is a third party, Lee is unlikely to be awarded visitation absent some showing of likely harm that would occur were visitation not permitted. *See In re Victoria C.*, 88 A.3d 749, 750 (Md. 2014) ("[T]hird parties seeking visitation contrary to the parents' wishes must make a *prima facie* showing that the absence of such visitation would have a 'significant deleterious effect' on the child.").

Answer (B) is not the best answer. It is not even likely that Lee will be awarded visitation, absent some showing of harm, much less shared custody. *See In re Victoria C.*, 88 A.3d 749, 750 (Md. 2014).

Answer (D) is not the best answer. Even if no other adults seek visitation, e.g., because Robin's former partner had died, Lee would still be unlikely to be awarded visitation absent some showing of harm. *See In re Victoria C.*, 88 A.3d 749, 750 (Md. 2014).

191.   **Answer (C) is the best answer.** As a general matter, stepparents who seek post-separation contact will not be ordered to pay support. *A.S. v. I.S.*, 130 A.3d 763, 770 (Pa. 2015) ("[R]easonable acts to maintain a post-separation relationship with stepchildren are insufficient to obligate a stepparent to pay child support for those children."). However, where the stepparent has done something unusual, such support might be ordered. *See id.* at 770–71 (Where "he has insisted upon and became a full parent in every sense of that concept, . . . Stepfather has taken sufficient affirmative steps legally to obtain parental rights and should share in parental obligations, such as paying child support.").

Answer (A) is not the best answer. A psychological parent might be awarded visitation without also being required to pay child support. *See Weinand v. Weinand*, 616 N.W.2d 1, 3 (Neb. 2000) (rejecting that an "ex-stepparent who is awarded rights of reasonable visitation in a divorce decree must pay child support as a consequence of such an award").

Answer (B) is not the best answer. A psychological parent might well be awarded visitation, the legal parent's wishes notwithstanding. *See McAllister v. McAllister*, 779 N.W.2d 652 (N.D. 2010).

Answer (D) is incorrect. Kelly might well be awarded visitation, Jan's wishes notwithstanding. *See McAllister v. McAllister*, 779 N.W.2d 652 (N.D. 2010). Further, unless having done something unusual, Kelly is unlikely to be ordered to pay support. *See A.S. v. I.S.*, 130 A.3d 763, 770 (Pa. 2015).

192.   **Answer (B) is the best answer.** The custodial parent determines the children's religious training, *see S.E.L. v. J.W.W.*, 541 N.Y.S.2d 675, 676 (Fam. Ct. 1989) ("[T]he custodial parent has the right to determine a child's religious upbringing and training."), and the refusal to teach Dana's beliefs to the children would not constitute a material change in circumstances. *Cf. In re Marriage of Lahart*, 2002 WL 1332971, at *2 (Iowa App. 2002) ("The record reflects that the children have been allowed to remain active in the Catholic Church although also attending church activities of the protestant church attended by Ann. Religion appears from the record to remain a significant part of the children's upbringing, and the broadening of the experience of the children does not represent a substantial change of circumstances in this case.").

Answer (A) is not the best answer. The custodial parent has the right to determine the children's religious upbringing. *See S.E.L. v. J.W.W.*, 541 N.Y.S.2d 675, 676 (Fam. Ct. 1989). Further prior agreements about the religious training of the children are not enforceable. *See In re Marriage of Bennett*, 587 N.E.2d 577, 581 (Ill. App. 1992).

Answer (C) is not the best answer. While the court will not order Casey to teach Dana's beliefs after Casey's beliefs had changed, *see S.E.L. v. J.W.W.*, 541 N.Y.S.2d 675, 676 (Fam. Ct. 1989), the court also would not have ordered Casey to teach those beliefs even had there been no change in Casey's beliefs, because Casey determines the children's religious upbringing, *id.*, and prior agreements about religious training are not enforceable. *See In re Marriage of Bennett*, 587 N.E.2d 577, 581 (Ill. App. 1992).

Answer (D) is incorrect. Casey's decision about religious upbringing would not constitute a material change in circumstances. *Cf. In re Marriage of Lahart*, 2002 WL 1332971, at *2 (Iowa. App. 2002).

193. **Answer (B) is the best answer.** Courts can constrain the noncustodial parent's religious instruction where such instruction is harming the children. *See In re Marriage of Murga*, 163 Cal. Rptr. 79, 82 (Ct. App. 1980) ("[T]he courts have refused to restrain the noncustodial parent from exposing the minor child to his or her religious beliefs and practices, absent a clear, affirmative showing that these religious activities will be harmful to the child."). *See also Khalsa v. Khalsa*, 751 P.2d 715, 721 (N.M. App. 1988) ("[A]lthough the courts are reluctant to enjoin a non-custodial parent from practicing his religion with his children, the courts can and will enjoin such practice where the testimony concerning physical or emotional harm to the child is detailed and the best interests of the child will be served through the prohibition.").

Answer (A) is not the best answer. While the custodial parent has the right to determine the children's religious instruction, *see S.E.L. v. J.W.W.*, 541 N.Y.S.2d 675, 676 (Fam. Ct. 1989) ("[T]he custodial parent has the right to determine a child's religious upbringing and training."), the custodial parent does not as a general matter have the right to preclude the noncustodial parent from teaching the children about his or her beliefs. *See Pater v. Pater*, 588 N.E.2d 794, 795 (Ohio 1992) ("A court may not restrict a non-custodial parent's right to expose his or her child to religious beliefs, unless the conflict between the parents' religious beliefs is affecting the child's general welfare.").

Answer (C) is not the best answer. Courts can limit a parent's speech where the speech is causing or likely to cause substantial harm. *See Shepp v. Shepp*, 906 A.2d 1165, 1173 (Pa. 2006) ("The state's compelling interest to protect a child in any given case, however, is not triggered unless a court finds that a parent's speech is causing or will cause harm to a child's welfare.").

Answer (D) is not the best answer. A parent's free exercise rights do not include the right to harm a child. *See In re Marriage of McSoud*, 131 P.3d 1208, 1215 (Colo App. 2006) ("[A]bsent a clear showing of substantial harm to the child, a parent who does not have decision-making authority with respect to religion nevertheless retains a constitutional right to educate the child in that parent's religion.").

194. Norman is unlikely to be successful. Because he was not married to Mary, had been told of the pregnancy but did not provide any support for Mary during the pregnancy, did not even attempt to establish a relationship with any child that might have been born, and did not manifest any interest until after the adoption had been finalized, he is unlikely to be successful in undoing the adoption. The adoption will likely be held valid. *See K.L.V. v. Florida Dep't of Health & Rehabilitative Servs.*, 684 So. 2d 253, 254 (Fla. App. 1996) ("A final judgment of adoption is presumptively valid."). It is unlikely that he will be able to establish parental rights now, when he did not take any steps to protect his parental interests even after learning of the pregnancy. *See In re Adoption of A.A.T.*, 287 Kan. 590, 592, 196 P.3d 1180, 1184 (Kan. 2008) ("A natural father has a liberty interest affording a right to notice of proceedings to adopt his newborn child if he: (1) diligently took affirmative action that manifested a full commitment to parenting responsibilities and (2) did so during the pregnancy and in a prompt and timely manner.").

195. Andrew may well be successful. He supported Barbara during the pregnancy and made clear that he would raise the child alone if she did not wish to play a part in raising the child. He did all that he could to establish and protect his parental rights, including acting in a timely way. *See Matter of Adoption of BBC*, 831 P.2d 197, 200–01 (Wyo. 1992) ("[H]e objected to putting the child up for adoption and told the mother that he would pay for the birth and support of the child. The record indicates that the father did about all he could do to determine when and where his child was to be born. In addition, within thirty days after the child's birth, the father attempted to locate the whereabouts of his child, petitioned the court for a writ of habeas corpus to obtain custody of his child, and objected to his child's adoption.").

Tort Actions

196. **Answer (A) is the best answer because it accurately describes the tort of criminal conversation, which involves sexual relations between a married party and someone other than his or her spouse.** *See Lynn v. Shaw*, 620 P.2d 899, 901–02 (Okla. 1980) ("Although adultery is the sine qua non for criminal conversation, it may be defined more precisely as adultery in the aspect of a tort. . . . The fundamental right violated by criminal conversation is the right of exclusive sexual intercourse which the law grants as a necessary consequence of the relationship. The foundation of the action is tortious injury to marital rights by invasion of the conjugal relationship. Recovery is granted on the basis of loss of consortium and services, injury to social position, impairment of family honor and mental suffering.").

   Answer (B) is incorrect because criminal conversation is a tort action rather than the basis for a prosecution. *See Lynn v. Shaw*, 620 P.2d 899, 901 (Okla. 1980) ("The foundation of the action is tortious injury to marital rights by invasion of the conjugal relationship.").

   Answer (C) is incorrect because criminal conversation is a tort rather than a basis for a criminal prosecution, *see Lynn v. Shaw*, 620 P.2d 899, 901–02 (Okla. 1980), **and because it is based on one of the parties having sexual relations outside of marriage rather than other kinds of wrongful conduct.** *See id.* at 901–02.

   Answer (D) is incorrect because the tort of criminal conversation does not provide damages for conversations about wrongful conduct as a general matter, but instead provides damages for having sexual relations outside of marriage. *See Lynn v. Shaw*, 620 P.2d 899, 901–02 (Okla. 1980).

197. While the state permits individuals to sue for alienation of affections, which involves the claim that someone stole the affections of a spouse, *see Nelson v. Jacobsen*, 669 P.2d 1207, 1215 (Utah 1983) ("[A]n action for alienation of affections is . . . [based] on the premise that each spouse has a valuable interest in the marriage *relationship,* including its intimacy, companionship, support, duties, and affection."), a plaintiff will not be successful merely by establishing that the marriage is no longer intact. Instead it will be necessary to show that the destruction of the marriage was due to the actions of the third party rather than the actions of the parties to the marriage. *See id.* at 1219 ("[T]he requirement that the defendant's acts must have constituted the 'controlling cause' of the alienation of affections means that the causal effect of the defendant's conduct must have outweighed the combined effect of all other causes, including the conduct of the plaintiff spouse and the alienated spouse."). Here, if the marriage was not salvageable before Casey's affair began, then Dallas will not be successful when bringing this cause of action.

198.   **Answer (B) is the best answer.** While this is a matter of state law, many states recognize a loss of consortium action for loss of parental services. *See Lake Cumberland Reg'l Hosp., LLC v. Adams*, 536 S.W.3d 683, 689 (Ky. 2017) (noting that the state "recognize[s] a cause of action for loss of parental consortium by a child"); *Campos v. Coleman*, 123 A.3d 854, 859 (Conn. 2015) ("[T]he unique emotional attachment between parents and children, the importance of ensuring the continuity of the critically important services that parents provide to their children, society's interest in the continued development of children as contributing members of society, and the public policies in favor of compensating innocent parties and deterring wrongdoing provide compelling reasons to recognize such a cause of action."). *But see Kane v. Quigley*, 203 N.E.2d 338, 339 (Ohio 1964) ("No right of consortium exists between a parent and child.").

       Answer (A) is not the best answer. While loss of consortium was traditionally a cause of action to compensate spouses for loss of society, *see Kane v. Quigley*, 203 N.E.2d 338, 339 (Ohio 1964) ("The basis for such action is the right of consortium or conjugal society, a right growing out of the marital relation and limited to the spouse."), many states permit children to bring a claim for loss of consortium. *See*, for example, *Campos v. Coleman*, 123 A.3d 854, 859 (Conn. 2015).

       Answer (C) is incorrect. Many states limit the cause of action to spouses and children, and will not permit an action for someone who was planning to marry the victim. *See*, for example, *Childers v. Shannon*, 444 A.2d 1141, 1142–43 (N.J. Super. 1982) ("Marriage, however, is the only legal touchstone by which the strength of a male-female relationship may be tested. It is not the function of this court to sift through the myriad relationships of a party in a negligence action to determine which of those near and dear have suffered an injury proximately caused by tortious conduct."); *Mills v. Lake Quassapaug Amusement Park, Inc.*, 1995 WL 317026, at *1 (Conn. Super. 1995) ("Our Supreme Court has denied a fiance's claim for a loss of consortium with his injured fiancee, with whom he co-habitated, since the parties were not married at the time of the alleged accident.").

       Answer (D) is not the best answer. Many states do not permit those planning to marry to maintain such a cause of action. *See*, for example, *Childers v. Shannon*, 444 A.2d 1141, 1142–43 (N.J. Super. 1982). *See also Morales v. Davis Bros. Const. Co.*, 706 So. 2d 1048, 1049 (La. App. 1998) ("[T]here can be no recovery for loss of consortium damages for a prenuptial injury that manifested itself before the marriage.").

199.   **Answer (A) is the best answer.** Many jurisdictions view an engagement ring as a gift that is conditioned on the wedding taking place such that the ring must be returned if the wedding does not take place, regardless of fault. *See Heiman v. Parrish*, 942 P.2d 631, 634 (Kan. 1997) ("In the absence of a contrary expression of intent, it is logical that engagement rings should be considered, by their very nature, conditional gifts given in contemplation of marriage. Once it is established the ring is an engagement ring, it is a conditional gift."). However, some jurisdictions take a different view. *See Clippard v. Pfefferkorn*, 168 S.W.3d 616, 620 (Mo. App. 2005) ("[A]s donee of the conditional gift in contemplation of marriage,

Defendant was entitled to retain the ring because the engagement was terminated by Plaintiff for no fault of Defendant.").

Answer (B) is not the best answer. Many jurisdictions require the ring (or the value thereof) to be returned if the wedding does not take place. *See Heiman v. Parrish*, 942 P.2d 631, 634 (Kan. 1997).

Answer (C) is not the best answer. Many jurisdictions treat the engagement ring as a conditional gift that should be returned if the couple does not marry. *See Heiman v. Parrish*, 942 P.2d 631, 634 (Kan. 1997). Even those that use a fault-based approach would not simply look at who called the wedding off, but instead would look at who was responsible. *See Clippard v. Pfefferkorn*, 168 S.W.3d 616, 620 (Mo. App. 2005) ("Plaintiff would have been entitled to the return of the ring if the engagement had been terminated by Defendant for no fault of Plaintiff.").

Answer (D) is not the best answer. Neither of the approaches used by the states suggests that there are no conditions under which the ring should be returned. *See Thorndike v. Demirs*, 2007 WL 2363411, at *9 (Conn. Super. 2007) ("[T]here are two very different viewpoints. One view, which is described as the fault approach, provides that if the marriage does not take place due to the fault of the donee or with the mutual consent of both parties, the ring must be returned to the donor. In the event that the marriage does not take place due to the fault of the donor, then he is not entitled to the return of the ring. . . . Other jurisdictions have adopted what is called a 'no fault' approach, i.e., the modern trend, holding that once an engagement is broken, the engagement ring should be returned to the donor regardless of fault.").

200. **Answer (A) is the best answer.** The genetic counselor will likely be liable for damages as long as the Oppenheimers can show that the negligent reporting played a causal role in their conceiving a child, e.g., because they would otherwise have adopted a child or perhaps have used donated eggs or sperm, etcetera. *See Molloy v. Meier*, 679 N.W.2d 711 (Minn. 2004) (holding physician liable for failing to tell parents of a genetic condition that any children they conceived might have).

Answer (B) is not the best answer. Liability may well be imposed where, but for the negligence of a medical professional, a child would not have been conceived. *See Molloy v. Meier*, 679 N.W.2d 711 (Minn. 2004).

Answer (C) is not the best answer. The difficulty is not merely that the child had the dread disease. *See State in Interest of DEM*, 441 So. 2d 514, 515 (La. Ct. App. 1983) ("The law does not guarantee perfect parents or children."). It is also important that the parents sought genetic counseling, the counseling was performed negligently, and that the parents relied on what they were told. *See Lininger By & Through Lininger v. Eisenbaum*, 764 P.2d 1202, 1214 (Colo. 1988) ("The Liningers sought the genetic counseling not only for themselves but also for their future children. Neither they nor Pierce can claim any right that Pierce be born a perfect child. What both Pierce and his parents can and do claim is that, in reliance on the physicians' advice, they intended to assume only the ordinary risks inherent in any decision to bear children.").

Answer (D) is not the best answer. While it is true that there are no guarantees, the Oppenheimers sought genetic counseling precisely because they wanted to decide what to do in light of all available information. They were denied that opportunity because of the negligent counseling. *See Lininger By & Through Lininger v. Eisenbaum*, 764 P.2d 1202, 1214 (Colo. 1988).

201.   **Answer (D) is the best answer.** Assuming that the state recognizes the cause of action, the physician might well be held liable if his or her negligence prevented Abby and Blair from securing a legal abortion, which resulted in their incurring various costs. *See Plowman v. Fort Madison Cmty. Hosp.*, 896 N.W.2d 393, 409 (Iowa 2017) ("The parents must prove the defendant's negligence deprived them of the opportunity to *lawfully* terminate the pregnancy in Iowa.").

Answer (A) is not the best answer. The physician might nonetheless be liable if his or her negligence caused Abby to choose not to abort the pregnancy when she would have aborted had she been apprised of the relevant information. *See Plowman v. Fort Madison Cmty. Hosp.*, 896 N.W.2d 393, 409 (Iowa 2017).

Answer (B) is not the best answer. States that recognize a wrongful birth action recognize the possibility that parents might incur emotional and financial costs when they are not given relevant information about the fetus. *See Smith v. Cote*, 513 A.2d 341, 348 (N.H. 1986) ("When parents are denied the opportunity to make this decision, important personal interests may be impaired, including an interest in avoiding the special expenses necessitated by the condition of a child born with defects, an interest in preventing the sorrow and anguish that may befall the parents of such a child, and an interest in preserving personal autonomy, which may include the making of informed reproductive choices.").

Answer (C) is not the best answer. While Abby and Blair would need to establish the physician's negligence, they also would need to show that the negligence caused them not to abort when they would have aborted if they had been apprised of the relevant facts. *See Plowman v. Fort Madison Cmty. Hosp.*, 896 N.W.2d 393, 409 (Iowa 2017).

202.   **Answer (D) is the best answer.** Those jurisdictions permitting recovery for wrongful conception tend to limit the damages. *See Pressil v. Gibson*, 477 S.W.3d 402, 409 (Tex. App. 2015) ("As an initial matter, in Texas, a plaintiff cannot recover damages related to the support and maintenance of a healthy child born as a result of the medical provider's negligence. . . . This is because the intangible benefits of parenthood far outweigh the monetary burdens involved."); *Chaffee v. Seslar*, 786 N.E.2d 705, 709 (Ind. 2003) ("We hold that the costs involved in raising and educating a normal, healthy child conceived subsequent to an allegedly negligent sterilization procedure are not cognizable as damages in an action for medical negligence."). *But see Cichewicz v. Salesin*, 854 N.W.2d 901, 910 (Mich. App. 2014) ("[W]rongful-conception claims remain actionable in Michigan, and damages related to the costs of raising the child to the age of majority may be recovered on a showing of an intentional or grossly negligent act or omission.").

Answer (A) is incorrect. Jurisdictions may permit limited recovery in this kind of case. *See Simmerer v. Dabbas*, 733 N.E.2d 1169, 1172 (Ohio 2000) ("[T]he plaintiffs could recover the medical costs of the pregnancy and delivery, damages for emotional distress due to pregnancy, lost wages due to pregnancy, damages for the husband's loss of consortium during pregnancy, and damages for the mother's pain and suffering during pregnancy and delivery. . . . [We] foreclose[] recovery of the costs of raising the child, however.").

Answer (B) is not correct. While many jurisdictions permit limited recovery on these facts, they tend not to permit the costs of raising a child. *See Pressil v. Gibson*, 477 S.W.3d 402, 409 (Tex. App. 2015); *Simmerer v. Dabbas*, 733 N.E.2d 1169, 1172 (Ohio 2000); *Chaffee v. Seslar*, 786 N.E.2d 705, 709 (Ind. 2003).

Answer (C) is not the best answer. While Teresa could have aborted, states as a general matter do not require abortion as a means of mitigating damages. *See Lovelace Med. Ctr. v. Mendez*, 805 P.2d 603, 621 (N.M. 1991) ("[A]s a matter of law, neither abortion nor adoption is an ordinary or a reasonable measure as that phrase is used in the law relating to mitigation of damages.").

203. **Answer (B) is the best answer.** If Samantha can show that she would have aborted once she knew that severe birth defects might result from the exposure, then she will likely be successful in her suit for wrongful birth damages. *See Dumer v. St. Michael's Hosp.*, 233 N.W.2d 372, 377 (Wis. 1975) ("[T]he doctor was negligent in not diagnosing the rubella the plaintiff-wife was suffering and inquiring [about the] pregnancy. If the doctor is found at the trial to have been negligent in those respects, it follows he had a duty to inform the plaintiff-mother of the effects of rubella.").

Answer (A) is not the best answer. While Samantha made clear that one of her students had been sick, that would not establish that she had been sick, let alone at a time that would be dangerous for the fetus. Nonetheless, the doctor would have been on notice that it would be important to find out whether the fetus had been exposed. *See Dumer v. St. Michael's Hosp.*, 233 N.W.2d 372, 377 (Wis. 1975).

Answer (C) is incorrect. Samantha's likelihood of success does not depend upon her having been exposed to rubella in the doctor's office. Rather, the focus will be on what the doctor failed to do after being notified that Samantha may have been exposed, given the great dangers posed for the fetus about which Samantha had no knowledge. *See Dumer v. St. Michael's Hosp.*, 233 N.W.2d 372, 377 (Wis. 1975).

Answer (D) is incorrect. Even if there was nothing that could have been done during the pregnancy to reduce or eliminate the harm caused by fetal exposure to rubella, the doctor still might be liable for failing to inform Samantha about the great risks to fetal health associated with exposure. *See Dumer v. St. Michael's Hosp.*, 233 N.W.2d 372, 377 (Wis. 1975).

204. **Answer (C) is the best answer.** Jurisdictions vary with respect to whether they will recognize a cause of action for negligent supervision by a parent. *Compare Smelser v. Paul*, 398 P.3d 1086, 1087 (Wash. 2017) ("[N]o tort or fault exists based on the claim of negligent supervision by a parent.") and *Beddingfield v. Linam*, 127 So. 3d 1178, 1189 (Ala. 2013) ("We decline to extend our holdings in negligent-supervision cases to recognize a cause of action based on a

parent's negligence or wantonness in supervising his or her own child.") *with Hartman by Hartman v. Hartman*, 821 S.W.2d 852, 858 (Mo. 1991) ("[T]his Court abrogates the parental immunity doctrine . . . . Minor unemancipated children are authorized to bring actions sounding in negligence against their parents. The actions of parents are to be measured by a reasonable parent standard.") and *Rousey v. Rousey*, 528 A.2d 416, 420 (D.C. 1987) ("[W]e simply decline to adopt the doctrine of parental immunity as the law of the District of Columbia.").

Answer (A) is not the best answer. Many states have abrogated the parental immunity doctrine wholly or in part, *see Rousey v. Rousey*, 528 A.2d 416, 419 (D.C. 1987) ("[A] substantial majority of states have now abandoned the doctrine in whole or in part."), and this has not caused the floodgates to open.

Answer (B) is not the best answer because it fails to account for jurisdictions that retain parental immunity. *See Smelser v. Paul*, 398 P.3d 1086, 1087 (Wash. 2017) and *Beddingfield v. Linam*, 127 So. 3d 1178, 1189 (Ala. 2013).

Answer (D) is not the best answer. It is unlikely that a court would accept that a four-year-old had assumed the risk. *Cf. Roberts v. New York City Hous. Auth.*, 685 N.Y.S.2d 23, 24 (App. Div. 1999) ("[A]s a matter of law, the doctrine of assumption of risk, which contemplates the voluntary assumption of fully appreciated, 'perfectly obvious' risks . . . can have no application to a six-year old . . . .").

205.   **Answer (D) is the best answer.** Many of the states recognizing parental immunity do not extend that immunity to bar suits involving intentional torts. *See Cates v. Cates*, 619 N.E.2d 715, 729 (Ill. 1993) ("[T]here is no immunity as applied to the area of intentional torts."); *Sepaugh v. LaGrone*, 300 S.W.3d 328, 334 (Tex. App. 2009) (noting that parental immunity "bars suits for intentional torts committed by a parent against his child"); *Wood ex rel. Wood v. Berean Baptist Church*, 1997 WL 33343376, at *1 (Mich. App. 1997) ("Claims of intentional torts are outside of the parental immunity doctrine."). Even jurisdictions extending parental immunity to some intentional torts might nonetheless refuse to extend it to cases involving sexual abuse. *See Henderson v. Woolley*, 644 A.2d 1303, 1309 (Conn. 1994) ("[T]he purpose of the doctrine would not be served by extending it to intentional acts of sexual abuse.").

Answer (A) is not the best answer. In many states, the parental immunity doctrine does not provide immunity for intentional torts. *See Cates v. Cates*, 619 N.E.2d 715, 729 (Ill. 1993); *Wood ex rel. Wood v. Berean Baptist Church*, 1997 WL 33343376, at *1 (Mich. App. 1997).

Answer (B) is not the best answer. Many states will extend parental immunity to stepparents. *See Zellmer v. Zellmer*, 188 P.3d 497, 504 (Wash. 2008) ("[A] majority of states addressing the issue hold it applies to stepparents who stand in loco parentis to the same extent as to legal parents.").

Answer (C) is not the best answer. His being liable would not depend upon his being prosecuted successfully, especially because the standards for liability differ. *See*, for example, *Cardillo v. Aron*, 2010 WL 986503, at *6 (Mass. Super. 2010) ("[T]he plaintiff need not, however, conclusively exclude all other possible explanations, and so prove his case beyond a reasonable doubt. Such proof is not required in civil cases, in contrast to criminal cases.").

206.   **Answer (B) is the best answer.** Because interspousal immunity has been abolished, Casey could have sued Cameron, which means that Nancy can seek contribution from Cameron. *See Wirth v. City of Highland Park*, 430 N.E.2d 236, 240 (Ill. App. 1981) (noting that "a trend began . . . to abrogate the doctrine of interspousal immunity and allow contribution to the third-party against the tortfeasor-spouse").

    Answer (A) is incorrect. The abrogation of interpousal immunity does not negate the spousal testimonial privilege. *Compare J.S. v. R.T.H.*, 714 A.2d 924, 931–32 (N.J. 1998) (discussing the common-law doctrine of interspousal immunity wherein one spouse could not sue or be sued by another) *with Meyers v. Com.*, 381 S.W.3d 280, 284 (Ky. 2012) (explaining that the spousal testimonial privilege affords a party "a privilege to prevent his or her spouse from testifying against the party as to events occurring after the date of their marriage . . . [unless the] spouse is charged with wrongful conduct against the person or property of . . . [t]he other . . . .").

    Answer (C) is incorrect. Because Casey could have sued Cameron, Nancy can seek contribution from Cameron. *See Wirth v. City of Highland Park*, 430 N.E.2d 236, 240 (Ill. App. 1981).

    Answer (D) is incorrect. Because Cameron is partially responsible, Casey's recovery will be diminished rather than barred. *See Wirth v. City of Highland Park*, 430 N.E.2d 236, 242 (Ill. App. 1981).

207.   **Answer (C) is the best answer.** If, as is implied, Gladys was on notice that her son was causing others injury, then she should have taken steps to prevent his harming others. *See Stein v. Lee*, 2011 WL 522886, at *3 (Conn. Super. 2011) ("A parent is under a duty to exercise reasonable care so to control his minor child as to prevent it from intentionally harming others or from so conducting itself as to create an unreasonable risk of bodily harm to them, if the parent (a) knows or has reason to know that he has the ability to control his child, and (b) knows or should know of the necessity and opportunity for exercising such control.").

    Answer (A) is not correct. Absent a statute imposing strict liability, *see Penton v. Castellano*, 127 So. 3d 944, 947 (La. App. 2013) ("This is legally imposed strict liability, and fault is determined regardless of whether the parent could or could not have prevented the child's act."), parents will not as a general matter be held strictly liable for harms caused by their children. *See Boyd v. Watson*, 680 N.E.2d 251, 253 (Ohio Com. Pl. 1996) ("Parents are generally not liable for the wrongful conduct of their children.").

    Answer (B) is not correct. As a general matter, parents are not liable for all harms caused by their children intentionally or negligently. *See Boyd v. Watson*, 680 N.E.2d 251, 253 (Ohio Com. Pl. 1996).

    Answer (D) is incorrect. Gladys can be held liable for harms caused by Frank when she is on notice about his harmful propensities, even if she discourages rather than encourages such behavior. *See Stein v. Lee*, 2011 WL 522886, at *3 (Conn. Super. 2011).

208. **Answer (D) is the best answer.** While the adoption agency might well be found liable, the jurisdiction might well limit the extent of the agency's liability. *See,* for example, *Ross v. Louise Wise Servs., Inc.,* 812 N.Y.S.2d 325 (App. Div. 2006) ("limit[ing] plaintiffs' potential recovery of compensatory damages to the extraordinary out-of-pocket expenses of raising their adopted child to age 21").

Answer (A) is not the best answer. While no parent is guaranteed a perfect child, *see State in Interest of DEM,* 441 So. 2d 514, 515 (La. App. 1983) ("The law does not guarantee perfect parents or children."), the allegation is that Your Loving Family affirmatively misrepresented what it knew about David. *See M.H. v. Caritas Family Servs.,* 488 N.W.2d 282, 286 (Minn. 1992) ("[T]he cases seem to agree that adoption agencies may be held liable for damages caused by intentional, affirmative misrepresentations of facts regarding the child to the adopting parents.").

Answer (B) is not the best answer. The court is more likely to limit damages in some way, e.g., to extraordinary expenses. *See Juman v. Louise Wise Servs.,* 608 N.Y.S.2d 612, 616 (Sup. Ct. 1994) ("In recognizing wrongful adoption in Wisconsin, the court . . . limited plaintiffs' recovery to the extraordinary medical expenses they would incur as a result of the agency's negligent misrepresentation").

Answer (C) is not the best answer because the court would likely limit the damages. *See Ross v. Louise Wise Servs., Inc.,* 812 N.Y.S.2d 325 (App. Div. 2006).

209. **Answer (D) is the best answer.** Some jurisdictions permit an adoption to be set aside where there has been an affirmative misrepresentation of material facts. *See Matter of Adoption of T.B.,* 622 N.E.2d 921, 925 (Ind. 1993) ("In order to set aside the order of adoption based on fraud, there must be a material misrepresentation of past or existing fact made with knowledge or reckless disregard for the falsity of the statement, and the misrepresentation must be relied upon to the detriment of the relying party."). However, the negligent failure to discover relevant information is unlikely to be enough to justify undoing an adoption. *See id.* ("Although the record may support a finding that FCS acted negligently in failing to discover the alleged sexual abuse, it does not support a finding that FCS committed fraud. Consequently, the attempt to set aside the adoption based upon fraud must fail.").

Answer (A) is incorrect. While a court's undoing an adoption is viewed as an extreme measure, *see Knox' Adoption v. Reid,* 165 N.W.2d 1, 3 (Mich. 1969) (noting an "extreme reluctance to set aside adoptions"), adoptions will sometimes be abrogated. *See Matter of Adoption of T.B.,* 622 N.E.2d 921, 925 (Ind. 1993).

Answer (B) is not the best answer. Under certain circumstances such as fraud, an adoption can be set aside. *See Matter of Adoption of T.B.,* 622 N.E.2d 921, 925 (Ind. 1993).

Answer (C) is not the best answer. The Andersons' child having even severe difficulties would not suffice as a basis for undoing the adoption if the agency had merely negligently failed to discover that the child had those difficulties. *See Matter of Adoption of T.B.,* 622 N.E.2d 921, 925 (Ind. 1993). In addition, it would be necessary to show that the agency made an affirmative misrepresentation of important information. *See id.*

210. **Answer (B) is the best answer.** Both are potentially liable, absent some legal justification for their actions. *See Wyatt v. McDermott*, 725 S.E.2d 555, 562 (Va. 2012) (explaining that the tort involves the following: "(1) the complaining parent has a right to establish or maintain a parental or custodial relationship with his/her minor child; (2) a party outside of the relationship between the complaining parent and his/her child intentionally interfered with the complaining parent's parental or custodial relationship with his/her child by removing or detaining the child from returning to the complaining parent, without that parent's consent, or by otherwise preventing the complaining parent from exercising his/her parental or custodial rights; (3) the outside party's intentional interference caused harm to the complaining parent's parental or custodial relationship with his/her child; and (4) damages resulted from such interference.").

Answer (A) is incorrect. If Steven conspired with Dana to deprive Blair of custody, then Steve may be liable as well. *See Stone v. Wall*, 734 So. 2d 1038, 1047 (Fla. 1999) (holding that a grandparent may be liable for intentional interference with a custodial relationship).

Answer (C) is not the best answer. While some states limit the cause of action to non-parents, *see Stone v. Wall*, 734 So. 2d 1038, 1047 (Fla. 1999) ("giving judicial recognition in Florida to the common law cause of action for intentional interference with the custodial parent-child relationship by a third party non-parent"), other states permit the noncustodial parent to be subject to suit as well. *See*, for example, *Khalifa v. Shannon*, 945 A.2d 1244 (Md. 2008).

Answer (D) is incorrect. Various jurisdictions recognize this tort. *See Wyatt v. McDermott*, 725 S.E.2d 555, 562 (Va. 2012); *Khalifa v. Shannon*, 945 A.2d 1244, 1268 (Md. 2008); Kessel v. Leavitt, 511 S.E.2d 720 (W. Va. 1998).

211. **Answer (C) is the best answer.** While some jurisdictions recognize a cause of action for interference with the parental relation whether or not that parent is the custodial parent, *see Khalifa v. Shannon*, 945 A.2d 1244 (Md. 2008), many do not. *See Cosner v. Ridinger*, 882 P.2d 1243, 1246 (Wyo. 1994) (noting that many of "[t]he jurisdictions recognizing this tort have limited the cause of action to the custodial parent and have not extended it to a non-custodial parent who is somehow deprived of visitation privileges").

Answer (A) is not the best answer. Many jurisdictions only recognize this cause of action for the custodial parent. *See Cosner v. Ridinger*, 882 P.2d 1243, 1246 (Wyo. 1994).

Answer (B) is incorrect. Merely because a jurisdiction recognizes a cause of action of interference with the custodial parent's relationship does not mean that it will also recognize such a cause of action for interference with the non-custodial parent's relationship. *See Cosner v. Ridinger*, 882 P.2d 1243, 1246 (Wyo. 1994).

Answer (D) is not the best answer. Several jurisdictions recognize a cause of action for interference with the custodial parent's relationship. *See Cosner v. Ridinger*, 882 P.2d 1243, 1246 (Wyo. 1994).

212. Many states have abolished the tort actions of criminal conversation and alienation of affections. *See*, for example, *McGrath v. Dockendorf*, 793 S.E.2d 336, 338 (Va. 2016) ("In 1968, the

Virginia General Assembly enacted Code §8.01-220, which currently provides in subsection (A): Notwithstanding any other provision of law to the contrary, no civil action shall lie or be maintained in this Commonwealth for alienation of affection, breach of promise to marry, or criminal conversation upon which a cause of action arose or occurred on or after June 28, 1968."). Suppose that Alabippi recognizes these causes of action. To be successful on the alienation of affections claim, Lynn will have to show that Casey was responsible for Dana's loss of affection for Lynn. *See Richardson v. Richardson*, 906 N.W.2d 369, 380 n.9 (S.D. 2017) ("The tort of alienation of affections has three elements: (1) wrongful conduct by the defendant with specific intent to alienate one spouse's affections from the other spouse; (2) loss of affection or consortium; and (3) a causal connection between such intentional conduct and loss."). If Dana's loss of affection for Lynn had already occurred prior to Dana's meeting Casey, then Casey would not be liable for alienation of affections. *Cf. Anderson v. Ladner*, 198 So. 3d 381, 386 (Miss. Ct. App.) ("[W]e find that the record reflects a dispute of material fact as to when Angela finally abandoned the marital relationship and when her affections were finally severed based upon the facts presented in this case."). In some states, a claim for criminal conversation could be maintained if Dana and Casey had had sexual relations before Lynn and Dana's divorce was final. *See Rodriguez v. Lemus*, 810 S.E.2d 1 (N.C. App. 2018) ("[E]vidence of sexual intercourse between the defendant and the plaintiff's spouse after the date of separation, but before the date of divorce, was sufficient to support a claim for criminal conversation."). To be successful on the criminal conversation claim, Lynn will have to establish that Dana and Casey had sexual relations, assuming that Alabippi will entertain criminal conversation suits when based on post-separation sexual relations.

213. The first question is whether New Colorona recognizes parental immunity for negligent supervision claims. If so, then Delores will not be able to seek contribution from Rory and Tate. *See Vincent Delmedico PPA v. Panda Properties, LLC*, 2017 WL 4106088, at *2 (Conn. Super. 2017) ("The doctrine [of parental immunity] prevents not only direct actions by a child against a parent, it also operates to preclude the parent of a minor plaintiff from being joined as a third-party defendant for purposes of apportionment of liability, contribution or indemnification based on the parent's allegedly negligent supervision of the minor plaintiff."); *see also Smelser v. Paul*, 398 P.3d 1086, 1089 (Wash. 2017) ("[A] parent is *not liable* for ordinary negligence in the performance of parental responsibilities."). However, other states permit a contribution action. *See Ankiewicz v. Kinder*, 563 N.E.2d 684, 687 (Mass. 1990) (recognizing that the state permits "contribution actions against parents for negligent supervision"). If New Colorona permits a claim for negligent supervision and has abrogated parental immunity, then Delores may well be successful when seeking contribution.

214. Sarah has committed adultery during the marriage at least twice. Yet adultery alone might not provide the basis for an intentional infliction claim, e.g., because adultery is not itself thought sufficiently extreme and outrageous. *See Poston v. Poston*, 436 S.E.2d 854, 856 (N.C. App. 1993) ("[A]ppellant's allegation of adultery does not evidence the extreme and outrageous conduct which is essential to this cause of action"). If South Georgiana has abolished the heart balm torts such as alienation of affections and criminal conversation, then the court might find this cause of action sufficiently close to those that this action must also be barred.

See Quinn v. Walsh, 732 N.E.2d 330, 337 (Mass. App. 2000) ("By abolishing these common law torts, the Legislature has registered its intent to preclude recovery for emotional distress resulting from adultery."). Yet Thomas may well have been claiming that it was not Sarah's adultery alone that is the basis for his intentional infliction claim. Rather, it is her having committed adultery at least two times and her having pretended that he was the biological father of Alex and Bevan when Sarah knew all along that he was not their biological father. Some jurisdictions would permit this cause of action to proceed (notwithstanding their having abolished the heart balm statutes), while others would not. *Compare Koestler v. Pollard*, 471 N.W.2d 7 (Wis. 1991) (action barred) *with Miller v. Miller*, 956 P.2d 887 (Okla. 1998) (permitting action based on false representations of paternity). *See also Mansfield v. Neff*, 2014 WL 458207, at *2 (Mass. Super. 2014) ("Many courts have recognized a tort of paternity fraud or have applied traditional tort claims in the context of false representations of biological paternity.").

215.   Many states will only permit a bystander negligent infliction of emotional distress claim to be brought by a legally recognized family member. *See Smith v. Toney*, 862 N.E.2d 656, 660 (Ind. 2007) ("Most courts that have considered this issue have disallowed bystander recovery for negligent infliction of emotional distress by persons engaged to be married or involved in cohabiting but unmarried relationships."). If New Vermshire follows that approach, then Kelly's negligent infliction claim might be barred because Jordan and Kelly are in a cohabiting but not a marital relationship. However, other jurisdictions use a more functional approach in which case Kelly might well be permitted to bring this cause of action. *See Graves v. Estabrook*, 818 A.2d 1255, 1262 (N.H. 2003) ("We thus recognize that unmarried cohabitants may have a close relationship, i.e., a relationship that is stable, enduring, substantial, and mutually supportive . . . cemented by strong emotional bonds and provid[ing] a deep and pervasive emotional security."). A separate issue is whether Kelly suffered the requisite degree of harm. *See White v. Bhatt*, 2017-Ohio-9277, ¶ 19 (Ct. App.) ("To prevail on a claim for negligent infliction of emotional distress arising out of witnessing trauma to another, a plaintiff must prove: . . . [he or she] was a bystander [who] . . . reasonably appreciated the peril that took place . . . [and who] suffered serious emotional distress as a result of this cognizance.").

Professional Responsibility

216. **Answer (C) is the best answer.** Once Alex had talked to each individual after assuring each that the information would remain confidential and after charging a fee, he arguably induced each to believe that there was an attorney-client relationship. *See Kuntz v. Disciplinary Bd. of Supreme Court of N. Dakota*, 869 N.W.2d 117, 124 (N.D. 2015) ("[A] lawyer may charge an initial consultation fee without necessarily creating a lawyer-client relationship and the payment of an initial consultation fee, by itself, does not establish a lawyer-client relationship. Rather, the existence of a lawyer-client relationship depends on the particular circumstances of the case, including the conduct of the parties, the circumstances of the consultation, the nature of information exchanged, and any agreements between the parties."). If an attorney-client relationship was thereby created, he would need permission from both Shannon and Tracy before Alex could represent either. *See State ex rel. Oklahoma Bar Ass'n v. Berry*, 969 P.2d 975, 979 (Okla. 1998) ("Rule 1.7(a) states: (a) A lawyer shall not represent a client if the representation of that client will be directly adverse to another client, unless: (1) the lawyer reasonably believes the representation will not adversely affect the relationship with the other client; and (2) each client consents after consultation."). *See also In re Braun*, 227 A.2d 506, 507–08 (N.J. 1967) ("[A]fter respondent had attempted to counsel both husband and wife with a view to reconciliation at the meeting of June 1964, he could not thereafter with propriety represent either in a divorce action.").

Answer (A) is not the best answer. Alex may well have created an attorney-client relationship after the first consultation, *See Kuntz v. Disciplinary Bd. of Supreme Court of N. Dakota*, 869 N.W.2d 117, 124 (N.D. 2015), which would mean that he would have to take certain actions before he could represent either Shannon or Tyler in this divorce. *See State ex rel. Oklahoma Bar Ass'n v. Berry*, 969 P.2d 975, 979 (Okla. 1998).

Answer (B) is not the best answer. Alex may well have received confidential information from Shannon at their first meeting and may well have induced Shannon to believe that Alex and Shannon had an attorney-client relationship. *See Kuntz v. Disciplinary Bd. of Supreme Court of N. Dakota*, 869 N.W.2d 117, 124 (N.D. 2015).

Answer (D) is incorrect. Alex may well have been precluded from representing either against the other after the first meeting, absent informed consent from each. *See State ex rel. Oklahoma Bar Ass'n v. Berry*, 969 P.2d 975, 979 (Okla. 1998).

217. **Answer (D) is the best answer.** Some jurisdictions impose a per se bar on dual representation in divorce cases. *See Walden v. Hoke*, 429 S.E.2d 504, 509 (W. Va. 1993) ("[I]t is improper for a lawyer to represent both the husband and the wife at any stage of the separation and

divorce proceeding, even with full disclosure and informed consent. The likelihood of prejudice is so great with dual representation so as to make adequate representation of both spouses impossible, even where the separation is 'friendly' and the divorce uncontested."). Other jurisdictions do not. *See Rowland v. Rowland*, 599 N.E.2d 315, 319 (Ohio App. 1991) ("Dual representation is not invalid *per se*."). Laura may be subject to discipline depending upon local law.

Answer (A) is incorrect, since the jurisdiction might have a per se ban on dual representation. *See Walden v. Hoke*, 429 S.E.2d 504, 509 (W. Va. 1993).

Answer (B) is incorrect. Even written, informed consent will not immunize an attorney from sanction if the jurisdiction has a per se ban on the representation at issue. *See Walden v. Hoke*, 429 S.E.2d 504, 509 (W. Va. 1993).

Answer (C) is not the best answer. The mere possibility of dissatisfaction, like the mere possibility of conflict, would not make Laura subject to sanction if she had secured informed, written consent where the jurisdiction permitted dual representation under those conditions. *Cf. Klemm v. Superior Court*, 142 Cal. Rptr. 509, 512 (Ct. App. 1977) ("[I]f the conflict is merely potential, there being no existing dispute or contest between the parties represented as to any point in litigation, then with full disclosure to and informed consent of both clients there may be dual representation at a hearing or trial.").

218.   **Answer (D) is the best answer.** Contingency fee arrangements in the context of divorce are prohibited in some jurisdictions. *See In re Jarvis*, 349 P.3d 445, 455 (Kan. 2015) (noting that "the respondent . . . violated rule 1.5(f)(1), [by] entering into a contingency fee agreement in a divorce case"). In other jurisdictions, they are permitted. *See Alexander v. Inman*, 974 S.W.2d 689, 693 (Tenn. 1998) ("contingent fee agreements are begrudgingly permitted in domestic relations cases"). Ann's likelihood of success will depend upon local law.

Answer (A) is not the best answer. Many jurisdictions prohibit contingency fee agreements in the context of divorce at least in part because they may discourage an attorney from promoting reconciliation. *See State ex rel. Oklahoma Bar Ass'n v. Fagin*, 848 P.2d 11, 14 (Okla. 1992) ("[A] contingency fee arrangement based upon the amount recovered in a divorce case gives the attorney a personal interest in the litigation thus serving as an impediment to reconciliation.").

Answer (B) is not the best answer. While some jurisdictions preclude contingency fee agreements in divorce because such agreements provide a disincentive for the attorney to promote the reconciliation of the parties, *see State ex rel. Oklahoma Bar Ass'n v. Fagin*, 848 P.2d 11, 14 (Okla. 1992), other jurisdictions permit such agreements. *See Alexander v. Inman*, 974 S.W.2d 689, 693 (Tenn. 1998).

Answer (C) is incorrect. A jurisdiction prohibiting contingency fee agreements in divorce may well make them unenforceable and will likely not consider whether the particular couple would have reconciled. *See McCrary v. McCrary*, 764 P.2d 522, 525 (Okla. 1988) ("There can be no doubt that if this arrangement was intended as a contingency fee in a divorce case, the agreement to convey the property in question would be against public policy and void and unenforceable.").

219.   The scrivener is merely writing up a document, *see Griffith v. Taylor*, 937 P.2d 297, 305–06 (Alaska 1997) ("the scrivener's exception . . . will only apply to purely clerical tasks which attorneys perform"); *Keegan v. First Bank of Sioux Falls*, 519 N.W.2d 607, 612 n.4 (S.D. 1994) ("[A] 'scrivener' is defined as a 'writer; scribe; conveyancer. One whose occupation is to draw contracts, write deeds and mortgages, and prepare other species of written instruments.'"), and is not providing legal advice. *See Eley v. Miller*, 34 N.E. 836, 838 (Ind. App. 1893) ("[T]he mere act of a scrivener who writes something dictated by another would not be practicing law."). A scrivener does not have the same duties to a client that an attorney has. *See Griffith v. Taylor*, 937 P.2d 297, 305 (Alaska 1997); *Marker v. Davis*, 204 N.W. 287, 289 (Iowa 1925) ("Davis admittedly acted as a mere scrivener. The work was purely gratuitous. Likewise all that he did later was done as a mere gratuity, and done at the request of the plaintiff. He was not the plaintiff's advisor. He owed him no other duty than to perform the particular acts which had been requested of him, and which he had promised to do. He owed the plaintiff no duty of watchfulness or of foresightedness."). While Larry does not have a duty to advise Bettina about how to protect her interests, he may have a duty to withdraw and advise the parties to seek representation. *See Matter of Marriage of Eltzroth*, 679 P.2d 1369, 1373 n.7 (Or. App. 1984) ("When the proposed 'agreement' between the parties presents obvious inequities on its face and raises questions and conflicts over the disposition of a substantial marital asset, it is the clear duty of the attorney to withdraw and advise the parties to seek independent counsel.").

Federal-State Power Distribution

220. **Answer (D) is the best answer.** Dana has mischaracterized the domestic relations exception. That exception does not permit federal courts "to issue divorce, alimony, and child custody decrees." *See Ankenbrandt v. Richards*, 504 U.S. 689, 703 (1992). However, because this suit does not involve any of those, the exception would not prevent a federal court from hearing this matter.

    Answer (A) is incorrect. The domestic relations exception is much more limited than that. *See Ankenbrandt v. Richards*, 504 U.S. 689, 703 (1992).

    Answer (B) is incorrect. Federal courts are not divested of jurisdiction merely because members of an intact family are involved. *See Drewes v. Ilnicki*, 863 F.2d 469, 471 (6th Cir. 1988) ("[A] district court does not lose jurisdiction merely because intra-family aspects are involved, particularly when the cause of action is cognizable in tort.").

    Answer (C) is incorrect. The domestic relations exception does not involve all family matters, but only those related to divorce, spousal support, and child custody. *See Ankenbrandt v. Richards*, 504 U.S. 689, 703 (1992). *See also Drewes v. Ilnicki*, 863 F.2d 469, 471 (6th Cir. 1988).

221. In order for federal law to displace state law, the state law "must do major damage to clear and substantial federal interests." *Hillman v. Maretta*, 569 U.S. 483, 491 (2013). Congress thought it important to have a "a clear and predictable procedure for an employee to indicate who the intended beneficiary of his life insurance shall be." *See id.* at 495. The court is likely to hold the state law preempted by the federal law, which means that Riley is unlikely to be successful. *See Hillman v. Maretta*, 569 U.S. 483 (2013).

Answers

Practice Final Exam

222. **Answer (B) is the best answer.** A minor marriage will be treated as valid until declared void by a court as long as the jurisdiction treats minor marriages as voidable rather than void. *See In re J.M.N.*, 2008 WL 2415490, at *8 (Tenn. Ct. App. 2008). Further, it is unlikely that a court would annul the marriage after Simon's death. *See Matter of Davis' Estate*, 640 P.2d 692, 693 (Or. App. 1982) ("[A] suit for annulment does not survive the death of one of the parties.").

    Answer (A) is incorrect. A voidable marriage does not have to be ratified before coming into being. Rather, a voidable marriage will be treated as valid until annulled by a court. *See In re J.M.N.*, 2008 WL 2415490, at *8 (Tenn. App. 2008).

    Answer (C) is incorrect. While one of the requirements for a common law marriage to exist is that others in the community knew of the marriage, *see In re Estate of Ober*, 62 P.3d 1114, 1117 (Mont. 2003) ("A common-law marriage cannot exist if the parties have kept their marital relationship a secret."), there is no such requirement for a ceremonial marriage. *See Cohen v. Shushan*, 212 So. 3d 1113, 1124 (Fla. App. 2017) ("A ceremonial marriage is effectuated pursuant to a marriage license and marriage ceremony conducted by a minister or authorized civil officer in the presence of witnesses.").

    Answer (D) is incorrect. A marriage valid in the state of celebration but void in the state of domicile is not likely to be recognized as valid. *See In re Mastrogiacomo*, 2003 WL 21436099, at *2 (N.Y. Sur. 2003) ("In conflicts of law the general rule is that a marriage which satisfies the requirements of the state where it was contracted will everywhere be recognized as valid unless it violates the strong public policy of another state which had the most significant relationship to the spouses and the marriage at the time of the marriage.").

223. **Answer (D) is the best answer.** If the marriage is void in the domicile at the time of its purported celebration, it will likely be treated as never having existed and not amenable to ratification. *See Lindsley v. Lindsley*, 2010 WL 2349200, at *3 (Tenn. App. 2010) ("Under the laws of Tennessee, a . . . marriage [that] is void *ab initio* . . . is neither given recognition by the courts nor is such a marriage capable of ratification by the parties."). If not a member of the decedent's family, Reese would likely be barred from seeking wrongful death damages. *See Del Ciotto v. Pennsylvania Hosp. of the Univ. of Penn Health Sys.*, 177 A.3d 335, 355 (Pa. Super. 2017) ("An action for wrongful death may be brought only by specified relatives of the decedent to recover damages in their own behalf, and not as beneficiaries of the estate.").

    Answer (A) is not the best answer. While voidable marriages are subject to ratification, *see State ex rel. Dep't of Econ. Sec. v. Demetz*, 130 P.3d 986, 989 (Ariz. App. 2006) ("A 'voidable' marriage, on the other hand, is one in which an impediment to marriage exists but the marriage is nevertheless subject to ratification."), void marriages are not subject to ratification. *See Lindsley v. Lindsley*, 2010 WL 2349200, at *3 (Tenn. App. 2010).

Answer (B) is not the best answer. While voidable marriages are valid until annulled by a court, *see In re J.M.N.*, 2008 WL 2415490, at *8 (Tenn. App. 2008), a void marriage will be treated as never having existed and not subject to ratification. *See Lindsley v. Lindsley*, 2010 WL 2349200, at *3 (Tenn. App. 2010).

Answer (C) is incorrect. No formal action is required in order for a voidable marriage to be treated as valid. Instead, the voidable marriage has to be annulled by a court in order not to be recognized. *See In re J.M.N.*, 2008 WL 2415490, at *8 (Tenn. App. 2008). Here, the marriage is void under the domicile's law rather than voidable, which is why the marriage will not be recognized. *See Lindsley v. Lindsley*, 2010 WL 2349200, at *3 (Tenn. App. 2010).

224. Storm and Tate's marriage is voidable rather than void, and a voidable marriage can be annulled by a court. *See Macias v. Sabillon*, 2017 WL 4274919, at *5 (N.Y. Sup. Ct. 2017) ("In cases of a voidable marriage—including fraudulent marriages—the marriage is legal until annulled by the Court and it only becomes void from the time its nullity is determined by the judgment of the Court."). However, once Storm and Tate ratify the marriage by living together when both have attained majority, the marriage becomes valid and is no longer voidable. *See Levick v. MacDougall*, 805 S.E.2d 775, 797 (Va. 2017) ("[A] voidable marriage may be afterwards ratified by the parties and become valid."). The parties to a valid marriage may seek a divorce. *See In re Estate of Laubenheimer*, 2012 WL 2336246, at *3 (Wis. App. 2012) ("Where a marriage is valid, the judgment is for a divorce."), whereas the parties to a voidable marriage might seek to have it annulled. *See id.* ("[A]nnulment is the proper remedy to set aside . . . the voidable marriage."). Because their marriage is valid, Storm and Tate will have to get a divorce or dissolution rather than an annulment. *See United Timber & Lumber Co. v. Alleged Dependents of Hill*, 84 So. 2d 921, 924 (Miss. 1956) ("The term 'divorce', confined strictly to the legal sense of the term, means the legal dissolution of a lawful union for a cause arising after marriage, while an annulment proceeding is one maintained upon the theory that for some reason existing at the time of a pretended marriage, no valid marriage ever existed. In the common wider use the term 'divorce' includes the dissolution of a valid marriage.").

225. **Answer (B) is the best answer.** Most jurisdictions do not allow siblings to marry, even if one of them has been adopted and the two are not related by blood. *See*, for example, *Arteaga v. State*, 521 S.W.3d 329, 333–34 (Tex. Crim. App. 2017) ("A marriage is void if one party to the marriage is related to the other as: . . . (2) a brother or sister, of the whole or half blood or by adoption."). *See also In re Marriage of MEW*, 4 Pa. D. & C.3d 51, 59 (Com. Pl. 1977) ("To authorize and encourage marriages of brothers and sisters by adoption would undermine the fabric of family life and would be the antithesis of the social aims and purposes which the adoption process is intended to serve."). However, there is case law permitting such a marriage where the individuals never lived together. *See Israel v. Allen*, 577 P.2d 762, 764 (Colo. 1978) ("We hold that it is just as illogical to prohibit marriage between adopted brother and sister.").

Answer (A) is incorrect. If the jurisdiction bars adoptive siblings from marrying, the marriage will not be recognized, even if no family member objects. Va. Code Ann. § 20-38.1 (a) (2) (West) ("The following marriages are prohibited: . . . . A marriage between an ancestor and descendant, or between a brother and a sister, whether the relationship is by the half or the whole blood or by adoption.").

Answer (C) is incorrect. Individuals who are of age and not related by blood may nonetheless be barred from marrying if they are too closely related by affinity. *See Summers v. Summers*, 2007 WL 4125339, at *1 (Mich. App. 2007) ("MCL 552.1 provides that a marriage is 'absolutely void' if it is 'prohibited by law' because of the relationship by consanguinity or affinity of the parties."). *See also Beam v. State*, 1 So. 3d 331, 333 (Fla. App. 2009) ("The term 'consanguinity' means related by blood; its antonym is 'affinity,' which means related by marriage.").

Answer (D) is incorrect. Some states permit first cousins to marry if unable to have a child through their union, *see*, for example, Utah Code Ann. § 30-1-1 (2) West ("First cousins may marry under the following circumstances: (a) both parties are 65 years of age or older; or (b) if both parties are 55 years of age or older, upon a finding by the district court, located in the district in which either party resides, that either party is unable to reproduce."), but jurisdictions have not adopted a similar approach with respect to adoptive siblings. *See* Va. Code Ann. § 20-38.1 (a) (2) (West).

226. The first question is whether Alex and Blair contracted a valid marriage in Anythinggoesland. Even if so, a separate question is whether Traditionaland will recognize that marriage. If Traditionaland permits such marriages, then their marriage will be recognized. Even if Traditionaland does not permit such marriages to be contracted within the state, it might recognize such a marriage if contracted in a state permitting such unions. *See Matter of Loughmiller's Estate*, 629 P.2d 156, 161 (Kan. 1981) ("Although our statutes prohibit first cousin marriages and impose criminal penalties where such marriages are contracted in Kansas, we cannot find that a first cousin marriage validly contracted elsewhere is odious to the public policy of this state."). If neither Anythingoesland nor Traditionaland recognizes first-cousin marriages, then the attorney might recommend that the couple move to a state that does recognize such marriages where they can again marry, so that they will be sure that their marriage will be recognized.

227. **Answer (A) is the best answer.** The issue to be determined first is whether Casey and Ellis were so inebriated that they did not know what they were doing when they exchanged vows. *See Christoph v. Sims*, 234 S.W.2d 901, 903 (Tex. Civ. App. 1950) ("A judgment decreeing incapacity because of drunkenness to invalidate a marriage must be based upon pleading and evidence that at the time of the marriage one of the parties did not have sufficient mental capacity to make a contract. . . . [T]he rule has been laid down that if a person, when married, is so much intoxicated as to be non compos mentis, and does not know what he is doing, being, for the time, deprived of reason, the marriage is invalid, but it is not invalid if the intoxication is of a less degree than that stated."). That they kissed after they were pronounced married undercuts that they were so drunk that they did not understand what they were

doing. Even if they were not competent to contract a marriage, a separate question would be whether the marriage would be treated as voidable rather than void. If such a marriage is treated as voidable by Washtana, then it will likely be treated as valid until annulled by a court. *See Estate of Wild v. Wild*, 2013 WL 2371190, at *3 (Iowa App. 2013) ("[W]hen a marriage is voidable it is legally valid for all civil purposes until it is judicially annulled."). Further, if one of the parties to a voidable marriage dies, that marriage may no longer be subject to annulment. *See Smith v. Smith*, 224 So. 3d 740, 746 (Fla. 2017) ("[A] voidable marriage is good for every purpose until avoided.... Upon the death of either party, the marriage is good *ab initio*.").

Answer (B) is not the best answer. While many states will permit a marriage that was celebrated by individuals too drunk to know what they were doing to be ratified when the parties become sober, *see Smith v. Smith*, 224 So. 3d 740, 746 (Fla. 2017) ("[A] marriage entered into where a party lacks mental capacity (due to intoxication, for example) may later be ratified upon regaining capacity."), the ratification would make the marriage valid and no longer subject to annulment. *See id.* ("[I]t is possible for a voidable marriage to ripen into a valid marriage if it is ratified by the parties."). But even if not ratified, the voidable marriage is valid until annulled by a court. *See Estate of Wild v. Wild*, 2013 WL 2371190, at *3 (Iowa App. 2013).

Answer (C) is not the best answer. Consummation is not necessary for a marriage to be treated as valid. *See Berdikas v. Berdikas*, 178 A.2d 468, 470–71 (Del. Super. Ct. 1962) ("[W]here the parties have been wed in compliance with the requirements of the statute ... a valid marriage is effected and no consummation of the marriage, as by coition is necessary."). Nonconsummation might be a basis for annulment. *See Patel v. Patel*, 11 N.E.3d 800 (Ohio App. 2014) (annulment granted because of lack of consummation). However, a voidable marriage is still valid until annulled by a court. *See Estate of Wild v. Wild*, 2013 WL 2371190, at *3 (Iowa App. 2013).

Answer (D) is not the best answer. The mere appearance of an exchange of vows would not require recognition of the marriage if it could be established that one of the parties was so drunk as to not understand what he or she was doing. If a marriage involving a party who did not understand the proceedings is treated as void rather than voidable, *see Krukowsky v. Krukowsky*, 49 Pa. D. & C.2d 651, 653 (Com. Pl. 1970) ("[A] marriage performed while one of the parties is non compos mentis is a void marriage."), then the marriage would be void, appearances notwithstanding.

228. **Answer (D) is the best answer.** Remaining in a marriage rather than immediately seeking a divorce can constitute consideration. *See Bratton v. Bratton*, 136 S.W.3d 595, 600 (Tenn. 2004) ("[R]econciliation in the face of an impending separation or divorce may be adequate consideration."). Further, threatening to get a divorce is not coercion when there is justification for seeking a divorce. *See Gilley v. Gilley*, 778 S.W.2d 862, 864 (Tenn. App. 1989) ("Perhaps husband was under duress due to the discovery of his own miscreant conduct, but in order for the agreement to be defeated, we must find legal duress. Whatever perceived pressures constrained him to sign the agreement against his free will were internal and of his own making, and whatever external pressures there may have been were not improper. The wife

clearly had a legal basis and right to prosecute a divorce and did nothing improper in negotiating an agreement in consideration of forgoing her claim.").

Answer (A) is incorrect. Remaining married rather than seeking a divorce immediately can constitute consideration. *See Bratton v. Bratton*, 136 S.W.3d 595, 600 (Tenn. 2004).

Answer (B) is not correct. While Dana did sign the agreement to avoid an immediate divorce, Phoenix had a right to seek a divorce and so was not imposing improper pressure. *See Gilley v. Gilley*, 778 S.W.2d 862, 864 (Tenn. App. 1989).

Answer (C) is incorrect because there was adequate consideration, *see Bratton v. Bratton*, **136 S.W.3d 595, 600 (Tenn. 2004), and because there was no improper coercion.** *See Gilley v. Gilley*, 778 S.W.2d 862, 864 (Tenn. App. 1989).

229. Based on the above, it is unlikely that Finley will be able to show that Ellis knowingly misrepresented the assets to induce detrimental reliance. *See In re Sertz v. Sertz*, 2012-Ohio-2120, ¶ 35 (Ct. App.) (noting that the standard for voiding the separation agreement is "whether there has been a knowing, material misrepresentation with the intent to induce reliance by the other party and the other party has relied upon the misrepresentation to his or her detriment"). Even if unable to establish that the omission was intentional, Finley might be able to have the agreement voided if Ellis omitted a substantial amount of assets. *See Hunter v. Hunter*, 2011-Ohio-3094, ¶ 26 (Ohio App) ("[W]here a separation agreement omits assets that are both substantial in relative amount and material to an informed and deliberate agreement about equitable division of property, such omissions render the dissolution decree voidable."). Ultimately, this may well be left to the discretion of the trial court. *See In re McLoughlin v. McLoughlin*, 2006-Ohio-1530, ¶ 31 (Ohio App.) ("[W]hether equity demands that the judgment be set aside remains a question within the court's discretion.").

230. **Answer (D) is the best answer.** Many states will not enforce a prenuptial agreement if it was unconscionable when made or unconscionable at the time enforcement was sought. *See O'Daniel v. O'Daniel*, 419 S.W.3d 280, 286 (Tenn. App. 2013) ("[W]here circumstances have changed over the course of the marriage such that enforcement of the agreement would be unconscionable or unfair because enforcement would likely result in a disadvantaged spouse being unable to provide for his or her reasonable needs, the courts will set aside the relevant portions of the agreement and award alimony."). A paradigmatic example would involve someone who would have to become a public charge if the prenuptial agreement were enforced. *See Taha v. Elzemity*, 68 N.Y.S.3d 493, 495 (App. Div. 2018) ("[T]he defendant sustained her burden of establishing that the prenuptial agreement was, at the time this action was before the court, unconscionable. Enforcement of the agreement would result in the risk of the defendant's becoming a public charge.").

Answer (A) is not the best answer. Many states will refuse to enforce a prenuptial agreement that is unconscionable at the time of enforcement, even if the agreement was not unconscionable at the time it was made. *See Hobbs v. Hobbs*, 2017 WL 603555, at *5 (Mich. App. 2017) ("A prenuptial agreement may be voided ... when the facts and circumstances are so changed since the agreement was executed that its enforcement would be unfair and unreasonable.").

Answer (B) is not the best answer. While a prenuptial agreement might be held unenforceable because of fraud, duress, or misrepresentation, *see Hobbs v. Hobbs*, 2017 WL 603555, at *5 (Mich. App. 2017) ("A prenuptial agreement may be voided (1) when obtained through fraud, duress, mistake, or misrepresentation or nondisclosure of material fact."), a prenuptial agreement might also be held unenforceable even if there was no coercion, fraud, or misrepresentation. *See id.*

Answer (C) is not the best answer. While a prenuptial agreement will not be enforced if its enforcement "would be unfair and unreasonable," *see Hobbs v. Hobbs*, 2017 WL 603555, at *5 (Mich. App. 2017), that should not be thought to mean that an agreement will be held unenforceable if one of the parties might have struck a better deal. *See H.T. v. A.E.*, 9 N.Y.S.3d 593 (Sup. Ct. 2014) ("Although the application of the parties' prenuptial agreement would arguably result in Husband retaining most of the property at issue, it is well settled that courts will not set aside an agreement on the ground of unconscionability simply because, in retrospect, the agreement proves to be improvident or one-sided. Here the agreement, while arguably favorable to Husband, is not so one sided as to appear manifestly unfair such that it shocks the conscience of the Court.").

231. **Answer (B) is the best answer.** Jurisdictions differ about whether a premarital agreement presented shortly before a wedding is to take place makes such an agreement unenforceable. *Compare In re Estate of Hollett*, 834 A.2d 348, 354 (N.H. 2003) (signing of premarital agreement shortly before the wedding as not voluntary as a matter of law) *with In re Marriage of Miller*, 2002 WL 31312840, at *2 (Iowa App. 2002) (upholding the validity of a prenuptial agreement presented shortly before the wedding).

Answer (A) is not the best answer. While there should be financial disclosure, *see Cole v. Cole*, 2017 WL 1450078, at *4 (Pa. Super. 2017) ("A premarital agreement shall not be enforceable if the party seeking to set aside the agreement proves, by clear and convincing evidence, that . . . the party . . . was not provided a fair and reasonable disclosure of the property or financial obligations of the other party"), jurisdictions differ about whether the presentation of a prenuptial agreement shortly before a marriage will make that agreement unenforceable. *Compare In re Estate of Hollett*, 834 A.2d 348, 354 (N.H. 2003) *with In re Marriage of Miller*, 2002 WL 31312840, at *2 (Iowa App. 2002).

Answer (C) is not correct. Jurisdictions distinguish between procedural and substantive unconscionablility, so the terms of an agreement will not alone determine whether that agreement is enforceable. *See Rivera v. Rivera*, 243 P.3d 1148, 1154 (N.M. App. 2010) ("Substantive unconscionability relates to the content of the contract terms and whether they are illegal, contrary to public policy, or grossly unfair, while [p]rocedural unconscionability is determined by analyzing the circumstances surrounding the contract's formation, such as whether it was an adhesive contract and the relative bargaining power of the parties.").

Answer (D) is not the best answer. Some jurisdictions would hold the agreement enforceable because Morgan could always have canceled or delayed the wedding. *See In re Marriage of Miller*, 2002 WL 31312840, at *2 (Iowa App. 2002) ("In the present case, Debra had a reasonable alternative: she could have canceled the wedding."). Further, Pat's refusal to marry without the agreement being signed as is would not constitute a threat or be thought unlawful. *See id.* at *3 ("[I]nsistence on a prenuptial agreement as a condition of marriage is not a threat or unlawful.").

232. At least part of the prenuptial agreement will be treated as unenforceable. Couples cannot make an enforceable prenuptial agreement about who will have custody even before the children are born because such a provision would not be based on whose having custody would best promote the children's interests. *See Edwardson v. Edwardson,* 798 S.W.2d 941, 946 (Ky. 1990) ("[A]ntenuptial agreements may apply only to disposition of property and maintenance. Questions of child support, child custody and visitation are not subject to such agreements."). However, the invalidity of one provision need not make the entire prenuptial agreement unenforceable. *See Sanford v. Sanford,* 694 N.W.2d 283, 291 (S.D. 2005) ("Those portions of a prenuptial agreement that are valid will be enforced despite the presence of invalid provisions within the agreement."). *But see Rivera v. Rivera,* 243 P.3d 1148, 1155 (N.M. App. 2010) ("The agreement does not contain a severability clause, and Wife makes no argument that the remainder of the agreement should not be affected by the invalidity of the support provisions. Because Wife makes no argument and because we are unable to discern whether the parties bargained for the waiver of spousal support in exchange for other benefits or concessions, we are unable to conclude that any portion of the agreement is valid without the unconscionable provisions."). As to whether the provision denying spousal support is enforceable, this will be a matter of state law. Some states treat such provisions as unenforceable. *See Sanford v. Sanford,* 694 N.W.2d 283, 287 (S.D. 2005) ("[P]rovisions in a prenuptial agreement purporting to limit alimony obligations are against public policy and therefore not enforceable."). Others might treat such a provision as unenforceable if its enforcement would mean that the non-supported spouse would have to get public support. *See Taha v. Elzemity,* 68 N.Y.S.3d 493, 495 (App. Div. 2018) ("[T]he defendant sustained her burden of establishing that the prenuptial agreement was, at the time this action was before the court, unconscionable. Enforcement of the agreement would result in the risk of the defendant's becoming a public charge.").

233. **Answer (D) is the best answer.** In many jurisdictions, not only will Dallas have to have fraudulently induced Erin to marry, but the fraud will have to go to the essentials of marriage. *See Matter of Geraghty,* 150 A.3d 386, 394 (N.H. 2016). *See also In re Marriage of Igene,* 35 N.E.3d 1125, 1128 (Ill. App. 2015) ("Courts in most jurisdictions have determined that the concealment of a prior marriage which has been dissolved by the death of, or divorce from, a spouse does not amount to fraud going to the essentials of the marriage contract.").

Answer (A) is not the best answer. If this is viewed as a fraud going to the essentials of marriage, then an annulment might well be granted, children notwithstanding. *See Matter of Geraghty,* 150 A.3d 386, 394 (N.H. 2016) ("The fraudulent representations for which a marriage may be annulled must be of something essential to the marriage relation — of something making impossible the performance of the duties and obligations of that relation or rendering its assumption and continuance dangerous to health or life."). State law might treat the children as legitimate even if the marriage is annulled. *See*, for example, S.C. Code Ann. § 20-1-90 ("When either of the contracting parties to a marriage that is void under the provisions of Section 20-1-80 entered into the marriage contract in good faith on or after April 13, 1951 and in ignorance of the incapacity of the other party, any children born of the marriage shall be deemed legitimate and have the same legal rights as a child born in lawful wedlock.").

Answer (B) is not the best answer. In many states, the marriage will be subject to annulment only if Dallas made a fraudulent misrepresentation going to the essentials of marriage. *See Matter of Geraghty*, 150 A.3d 386, 394 (N.H. 2016); *In re Marriage of Igene*, 35 N.E.3d 1125, 1128 (Ill. App. 2015). Dallas's having knowledge of Erin's views would not show that Dallas had made an affirmative representation upon which Erin had relied. *See id.* at 1129 (noting that in those cases where an annulment had been secured because one of the parties had been previously married, "the party [who had] fraudulently concealed a prior marriage made false representations").

Answer (C) is not the best answer. An annulment might be granted for a fraud going to the essentials of marriage, even if the perpetrator had reasonably believed that the fraud would never be discovered. A different rule would reward the person imposing the fraud at the expense of the innocent spouse. *See Masters v. Masters*, 108 N.W.2d 674, 678 (Wis. 1961) ("[T]o deny an annulment would reward the defendant for a palpable fraud and punish the plaintiff for being victimized.").

234.   **Answer (C) is the best answer.** Because Caleb was born into an existing marriage, the parties to the marriage may well be able to prevent Alex from establishing parental rights. *See*, for example, *Slowinski v. Sweeney*, 64 So. 3d 128, 129 (Fla. App. 2011) ("The statutes governing paternity contain language indicating biological fathers may not challenge the paternity of children born to intact marriages").

Answer (A) is incorrect. Biological connections notwithstanding, Alex may have great difficulty in establishing parental rights. *See Slowinski v. Sweeney*, 64 So. 3d 128, 129 (Fla. App. 2011) ("Paternity is 'otherwise' established when the child is born to an intact marriage and recognized by the husband as his own child. In such circumstances, the husband is considered to be the child's 'legal' father, regardless of whether he is the biological father.").

Answer (B) is incorrect. Alex may well have great difficulty in establishing parental rights even if there has been no formal adoption, because the child was born into an intact marriage. *See Slowinski v. Sweeney*, 64 So. 3d 128, 129 (Fla. App. 2011).

Answer (D) is not the best answer. Merely because Alex once suggested that Brett obtain an abortion would not foreclose his having parental rights. For example, he might later have changed his mind. Had he done so, he presumably would have continued to live with Brett. Had he acknowledged paternity upon Caleb's birth and committed to being Caleb's parent, he then would presumably have been recognized as one of Caleb's parents (assuming that he was a fit parent). *See In re Adoption of S.C.D.*, 742 So. 2d 1058, 1060 (La. App. 1999) ("[I]n order to establish his parental rights under the statutory scheme, the alleged father must acknowledge that he is the father of the child. He must also prove that he has manifested a substantial commitment to the child and that he is a fit parent of the child.").

235. **Answer (B) is the best answer.** Gene is likely to be successful because although he is not biologically related to Georgette, Georgette was born and conceived during the marriage. Further, Greer encouraged the relationship between the two of them, and he is embracing the legal rights and responsibilities of parentage. *See Atkinson v. Atkinson*, 408 N.W.2d 516, 519 (Mich. App. 1987) ("[W]e adopt the doctrine of 'equitable parent' and find that a husband who is not the biological father of a child born or conceived during the marriage may be considered the natural father of that child where (1) the husband and the child mutually acknowledge a relationship as father and child, or the mother of the child has cooperated in the development of such a relationship over a period of time prior to the filing of the complaint for divorce, (2) the husband desires to have the rights afforded to a parent, and (3) the husband is willing to take on the responsibility of paying child support.").

Answer (A) is incorrect because it mischaracterizes the doctrine at issue. Equitable parent doctrine recognizes the parental status of an individual who was married to the child's mother who had encouraged her spouse to establish a parent-child relationship with that child. *See Atkinson v. Atkinson*, 408 N.W.2d 516, 519 (Mich. App. 1987).

Answer (C) is not the best answer. While Gene must already have a parent-child relationship with Georgette and the status would not be recognized if that recognition would be detrimental to Georgette's interests, *see York v. Morofsky*, 571 N.W.2d 524, 527 (Mich. App. 1997) ("[T]he child's best interests are also of major concern in determining whether a party is an equitable parent as well."), there are additional requirements as well. *See Atkinson v. Atkinson*, 408 N.W.2d 516, 519 (Mich. App. 1987).

Answer (D) is incorrect. Equitable parent status can be conferred over the current objections of the child's other parent. *See York v. Morofsky*, 571 N.W.2d 524 (Mich. App. 1997) (equitable parent status recognized, objections of child's mother notwithstanding).

236. **Answer (B) is the best answer.** If local law requires that sperm donor give the sperm to a doctor in order for the donor to be viewed as having neither the rights nor obligations of parenthood, then the failure to use a doctor might mean that the individual providing sperm will not be viewed as a donor and thus might be awarded parental rights and obligations. *See In Interest of P.S.*, 505 S.W.3d 106, 108 (Tex. App. 2016) ("Because Father did not provide sperm to a licensed physician for the purpose of artificial insemination, we hold that Father is not a donor as that term is defined in section 160.102(6) and therefore may be named as a parent to Pamela. Consequently, we will affirm the trial court's order establishing Father's paternity of Pamela."). Or, the individual providing sperm might be recognized as having parental rights if that were the agreement of the parties. *See In Interest of R.C.*, 775 P.2d 27, 35 (Colo. 1989) (recognizing parental rights of man because "the known semen donor and the unmarried recipient agreed that the known donor would have parental rights and expressly agreed at the time of insemination that he would be treated as the natural father of any child so conceived").

Answer (A) is not the best answer. Robert might well be recognized as having parental rights if that was their agreement, *see In Interest of R.C.*, 775 P.2d 27, 35 (Colo. 1989), or if local law required that sperm donors provide their sperm to licensed physicians to avoid the imposition of parental rights and obligations. *See In Interest of P.S.*, 505 S.W.3d 106, 108 (Tex. App. 2016).

Answer (C) is not the best answer. An individual who provides his sperm to a physician so that a woman (not his wife) can become pregnant will not be recognized as the child's father. *See Jhordan C. v. Mary K.*, 224 Cal. Rptr. 530, 531 (Ct. App. 1986) ("[I]n California a donor of semen *provided to a licensed physician* for use in artificial insemination of a woman other than the donor's wife is treated in law as if he were not the natural father of a child thereby conceived.").

Answer (D) is not the best answer. A man providing sperm to a woman who uses that sperm to become pregnant via artificial insemination may be recognized as the child's father if certain procedures specified by law are not followed, even if the woman does not want the man to have parental rights. *See In Interest of P.S.*, 505 S.W.3d 106, 108 (Tex. App. 2016).

237.   Vick is unlikely to be recognized as an equitable parent if the jurisdiction has rejected that doctrine, *see Randy A.J. v. Norma I.J.*, 677 N.W.2d 630, 642 (Wis. 2004) ("We do not employ the equitable parent doctrine."). Even if that is not a viable option, Vick has other options. Because Sarah was born into their marriage, he might not only be presumed to be her father, but the time during which that presumption was rebuttable may already have passed. *See* Okla. Stat. Ann. tit. 10, § 7700-607 (West) ("[A] proceeding brought by a presumed father, the mother, or another individual to adjudicate the parentage of a child having a presumed father shall be commenced not later than two (2) years after the birth of the child."). Even if he were not presumed to be Sarah's father, Whitney might be estopped from challenging his paternity. *See Tregoning v. Wiltschek*, 782 A.2d 1001, 1004 (Pa. Super. 2001) ("[W]hen it suited appellee's interests she accepted appellant's role as the father of Jazmin. That position having been accepted and promoted by both parties requires the conclusion that appellee is now legally estopped from asserting a challenge to the paternity of appellant.").

238.   In order for an annulment to be granted, Bernard would have to establish that Alice had made a fraudulent misrepresentation about an essential to marriage. *See Royal v. Kukharenko*, 2010 WL 3447867, at *5 (Alaska 2010) ("A marriage may be declared void if the consent of either party was obtained by fraud. A party seeking to annul based on fraud must show by clear and convincing evidence that his or her consent to marriage was obtained by the fraud alleged . . . [and that] the fraud concerns an issue essential to the marriage."). Even if Bernard can establish with clear and convincing evidence that he had detrimentally relied on Alice's false representation that he was Tommy's biological father, he still may have great difficulty in having the marriage annulled. The jurisdiction may impose a duty on the victim to discover the fraud within a reasonable period, *see Mienik v. Mienik*, 456 N.Y.S.2d 424, 426 (App. Div. 1982) (discussing the "obligation imposed upon the victim of the fraud to discover the fraud within a reasonable time after the marriage and to disavow the marriage"), and here Bernard is seeking to annul the marriage 10 years later. *See id.* ("We find his belated

inquiry, which took the form of a request that the parties and the infant child submit to a blood grouping test, more than 13 years after the child's birth, was untimely as a matter of law."). Bernard might be viewed as having been on constructive notice that he was not Tommy's biological father—Tommy was born full term, which means that his conception occurred a few months before Alice and Bernard had started dating.

239. **Answer (C) is the best answer.** Dissipation occurs when a party uses marital assets for his or her own purposes when the marriage has broken down. *See Reed v. Reed*, 763 N.W.2d 686, 695 (Neb. 2009) (explaining that "'[d]issipation of marital assets' is defined as one spouse's use of marital property for a selfish purpose unrelated to the marriage at the time when the marriage is undergoing an irretrievable breakdown"). A party who dissipates marital assets can have those assets credited to his or her account when the marital assets are being distributed at the time of divorce. *See Duffy v. Duffy*, 2018 WL 472634, at *6 (Ky. App. 2018) ("If dissipation is found to have occurred, the court will deem the wrongfully dissipated assets to have been received by the offending party prior to the distribution."). Here, Ned will likely have the $40,000 credited to his side of the ledger when the marital assets are being distributed.

Answer (A) is not the best answer. While it is true that Ned's share of the remaining assets will be diminished if Pat's approach is adopted, that is something that he should have thought about before wasting the marital assets. He will likely be forced to bear the burden of his having wasted those monies. *See Tamba v. Tamba*, 1991 WL 318791, at *14 (Del. Super. 1991) ("To the extent that the Husband has already squandered a portion of his . . . share of the marital assets, that is a problem which he will have to live with since he has only himself to blame for the plight in which he finds himself.").

Answer (B) is not the best answer. While it is true that gambling winnings during a marriage will likely be treated as marital assets subject to distribution, *see Goodman v. Goodman*, 2018 WL 1163188, at *10 (Ind. App. 2018) ("Husband earned $140,961 in gambling winnings. As these amounts were acquired after the marriage and before the final separation of the parties, they are part of the marital estate."), that does not mean that Pat should be forced to share the burden of Ned's having wasted the assets. *See Duffy v. Duffy*, 2018 WL 472634, at *6 (Ky. App. 2018).

Answer (D) is incorrect. Gambling losses need not be viewed as waste or dissipation if the family goes on a gambling vacation together. But where an individual goes gambling purely for his own enjoyment once the marriage is over, gambling losses will likely be treated as dissipation. *See Lowrey v. Lowrey*, 25 So. 3d 274, 288 (Miss. 2009) ("[G]ambling losses can be considered as dissipation in an equitable distribution of marital assets.").

240. **Answer (D) is the best answer.** The necklace might be viewed as Sally's separate property or as marital property, depending upon local law and Wanda's intent. Some states treat interspousal gifts as marital property. *See Marshall-Beasley v. Beasley*, 77 So. 3d 751, 758 (Fla. App. 2011) ("Any gift of jewelry from Former Husband to Former Wife bought with marital assets remains a marital asset."); *McMillan v. McMillan*, 790 S.E.2d 216, 224 (S.C. App. 2016)

("Interspousal gifts of property . . . are marital property which is subject to division."). Some states will treat interspousal gifts as separate property only if there is a clear showing of donor intent to that effect. *See McCreery v. McCreery*, 2005 WL 2249594, *2 (Va. Cir. Ct. 2005) ("[T]here simply is no clear and unambiguous evidence that Husband expressed an intent to transfer the jewelry into Wife's name as her sole property. The jewelry was simply a gift between the parties as spouses, and, as a result, the jewelry cannot be considered Wife's separate property."). Yet others will treat such personal gifts as the separate property of the donee. *See Fleishhacker v. Fleishhacker*, 39 So. 3d 904, 914 (Miss. App. 2009) ("[W]e again addressed whether gifts of jewelry between spouses should be considered marital property. We held that '[e]ven though acquired during the marriage with marital assets, personal gifts of this nature are separate personal property of the donee.'").

Answer (A) is not the best answer. Gifts received during the marriage may well be treated as separate property. *See Robbins v. Townsend*, 2018 WL 1078896, at *1 (Ariz. App. 2018) ("If the property acquired during marriage was acquired by gift, devise, or descent, then the property is characterized as separate.").

Answer (B) is not the best answer. Property purchased with marital funds might be treated as separate if that was the clear intent of the individual making the gift. *See McCreery v. McCreery*, 2005 WL 2249594, *2 (Va. Cir. Ct. 2005).

Answer (C) is not the best answer. Some states treat interspousal gifts as marital property. *See Marshall-Beasley v. Beasley*, 77 So. 3d 751, 758 (Fla. App. 2011). Further, insofar as intent is determinative, the important issue is not Wanda's current intent but her intent at the time the gift was made. *See In re Balanson*, 25 P.3d 28, 37 (Colo. 2001) ("[W]hen determining whether transfers of property from one spouse to the other, such as that of the jewelry and furs at issue in this case, constitute marital property, a court must first determine whether the transfer was a gift to the other spouse, and therefore excluded from the definition of marital property under the Act. In order to qualify as a 'gift,' a transfer of property must involve a simultaneous intention to make a gift, delivery of the gift, and acceptance of the gift.").

241. **Answer (D) is the best answer.** Property inherited by one individual during the marriage is separate property. *See In re Marriage of Thomas*, 2017 WL 2684359, at *2 (Iowa App. 2017) ("All property of the marriage at the time of the divorce, except gifted or inherited property, is divisible property."). However, property purchased during the marriage using funds earned during the marriage is marital property subject to distribution. *See Doyle v. Doyle*, 786 S.W.2d 620, 622 (Mo. App. 1990) ("Wages earned by Matthew during the marriage are marital property."); *Sanon v. Sanon*, 2016 WL 1688596, at *3 n.8 (N.Y. Sup. 2016) ("If the gifts were purchased with . . . 'marital'—funds, then the items (rings, cars, houses, other goods) are marital property and the wife has a marital interest in them and they must be disclosed and are subject to equitable distribution.").

Answer (A) is incorrect. Because Taylor's car was purchased with marital funds, it is marital property subject to distribution. *See Doyle v. Doyle*, 786 S.W.2d 620, 622 (Mo. App. 1990); *Sanon v. Sanon*, 2016 WL 1688596, at *3 n.8 (N.Y. Sup. Ct. 2016).

Answer (B) is incorrect. Property inherited during a marriage is separate property not subject to distribution. *See In re Marriage of Thomas*, 2017 WL 2684359, at *2 (Iowa Ct. App. 2017).

Answer (C) is incorrect. Property inherited during the marriage is separate property. *See In re Marriage of Thomas*, 902 N.W.2d 593 (Iowa App. 2017). However, property purchased using marital funds is marital property subject to distribution. *See Doyle v. Doyle*, 786 S.W.2d 620, 622 (Mo. App. 1990); *Sanon v. Sanon*, 2016 WL 1688596, at *3 n.8 (N.Y. Sup. 2016).

242.   **Answer (D) is the best answer.** *See Curley v. Curley*, 2012 WL 1605207, at *16 (N.J. Super. App. Div. 2012) (noting that the increase in value of a pre-owned asset during the marriage will be separate as long as the appreciation is passive, e.g., due to market forces, rather than active).

Answer (A) is not the best answer. Separate property used as the marital domicile may nonetheless retain its characterization as separate property. *See Bridgewater v. Bridgewater*, 360 So. 2d 219, 219 (La. App. 1978) (husband's separate property, used as marital domicile during the marriage, remained his separate property).

Answer (B) is not the best answer. Purely passive appreciation of a separate asset is not subject to distribution. *See Price v. Price*, 496 N.Y.S.2d 455, 462 (App. Div. 1985) ("[P]assive appreciation of a separate property asset during the marital relationship would not be subject to a claim by the nontitled spouse.").

Answer (C) is not the best answer. Merely because the house was titled in Robin's name would not make the appreciation separate property if the increase in value was due to the investment of marital funds. *See Harrower v. Harrower*, 71 P.3d 854, 858 (Alaska 2003) ("[T]he asset's value at the inception of the marriage retains its separate character, but any subsequent increase in value is treated as marital property to the extent that it results from active marital conduct: Appreciation in separate property is marital if it was caused by marital funds or marital efforts; otherwise it remains separate.").

243.   **Answer (B) is the best answer.** Where there has been a negligent failure to inform the parents, the parents must show that the failure caused them harm, e.g., deprived them of the opportunity to abort. *See Plowman v. Fort Madison Cmty. Hosp.*, 896 N.W.2d 393, 409 (Iowa 2017) ("The parents must prove the defendant's negligence deprived them of the opportunity to *lawfully* terminate the pregnancy in Iowa."). In addition, the parents will show that they suffered harm as a result of that lost opportunity. *See id.* at 402 ("[T]he resulting injury to the parents lies in their being deprived of the opportunity to make an informed decision to terminate the pregnancy, requiring them to incur extraordinary expenses in the care and education of their child afflicted with a genetic abnormality.").

Answer (A) is not the best answer. Unless Mary can establish that she would have aborted the pregnancy, her not having been given the correct test results would not have played any causal role in her being forced to incur those extraordinary expenses. *See Plowman v. Fort Madison Cmty. Hosp.*, 896 N.W.2d 393, 399 (Iowa 2017) ("In a wrongful-birth action, parents of a child born with a detectable birth defect allege that they would have avoided conception or terminated the pregnancy but for the physician's negligent failure to inform them of the likelihood of the birth defect.").

Answer (C) is not correct. Mary will need to show that she would have gotten an abortion had she been given the results in a timely way. *See Plowman v. Fort Madison Cmty. Hosp.*, 896 N.W.2d 393, 409 (Iowa 2017). The claim that the child would have been better off never having lived is part of a wrongful life claim rather than a wrongful birth claim. *See Greco v. United States*, 893 P.2d 345, 347 (Nev. 1995) ("Implicit in this argument is the assumption that the child would be better off had he never been born.").

Answer (D) is incorrect. It is not necessary to show that the Down Syndrome could have been corrected in utero. Here, the claim is that Mary was denied the opportunity to make an informed decision about continuing the pregnancy. *See Plowman v. Fort Madison Cmty. Hosp.*, 896 N.W.2d 393, 403 (Iowa 2017) ("The compensable injury in a wrongful-birth claim is the parents' loss of the opportunity to make an informed decision to terminate the pregnancy.").

244. West Kanowa can grant the divorce, assuming that Pat has established domicile and met the residence requirement. *See Falah v. Falah*, 87 N.E.3d 763, 767 (Ohio App. 2017) ("[A] trial court has subject matter jurisdiction to hear a divorce action if the plaintiff has been an Ohio resident for at least six months . . . The word 'resident' . . . means one who possesses a domiciliary residence, a residence accompanied by an intention to make the state of Ohio a permanent home."). *See also Lacroix v. Lacroix*, 742 So. 2d 1036, 1038 (La. App. 1999) (discussing indicia of domicile). However, West Kanowa does not have sufficient contacts with Parker to distribute property located in East Minnegan. *See Davis v. Davis*, 293 N.E.2d 399, 405 (Ill. App. 1973) ("Having decided that competent evidence supports the finding that Shelley was a resident of Illinois for the necessary one year prior to filing of the complaint and that Laura's special appearance did not confer personal jurisdiction on the trial court, we affirm the part of the decree granting the divorce but reverse . . . any portions of the decree disposing of the property rights of Laura or Shelley."). In short, Parker's challenge to the court's jurisdiction to distribute the property is likely to be successful.

245. When there is a substantial change of circumstances in the life of a noncustodial parent resulting in that parent's earning substantially less, that parent may be able to have a child support obligation reduced. *See Sullivan v. Tardiff*, 124 A.3d 652, 657 (Me. 2015) ("A party moving to decrease the amount of child support . . . must prove by a preponderance of the evidence that the decrease is necessitated by a substantial change in circumstances that either reduces the payor spouse's ability to contribute to the support of the minor child or reduces the payee spouse's need to receive support."). However, a parent who is voluntarily underemployed may well not be able to have the child support obligation modified. *See Incontro v. Jacobs*, 761 N.W.2d 551, 559–60 (Neb. 2009) ("[T]he record indicates that Incontro's income decreased due to his own personal wishes, and not as a result of unfavorable or adverse conditions in the economy, his health, or other circumstances that would affect Incontro's earning capacity. While the amount of Incontro's income has changed from the entry of the original child support order, he has failed to prove a change in his earning capacity. . . . For these reasons, the district

court abused its discretion when it modified Incontro's child support payments based upon Incontro's change in income."). Here, Casey may well be found to be voluntarily underemployed and his request to have his child support obligation reduced may well be rejected.

246. **Answer (D) is the best answer.** Because Roberto and the children continue to live in Georgiana, which is the state issuing the initial decree, a Georgiana rather than a Calington court would have jurisdiction to modify the support obligation. *See Draper v. Burke*, 881 N.E.2d 122, 125 (Mass. 2008) ("Under UIFSA, once one court enters a support order, no other court may modify that order for as long as the obligee, obligor, or child for whose benefit the order is entered continues to reside within the jurisdiction of that court unless each party consents in writing to another jurisdiction.").

Answer (A) is not the best answer. While it is true that Juan might be able to find a better paying job later, that does not preclude his having a reduced obligation now in light of his new lower-paying job. *See Grady v. Grady*, 640 So. 2d 157, 157 (Fla. App. 1994) ("The trial court essentially concluded that the father was a mid-level manager who, in a difficult job market, had been unable to find employment equivalent to his previous job. There is sufficient evidence to support the trial court's finding that the father was not voluntarily underemployed. Thus, the trial court was not obligated to impute income to the father under these circumstances.").

Answer (B) is not the best answer. Juan is not likely to be successful because the Calington court would likely not have jurisdiction to hear the case. *See Draper v. Burke*, 881 N.E.2d 122, 125 (Mass. 2008).

Answer (C) is not the best answer. Juan is not likely to be successful because the Calington court would likely not have jurisdiction. *See Draper v. Burke*, 881 N.E.2d 122, 125 (Mass. 2008). He might well have been successful had he sought relief in a Georgiana court, notwithstanding that the children's needs have not changed. *See Grady v. Grady*, 640 So. 2d 157, 157 (Fla. App. 1994).

247. **Answer (C) is the best answer.** Cameron will likely be able to rebut the presumption of paternity because his challenge to paternity is timely, he will have no difficulty in showing a lack of genetic connection, and he has never bonded with Cassandra nor held her out as his own. *See Rydberg v. Rydberg*, 678 N.W.2d 534, 541 (N.D. 2004) ("genetic tests are enough to rebut the presumption of paternity"); *Justin P. v. Jennifer L.*, 2011 WL 7006508, at *2 (N.Y. Fam. 2011) ("The child's attorney has not presented any genuine issue of fact that the child has formed any bond with the petitioner sufficient to defeat the petitioner's motion for summary judgment."); *D.I. v. I.G.*, 2018 WL 1222720, at *2 (Ala. Civ. App. 2018) ("A man is presumed to be the father of a child if . . . while the child is under the age of majority, he receives the child into his home and openly holds out the child as his natural child or otherwise openly holds out the child as his natural child and establishes a significant parental relationship with the child by providing emotional and financial support for the child.").

Answer (A) is incorrect. A child support obligation can be imposed under other circumstances, e.g., if the child is adopted. *See In re Adoption of S.B.*, 2017 WL 3077068, at *5 (Ill.

App. 2017) ("The formality of an adoption provides financial support, inheritance rights, and legal protections that are simply not present without the adoption process.").

Answer (B) is not the best answer. While Cameron will not be able to claim that he had been deceived about his having fathered Cassandra, he also neither claimed the child as his own nor formed a bond with the child. *Justin P. v. Jennifer L.*, 2011 WL 7006508, at *2 (N.Y. Fam. 2011); *D.I. v. I.G.*, 2018 WL 1222720, at *2 (Ala. Civ. App. 2018).

Answer (D) is not the best answer because that presumption is rebuttable. *See Rydberg v. Rydberg*, 678 N.W.2d 534, 541 (N.D. 2004).

248. **Answer (B) is the best answer.** Even if Tortington permits minor children to sue for loss of consortium when a parent dies through another's negligence, a separate issue is whether the jurisdiction will permit adult children to bring such an action. *Compare Roth v. Evangelical Lutheran Good Samaritan Soc.*, 886 N.W.2d 601 (Iowa 2016) (adult children permitted to bring loss of consortium claim) and *N. Pac. Ins. Co. v. Stucky*, 338 P.3d 56 (Mont. 2014) (same) *with Campos v. Coleman*, 123 A.3d 854, 868 (Conn. 2015) ("[A] loss of parental consortium claim may be raised only by a person who was a minor on the date that the parent was injured.") and *Clements v. Moore*, 55 S.W.3d 838 (Ky. App. 2000) (adult children cannot bring a claim for loss of consortium).

Answer (A) is not the best answer. In many states, both minor and adult children can bring a cause of action for loss of parental consortium. *See Roth v. Evangelical Lutheran Good Samaritan Soc.*, 886 N.W.2d 601 (Iowa 2016) and *N. Pac. Ins. Co. v. Stucky*, 338 P.3d 56 (Mont. 2014).

Answer (C) is not the best answer. Some jurisdictions permit minor but not adult children to bring a cause of action for loss of consortium. *See Campos v. Coleman*, 123 A.3d 854, 868 (Conn. 2015) and *Clements v. Moore*, 55 S.W.3d 838 (Ky. App. 2000).

Answer (D) is not the best answer. While the closeness between parent and child may be a factor, *see Jordan v. Baptist Three Rivers Hosp.*, 984 S.W.2d 593, 601 (Tenn. 1999) ("The age of the child does not, in and of itself, preclude consideration of parental consortium damages. The adult child inquiry shall take into consideration factors such as closeness of the relationship and dependence (i.e., of a handicapped adult child, assistance with day care, etc.)."), some jurisdictions simply do not permit adult children to bring such a cause of action. *See Campos v. Coleman*, 123 A.3d 854, 868 (Conn. 2015) and *Clements v. Moore*, 55 S.W.3d 838 (Ky. App. 2000).

249. **Answer (C) is the best answer.** Paychecks earned during the marriage are marital assets. *See Sitz v. Sitz*, 749 N.W.2d 470, 475 (Neb. 2008) (noting that the "paycheck . . . was marital property"). Ellis's share of the marital assets used to improve the house will likely be credited in some way such as a portion of the costs expended, *see Callender v. Callender*, 625 So. 2d 257, 261 (La. App. 1993) ("[T]he husband was entitled to reimbursement for his share of community funds spent to improve his wife's house."), or a portion of the value of the house's improvement. *See Hall v. Hall*, 462 A.2d 1179, 1182 (Me. 1983) ("The marital share is the

amount by which the use of marital funds has enhanced the value of the property, rather than merely the cost of the improvements.").

Answer (A) is not the best answer. Darby's paychecks are a marital asset. *See Sitz v. Sitz*, 749 N.W.2d 470, 475 (Neb. 2008), and Ellis is likely to be credited in some way for the use of marital assets to improve Darby's property. *See Callender v. Callender*, 625 So. 2d 257, 261 (La. Ct. App. 1993) and *Hall v. Hall*, 462 A.2d 1179, 1182 (Me. 1983).

Answer (B) is not the best answer. The home will likely continue to be viewed as separate property, although the value of the improvement to the home will likely be distributed. *See Matter of Marriage of Benson*, 406 P.3d 148, 151 (Or. App. 2017) (wife awarded 75% of the value of the house's increased value even though the house itself was husband's separate property).

Answer (D) is not the best answer. More would have to be shown to establish that Ellis's share of the marital funds was gifted to Darby. *See Bordelon v. Bordelon*, 942 So. 2d 708, 713 (La. App. 2006) ("[W]here community property or community funds have been used to improve or benefit the separate property of the owner spouse, the non-owner spouse is entitled, upon termination of the community, to one-half of the improvement costs.").

250. **Answer (C) is the best answer.** Even if New Vermshire treats first cousin marriage as void, the marriage might nonetheless be recognized if such a marriage is permitted where it was celebrated. *See Ghassemi v. Ghassemi*, 998 So. 2d 731, 743 (La. App. 2008) ("[T]he mere fact that a marriage is absolutely null when contracted in Louisiana does not mean that such a marriage validly performed elsewhere is automatically invalid as violative of a strong public policy."). Recognition of the marriage would be even more likely where the couple had married in accord with their domicile's law. *See State Dep't of Human Res. v. Lott*, 16 So. 3d 104, 106 (Ala. Civ. App. 2009) ("[T]he validity of a marriage is determined by the law of the place where it is contracted; if it is valid there, it will be recognized as valid everywhere, unless recognition is contrary to a strong public policy of the state of the parties' domicile.").

Answer (A) is not the best answer. When evasive marriages are discussed in the case law, they usually involve individuals domiciled in one state who marry in another state where the marriage is permitted but who return to live in their domicile. *See In re Estate of Toutant*, 633 N.W.2d 692, 698 (Wis. App. 2001) (holding marriage celebrated in Texas void where Wisconsin domiciliaries had married in Texas even though they were precluded under Wisconsin law from marrying). In this case, the parties were domiciled in the state where they married.

Answer (B) is not the best answer. A couple that cannot currently marry in the domicile might marry elsewhere and have the marriage recognized in the domicile if that marriage is not treated by the domicile as void *ab initio*. *See Mazzolini v. Mazzolini*, 155 N.E.2d 206, 209 (Ohio 1958) ("[T]he marriage herein between the Mazzolinis was not proscribed by the laws of Massachusetts where it was regularly solemnized, and since it would not have been void *ab initio* in Ohio, we think the lower courts correctly decided that the suit for annulment did not lie.").

Answer (D) is not the best answer. While many jurisdictions do not consider first cousins immediate family members, *see Blanyar v. Pagnotti Enterprises, Inc.*, 679 A.2d 790, 791 (Pa. Super. 1996) (cousin not considered immediate family member for purposes of negligent infliction claim); *Trapp v. Schuyler Constr.*, 197 Cal. Rptr. 411, 412 (Ct. App. 1983) (same), and many jurisdictions limit loss of consortium claims to members of the nuclear family, *see Hibpshman v. Prudhoe Bay Supply, Inc.*, 734 P.2d 991, 996 n.16 (Alaska 1987) ("Several courts have dealt with this issue by expressly confining loss of consortium claims to the nuclear family, to husband-wife and parent-child relationships."), the issue here is whether the marriage will be recognized. If so, then Robin may well be successful.

Index